Criminal Law

2nd Edition

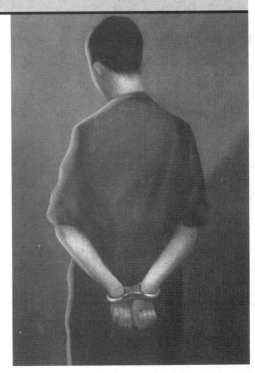

Diana Roe

Hodder & Stoughton

A MEMBER OF THE HODDER HEADLINE GROUP

Orders: please contact Bookpoint Ltd, 130 Milton Park, Abingdon, Oxon OX14 4SB. Telephone: (44) 01235 827720, Fax: (44) 01235 400454. Lines are open from 9.00 to 6.00, Monday to Saturday, with a 24-hour message answering service. Email address: orders@bookpoint.co.uk

A catalogue record for this title is available from the British Library

ISBN 0 340 848197

First published 1999
Impression number   10 9 8 7 6 5 4 3
Year   2007 2006 2005 2004 2003

Cover artwork by Mark Moran
Typeset by Dorchester Typesetting Group Ltd
Printed in Great Britain for Hodder & Stoughton Educational, a division of Hodder Headline Ltd, 338 Euston Road, London NW1 3BH
by Martins The Printers, Berwick-upon-Tweed

Criminal Law

CONTENTS

ACKNOWLEDGEMENTS

Every writer on Criminal Law (and indeed almost every judge and practitioner), owes an enormous debt of gratitude to Professor Sir John Smith for his insight into criminal law.

The author would also like to thank the other authors of articles in the *Criminal Law Review* who have been mentioned in this book. Many thanks also to the editorial team at Hodder & Stoughton Educational, particularly Alexia Chan and Diana Bateman for all their help and guidance, to my students for their enthusiastic contributions, and finally to my husband Peter, for all his love, support and delicious meals. Move over Jamie!

The author and publisher would like to thank the following for their permission to reproduce copyright text material:

The Daily Telegraph for the articles on pages 8, 48, 68, 87, 101, 152, 177, *The Evening Standard* for the articles on pages 53, 113, 229, 238, 241; *The Times* for the articles on pages 69, 258, 288.

Pat Murray for the cartoons on pages 17, 112, 136, 156, 183, 217, 267.

Every effort has been made to trace copyright holders; any omissions brought to our attention will be corrected in future printings.

Chapter 1

INTRODUCTION TO CRIMINAL LAW

1.1 Introduction

Welcome to the second edition of this textbook and your study of Criminal Law. In this chapter we will begin by looking at certain preliminary matters, including the definition of a crime, the way such offences are classified and the courts in which they are tried. We will go on to discuss the reasons for citing cases in English law and conclude with an investigation into ways in which the criminal law is updated and reformed.

The elements of a crime will be looked at in Chapter 2 and then, in Chapters 3 to 9, there will be a discussion of the main criminal offences required for most examination boards. Chapters 10 and 11 deal with general defences and are followed by chapters on the various parties to a crime, a discussion of inchoate (incomplete) offences and the subject of vicarious and corporate liability. Chapter 15 endeavours to bring everything together into a comprehensive whole and to give advice on revision and examination technique.

1.1.1 The reasons for writing this book

Criminal law, which affects all our lives in one way or another, is an enthralling subject, and most students beginning their A Level studies or embarking on their law degree courses will be looking forward to studying it.

Sometimes, however, this initial enthusiasm can wane as the student becomes drowned in a sea of detail and cannot see the wider position or, alternatively, cannot find the answers to the questions posed. At times like this, you should remind yourselves that the fault might not be yours at all! Some of the judges might also have experienced difficulties with the matter in hand, have come to different conclusions on it, and, in this way caused the confusion in that particular area of law. In other cases, the material studied seems to assume a basic knowledge of the law that you might not possess at the beginning of your studies, necessitating a visit to the law library to try to discover the outcome of a case or further detail. In addition, it is often difficult to discover the current state of the law or information about the reforms that are being planned.

My aim in writing this book, therefore, is to try to address some of these issues and hopefully, in the process, to make your life a little easier.

- I aim to provide a clear explanation of the law, backed up by informed comment on the more controversial aspects of it.
- Reports from newspapers are included to help such discussion and show the relevance of the legal issues.
- Key Facts charts will clearly sum up the current state of the law in a particular area and indicate the cases and statutes in which the law is laid down.
- Problem questions and topics for discussion are included in the Activities section. The aim here is to persuade you to study the material in the chapter, (there are no tricks; the information is all there!) and, hopefully, get you to enjoy tackling the topics chosen, rather than regarding them as a chore.
- Lastly, at the end of each chapter, there are five or ten self-assessment questions to help you test your understanding of the issues.

1.1.2 Who will benefit from this book?

The book is designed as a companion volume to Jacqueline Martin's best-selling book on the English Legal System and is geared specifically for students studying criminal law as the whole at AS/A2 Level. It is in sufficient depth to enable such students to reach the very highest grades and also to be of great value to students on law degree courses or for those studying for the Common Professional Examination or an ILEX qualification. Hopefully, therefore, the book will assist students of all abilities and varying amounts of time.

1.2 The nature and definition of a crime

One of the most important differences between civil and criminal law is that, in the latter, the State plays a major role in the proceedings. It will be noted in 1.4 that nearly all prosecutions are initiated by the State in one form or another in order to protect the public from harm. Criminal wrongs are dealt with by the State for the following reasons:

- They often concern matters that are so serious, both for the victim and for the public at large, that it is felt that they cannot just be left to the individuals concerned.
- A claim for compensation would often be seen as totally inadequate.
- The victim and the public may wish to see the perpetrator put in custody and thereby be rendered harmless.
- Even where the matter could be dealt with by way of compensation, it would be unfair for the victim to bear the expense of such a move.
- With other wrongs, such as some of the minor public order offences, there may be too little interest on the part of individuals in getting the matter dealt with.

The State therefore is called upon to deal with these problems. It now needs to be established which of the wrongs fall into this category.

There have been many attempts to define the meaning of a crime, most of them extremely lengthy. My own simple definition would be to describe a crime as a wrong against the State, either by commission or omission, regarded by that body as criminal and one to which a punishment has been attached. This helps to explain the nature of a crime but, it should be noted, still fails to address the issue of why it comes into this category. Many crimes are also moral wrongs, such as the crimes of murder and theft, but crime and morality do not always combine in such a definite way. A large section of the community would argue that it is morally wrong to tell lies or to commit adultery but, unless the lies are told under oath or the adultery committed in public so as to offend against public decency, the criminal law will not become involved. Conversely, illegal parking or drinking after hours, while thought to be anti-social and thoughtless acts, would not normally be regarded as moral wrongs. A study of criminal law will also show that, while certain crimes remain constant, views about other behaviour may change over the years. For example, acts classed as criminal 40 years ago are not offences today, such as suicide, which was decriminalised in 1961 and homosexual acts between consenting adults for which the law changed in 1967. The Wolfenden Committee in 1957 decided that it was not the function of the criminal law to interfere into the private lives of citizens in order to try to impose certain standards of behaviour more than was considered necessary. It was felt that this should only be done:

> to preserve public order and decency, to protect the citizen from what is offensive or injurious, and to provide sufficient safeguards against exploitation and corruption of others, particularly those who are especially vulnerable.

The law, however, did not change until 10 years later, and even then there was still a continuing debate as to whether the age limit imposed by the State should remain as it was in order to protect the young or, instead, be lowered to give the latter more freedom of choice.

The **Sexual Offences (Amendment) Act 2000** had a very rough ride through Parliament but eventually the latter route was chosen, with some safeguards built into the Act to protect more vulnerable groups. **S1** of the Act lowers the age of consent from 18 to 16 in England, Wales and Scotland and from 18 to 17 in Northern Ireland, equalising it with the relevant age of consent for heterosexual activity in these countries.

1.3 Sources of criminal law

In addition to trying to identify whether a particular form of conduct should be regarded as criminal, there are also difficulties in finding the existing law. Criminal law is an uneasy mixture of common law rules, i.e. rules laid down by the judges over the years, and legislation. The latter is the law coming from Parliament in the form of Acts of Parliament and delegated legislation. Some statutes are of very ancient origin; for example, the **Treason Act** was passed in 1361. Before the last century, however, the law coming from Parliament was fairly limited and large areas of the criminal law were developed by the judges. Much of this has subsequently been put into statutory form, such as the law of theft, which is now to be found in the **Theft Act 1968**. Our judges decided in the case of **Knuller v DPP 1973**, that it is not now their province to make new law so this will normally be done by Parliament.

Between 30 to 80 new Acts of Parliament are therefore enacted every year. One with far-reaching consequences for criminal law and

even more for criminal procedure, is the **Human Rights Act 1998.** This incorporated the provisions of the *European Convention on Human Rights* into English law, helping to guard certain fundamental freedoms. A glance through the criminal appeal reports shows that defendants are not being slow to invoke appropriate sections of this Act, although the move was unsuccessful in the case of **Diane Pretty**, described in Chapter 3. At the other end of the scale one should note the *Anti-Terrorism, Crime and Security Bill*, having a very turbulent passage through the House of Lords at the time of writing. Certain controversial provisions, such as detention without trial and the proposed creation of new criminal offences, are being hotly debated.

Despite all these new laws however, reform of existing criminal law can be a slow and laborious process; large pockets of this remain largely judge-made but, where deemed appropriate, Parliament might decide to 'tidy up' the provisions. A notable example of this interaction between the judges and Parliament intervention can be seen in the crimes of murder and voluntary manslaughter. For example, until the middle of the twentieth century, the death penalty was imposed for the crime of murder. Parliament then stepped in with the **Murder (Abolition of Death Penalty) Act 1965**, which suspended the death penalty for murder, except for treason and certain forms of piracy. A later piece of delegated legislation made this permanent. The **Crime and Disorder Act 1998** then removed the death penalty for treason and piracy. In addition, there is no Act of Parliament laying down a definition of murder; instead, the judges have developed this over the years. Their definition originally stated that death had to occur within a year and a day. This prevailed until 1996 when Parliament abolished it by passing the **Law Reform (Year and a Day Rule) Act 1996.** With regard to voluntary manslaughter, the **Homicide Act 1957**, which a layman might reasonably assume to give information on the crime of murder, lays down instead three partial defences, reducing the crime from murder to manslaughter if certain circumstances are made out. These include cases where the defendant suffered from diminished responsibility at the time of the killing, had been provoked in some way or was the survivor of a suicide pact. It can thus be seen that the law on these two offences is a confusing mixture of judge-made rules and statutory provisions. The law on involuntary manslaughter, on the other hand, remains completely judge-made.

Even in cases where all the law on the subject is in statutory form, such as in theft and criminal damage, the judges may still become involved. They may be called upon to decide the meaning of a particular word or phrase in the act, if this should be unclear.

Discovering the source of much of criminal law is not, therefore, an easy process. There have been increasing calls for a special criminal code to deal with this problem and update the law. This is not a new request! A draft code was put before Parliament as long ago as 1878 and, again, in the following two years but was never brought into law. A similar fate seems to await the Draft Criminal Code drawn up in 1989, discussed later in this chapter, although it now appears that some of its provisions may be enacted in a gradual way.

1.4 The prosecution process

1.4.1 The decision to prosecute

As stated earlier in this chapter, the decision to prosecute comes from the State via the Director of Public Prosecutions, who is the head of the Crown Prosecution Service. In most cases, the police will start the investigation and until 1985, they carried on to prosecute. The

Prosecution of Offences Act 1985 changed the position because it was believed that a separate body should be involved in this process. Despite this laudable aim, the CPS has had a poor press, with complaints being made about the poor administration and the quality of its lawyers. The current Lord Chancellor is taking action on this. The CPS is not the only body involved in the process; officials from local authorities, such as Trading Standards Officers, and the Serious Fraud Office may decide to start a prosecution. In addition, a private prosecution may be launched, although these are rare. With regard to serious offences under the **Official Secrets Acts**, the Attorney-General, who is higher in the power structure than the DPP, must give permission for these to progress.

When making the decision to prosecute, regard must be given to the evidence available, which needs to be substantial and reliable, and whether it is in the public interest to do so. When there is doubt, the accused should be given the benefit of it, which inevitably means that some offenders are never brought to trial.

1.4.2 The classification of offences

Offences are put into two broad categories, summary offences, the more minor ones, and indictable offences, which are more serious. The James' Committee however, recommended dividing cases into three: offences triable summarily, offences to be tried on indictment only and a third category of cases that could be tried either way.

Summary offences

These offences must be tried in the magistrates' court because an Act of Parliament decrees that they will be dealt with summarily. Normally three lay magistrates try the case although, in some of the larger towns, a legally qualified, paid magistrate, now called a District Judge (Magistrates' Court), will decide the case alone. If the defendant pleads not guilty, the magistrates act as both judge and jury, deciding the matter of guilt or innocence and fixing the sentence. Most of these offences are fairly minor, including minor traffic offences but, periodically, they are added to by Parliament and more serious ones have been included. Examples of summary offences are speeding, illegal parking, careless driving, assaulting a police officer in the execution of his duty, minor criminal damage, assault and battery and driving or being in control of a vehicle with excess alcohol in the blood.

Indictable offences

Offences tried on indictment are the more serious or complicated ones which must be dealt with by the Crown Court. Such offences include offences under the **Official Secrets Act**, murder, manslaughter, robbery, blackmail, arson and causing death by dangerous driving. The case will normally start in the magistrates' court, but will then be transferred for trial in the Crown Court.

The magistrates still have the important task of deciding whether the accused will be remanded in custody or released on bail until his trial takes place. The **Bail Act 1976**, as amended, states that everyone has a general right to bail, unless the offence is a serious violent one, in which case the magistrates must state in open court why they are giving bail. In other cases, bail will be allowed unless there is a good reason why it should be refused, such as the likelihood of the defendant committing further offences or absconding.

Offences triable either way

As the name suggests, it is possible for such offences to be tried summarily in the magistrates' courts or, on indictment in the Crown Court. Under the **Magistrates' Court Act 1980**, it is for the courts to decide this matter. If it is decided that the case is more

suitable for trial on indictment, then it must be dealt with in this way; the accused has no say in the matter. If, however, the magistrates decide that they do have enough power, the defendant, if pleading not guilty, may choose whether he wants this form of trial or would prefer to take his case to the Crown Court. The vast majority of offenders choose summary trial but in a dangerous driving or theft case, for example, the accused may believe, (often wrongly), that a jury trial will give him a better chance of an acquittal. If he chooses such a trial, committal proceedings will take place and the case will be set down for trial in the Crown Court.

If the accused chooses magistrates' court trial, he must first be warned that the magistrates have the power to send him to the Crown Court for sentencing, if they have found him guilty and believe that their powers are insufficient to deal with him. It should be remembered that magistrates only have the power to impose a fine of £5000 or less and/or a sentence of imprisonment of six months for any one offence.

Examples of triable either way offences include the ones just mentioned of theft and dangerous driving, burglary, actual bodily harm, criminal damage over £5000, indecent assault and obtaining property or services by deception. The current government tried to curtail jury trial in such cases, but twice faced defeat in the House of Lords. It has since had a change of heart on this issue.

1.5 The system of criminal courts

1.5.1 Courts of first instance

We have already noted these courts in the last section; they consist of the magistrates' courts and the Crown Court with over 90 branches. As stated, magistrates' courts, on the criminal side of the law, will deal with all the summary offences and with the triable either way offences where the defendant has chosen summary trial. The Crown Court is reserved for indictable offences and those triable either way offences where the magistrates decide that they have insufficient power to deal with them and cases where the accused opts for this form of trial. Trial in the Crown Court will be by a single judge, if the defendant pleads guilty, or by judge and jury if the defendant pleads not guilty. In the latter case, a jury of 12, who are selected at random, will decide upon the verdict, after listening to the facts and hearing advice on the points of law involved from the judge. The latter will be a circuit judge or a recorder (a part-time judge) for the less serious indictable or triable either way cases dealt with in this court. For the most serious cases, a High Court judge will officiate. This judge normally sits in the Queen's Bench Division of the High Court but makes periodical visits to the branches of the Crown Court on his circuit. He is sometimes known as the 'Red Judge', because of the colour of his robe.

Deliberations in the jury room are secret and, when they are complete, the foreman delivers the verdict in open court. Majority verdicts, of 11-1 or 10-2 are now accepted. If the defendant is acquitted, he will walk free from the court and cannot be retried for the same offence. If the jury finds the defendant guilty, the judge will do the sentencing. Most offences have a maximum sentence laid down, but no minimum, giving the judge a large measure of discretion. Exceptions to this are certain forms of treason and piracy and the crime of murder, which have a fixed sentence of life imprisonment. Until 1998, the first two crimes were, theoretically, punishable by death but this position changed with the passing of the **Crime and Disorder Act 1998.** In addition to these crimes with a sentence fixed by law, the controversial **Crime (Sentences) Act 1997** lays down an automatic sentence of life

imprisonment, save in exceptional circumstances, where the defendant is found guilty of a second, serious violent offence.

This Act has been the subject of great criticism. Professor Smith roundly calls it 'an absurd piece of legislation'. It is certainly generating a large number of appeals, particularly on the subject of what constitutes 'an exceptional circumstance'.

Most judges, too, are opposed to the **Crime (Sentences) Act**, which fetters their discretion so drastically. A large body of them would like also to remove the mandatory life sentence for murder. In a lecture to the police back in 1998, Lord Bingham, a former Lord Chief Justice, stated that the mandatory life sentence for murder should be abolished and declared that it should be left to the judges to fix a minimum jail term. He claimed that his views were endorsed by Lord Irvine, the Lord Chancellor, and had 'the overwhelming support' of the judges of the Queen's Bench Division, who are the ones to sentence murderers.

Lord Bingham favoured the introduction of a discretionary life sentence where the judge would specify in open court the minimum sentence to be served before there was any prospect of release. (If the circumstances warranted it, he could order that the defendant should never be released.) The judge's decision would be open to challenge on the grounds of excessive severity or leniency. After the minimum period laid down had been served, the Parole Board, rather than the Home Office, would then decide when it was safe to release the offender on licence.

Parliament, on the other hand, has so far been opposed to what it perceives as the further 'watering down' of punishment for this most serious of crimes, even though one of its own Select Committees investigated the matter and sided with the judges on this point. This matter is returned to in Chapter 3.

Possible reform of the criminal courts

The eagerly awaited Auld Report, published in October 2001, suggested major changes to the courts of first instance, recommending the insertion of a middle tier of courts, where a tribunal would decide the issue. It remains to be seen whether such sweeping changes will be adopted.

1.5.2 The appeal courts in criminal law

It is very important to gain an understanding of this area before you go on to study the main offences and defences in criminal law. It will enable you to understand why an appeal has been made and to appreciate the status of the appeal court.

Appeals from the magistrates' courts

There are two main ways to appeal. The normal appeal route allows the defendant to appeal to the Crown Court, against the verdict or the sentence decided by the magistrates. In the Crown Court, there will be a complete rehearing of the case by a circuit judge and at least two magistrates. Only the accused is permitted to appeal by this method. The verdict may be affirmed or changed. The sentence may be increased or, (perhaps more often) decreased.

The other route only concerns points of law or claims that the magistrates have acted 'ultra vires', i.e. outside the scope of their powers. Either the prosecution or defence may appeal by way of 'case stated', i.e. by a written statement asking for an opinion on the point of law involved, to the Divisional Court of Queen's Bench Division. Two or three judges of the court will give their view of the law, which will then be followed by the lower court. If the case has reached the Crown Court, this court, too, may make such an appeal if the parties require advice on a point of law.

There is a further appeal from the Divisional Court straight to the House of Lords.

Appeals from the Crown Court

Such appeals are made to the Court of Appeal (Criminal Division), which sits in the Royal Courts of Justice in the Strand. The main rules are to be found in the **Criminal Appeal Act 1995**, which simplified the existing system.

Against sentence

An appeal may be made by the accused against the sentence imposed by the Crown Court. Leave to appeal is needed from the Court of Appeal or the trial judge, and only in a quarter of all appeals to this court is such permission granted. Only in rare circumstances will the sentence be increased. The **Criminal Justice Act 1988** gave such a right to the Attorney General, who is allowed to appeal against an unduly lenient sentence. Between 1989 and 1997, 367 such sentences were reviewed.

Against the verdict

Only the defendant may challenge the actual verdict in a case, except in an exceptional case where the prosecution can show that the jury has been 'nobbled'. The defendant may appeal, either on a point of law, or because there are other reasons to suggest that the verdict may be 'unsafe'. It has now become easier to bring such evidence before the court. Leave is required for this. You will discover as you progress through this book that most appeals are on the grounds that the judge has misdirected the jury in some material way on the law relating to the crime in question.

Woman jailed for killing aunt loses second appeal

By David Millward

A WOMAN convicted of killing her elderly aunt lost her second appeal amid uproar in the Appeal Court yesterday.

Shouts of "shame" and "this is injustice" from supporters of Susan May greeted the decision by Lord Justice Kennedy, Mr Justice Buckley and Mr Justice Grigson, May was jailed for life at Manchester Crown Court in May 1993 after being convicted of murdering Hilda Marchbank, 89. The case was referred to the Appeal Court by the Criminal Cases Review Commission two years ago.

Campbell Malone, her solicitor, said: "Susan is determined to fight on." The court had been told that May, 55, was the principal carer of her mother, with whom she lived in Royton, near Oldham, Greater Manchester, and Mrs Marchbank, who lived nearby.

On March 12, 1992, after going to Mrs Marchbank's house, May told police she had found her body in bed. May claimed that Mrs Marchbank had been killed during a burglary that went wrong. But the prosecution said the robbery was faked. Police found that May had debts of £7,000. The prosecution said that May was a beneficiary of Mrs Marchbank's estate.

She was alleged to have left a bloody handprint on the wall. But this was challenged by Michael Mansfield, QC. He told the court that there was no evidence that the three bloodstains were on the wall on the day Mrs Marchbank's body was discovered. Rejecting the appeal, Lord Justice Kennedy said the court accepted evidence from the police and the forensic scientist that the bloodstains were on the wall when they arrived at the scene.

The jury had been right to infer that the marks were left at the time of the murder. The identification of May's right hand as the source of one of the prints was therefore "damning evidence against her".

Daily Telegraph, 8 December 2001

The Court of Appeal may allow the appeal, dismiss it or order a retrial, as shown in the cases of **Ahluwalia** and **Thornton**, seen in Chapter 4 under voluntary manslaughter.

While the prosecution cannot overturn an acquittal, the Attorney General has power to ask the Court of Appeal to look at the point of law involved and set a precedent for the future. The original acquittal will not be touched. This process is called an Attorney General's Reference and several examples of these are shown throughout the book.

Appeals to the House of Lords

Either the prosecution or the defence may appeal from the Court of Appeal to the House of Lords if a point of law has been certified as one of general public importance. Such appeals rarely reach double figures each year, but have a very important influence on the law. Examples can be seen in Chapter 2, in the cases of **Hancock and Shankland** and **Woollin**, when the meaning of the word 'intention' in murder cases caused problems.

It should also be noted that, following recent concern about miscarriages of justice and the report on this from the Runciman Commission, the Criminal Cases Review Commission was set up by the **Criminal Appeal Act 1995** to make it easier for such cases to be investigated. This became operational in April 1997. The article (left) shows that not all defendants succeed after such an appeal.

1.6 The operation of binding precedent in criminal law

Most of you will be studying the rules relating to the English legal system as part of your course and will learn of the importance of the doctrine of precedent in English law. Our system differs from that in many other countries in Europe in that the decisions of some courts are binding on others in the system.

The general rule is that the decisions of the higher courts will bind the courts lower in the hierarchy. In criminal law, this means that the magistrates' courts and Crown Court are bound by the decisions of the Court of Appeal and the House of Lords, unless the case can be distinguished in some way. The Court of Appeal is bound by decisions of the House of Lords and is also generally bound by its own earlier decisions, unless one of the three exceptions laid down in **Young v Bristol Aeroplane 1944** can be put forward:

- If there are two conflicting earlier decisions. The current court may choose which of the earlier cases to follow.
- If the decision conflicts with a House of Lords' decision.
- If the decision was made 'per incuriam', i.e. by mistake, because a relevant precedent or statutory provision was not brought to the court's attention in the earlier case.

The Criminal Division also has more freedom than the Civil Division, to depart from its own earlier decisions where they are clearly thought to be wrong and the liberty of the subject is at stake. This was stated in **Taylor 1950.**

The House of Lords is the final appeal court in criminal matters unless community law is involved. The House of Lords binds all the courts below it and, until 1966, was bound by its own earlier decisions. Lord Gardiner then issued his famous Practice Statement declaring that, while their Lordships still considered the doctrine of binding precedent to be an essential part of English law, the House of Lords from that time on would be prepared to depart from its own earlier decisions 'when it appears right to do so'. Lord Gardiner did go on to say that the House would bear in mind 'the especial need for certainty as to the criminal law', a statement that may have come back to haunt him after some later decisions of the Lords rendered the law anything but certain!

While the House of Lords is now permitted to overrule its own earlier decisions, it was made very clear in the Practice Statement that the lower courts were not to be given the same freedom. The Court of Appeal, therefore will be bound by the decisions of the House of Lords and, generally, by its own decisions. It is not, however, bound by decisions of the Judicial Committee of the Privy Council. This body sits to hear appeals from other countries, which still retain this court as the one for final appeals. The precedents set by the Privy Council are highly persuasive as, in many cases, the judges are the same as those who sit in the House of Lords, but they are not binding.

The operation of the doctrine of binding precedent explains why the citing (or quoting) of cases is so important in criminal law. Certain cases lay down precedents that the later courts are then obliged to follow. The facts of the case are relatively unimportant, although often very interesting; it is the principle of law coming from the case which is vital and which will be binding on other judges. When answering problem questions, therefore, you need to be aware of the cases laying down the rules, or interpreting the ones laid down by Parliament, and show the ability to apply these rules to the facts you are given. This is exactly what the judges are doing as the new cases come before them!

Most criminal cases start with the word Regina, (the Latin for Queen), or 'R' v the defendant. When this is the case, only the defendant's name will be shown in this book. If the case involves a prosecutor's name, this will be included in the citing. If the case concerns the Attorney General, the Director of Public Prosecutions or the Metropolitan Police Commissioner, the initials will indicate this. It should also be noted that, when an appeal is made, the defendant becomes known as the appellant or the respondent. For ease, however, I have retained the words 'defendant' or 'accused'.

1.7 Ways of reforming criminal law

The currrent main law-making body is, of course, Parliament but, before Parliament can legislate, someone else must have made the decision that the law needs to be changed. The government of the day introduces Bills to deal with particular topics, often in relation to procedural matters or sentencing, the **Crime (Sentences) Act 1997** being an example, or in response to a particular problem, as shown by the **Dangerous Dogs Act 1991** and the **Protection from Harassment Act 1997**. In addition, ad hoc Royal Commissions are sometimes set up to make recommendations on a specific topic as, for example, the Royal Commission on Criminal Justice (known more often as the Runciman Commission, after the name of its chairman). On a longer-term basis, two other bodies have made vital contributions towards reforming the criminal law. The first

one is the Criminal Law Revision Committee, a part-time body, set up in 1957, which has been instrumental in instigating several important reforms. One example of its work was its proposals for rationalising the law of theft, which led to the passing of the **Theft Act 1968**.

The Law Commission

In 1965, it was decided that a full-time body should be set up to undertake more comprehensive law reform, and the Law Commission was created. Its remit is extensive as shown in **s3 Law Commissions Act 1965** (there was a separate one for Scotland). The two Law Commissions were charged with keeping:

> under review all the law, . . . with a view to its systematic development and reform, including in particular the codification of such law, the elimination of anomalies, the repeal of obselete and unnecessary enactments, the reduction of the number of separate enactments and generally the simplification and modernisation of the law.

The English Law Commission saw the codification of the criminal law as a pressing issue. It recognised that the rules are an untidy mixture of judge-made rules and statutory provisions, and that even where there are Acts of Parliament, some of these are inadequate because of their age and style of language. A great deal of work, therefore, went into producing a Draft Code in 1989, along with a Bill to implement its proposals. This Code is referred to in the following chapters, in cases where other reforms have not overtaken it. Unfortunately, it is gathering dust. Parliament has shown little will to implement it. Undefeated, the Law Commission decided to try to implement changes in key areas in a more piece-meal fashion. This, too, has been largely unsuccessful and the patience of the Commissioners now seems to be coming to an end. In 1993, the Chairman, Mr Justice Brooke, launched a stinging attack on the government of the day, and declared that the failure by Parliament to implement any of the reforms was 'a disgrace'.

In August 1999, Professor Sir John Smith writing in the *Criminal Law Review* also felt a pressing need to remind Parliament of its role, when he argued that:

> *Major parts of English criminal law are in a thoroughly unsatisfactory state – the criticisms that the law is archaic, obscure, incoherent and inconsistent are familiar and have been rehearsed on numerous occasions. The law is increasingly inefficient, and is increasingly failing to deliver justice. The case for a modern criminal code, a strong one when first made by the Law Commission in 1968, is overwhelming thirty years on.*

In your study of criminal law, therefore, you not only need to acquire knowledge of the existing state of the law on each topic, but also to be aware of any imperfections in these rules and of any suggestions for future reform. Happy studying!

Self-Assessment Questions

1. Define a crime. Give two examples where the criminal law seems to combine with more general views of morality and two instances where there may be a conflict with at least some members of society.
2. Describe two sources of criminal law, giving examples to support your answer.
3. What was the effect of the **Prosecution of Offences Act 1985**?
4. Give two examples each of a summary offence and an indictable offence and state where and by whom such offences are tried.
5. What is a triable either way offence and how is it currently dealt with?
6. Why have the **Crime (Sentences) Act 1997**, the **Sexual Offences Act 2000,** and the **Anti-Terrorism, Crime & Security Bill** been criticised?
7. To which court will a defendant in a magistrates' court appeal against a) the sentence or verdict or b) on a point of law?
8. To which courts may an appeal be made from the Crown Court?
9. Discuss the position of the House of Lords and the Court of Appeal with regard to their own earlier precedents.
10. Name two bodies involved with reforming the criminal law before the matter reaches Parliament and explain why there has been criticism of this process.

Chapter 2

THE ELEMENTS OF A CRIME

2.1 Introduction

Before we start our study of the specific criminal offences in Chapters 3–9, we need to establish when a person is said to possess the necessary criminal liability. This will not arise until the constituents of the offence have been established and the requisite state of mind for committing such a crime has been proved. This chapter therefore begins by examining the burden of proof in criminal law and then goes on to discuss the elements of a crime. It ends by looking at certain crimes, often of a regulatory nature, for which liability can arise even though the party claims that he was not at fault in the normal sense. These are known as offences of strict liability.

The burden of proof in criminal law

Before the defendant can be convicted of a wrong against the State, the case has to be proved against him. In **Woolmington v DPP 1935**, the House of Lords clearly established that this has to be beyond reasonable doubt and that the onus is on the prosecution to prove this.

In the above quoted case, the defendant claimed that he took a gun with him to the home of the victim's mother, not for any criminal intent against them, but to show his estranged wife that he planned to commit suicide if she failed to return to him. He alleged that the gun then went off by accident, as he was showing it to her. Despite this claim, the defendant was convicted of murder.

The House of Lords allowed the appeal on the grounds that the judge had misdirected the jury by suggesting that the defendant had to prove that the killing was accidental, rather than the prosecution having to show that it was murder.

The elements of a crime

When trying to establish the requisite criminal liability, the prosecution will normally have to prove two things. Put briefly, the prosecutor must show that the defendant had actually committed the offence in question, and that he had done so with the mental element required by the law, i.e. with the necessary 'guilty mind'. These two elements of a crime are expressed in Latin, the term *actus reus* being used to describe the wrongful act and the words *mens rea* describing the mental element. It should be noted that not all judges like the retention of these archaic terms. Lord Diplock said that it would be preferable, 'to avoid bad Latin . . . and speak about the conduct of the accused and his state of mind at the time of that conduct.' Despite his efforts, however, the expressions remain in common use and need to be studied.

The diagram on the next page might help you recognize the difference between the two terms.

2.2 The *actus reus*

The existence of the *actus reus* is essential for criminal liability. Each crime has its own *actus reus*, laid down by statute or by the judges. For example, under statute, the *actus reus* of s18 **Offences Against the Person Act 1861** occurs where a person unlawfully wounds or causes grievous bodily harm to another. The *actus reus* of theft under the **Theft Act 1968** arises when a party 'appropriates property belonging to another'. At common law (i.e. where the

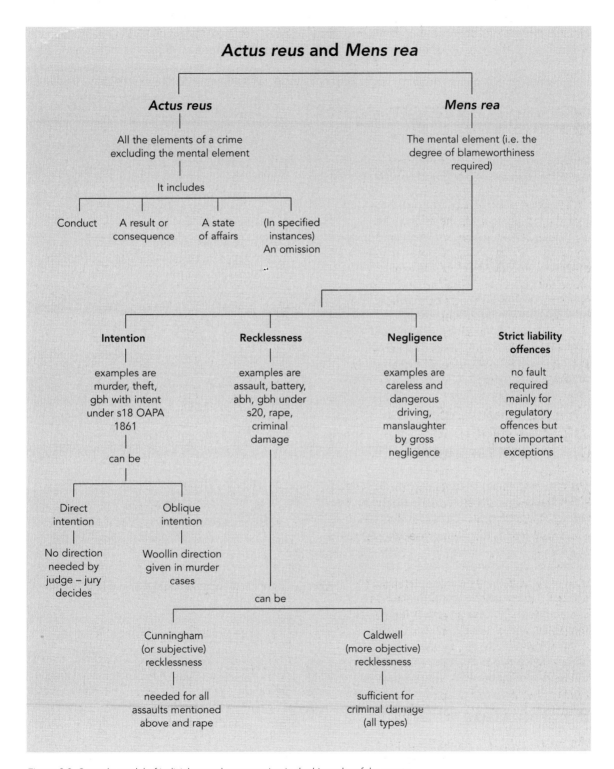

Actus reus and Mens rea

Actus reus

All the elements of a crime excluding the mental element

It includes

Conduct | A result or consequence | A state of affairs | (In specified instances) An omission

Mens rea

The mental element (i.e. the degree of blameworthiness required)

Intention

examples are murder, theft, gbh with intent under s18 OAPA 1861

can be

Direct intention

No direction needed by judge – jury decides

Oblique intention

Woollin direction given in murder cases

Recklessness

examples are assault, battery, abh, gbh under s20, rape, criminal damage

Negligence

examples are careless and dangerous driving, manslaughter by gross negligence

Strict liability offences

no fault required mainly for regulatory offences but note important exceptions

can be

Cunningham (or subjective) recklessness

needed for all assaults mentioned above and rape

Caldwell (more objective) recklessness

sufficient for criminal damage (all types)

Figure 2.3 *Cascade model of judicial precedent operating in the hierarchy of the courts*

criminal offence has been developed by the judges, rather than by Parliament), the *actus reus* of murder has been established as 'the unlawful killing of a person in being under the Queen's peace'. These definitions will be explained in detail when the relevant offences are dealt with later.

In many cases, the actions of the accused will speak for themselves and the *actus reus* will be easy to establish but occasionally the matter is more complex as can be seen in the following subsections.

2.2.1 Conduct

In many instances, the mere conduct of the accused may be enough to show that the *actus reus* has been committed. A classic example of this is perjury, i.e. lying under oath. Another example is the conduct of 'appropriating property belonging to another' as laid down in the crime of theft.

2.2.2 A result or consequence

For the commission of some crimes, however, it is necessary to show more than just conduct; the result or consequence of that conduct must also be assessed. For example, in the crime of murder, an unlawful killing has to have arisen as a result of the defendant's violent act.

Similarly, under **s20 Sexual Offences Act 1956**, it is an offence to take an unmarried girl out of the possession of her parent or guardian without lawful authority. Should such a consequence occur, the *actus reus* of the crime will be established.

2.2.3 A state of affairs

In rare cases, the unfortunate defendant may be found guilty of a crime simply by being in a particular place when this state of affairs has

been declared to be wrong. An example is the case of **Larsonneur 1933**. The defendant had gone to Ireland when her permission to be in the UK had expired. She was then deported from Ireland and brought back to England against her will by the police.

Despite the fact that she had no wish to return to this country, she was found guilty of 'being an alien to whom leave to land in the United Kingdom has been refused', which was an offence under the **Aliens Order 1920.**

Despite widespread criticism of the unfairness of this decision, certain later Acts of Parliament have also adopted this strict approach. A modern example is **s4 Road Traffic Act 1988**, under which it is an offence to be in charge of a motor vehicle on a road or public place while unfit to drive through drink or drugs. The *actus reus* of the offence will be present even if the defendant has decided not to drive the vehicle in question and has planned to sleep in the car instead. The state of affairs of being in charge of the vehicle is enough to establish liability under this section of the Act.

Activity

- Read the following extract and decide how the *actus reus* of the crime was established by the prosecution:

  In **Winzar v Chief Constable of Kent 1983**, the defendant had been taken to hospital, but once there it was discovered that he was not ill, merely drunk. He was therefore requested to leave the premises. He failed to comply with this order and was later found in a corridor of the hospital. The police were called and he was removed from the premises against his will and taken to a police car on the highway. He was then charged with being found drunk in the highway.

2.2.4 An omission

The first point to note is that normally, in English law, a person will not be found to be criminally liable merely because he failed to act.

Stephen L J made this position clear back in the nineteenth century, when he stated:

It is not a crime to cause death or bodily injury, even intentionally, by any omission.

He went on to describe the situation where a person sees another man drowning but does nothing to help him, even though, if he had merely reached out his hand, the man who could not swim would have been saved. Under English law, the person failing to act has committed no crime.

There are, however, limited exceptions to this rule where the law has decided that a person should be criminally liable for failing to act. They include the following situations:

- **Where a statute lays this down**
  A limited number of statutory provisions create liability for omissions in specified circumstances. The following are examples under the **Road Traffic Act 1988**, as amended: (i) Failing to provide a breath specimen as required; (ii) Failing to give details to someone entitled to receive them, after a traffic accident; (iii) Failing to report an accident as required.

  It is also a statutory offence under the **Children and Young Persons Act 1933** to fail to provide a child with adequate food, clothing, housing or medical help.

- **Where there is a contractual duty to act**
  There may be a specific duty to act laid down in a person's contract. For example, a lifeguard is employed to save lives, so would obviously be failing in his duty if he observed someone in difficulties but took no

steps to save him from drowning. The same rules would apply to a person employed to guard a level crossing, as the defendant in **Pittwood 1902** discovered to his cost. He was a railway employee who had opened the level crossing gates to let a cart pass across the line, but had failed to shut the gates again before going off to have his lunch. A few minutes later, a passing train hit a hay-cart crossing the track and the driver of this vehicle was killed.

The defendant was found guilty of 'gross and criminal negligence' after the judge made it clear that 'a man might incur criminal liability from a duty arising out of contract'.

- **Where there is a duty imposed by law**
  The judges themselves have imposed a duty to act in certain situations. The following are examples:

(i) *Where the person is guilty of misconduct in a public office*
  In **Dytham 1979**, a police officer was found to be criminally liable when he failed to preserve the Queen's peace and stood by while a man was kicked to death.

(ii) *Where there is a special relationship between the parties*
  A party may be found guilty of failing to act if there is duty imposed upon him by virtue of the special relationship between him and the victim. An early case on this subject was **Instan 1893**, where a niece failed to obtain help for her aunt, with whom she was living. The aunt had contracted gangrene in her leg and died.

  The niece's conviction for manslaughter was upheld. The appeal court held that English law would be 'hopelessly deficient if the judges were unable to base liability on the common duty of care owed by one relative to another'.

Another case illustrating this is **Gibbins and Proctor 1918**, where a man and his common law wife were found guilty of homicide, when they failed to feed the man's child and she died from starvation.

The father obviously had a duty to look after his child. The woman was held to be liable because even though the child was not hers, she was living with the man and had accepted his money for food.

In **Khan 1998**, however, it was decided that drug dealers are not under any special duty to look after their clients, so a manslaughter conviction was quashed.

(iii) *Where the defendant has voluntarily accepted responsibility for the other*
This offer overlaps with the duty imposed by a special relationship, mentioned above, but is wider in that the law can impose liability in any case where the victim has relied upon the defendant and the latter then fails to help.

A particularly gruesome example of this was the case of **Stone and Dobinson 1977**. The sister of an elderly man came to stay with him and his woman friend. The man's sight, hearing and sense of smell were all deficient and his woman companion was of low intelligence. Fanny, the sister was said to be 'morbidly obsessed' with putting on weight. She refused to eat and became bed-bound and developed serious bedsores that became very badly infected. The couple made half-hearted attempts to get help for her but failed to obtain the proper medical aid and Fanny died.

The couple's conviction for manslaughter was upheld. The Court of Appeal held that they had assumed a duty to care for the sister, they knew that she was relying on them and they had failed to get her the assistance that she needed.

(iv) *Where there is a dangerous situation caused by the defendant and he has failed to put this right*
The House of Lords was of the opinion that the categories just mentioned did not cover all the situations where liability should be imposed. In the case of **Miller 1983** a squatter had fallen asleep while smoking and his cigarette caused the mattress to catch fire. The flames woke him but instead of putting out the fire, Miller merely moved to another room and went back to sleep. The house was badly damaged and the defendant's conviction for arson was upheld.

The House of Lords decided that 'failing to take measures that lie within one's power to counteract a danger that one has oneself created' could, in circumstances like this, create liability.

In some instances, the courts will avoid the difficulties of trying to establish liability for omissions and impose liability in another way. An example was the case of **Fagan v Metropolitan Police Commissioner 1969**, where the Court of Appeal decided that a battery could not be committed by an omission. To impose liability, therefore, the idea of a continuing act was used.

The defendant had been told to stop his car and pull in to the kerb. As he did so, he accidentally drove on to the policeman's foot. When he was shouted at to remove the car, the defendant swore at the policeman, told him he could wait and switched off the ignition. He was convicted of assaulting a police constable in the execution of his duty but later appealed stating that no liability could be incurred by merely failing to act.

The Court of Appeal held differently. The judges decided that driving onto the policeman's foot and then keeping the car there was one continuous act, not an act followed by an omission. Fagan's conviction, therefore, was upheld.

2.2.5 Suggested reform

The reform bodies appear to be very undecided on this subject. In 1980, the Criminal Law Revision Committee recommended that liability for omissions for offences against the person should be restricted to serious crimes. In 1989, however, the Law Commission took the opposite approach and suggested widening liability for omissions, proposing that some offences could be redrafted to allow for this.

The latest recommendations are in a Law Commission Report of 1993 *(No. 218)*. Attached to this report is the *Draft Criminal Law Bill*, ready to be put before Parliament. This ignores the earlier proposals of the Commission to widen liability and follows instead the reforms suggested in 1980!

Clause 19 of the Bill states that a party may be liable for omissions in the range of situations already laid down by the judges, but confines

liability to serious offences, such as intentional serious injury, torture, unlawful detention, kidnapping, abduction and aggravated abduction.

The *Draft Criminal Law Bill*, therefore, would not provide for more general liability for omissions. It does, however, recognise the '**Miller** principle', in *Clause 23*. This clause states that a person will commit an offence where he fails to act, which may not at that stage be unlawful, but then fails to take reasonable steps to deal with the results of that act.

Activity

- In groups or in written form, decide whether the right balance has been struck concerning liability for omissions.
- Assess whether the *actus reus* of a crime has been established in the following unrelated situation. Give cases to support your findings:

Des was in the habit of feeding his bedridden grandmother at lunchtime, before going to his part-time job. He was promoted suddenly, necessitating far greater hours at his place of work and totally forgot his grandmother's needs. His grandmother has just died of starvation.

Gary noticed that the wheel of the car in front of him was wobbling dangerously but failed to inform the driver because he was late for an appointment and did not wish to become involved. The wheel came off the car and the driver was killed.

Sue was staying illegally in college accommodation. She fell asleep while the bath was running and the bath water overflowed. Sue woke up, decided that the water was now too cold and went to bed, leaving the water running in the bathroom. The resulting flood seriously damaged the lower two floors of the college building.

Steve, an electrician employed by the local council, went off for his tea break, leaving all the wires exposed. Murray, the supervisor was electrocuted.

Comment

Some legal writers, like Professor Glanville Williams, favour a restrictive approach to imposing liability for omissions. Other academics, including Professor Ashworth, take the opposite view and state that the proposed reforms do not go far enough, as wider policy issues are involved.

Others also agree with this view and are dissatisfied with the current state of English law, which normally absolves a party from blame when he fails to help, even in extreme situations, such as where he stands watching, while a child drowns in a shallow pool of water. They would argue that there has been an unwelcome increase in the principle of non-involvement in the affairs of strangers, even when it is patently obvious that help is urgently needed. Harrowing reports of people ignoring cries for help from victims of muggers or rapists or closing their ears to the sounds of children being ill-treated are, unfortunately, all too common.

Education in good citizenship might be an alternative approach to creating further criminal offences.

FIVE KEY FACTS ON THE *ACTUS REUS*

- The *actus reus* comprises all the elements of a crime except the mental element.
- The *actus reus* may consist of conduct (as in appropriating property in theft), a result or consequence (e.g. a death in murder), or a state of affairs (**Larsonneur 1933, Winzar 1983**).
- Generally, there is no liability in criminal law for omissions, as stated by Stephen L J.
- There are limited exceptions to this rule, as where statute imposes liability (e.g. **Road Traffic Act 1988**), a contract of employment (**Pittwood 1902**), or a public duty (**Dytham 1979**). Liability may also be imposed where there is a special relationship between the parties (**Instan 1893, Gibbins and Proctor 1918**), where one party voluntarily accepts liability (**Stone and Dobinson 1977**), or where there is a dangerous situation that the person creating the danger fails to put right (**Miller 1983**).
- If liability cannot be imposed in this way, the courts may be prepared to say that there is a continuing act (**Fagan v MPC 1969**).

2.3 The *mens rea* of a crime

In addition to proving that the *actus reus* exists, in most cases it will also be necessary to show that the defendant has committed the offence with the relevant *mens rea*, i.e. the degree of blameworthiness required by the offence in question. It will be noted towards the end of this chapter, however, that some offences, usually those of a regulatory nature, do not require fault to be proved. These are offences of strict liability.

The latter crimes are increasing but are still in the minority. In the case of other offences, some form of *mens rea* will have to be established before guilt can be shown. The *mens rea* for each offence will be laid down in the relevant statute, or, in the case of common law offences will have been formulated by the judges developing the crime in question, as will be seen as you travel through this book.

2.3.1 The different degrees of *mens rea*

In relation to the most serious criminal offences, the prosecution will normally need to prove a high degree of blameworthiness. The defendant will only be found guilty if it is shown that he intended to commit the crime in question. This form of *mens rea* is necessary before the offence of murder is established. The person accused will only be convicted if the jury is convinced that he intended to kill or cause grievous bodily harm. Such a high degree of *mens rea* is also necessary to establish guilt under **s18 Offences Against the Person Act 1861**. The accused can only be convicted for this most serious non-fatal offence against the person if he maliciously wounds another or causes grievous bodily harm, 'with intent to do some grievous bodily harm'. Intention is also needed for the crime of

theft. The defendant will not be guilty of this offence unless it is shown that he appropriated property belonging to another, 'with the intention of permanently depriving the other of it'.

Other crimes do not necessarily require such a high degree of fault. They can be committed intentionally or recklessly. The other non-fatal offences against the person that we shall be studying in Chapter 6 all come into this category. These are the offences of assault, battery, assault occasioning actual bodily harm and malicious wounding or grievous bodily harm under **s20 Offences Against the Person Act**; other crimes are rape and criminal damage.

In a small number of cases, it is enough to establish mere negligence. This is comparatively common in civil law, which has laid down a duty not to be negligent in a wide variety of situations. In criminal law, however, the defendant will not normally be liable for careless acts, even where these cause harm to another person. There are, however, notable exceptions to this general rule, where criminal liability has been imposed. One example is driving without due care or attention. A much more serious offence that can be committed negligently is manslaughter although, as will be seen in Chapter 5 on involuntary manslaughter, the negligence in such a case must be 'gross'. It is now necessary to look at these three states of mind in more detail.

2.3.2 Intention

We noted earlier that liability for crimes like murder and theft can only be established if the jury is satisfied that the defendant intended to commit the offence. Unfortunately for law students, there is no statutory definition of the word 'intention' and it is normally left to the jury to decide whether such a state of mind exists.

The difference between intention, motive and desire

What has been made clear by the courts is that the word 'intention' is not to be equated with the word 'desire' or the word 'motive'. On occasion, we might have the desire to inflict a minor injury on a person who has upset us in some way or even to rob a bank if faced with grave financial problems. Provided that these remain as mere thoughts, we cannot be brought before a court, however strong the desire may be. It was clearly stated in **Cunliffe v Goodman 1950** that intention is a state of affairs 'that a person does more than merely contemplate'.

Intention should not normally be confused with motive. The motive for committing the crime in question may be a good one but if the intention is present, the *mens rea* will have been established and the defendant will have to hope that his motive is taken into account at the sentencing process. In **Chandler v DPP 1964**, the defendant was very much opposed to the use of nuclear weapons and had been involved in a 'sit in' at a military base with the purpose of preventing aircraft containing such missiles from taking off. He was charged with breaking into a prohibited place with a purpose prejudicial to the safety and interests of the state but argued that he did not have the appropriate *mens rea* for this offence. He claimed that his purpose was to save the State from the dangers of nuclear weapons.

The case reached the House of Lords, where it was established that the defendant's motive was irrelevant. The immediate purpose of the offender was to break into the airfield and cause an obstruction.

In the earlier case of **Steane 1947** the courts had been more prepared to consider the motive of the defendant. The latter appealed against a conviction for doing acts with the intention of assisting the enemy during the Second World

War. He had broadcast favourable propaganda for the Nazi regime but argued that he had only done this after being beaten and after threats that he and his family would be sent to a concentration camp if he refused to help. His conviction was quashed, despite the fact that his immediate purpose had been to help the enemy. Lord Goddard was obviously sympathetic and compared the defendant's action to those of prisoners of war who are also forced to do unpleasant acts to assist the captors.

Despite this case, which has not been expressly overruled, the current approach is to separate motive and intention, apart from in 'racially aggravated offences' and to use other methods, such as the defence of duress, or a reduced sentence to ensure that any special circumstances are taken into account.

Direct and oblique intention

In many cases it will not be too difficult for the jury to decide on the intention of the accused; it will be clear from the circumstances. This is referred to in law as a 'direct intent'.

For example, if a leader of a criminal gang took out a loaded gun and fired it straight at the heart of a rival gang leader, it would be obvious that he intended to kill or at least cause serious injury to that other person. Many would also argue that the purpose of the pilots on their suicide missions to New York and Washington on that fateful Tuesday, 11 September 2001, was just as clear. While fighting their alleged 'holy war', their immediate aim was not only to try to destroy the buildings in question but also to kill or injure the passengers inside the plane, staff and visitors in the World Trade Centre and people in the Pentagon. Most jurors would have little difficulty in finding the necessary intention to kill in such a situation.

It is another form of intent, known as 'oblique intent', that has caused the problems in this area of law. For example, some of the terrorists may not have known the full circumstances surrounding that terrible day and may have believed that there was to be an attack on American property. Should they, too, be found guilty of murder? Should an investor facing ruin from unwise dealings on the Stock Market be found guilty of murder if he starts a fire on the floor of the Stock Exchange in the early hours of the morning to draw attention to his losses and three cleaners perish in the blaze? He may never have given any thought to the fact that other people might be inside the building and claim that it was not his purpose to kill or injure anyone, merely to damage the building. Others, however, may well take the view that he should have foreseen that death or serious injury was likely in such circumstances. The word 'intention', therefore, has been widened and in some instances will also cover a situation where the defendant's avowed purpose was different from the actual consequences of his act. Ultimately, it will be up to the jury to decide on the question of guilt but what has caused great problems is trying to establish how much help the trial jury should give the jury in such a situation.

The current state of the law on intention in murder was expressed by the House of Lords in the case of **Woollin 1998**, which modified an earlier direction by the Court of Appeal in **Nedrick**. Their Lordships affirmed that it was the task of the jury to determine whether the defendant intended to kill or cause serious bodily harm. They went on to say, however, that where this simple direction was not enough, the jury should be further directed that they were not entitled to find the necessary intention in cases of murder, unless they felt sure that death or serious bodily harm was a virtually certain result of the defendant's action (barring some unforeseen intervention) and the defendant had appreciated that fact.

To understand how this direction was eventually reached, we need to look at six

major cases starting back in 1961, where the defendant was charged with murder but has alleged that it was not his purpose to commit such a crime.

In **DPP v Smith 1961**, the defendant had been ordered to leave his car, which contained stolen goods. Instead, he accelerated sharply and drove off at 60 miles per hour with the policeman clinging to the vehicle. The officer was thrown off and into the path of an incoming car and later died from his injuries. Smith was charged with murder and convicted. His appeal against this, on the grounds that he had not intended to cause the death, reached the House of Lords.

The House of Lords upheld the conviction, deciding that the defendant had the necessary intention for murder if an ordinary responsible man, in similar circumstances would have contemplated the end result.

At this stage, therefore, an objective test had been laid down for establishing intention in murder cases, a view that was strongly criticised by academics and later led to intervention from the newly formed Law Commission. On the advice of this body, **s8 Criminal Justice Act 1967** was enacted.

S8 states that the jury is not bound in law to infer that the defendant intended or foresaw a result of his actions just because it was a natural and probable consequence of them. It should, instead, make the decision about whether he did have such an intention or foresight by looking at all the evidence and drawing the proper conclusions from that.

It can be seen therefore, that others are not supposed to tell the jury what it must do in such a situation. The jurors must, instead look at the matter in a subjective way and decide what the actual defendant intended or foresaw, not look at the matter from the viewpoint of the reasonable man, as suggested in **Smith.**

In the case of **Hyam v DPP 1975**, the defendant became very jealous when another woman took her place in the affections of her man friend. In the early hours of the morning, therefore, she poured petrol through this woman's letterbox and set fire to it. In the resulting blaze, two children died.

Hyam argued that she had only intended to frighten the other woman and her case reached the House of Lords, which rejected her appeal.

The judges varied in their reasons for dismissing the appeal and two gave the impression that intention was established if it was shown that the defendant foresaw the result as highly probable. Lord Hailsham did not subscribe to this view and his words were picked up by judges of the Court of Appeal in two non-fatal injury cases, that of **Mohan 1975** and **Belfon 1976.** These judges decided that mere foresight that death or personal injury was highly probable was not the same as having the intention to cause the act in question. Instead, it was merely evidence for the jury to look at, when deciding whether an intention was present. This view of the law is the one that has prevailed, as will be seen from later cases.

The question of what constitutes intention resurfaced in the case of **Moloney 1985**. The defendant had been drinking late at night with his stepfather after the Ruby Wedding anniversary celebration of his grandparents. Evidence showed that the parties were on good terms when the others left but, later, a disagreement broke out over which of them could load a shotgun in the fastest time. The stepson won this argument and then claimed that his stepfather dared him to pull the trigger. He did so and the stepfather was killed. Moloney was convicted of murder but the House of Lords changed the verdict to manslaughter.

Lord Bridge delivered the main judgment. He made it clear that it was the jury's task to decide on the matter of intention. He stated:

The golden rule should be that, when directing a jury on the mental element necessary in a crime of specific intent, the judge should avoid any elaboration or paraphrase of what it meant by intent, and leave it to the jury's good sense to decide whether the accused acted with the necessary intent, unless the judge is convinced that . . . some further explanation or elaboration is strictly necessary to avoid misunderstanding.

He went on to say that he thought that such cases would be very rare, even where the death is more indirect.

This part of his judgment was approved of in later cases but problems arose over the form the direction to the jury should take when those 'rare occurrences' arose. He said that the jury should be asked to decide on two matters:

First, was death or really serious injury in a murder case . . . a natural consequence of the defendant's act? Secondly, did the defendant foresee that consequence as being a natural consequence of his act? The jury should then be told that if they answer yes to both questions it is a proper inference for them to draw that he intended that consequence.

These '**Moloney** guidelines' as they came to be called were themselves called into question in the case of **Hancock and Shankland 1986**. The case concerned two striking miners who were bitterly angry when another miner went back to work. They therefore pushed a heavy concrete block and post from a bridge onto the motorway in front of the taxi and police escort taking the miner to work. The taxi driver was killed. The trial judge diligently recited the **Moloney** guidelines to the jury and the defendants were convicted of murder. The Court of Appeal quashed the conviction and this was confirmed by the House of Lords.

The Court of Appeal had argued that the **Moloney** guidelines were deficient. In the

House of Lords, Lord Scarman agreed with this and stated that the Moloney guidelines were 'unsafe and misleading'. He declined to put others in their place, even though the Lord Chief Justice in the Court of Appeal had suggested rather lengthy ones! He did go on to reiterate, however, that it was the jurors who should decide whether the intention to kill existed, after looking at all the evidence in the case.

This case established that the **Moloney** guidelines should no longer be used. Both the appeal courts also stressed that even where there is a belief that the defendant must have known that the consequences of his act were virtually certain, this is not the same as saying that he has such an intention. The members of the jury must still decide on this point, after hearing that they are entitled to infer this if they wish to do so after looking at all the evidence.

The matter came up again in the case of **Nedrick 1986**, a case with very similar facts to **Hyam**, mentioned earlier. The defendant again poured petrol through a letterbox and set it alight and the death of an innocent child resulted. The jury convicted Nedrick of murder. The trial at first instance was heard before the case of **Moloney** reached the House of Lords and, was, of course, also before the modifications made in **Hancock and Shankland**. The judge had therefore directed the jury in a way that followed the House of Lords' decision in **Hyam**. The appeal against the conviction for murder was accepted because of this misdirection occasioned by the changes in the law.

Lord Lane decided that the correct direction to the jurors should now be to tell them that:

if they are satisfied that at the material time the defendant recognised that death or serious injury would be virtually certain, (barring some unforeseen intervention) to result from his voluntary act, then that is a

fact from which they may find it easy to infer that he intended to kill or do serious bodily harm, even though he may not have had any desire to achieve that result.

Lord Lane also stated that 'Where the charge is murder and in the rare cases where the simple direction is not enough, the jury should be directed that they are not entitled to infer the necessary intention unless they feel sure that death or serious bodily harm was a virtual certainty (barring some unforeseen intervention) as a result of the defendant's actions and that the defendant appreciated that this was the case.'

The cases, however, continued to confuse the issue. In **Walker and Hayles 1990**, an attempted murder case, the conviction was upheld, even though it was claimed that the judge had misdirected the jurors on the lines that they could also infer the necessary intention if the defendant foresaw the consequences of his act as being 'highly probable'. The Court of Appeal stated that:

once one departs from absolute certainty, there is bound to be a question of degree. We do not regard the difference of degree, if there is one, between a very high degree of probability on the one hand and virtual certainty on the other as being sufficient to render what the recorder said a misdirection.

The court did, however, go on to state that it would prefer the words 'virtually certain' to be used.

In the case of **Woollin 1996**, the defendant was alleged to have violently shaken his three-month-old baby and then thrown him across the room in the direction of his pram four or five feet away. Woollin admitted in later interviews that the baby had hit the floor hard but claimed that he 'did not think it would kill him', although he accepted that there was a risk of injury.

In addition to the model direction in **Nedrick**, the trial judge had later told the jurors that they might infer intention 'if they were satisfied that when the defendant threw the child he appreciated that there was a substantial risk that he would cause serious harm to it'. The defence claimed in the appeal that such a direction 'might therefore have served to confuse or mislead the jury as to the degree of foresight required'.

The Court of Appeal decided that there was no misdirection.

The issue was then referred to the House of Lords. Their Lordships disagreed with the Court of Appeal's decision. The point of law put before that court was quite a narrow one. It concerned murder cases where there is no direct evidence that D's purpose was to kill or inflict serious injury on V and asked:

> . . . is it necessary to direct the jury that they may only infer an intent to do serious injury if they are satisfied (a) that serious bodily harm was a virtually certain consequence of D's voluntary act and (b) that D appreciated that fact?

The answer was in the affirmative although Lord Steyn decided that the word 'find' should be used instead of the word 'infer'. Apart from this modification therefore, the middle part of the judgment of the Court of Appeal in **Nedrick** was considered to be a correct statement of the law. The jurors will still decide the issue but, where the charge is murder, their discretion has been fettered and they can only find intention when they are satisfied that death or serious bodily harm was virtually certain (barring some unforeseen intervention) and the defendant appreciated this fact.

Woollin's conviction for murder therefore, was quashed and one of manslaughter substituted instead. Even though the judge had, at an earlier time, given a correct direction under the **Nedrick** guidelines, the House of Lords

decided that he had later confused the jury by his comments the next day concerning 'a substantial risk', thus giving a wider direction. As it was impossible to know which of the two statements the jury had followed, this must therefore be considered a material misdirection that could not be cured by the inclusion of the earlier correct statement of the law.

Comment

The decision in **Woollin** has made the law more certain in some respects but, unfortunately, leaves many more issues unresolved.

Plus points
- The new direction in murder cases is mercifully brief and easy for a jury to understand. Their Lordships had stressed the need for any direction to be 'clear and simple and expressed in as few words as possible'. This modification by them of the middle part of the judgment in **Nedrick** has this advantage, particularly when compared to the lengthy statements formulated by Lord Bridge in **Moloney** and those suggested by the Court of Appeal in **Hancock and Shankland**, which could well have confused a jury.
- Following on from this, the line between intention and recklessness has now been firmly drawn. The fact that death or serious injury might have been 'highly probable' or that there was 'a substantial risk' of such harm arising, is no longer sufficient in cases of murder.
- There are now clear instructions as to what the members of the jury cannot do, i.e. they are not entitled to find a person guilty of murder unless they are sure that death or serious bodily harm was virtually certain and the defendant appreciated this fact.
- It appears that the case of **Hyam** has at last been put to rest. Professor Smith states forcefully:

Their Lordships have often been unnecessarily – and dangerously – coy about declaring that their brethren or predecessors have got it wrong. Lord Steyn now recognises the truth about Hyam. It was not materially different from Nedrick; and in Nedrick the conviction was rightly quashed.

Areas of confusion

- In **Nedrick**, the Court of Appeal's final direction appeared to be that foresight of a consequence as being virtually certain was not the same as intention. Part of the direction stated that the jury was merely entitled to infer intention if death or serious bodily harm was a virtual certainty. From this, it can be presumed that they were not compelled to do so.

  In **Woollin**, Lord Steyn appears to accept this fact by retaining the word 'entitled' in his revised direction. The amended direction states that the jurors are not entitled to find intention unless they are sure that the defendant foresaw that death or serious injury was virtually certain. Nevertheless, once they are decided on this issue, they appear to have some discretion about their eventual decision. It would appear from this that foresight of virtually certain consequences is not therefore the same as intention. It is still only evidence on which the jury may find it. Peter Mirefield, writing in the *Criminal Law Review* in 1999 supports this view. A P Simester and Stephen Shute in the March 2000 edition of the same journal also make this point when they state:

  The articulation of 'find' substituted by their Lordships in **Woollin** *suggests that the link between virtual certainty and intention is definitional; on the other hand, what remains of the model definition is expressed in negative*

terms . . . *which suggests that the jury can legitimately refuse to find intention even where foresight of virtual certainty is proved.*

- It is felt that such an approach could cause problems in the future. Professor Sir John Smith argues that, if this view of the law were taken, a jury could legitimately ask the following question of the trial judge:

  We are all quite sure that D knew it was virtually certain that his act would cause death. You tell us we are entitled to find that he intended it. Are we bound to find that? Some of us want to and some do not. How should we decide?

  A further direction would then be necessary!

- Others would stress the fact that Lord Steyn changed the word 'infer' which appeared in the **Nedrick** direction to that of 'find', and thus by this action was acknowledging the concerns expressed by academics like Glanville Williams and Ashworth over the use of the former word. They would argue that it follows from this that the House of Lords is now accepting the view that foresight that a consequence is a virtual certainty actually equates to intention. To support this, they would draw our attention to the fact that Lord Steyn quoted with apparent approval a statement in **Nedrick** declaring that 'A result foreseen as virtually certain is an intended result'. Professor Smith favours this approach. He stated in his commentary on the case:

  If that is right, the only question for the jury is 'Did the defendant foresee the result as virtually certain? If he did, he intended it.' That, it is submitted is what the law should be; and it now seems that we have at last moved substantially in that direction.

This is in line with a view expressed earlier by Professor Glanville Williams. He stated back in 1989 that:

The proper view is that intention includes not only desire of consequence (purpose) but also foresight of certainty of the consequence, as a matter of legal definition.

Unfortunately, after all the time and effort expended this issue still requires clarification. A good case can be made out for either of the arguments mentioned above.

- Such unresolved issues probably mean that further appeals will be inevitable. Alan Norrie, writing in the *Criminal Law Review* 1999 does not believe that **Woollin** constitutes the last word on indirect intention in murder cases. He argues persuasively that:

Another case with different moral facts, reflecting more manifest malice, could well let the Hyam genie out of the bottle.

- If no jury discretion exists in such cases, there could be problems where moral issues are involved. For example, a doctor might give strong drugs to a patient simply to relieve his dreadful suffering but with the knowledge that death or serious harm was virtually certain to result. Is such a man always to be found guilty of murder or should some sort of moral threshold have to be passed before such liability arises?

Effective, but hardly brief!
- The point of law certified for the House of Lords only related to murder and Lord Steyn stated that a different approach to the word 'intention' could be taken where other offences were concerned. This matter needs clarification.
- With regard to the crime of attempted murder, the case of **Walker & Hayles** was not expressly overruled. It would be strange however, if a less demanding standard were to apply to this lesser crime and an offender found guilty if he foresaw the consequences of his actions as being 'highly probable'. It is a matter of regret that such a simple issue was not addressed by their Lordships.
- It is also not clear whether the modified direction in **Woollin** had the endorsement of all five Law Lords. While two of the judges expressly agreed with the judgment of Lord Steyn, Lord Browne-Wilkinson and Lord Goff only agreed that the appeal should be allowed, thus suggesting that they may not have agreed with all of Lord Steyn's reasoning.

After all the difficulties the cases mentioned above have given to trial judges, academics and students, cynics might argue that it would be preferable not to give any additional guidance to the jury and merely draw its attention to **s8 Criminal Justice Act 1967**.

A more effective move would be to put pressure on Parliament to formulate a statutory definition of intention, perhaps on the lines suggested below. This would deal with the issue as a matter of law and take the pressure off the jury, which could then do the task asked of it, which is to apply the law, as stated by the judge, to the facts given to it.

Activity

- In essay form or in group discussion, assess the truth of the following statement:

  'A result foreseen as virtually certain is an intended result'.

- Lara belonged to a fringe animal rights group. She was very upset when a Private Member's Bill outlawing fishing was defeated in the House of Commons. She therefore decided to set fire to the building to draw attention to the cause. There was a late night sitting in Parliament at the time and two MPs were overcome with smoke and died. Lara has been charged with the crime of murder.

  Advise the judge and jury how they should approach the subject of deciding whether Lara had the necessary *mens rea* for this offence.

Suggested reform of intention

There have been three reports on this, a Law Commission Report in 1989, the accompanying *Draft Criminal Code*, a report from the Select Committee of the House of Lords on *Murder and Life Imprisonment*, which echoed the views of the Commission and, finally the definition of intention in the Law Commission's report *'Legislating the Criminal Code: Offences Against the Person and General Principles'* (*Law Com No. 218 1993*). The latter only applies to non-fatal offences but it is assumed that the same definition would be used for fatal offences. This states that a person is classed as acting 'intentionally' when 'it is his purpose to cause it, or, although it is not his purpose to cause that result, he knows it would occur in the ordinary course of events if he were to succeed in his purpose of causing some other result'.

TEN KEY FACTS ON INTENTION

- The *mens rea* of an offence usually consists of intention or recklessness, although in a small percentage of crimes, mere negligence will suffice. Manslaughter is one such crime, provided that the negligence is gross. In a small amount of criminal offences, often ones of a regulatory nature, liability might be strict.

- The word 'intention' is not defined by statute although there have been repeated calls for reform.

- The judges have made it clear that the word 'intention' is not normally to be equated with the words 'desire' (**Cunliffe v Goodman 1950**), or 'motive' (**Chandler v DPP**), but note the new 'racially aggravated' offences under the **Crime and Disorder Act 1998**, under which the defendant's motive may well be a factor.

- **S8 Criminal Justice Act 1967** is designed to help members of the jury and tells them that they should make the decision about whether the defendant had the necessary intention or foresight by looking at all the evidence and drawing the proper conclusions from that. The test, therefore, is a subjective one.

- Where it is obviously the purpose of the defendant to achieve the intended result he is stated to have a direct intent to commit the crime in question. In other cases, the actual consequence may not have been his original purpose. These are known as cases of oblique intent.

- In cases of direct intent, the jury will be asked to decide whether the defendant had the intention to commit the crime without any additional guidance from the judge. In cases where the defendant is claiming that it was not his purpose to kill or seriously injure the victim or cause him other harm but where nonetheless this has happened, a further direction from the judge may be deemed to be necessary (**Moloney 1986**).

- The wording of such a direction has changed several times, as seen in cases such as **Smith, Hyam, Moloney, Hancock and Shankland** and **Nedrick**. Part of the direction in the latter case was approved of, with some modification, by the House of Lords in **Woollin**. This amended direction states that, in cases where the charge is murder, the jury is not entitled to find intention unless it is sure that death or serious bodily harm was a virtual certainty and the defendant appreciated this fact. This is very similar to the direction suggested by Lord Lane in **Nedrick**, except that he used the word 'infer'. This has now been changed to the word 'find', which appears to give the jury less choice in the matter.

- In cases of murder it is not now sufficient to show a lesser degree of blameworthiness, such as the defendant being aware that death or serious bodily harm was 'highly probable' (**Walker and Hayles 1990**) or that he appreciated 'that there was a substantial risk' of this consequence (**Woollin 1998**). The **Nedrick** wording, as modified by the House of Lords in **Woollin**, must be used. The blurring of the lines between intention and recklessness has therefore been halted.

- It is still not clear, however, whether foresight of a consequence as virtually certain amounts to intention as a matter of law or merely permits the jury to find intention once this has been established. Other problems with the modified direction should also be noted.

- In **Woollin**, the House of Lords made it clear that the word 'intent' need not necessarily have the same meaning in lesser crimes.

2.3.3 Recklessness

The preceding part of this chapter showed how difficult it can be in some cases to prove that the defendant intended to commit the crime in question. For many offences, therefore, it is not necessary to show such a high degree of blameworthiness; it is sufficient to prove that the accused has been reckless as to whether the crime was committed.

Unfortunately for the poor law student, however, having just grappled with the complexities of the meaning of intention, it will now be discovered that there is similar uncertainty over the meaning of the word 'reckless' and that two meanings are currently in use for different types of crime. We therefore need to examine how such a situation came about.

The meaning of the word 'reckless'

Before we investigate the two different meanings of the word 'reckless', it is important to note that in all cases where this type of *mens rea* needs to be shown, it is essential to establish that the defendant took an unjustifiable risk. Not all risks come into this category. For example, a surgeon may perform a delicate operation on a patient, which only has a 50:50 chance of success but is one which may well give him a much better quality of life if it succeeds. There is obvious social utility in allowing the doctor to proceed without the fear of criminal liability if the operation is a failure.

Some actions have no such utility. The throwing of a firework into a crowd of people would be such a case; the offender would be taking an unjustifiable risk that someone in the crowd might be harmed and it would be felt right for such a person to face criminal charges if that happened.

The two types of recklessness

Confusion has arisen over the legal definition of the word 'reckless' because of the different opinions as to the degree of recklessness to be shown. Some would argue that a defendant should only be liable if he had actually foreseen that he was taking an unjustifiable risk, whereas others are of the belief that he should be liable if he ought to have foreseen such a risk. The latter is a more objective view under which it would be easier to establish guilt. These two types of recklessness are known respectively as Cunningham and Caldwell recklessness.

Cunningham recklessness

Before the case of **MPC v Caldwell 1982**, the judges had decided that the more subjective approach was the one to be used, i.e. before the defendant could be said to be liable, he must have been aware of the risk he was running.

This was established in the case of **Cunningham 1957**. It was stated that this type of recklessness had to be shown in any case where the old-fashioned word 'malicious' was used. The offence of malicious wounding is an example and another is shown in the case of **Cunnningham** itself, i.e. the crime of 'maliciously administering a noxious thing so as to endanger life', contrary to **s3 Offences Against the Person Act 1861.**

The defendant stole money from a gas meter and in so doing, tore the meter from the wall and left the gas pipes exposed. Gas then seeped through the porous walls into the basement of the house next door and affected a woman living there. Cunningham was convicted but made a successful appeal.

It was held that the judge had misdirected the jury by telling them that the word 'malicious' simply meant 'wicked', instead of giving it its more precise legal meaning.

The Appeal Court stated that when the word 'malicious' was used in a statute, it was necessary to establish that the defendant either intended to cause the harm in question or he had foreseen that such an event would occur. On this test, Cunningham could only be convicted if he knew of the risk from the gas but, nevertheless, went on to take it. It was not enough that he ought to have foreseen such a risk; the test was subjective. This ruling was therefore held to apply to all cases that had the word 'malicious' in the offence and in **Parmenter 1991**, a conviction for malicious wounding was quashed because such a direction had not been given.

For several years, this test was also felt to be of a more general application, even in newer statutes where the word 'reckless' was used, as in the case of the **Criminal Damage Act 1971**. In this statute, the word 'reckless' replaces the word 'malicious' in the preceding act which was the **Malicious Damage Act 1861**. Before the **Criminal Damage Act** had been passed, the

Law Commission had considered the mental element in this offence and had decided that the law was satisfactory in this respect, although it was admitted that it needed to be expressed more clearly. This was effected by using the words 'intentionally' and 'recklessly', instead of the word 'maliciously'. No definition of recklessness was provided in the Act, so it was therefore believed that the law remained substantially the same, despite the change in wording, i.e. it was believed that the **Cunningham** test continued to apply.

This view was followed in the case of **Stephenson 1979**. A conviction for criminal damage was quashed because the trial judge had stated that the defendant could be found guilty if he 'closed his mind to the obvious fact of risk from his act', a test which was more objective in approach.

The defendant was a schizophrenic and had decided to sleep in a haystack. He lit a fire to keep himself warm and caused £300 worth of damage. Such a result would obviously have been foreseen by an ordinary 'reasonable' man, but the Court of Appeal quashed the conviction. Lord Lane was emphatic that the test was subjective: 'we wish to make it clear that the test remains subjective, that the knowledge or appreciation of risk of some damage must have entered the defendant's mind even though he may have suppressed it'.

Caldwell recklessness

This then was the position until the cases of **Caldwell** and **Lawrence**, in **1982**. These two cases were decided by the House of Lords on the same day and, together, they introduced a high degree of uncertainty into this area of law.

In **MPC v Caldwell 1982**, the defendant had been engaged to work for the proprietor of a residential hotel but had been dismissed and nursed a grievance against the owner. When he was very drunk, Caldwell broke a window in the hotel and started a fire on the ground floor.

Fortunately, this was discovered and put out quite quickly and no serious harm was done, either in the form of personal injury to the ten people residing in the hotel, or in the form of property damage.

Caldwell was prepared to admit to the lesser charge of criminal damage but fiercely resisted the more serious charge of causing criminal damage with intent to endanger life or being reckless as to whether life would be endangered. Despite this, the jury found him guilty and he was sentenced to three years' imprisonment.

The case eventually reached the House of Lords where Lord Diplock gave the main speech and changed the law on recklessness, at least for the crime of criminal damage. Diplock argued:

> that the only person who knows what the accused's mental processes were at the time of committing the crime is the accused himself and probably not even he can recall them accurately when the rage or excitement under which he acted has passed or he has sobered up if he were under the influence of drink at the end of the relevant time.

He therefore believed that the test for recklessness should be widened to encompass a wider range of situations. He decided that a person is reckless under the **Criminal Damage Act 1971** if:

1. He does an act which in fact creates an obvious risk that property will be destroyed or damaged, and
2. when he does the act he either has not given any thought to the possibility of there being any such risk or has recognised that there was some risk involved and has nonetheless gone on to do it.

Caldwell's appeal therefore was dismissed and a wider test of recklessness had emerged on a three to two majority. Lord Edmund Davies and Lord Wilberforce dissented on this point but upheld the conviction.

It should be noted, however, that **Cunningham** recklessness had not disappeared in this new test; it is included in the second half of point two, i.e. the defendant has recognised that there may be some risk involved but has nonetheless gone on to take it. It is the other part of the test which has the effect of widening liability substantially. It includes situations where there is a risk, which would have been obvious to a reasonable man, but the defendant in question has not given any thought to it.

Lord Diplock believed that such an extension of liability was both necessary and justifiable, because of the difficulties of trying to gauge the state of the defendant's mind. He argued that **Cunningham**-style recklessness had been developed for a special purpose, i.e. to deal with statutes containing the word 'malicious', which seemed to indicate some foreseeability on the part of the defendant. The **Criminal Damage Act**, on the other hand, had substituted the word 'reckless', so he argued that the same approach was not necessary. He also stated that it was not helpful to classify types of recklessness into subjective and objective categories but, despite this plea, that is exactly what has happened.

Judgment in the case of **Lawrence** was also given by the House of Lords on the same day as **Caldwell** but after that decision, and by a differently constituted court, although Lord Diplock was included in both sittings. In **Lawrence**, the House, in a reckless driving case, upheld the wider definition of recklessness, laid down in **Caldwell**.

A motorcyclist had collided with and killed a pedestrian and the House held that there had been an obvious and serious risk, to which Lawrence had failed to advert. His conviction, therefore, was upheld. Later cases followed this new approach. In **Reid 1992**, discussed more fully below, Lord Keith stated that the: 'absence of something from a person's state of mind is as much part of his state of mind as is its presence'.

Lord Diplock's attempt to clarify the law on recklessness and, arguably, to make his new test one of universal application, attracted great criticism from both judges and academics. It was said that the change in the law was 'regrettable' (Professor Glanville Williams), that the test was 'not very helpful' (Lord Browne-Wilkinson) and was one which made the eyes of the jury 'glaze over' when it was put to them (Professor Smith).

The test, therefore, far from becoming of universal application, was attacked from the beginning and its use has been increasingly restricted. It was used, albeit in a strained way, in the case of **Pigg 1982**, an attempted rape case, but later abandoned in similar cases where it was decided that the decision in **Morgan** and the provisions in the **Sexual Offences (Amendment) Act 1976** had made it clear that a more subjective approach had to be taken in such cases. The case of **Satnam 1983** is an example of this.

The Court of Appeal also confirmed that **Cunningham** recklessness was still necessary for offences containing the word 'malicious', as in the offence of malicious wounding. In **W (a minor) v Dolbey 1983**, a boy of 15 pointed an airgun belonging to his brother at a man on a farm and, when told to put it down, fired it instead, wounding the man in question. The boy argued that he thought the gun was unloaded. His conviction for unlawful wounding was quashed because the more objective test had been applied and this was held to be incorrect for this type of offence. In **Parmenter 1991**, the House of Lords also agreed that **Cunningham** recklessness was necessary for cases of assault, as will be noted in Chapter 6.

It can be seen, therefore, that **Cunningham**, rather than **Caldwell** recklessness, must be shown for rape, attempted rape and for any cases where the word 'malicious' appears in the definition of the offence. In addition, the **Caldwell** test no longer has any application in driving offences because reckless driving has been replaced by dangerous driving. It will be noted in Chapter 5 that reckless manslaughter, for which **Caldwell** recklessness would have sufficed, has also disappeared and been replaced by manslaughter by gross negligence. Gradually, therefore, the cases to which **Caldwell** recklessness might have applied are disappearing or the judges are stating that the test should not be used.

When does Caldwell recklessness still apply?

We now need to investigate the situations in which it will still be relevant and these appear to be confined, at least in the areas we are studying, to offences of criminal damage. In these cases, however, the new test is strictly applied, sometimes with unjust results.

In **Elliott v C (a minor) 1983**, the defendant was only 14 and of low intelligence. She stayed out all night without sleep and entered a garden shed, where she poured white spirit over a carpet and set light to it and the whole shed was destroyed. The Divisional Court reluctantly upheld her conviction for aggravated criminal damage, because the court was bound by the precedent set in **Caldwell**, concerning the test of recklessness. Goff L J stated, however: 'I would be lacking in candour if I were to conceal my unhappiness about the conclusion which I feel compelled to reach.'

A possible loophole?

It is clear that the **Caldwell** test, when it is applied, is a strict one and its use will make more offenders liable. It has, however, been argued that there is a loophole, or lacuna as it is called, through which some offenders may escape. It would arise where it has been established that the defendant has considered the possibility of a risk, but has concluded that no risk exists and has then gone ahead with his action. If he had not decided to plead guilty may have been able to use such a loophole in **Crossman 1986**. He also ignored the advice from others that a load of heavy machinery was not suitably secured. He argued that 'it was as safe as houses'. Unfortunately, his judgement was wrong and the load fell off the lorry and killed a pedestrian. He had, however, given thought to the risk and erroneously decided that one did not exist, so *prima facie*, would seem to come under the alleged lacuna.

The matter was aired in the case of **Chief Constable of Avon and Somerset v Shimmen 1986**. The defendant possessed skills in martial arts and was demonstrating these to his friends. He intended to land a kick falling just short of a shop window, but his skills were not as great as he imagined and he put his leg through the window. The magistrates were not prepared to convict and the prosecution appealed to the Divisional Court. This court decided that the lacuna did not apply in this case. The judges argued that he had perceived that there was at least some risk and had then gone on to take it; he had not decided that no risk at all existed.

The Court of Appeal took a similar view in the case of **Merrick 1995**, where the defendant had gained permission to remove some old electrical equipment from a house and in so doing, had left a live cable exposed for six minutes before burying it. He argued that he had believed that there was no risk. Once again, the judges preferred to take the view that he must have known that there was some risk in the period while the cable was exposed but had thought that the risk was worth taking. That, they argued, was not the same as deciding that there was no risk at all.

Eventually, the House of Lords was called on to consider this problem. In **Reid 1992**, the defendant was driving in the centre of London and tried to overtake on an inside lane. This narrowed considerably near a junction to allow for a taxi driver's hut. Reid struck this hut and his passenger was killed. He appealed against his conviction for causing death by dangerous driving. The case reached the House of Lords, which laid down three situations in a driving case where someone might not be liable under the **Caldwell/Lawrence** test:

- Where the driver acted under an understandable or excusable mistake of fact, (as, for example, overtaking on a hill when driving a left-hand drive vehicle and being misinformed about the safety of such an act, or where a safe manoeuvre suddenly becomes unsafe because of a fuel blockage).
- Where the driver's ability to recognise a possible risk could have been affected by a condition which is not his fault, (as, for example, illness or shock).
- Where the driver was acting under duress.

Their Lordships accepted that it was not always essential to use the exact words laid down in **Caldwell/Lawrence** and agreed that there were limited exceptions where the rule would not apply. Reckless driving has now disappeared so the exception will no longer be necessary for those cases. Presumably, if relevant, they will apply to cases of criminal damage. They are, however, far narrower than at first believed. A wider lacuna has not been accepted by the courts.

To sum up, since the case of **MPC v Caldwell 1982**, there are two types of recklessness in English law, **Cunningham** recklessness, which is required for most of the offences we shall be studying and **Caldwell** recklessness which is now limited to criminal damage. These matters will be returned to in Chapters 6 and 9. The rules are summarised in the key facts chart on page 34.

Activity

- In groups or individually, discuss the following statement: 'The use of two tests to define recklessness in English law has caused both confusion and injustice.'
- Harry, aged 14, ran away from home two weeks ago. At night, when it was chilly, he slept in the doorway of Hermione's supermarket but was then moved on by the manager, Voldemort. Harry returned to the supermarket entrance the next evening and lit a small fire. Unfortunately for Harry the wind was strong and the fire spread rapidly. Much of the store was damaged and the late-evening staff had to be evacuated. No personal injury resulted. Using cases discussed in this section, discuss Harry's possible *mens rea*.

Comment

It is unfortunate that two types of recklessness exist in English law. One can perhaps understand why Lord Diplock wished to introduce a wider test and, arguably, this is not too unfair in basic criminal damage cases. What causes concern, however, is the use of the test for the aggravated offences of criminal damage, where the maximum sentence is life imprisonment. The judges have shown that they are prepared to sentence up to this maximum in these cases, especially arson, and it could be seriously questioned whether an objective view of the defendant's guilt should be taken. In other cases where the maximum sentence is life, a subjective approach is taken. Another criticism is that the **Caldwell** test blurs what was formerly a clear distinction between recklessness and negligence and creates a lack of uniformity over an important concept.

FIVE KEY FACTS ON RECKLESSNESS

- Recklessness is the taking of an unjustifiable risk. Before 1982, **Cunningham**, or subjective recklessness, was the test to be applied in all cases (**Cunningham 1957**). It seeks to discover whether the defendant was aware that there was an unjustified risk. A subjective approach is taken.
- The House of Lords' decisions on the same day in **MPC v Caldwell** and **Lawrence 1982**, restated the law and laid down a different test in cases of criminal damage and what was then reckless driving. This said that a person is reckless when he does an act which creates an obvious risk, in circumstances where he has either not given any thought to the possibility that a risk exists or has given the matter some thought but nevertheless has gone on to take it. It can be seen that this introduces a more objective element into the test and will thus make more people liable, as shown in **Elliot v C (a minor) 1983**.
- At first, it was suggested that the test would apply to all cases but, with the demise of reckless driving and reckless manslaughter, it now seems only to apply to offences of criminal damage.
- The subjective, **Cunningham** test is used for cases of rape (**Satnam 1983**), malicious wounding (**W (a minor) v Dolbey**), assault (**Parmenter 1991**).
- The use of a possible lacuna in the **Caldwell** test has been recognised by the House of Lords but has been strictly contained (**Reid 1992**).

Possible Reform of Recklessness

The Law Commission, in the *Draft Code* and in later Bills, favours a return to subjective recklessness. It proposes that a person acts recklessly with respect to:

(i) a circumstance, when he is aware of a risk that it exists or will exist; and
(ii) a result, when he is aware of a risk that it will occur, and it is unreasonable, having regard to the circumstances known to him, to take that risk.

2.3.4 Negligence

Negligence occurs when a person acts in a way that falls below the standard expected of the reasonable person in the same situation as the accused. Such carelessness often incurs liability in civil law but, in addition, there are certain situations where a person would also be liable under the criminal law.

As discussed in the last section, the distinction between recklessness and negligence used to be clearly defined; the former was the deliberate taking of an unjustifiable risk, while the latter was inadvertent risk taking. Since the decisions in **Caldwell** and **Lawrence**, however, the lines between the two forms of blameworthiness have become increasingly blurred.

Negligent acts may suffice to incur liability in driving offences. In **McRone v Riding 1938**, the defendant was a learner driver but, nonetheless, it was decided that he could be convicted of careless driving if his standard of driving fell below that of a reasonably competent driver.

Negligence, albeit negligence of a higher degree, will also suffice for the more serious offences of dangerous driving and causing death by dangerous driving. These offences were introduced by the **Road Traffic Act 1991**, which substituted new sections in to the **Road Traffic Act 1988**, and, at the same time, abolished the offences of reckless driving and causing death by reckless driving. The new **s2A Road Traffic Act 1988** states that a person will be guilty of dangerous driving if the way he drives falls far below what would be expected of a competent and careful driver and it would be obvious to the latter that driving in that way would be dangerous. He would also be driving dangerously if it would be obvious to a competent and careful driver that driving a vehicle in its current state would be dangerous. The test, therefore, is objective, i.e. would a competent and careful person drive in such a way?

In addition to these serious driving offences, grossly negligent behaviour that leads to the death of a person may result in a manslaughter charge. This area of law will be examined more fully in Chapter 5 on involuntary manslaughter. For the present, it should be noted that the offence of manslaughter by gross negligence has been revived and takes place where the defendant's conduct was 'so bad in all the circumstances as to amount . . . to a criminal act or omission', as stated by Lord Mackay, the former Lord Chancellor in **Adomako 1994**.

2.3.5 Offences of strict liability

There are many offences, often of a regulatory nature (but not necessarily so), which have been created as offences of strict liability. Most offences have been laid down by statute, but there are limited common law examples such as public nuisance and criminal libel.

This last offence had lain practically dormant for many decades but was dramatically resurrected in the case of **Lemon v Gay News Ltd 1979**, when the newspaper in question was convicted of blasphemous libel. The poem causing all the trouble had described various homosexual acts being performed on the body of Jesus Christ after his death. The editor and publisher appealed against the conviction, arguing that the blasphemous libel had to be proved.

The case reached the House of Lords, which affirmed the decision of the lower courts that the liability in such cases was strict.

It is commonly stated that no *mens rea* is needed for strict liability offences. This is not quite accurate; what should be stated is that *mens rea* does not have to be proved with regard to one or more of the elements of the *actus reus*. In many offences, it is obvious that *mens rea* is required. The words, 'intention' or 'recklessness', laid down for many offences, signify the degree of blameworthiness required. Other crimes will only be committed if the defendant acts 'wilfully', 'knowingly' or 'dishonestly'. He cannot, therefore, be convicted if such states of mind cannot be shown to the satisfaction of the magistrates or the jury. Should the offence be one of strict liability, however, the defendant may well be held to be criminally liable without any proof of fault on his part. It is now necessary to look at some examples of strict liability and then to consider the arguments for and against their imposition.

Examples of strict liability offences

An early example of liability without fault is illustrated in the case of **Prince 1875**. The defendant was charged under **s55 Offences Against the Person Act 1861**, with unlawfully taking an unmarried girl under the age of 16 out of the possession and against the will of her father, mother or any other person having lawful charge of her. Prince was found guilty, despite the fact that Annie Phillips, the girl in question, looked much older than her 13 years and despite evidence that she had told Prince that she was 18 and he had believed her.

The court stressed that the relevant section did not contain the words 'knowingly' or 'maliciously', so liability arose when Prince merely committed the act.

It will be noted below that this decision, which acted as an important precedent for well over 100 years has recently been affected by the case of **B (a minor) v DPP 2000** and has therefore been seriously challenged.

Another early example of a strict liability offence is **Cundy v Le Cocq 1884**. The unfortunate publican in this case was convicted of selling intoxicating liquor to someone who was drunk, contrary to **s13 Licensing Act 1872**, despite his claim that he had no knowledge that the customer was intoxicated.

On appeal, the judges were unsympathetic. It was stated that: 'the object of this part of the Act is to prevent the sale of intoxicating liquor to drunken persons and it is perfectly natural to carry that out by throwing on the publican the responsibility of determining whether the person comes within that category'.

With regard to such regulatory offences, the appeal courts are quite prepared to strike an equally uncompromising attitude today, as can be seen in **London Borough of Harrow v Shah & Shah 2000**. The defendants were charged with selling a National Lottery ticket to a boy under the age of 16, despite the fact that they had not been present when the transaction took place and had put up clear notices in the store warning employees not to sell tickets to under-age buyers, as well as warning them verbally. The employee who sold the offending ticket believed the boy to be over the requisite age limit. The magistrates dismissed the charge but the local authority then appealed against this decision.

The Divisional Court of Queen's Bench Division allowed this appeal. The court decided that liability under **s13 National Lottery Act 1993** and its attendant regulations was strict and that no defence of 'reasonable diligence' appeared in the section. The prosecution, therefore, did not have to prove that the defendant knew of the buyer's age or was reckless about this. It also claimed that the matter was not 'truly criminal in character' but dealt instead with a matter of social concern, i.e. access to gambling by young people. The judges therefore took the view that the imposition of strict liability would encourage greater vigilance in preventing the commission of such an offence, even in cases like this. The point of law was referred back to the magistrates to continue with the hearing but with an expectation that they would deal with the case in a lenient way.

We will see many similar 'regulatory' cases below, detailed in the arguments for and against the imposition of strict liability. With regard to more serious offences, like **Prince**, mentioned above, which have a greater stigma attached, an important change of opinion can be observed in the last 30 years, culminating in the potentially far-reaching decision of the House of Lords in **B (a minor) v DPP 2000**.

A strong move against strict liability was first observed in the case of **Sweet v Parsley 1969**. A teacher leased a farmhouse near Oxford, which she then rented out to students, while retaining a room for her occasional use. These students indulged in the use of recreational drugs and this resulted in Sweet being convicted of being concerned in the management of premises which were being used for the purpose of smoking cannabis, contrary to **s5 Dangerous Drugs Act 1965**. This section was silent on the matter of *mens rea* and both the court of first instance and the Divisional Court of Queen's Bench Division decided that she was strictly liable. Her case then reached the House of Lords.

Lord Reid made a distinction between regulatory criminal offences and ones which he decided were more 'truly criminal acts'. He acknowledged that the imposition of strict liability might well be appropriate for the former type of offence but felt that there was a strong presumption that *mens rea* was needed for the latter type of offence. Sweet's conviction was therefore quashed.

At a later time, the **Dangerous Drugs Act** was replaced by the **Misuse of Drugs Act 1971** and the section corresponding to the one affecting **Sweet** now requires knowledge before liability is imposed.

A potentially greater attack on this principle was made more recently in the case of **B (a minor) v DPP 2000**. The appeal concerned a boy of 15, who was charged with inciting a girl under the age of 14 to perform an act of gross indecency with him. In spite of her refusals, the boy had persistently tried to persuade her to perform oral sex on him. The Youth Court had asked advice on a point of law as to whether the boy would have a defence if he genuinely believed that the girl was over the age of 14. The relevant section of the **Indecency with Children Act 1960** made no mention of this. The matter reached the Divisional Court, which decided that the case was one of strict liability. There was a further appeal to the House of Lords, where a markedly different approach was taken.

Their Lordships noted that the relevant section of the **Indecency with Children Act 1960** made no mention of *mens rea*. They decided therefore, that their starting point should be the common law presumption that *mens rea* was an essential ingredient of an offence unless Parliament had expressly or by implication indicated otherwise. Their Lordships quoted with approval the case of **Sweet v Parsley 1970**, just discussed. They argued that there was no general consensus of opinion that strict liability was necessary to the enforcement of the law in sexual matters. They therefore decided that, if the interpretation of the current offence was being gleaned from an interpretation in another statute (in this case the **Sexual Offences Act 1956**), the relevant provisions in that other act had to 'give compelling guidance' and in this case did not. Steyn went on to state robustly that **Prince** 'is a relic from an age dead and gone'.

The House of Lords decided, therefore, that with regard to the **Indecency with Children Act 1960**, the prosecution needed to prove that the offence had taken place and to do this had to show an absence of genuine belief by the defendant that the girl was 14 or over. When deciding on this second issue there was another important development. The judges followed cases like **Morgan** and decided that such a belief did not have to be reasonably held.

They decided that there had been several such cases in recent years where the courts had departed from the traditional view that if the defence of mistake was put forward, it had to be shown that the honest mistake was reasonably held. The judges in the current case came to the conclusion that when *mens rea* was ousted by a mistaken belief, it was as well ousted by an unreasonable belief as by a reasonable one. This issue will be looked at more fully under General Defences in Chapter 11.

◣ *Comment*

It now appears that the common law presumption that *mens rea* is needed for most 'truly criminal' offences is stronger that ever.

Professor Sir John Smith thoroughly approves of the width of the decision in **B (a minor) v DPP**. He believes that it helps to counter the House of Lords' 'dismal record in criminal cases' and hails it as a 'good start to the new millennium'. It is, however, too early to ascertain exactly how far it will impact on other cases where age is a factor. At the very least, the precedent set in **Prince**, mentioned earlier, while not expressly overruled, is, as Smith notes, 'severely shaken as authority'.

What is equally certain is that the imposition of strict liability in 'truly criminal' cases has not yet received its death knell. This can be seen in the later case of **K 2001**, another sexual offence case where age was a factor. In this case the Court of Appeal distinguished the decision in **B (a minor) v DPP**.

The defendant was charged with indecent assault on a girl under the age of 16, contrary to **s14 Sexual Offences Act 1956**. The girl in question was 14 but the 26 year-old defendant argued that she had lied about her age and he had believed her claim that she was 16. He also alleged that she had also consented to the sexual activities. The girl, on the other hand, claimed that he had accosted her in the street and made sexual advances to her without her consent. She made a complaint against him to this effect two days later. The trial judge decided, on a preliminary point of law, that the prosecution now needed to prove that the defendant possessed *mens rea*. It therefore had the burden of proving that the defendant did not have a genuine belief that the girl was 16. This point was at issue in this appeal.

The Court of Appeal decided that 'in our judgment, the prosecution do not have to prove that the defendant at the time of the incident did not honestly believe that the complainant was 16 years or over', i.e. the court decided that the offence was one of strict liability. It decided that Parliament had excluded any express mention of such a defence in **s14**. The Court of Appeal felt that it also should not be implied because if a defence was meant to be included in **s14(1)**, then the draftsmen would not have then gone on to enact **ss14(3) and 14(4)**. As well as dealing with offences against children, **s14** also imposes similar liability if there is an indecent assault on a defective (of any age). **S14(4)** provides that the defendant only commits this second offence if he had reason to suspect that the other is a defective. If the approach in **B v DPP** were followed in this case, and *mens rea* had to be shown, it would make a nonsense of these other sections. The Court of Appeal therefore came to the conclusion that **s1** imposed strict liability. The judges did express the hope that Parliament 'might look again at this area of the law relating to sexual offences'.

Professor Sir John Smith, in his commentary in **B v DPP** had already envisaged problems in age-related sexual offences and had faced the fact that strict liability must still prevail in some cases. This appears to be one of them, at least until Parliament steps in and reforms the **Sexual Offences Act 1956**.

It can be seen from the above that the issues concerning the imposition of strict liability are not always as clear-cut as at first appears. Indeed, whether the offences are of a 'truly criminal' nature or ones of a more regulatory kind, which might be viewed less seriously, there are powerful arguments both for and against the imposition of such liability, as noted below.

Ten arguments in favour of retaining strict liability offences

- The public is protected against the selling of unfit food

Strict liability is imposed in such cases to ensure that the providers of food maintain control of their checking procedures and keep their standards high.

In **Callow v Tillstone 1900**, a butcher was convicted of selling meat which was held to be unfit for public consumption, even though a vet had declared the meat to be safe. Similarly, in **Smedleys v Breed 1974**, the manufacturer's conviction for selling unfit food was upheld by the House of Lords, when four tins of peas were found to contain caterpillars. Their Lordships were unimpressed with the argument that over three million tins of uncontaminated peas had been sold.

- The public gains greater protection from pollution

In **Alphacell v Woodward 1972**, the defendant's conviction for causing polluted matter to enter a river was upheld, despite the claims that the company was unaware of any obstruction to its pumps. Lord Salmon stated that, if the offence were not one of strict liability, 'a great deal of pollution would go unpunished and undeterred to the relief of many riparian factory owners. As a result many rivers which are now filthy would become filthier still and many rivers which are now clean would lose their cleanliness'. Fighting words!

- The countryside is better protected

In **Kirkland v Robinson 1987**, the Divisional Court of Queen's Bench refused to accept the defendant's claim that he was unaware he was in possession of wild birds, contrary to the **Wildlife and Countryside Act 1981**. The court decided that the protection of the environment was of 'outstanding social importance'.

- People are deterred from holding unlawful weapons

Both Parliament and the courts believe that the holding of weapons capable of causing harm, should be strictly controlled, even if this should result in occasional injustice. In **Howells 1977**, the defendant's conviction for failing to obtain a firearms' certificate was upheld, despite the fact that he believed that his gun was an antique and therefore did not need such certification. In **Bradish 1990**, the defendant argued that he was unaware that a canister in his possession contained prohibited CS gas. Once again, the conviction was upheld.

- There is greater protection from illegal broadcasts

In the case of **Blake 1997**, a conviction under the **Wireless Telegraphy Act 1949** was upheld, when the defendant operated a radio station without a licence, despite his claim that he thought he was merely making demonstration tapes. The court decided that the Act had been designed to deter such practices, which might otherwise interfere with emergency communications.

- There is more effective protection against dangerous drugs

Strict liability is imposed in some drug offences, both to protect the public and to make it more difficult for offenders to evade liability by arguing that they did not know the drugs were in their possession. In **Warner v MPC 1969**, the defendant had taken possession of some boxes, left for him at a café. He sold perfume as a sideline and argued that he thought that this was what boxes contained. In fact, prohibited drugs were found in one of them. Despite his allegations, the House of Lords upheld his conviction.

- **The public is protected from unsafe buildings**

In **Atkinson v Sir Alfred McAlpine 1974**, a building company was convicted under the **Asbestos Regulations 1969** for failing to state that it was using crocidolite, even though it was unaware of this fact. Similarly in **Gammon v AG for Hong Kong 1984**, the defendants were found liable when part of the building they were helping to construct collapsed, even though the company was unaware that the plans were not being followed. The Privy Council stressed that the main reason for enforcing strict liability in cases such as this was to protect the public.

- **Higher standards will be obtained**

In the above case, the Privy Council also went on to state that strict liability was necessary 'to encourage greater vigilance to prevent the commission of the prohibited act'. This, too, is seen as one of the main reasons for making liability strict. Manufacturers, builders, providers of food all know that they must keep to the highest standards or face possible prosecution.

- **A successful prosecution has a powerful deterrent value**

This could affect both the offending individual or company and others who become aware of the conviction. In cases where the company has been convicted, the attendant bad publicity is very unwelcome so again extra vigilance will be encouraged.

- **It allows a prosecution to be brought in difficult cases**

It would be very difficult, in many cases, to obtain a conviction if some form of *mens rea* had to be proved. It will be seen in Chapter 14 that the courts then have to resort to other methods such as the delegation principle, in order to maintain standards. It is also important to note that, in many cases, liability is strict, not absolute. This means that in these instances, the defendant may be able to put forward a limited defence, such as the fact that the offence was committed by another or under duress. This helps to lessen the unfairness of the rules.

Ten arguments against the imposition of strict liability

- **It can be unjust**

One of the main principles of criminal law is that a person or a company should only be liable if they are at fault in some way. In many of the cases described, the defendants were completely unaware that that an offence was being committed. For example, in **Pharmaceutical Society of Great Britain v Storkwain Ltd 1986**, a pharmacist's conviction for supplying drugs without a valid prescription was upheld, even though he did not know that the signature was forged. Surely it would be fairer in such cases only to impose liability for negligent behaviour, giving the truly innocent a defence.

- **It may not succeed in raising standards**

People cannot raise standards if they are not aware that they are doing wrong. The rationale behind the introduction of such legislation therefore, is not satisfied.

- **There is little concrete proof that strict liability works in other cases.**

It could instead, foster feelings of resentment and injustice, which might lead to a loss of respect for the law.

- The courts often face difficulties in identifying such offences

In many statutes, it is not always clear whether a strict liability offence has been created. Some guidance on this was given in the case of **Gammon v AG for Hong Kong 1984**, mentioned earlier. The Court of Appeal reiterated the view expressed in **Sweet v Parsley** that crimes could be divided into ones which were merely regulatory and those which were 'purely criminal' in character. For the latter type of offence, there is a clear presumption that *mens rea* is required before an individual or company can be convicted. In the case of regulatory offences also, there is still a presumption that *mens rea* is necessary and this would predominate unless it is felt that an issue of social concern, such as public safety, is involved. In such cases, it may then be necessary to impose liability in order to encourage greater vigilance and higher standards.

- The courts have been inconsistent in their attitude towards strict liability offences

In some instances they take a very harsh approach, as in **Cundy v Le Cocq 1884**, described earlier, whereas in other similar cases they are prepared to be more tolerant. In **Sheras v De Rutzen 1895**, a publican's conviction for serving alcohol to a police officer was quashed by the Divisional Court. The officer had not worn an armband, which would have identified him as being on duty. The court felt that the presumption against strict liability should be upheld, particularly as no amount of care would have prevented the commission of the offence.

As noted earlier, in **Warner v MPC 1969**, the House of Lords upheld the conviction of a defendant for being in possession of drugs. In **Sweet v Parsley 1970**, however, the same court quashed a similar conviction and stated that where a section in an Act is silent on the matter of *mens rea*, it should be presumed.

- There may also be a lack of clarity in some judgments

The courts may struggle to justify the imposition of liability and, in so doing arrive at decisions which affront notions of common sense and simple justice. The case of **Warner** was the first case on strict liability to go to the House of Lords. Smith and Hogan, in the Eighth Edition of their book *Criminal Law: Cases and Materials* (published by Butterworths) stated that 'The five speeches delivered in **Warner** differ so greatly and it is so difficult to make sense of parts of them that courts in later cases have found it impossible to extract a ratio decidendi.'

- Legal academics may criticise the decisions made by the judges

Professor Sir John Smith called the judgment in **Warner** 'another calamitous decision by the House'!

- Such decisions may also have the opposite effect of what is intended

They could lead to later action by Parliament, allowing a defence in some situations, as in the **Misuse of Drugs Act 1971**.

- A criminal conviction is imposed

Probably the most important argument against the creation of strict liability offences is that the stigma of a criminal conviction is imposed on the individual or company, sometimes for an act which he could not have foreseen or prevented.

- **The penalties for such infringement may be very severe**

Even though offences are often of a regulatory nature, with fairly minor fines, this is not always the case. In the case of **Gammon**, mentioned earlier, the maximum penalty was a $250,000 fine and imprisonment for three years. The offence committed in **Shah 2000**, if tried on indictment, carries a maximum sentence of two years' imprisonment. It has also been seen that strict liability still exists in several more 'truly criminal' cases, where an even lengthier custodial sentence is possible.

Possible reform of strict liability

We noted earlier that there has been a strong move away from the imposition of such offences for more serious crimes. It is submitted that Parliament now needs to address the anomalies in statutes relating to sexual offences, particular in view of the decision in B (a minor) v DPP 2000 and K 2000. With regard to regulatory offences also, confusion exists in several areas.

Reform of this area is indirectly incorporated into the Draft Criminal Code. The Code, if ever enacted, would lay down a presumption that all offences require either intention, recklessness or knowledge and, if offences are felt to be necessary which create liability for negligence or seek to impose strict liability, then Parliament must clearly state this in the relevant provision.

FIVE KEY FACTS ON STRICT LIABILITY

- These offences are ones for which no fault has to be shown for one or more parts of the *actus reus*. They are nearly always created by statute and are often for fairly minor infringements.
- The House of Lords' decision in **B (a minor) v DPP 2000** came out strongly in favour of the necessity for *mens rea* to be proved in 'truly criminal' cases. The long established precedent in **Prince**, though not expressly overruled, has now been seriously weakened.
- Despite this, strict liability may still be imposed for some age-related sexual offences, as can be seen in **K 2000**. There have been calls for Parliament to reform the **Sexual Offences Act 1956.**
- Strict liability offences may still be needed to protect the environment and to protect the public from unfit food, unsafe buildings, unnecessary pollution, unlawful weapons and drugs and illegal broadcasts. They may act as a deterrent to others and thus help to raise standards.
- On the negative side they can be unjust, ineffective, difficult to identify and lead to confusion. The stigma of a criminal conviction should not be underestimated.

On paper or in general debate, discuss the following propositions:

- In a just society, criminal liability should never be imposed without some degree of blameworthiness.
- The imposition of strict liability in certain criminal offences is a necessary evil in the fight to protect the public from harm.

2.3.6 The doctrine of transferred malice

Before leaving the subject of *mens rea*, it should be noted at this stage that if the defendant has the *mens rea* for one offence, it may be transferred to another offence of the same type. The case of **Latimer 1886**, provides an example. The defendant, a soldier, hit a customer in a pub with his belt after an attack by that other. The belt rebounded off the first victim and hit a woman in the pub, cutting her face open in the process. The court held that the *mens rea* from the first attack could be transferred to the second offence. The position would have been different if another type of offence had been planned in the first instance as, for example, criminal damage. In such a case, the *mens rea* of that offence could not be transferred. The case of **Pembliton 1874** illustrates this in reverse. In this case, the defendant intended to throw a stone at a fighting crowd but accidentally broke a window instead. He could not be found guilty of this offence under the doctrine of transferred malice; it would have to be the subject of a separate charge.

The House of Lords was not prepared to accept the doctrine of transferred malice in **Attorney General's Reference (No 3 of 1994)(1996)**. A man had stabbed his girlfriend in the stomach. The girl was over five months' pregnant, a fact known to the accused. It later came to light that in addition to the injuries to the girlfriend, the foetus had also been penetrated by the weapon. The baby was born very early and only lived for a few months. The man was convicted of grievous bodily harm in relation to the mother and was later charged with the murder of the baby.

The trial judge decided that there could not be a conviction for either murder or manslaughter in such circumstances and the man faced no further action on this charge. The Attorney General submitted a reference to the Court of Appeal. This court decided that, under the doctrine of transferred malice, the acts against the mother could be transferred to the child and charges of both murder and manslaughter were sustainable. This court decided that it was immaterial that the child had not yet been born.

The House of Lords took a different view and decided that only a manslaughter conviction could be obtained, due to an unlawful and dangerous act that caused a death, (as will be noted in Chapter 5 on Involuntary Manslaughter). The top appeal court judges did not approve of the extension of transferred malice to make it apply to a case such as this.

2.4 Coincidence of the *actus reus* and *mens rea*

We have noted that, normally, two elements have to be established before a crime can be committed, the *actus reus* and the requisite *mens rea*. In a small minority of cases, the courts have been willing to accept that the *actus reus* can be a continuing act, as in the case of **Fagan**, mentioned under the section on the *actus reus* in a crime. They may, instead, use the concept of a series of acts in which the *mens rea* may have been present some of the time. The case of **Thabo Meli 1954** provides an illustration of this.

In this case, a gang had severely beaten the victim and, believing him to be dead, had thrown him over a cliff. At that time, he was still alive but he died later from exposure. The *mens rea* for murder had existed at the beginning of the sequence of acts and this was held to suffice. The defendants were not allowed to argue that they did not possess the appropriate *mens rea* at the time of his death. The Privy Council decided that the men should not be allowed 'to escape the penalties of the law' and found them guilty of murder.

A similar view was taken in **Le Brun 1991** where the continuing act was held to last during the time the defendant was trying to cover up his crime. The man had been quarrelling with his wife and knocked her out. It was then alleged that, while trying to remove her from the scene of the crime in order to avoid discovery, he dropped her. She hit her head on a kerbstone and died. The Court of Appeal upheld the husband's conviction for manslaughter.

Self-Assessment Questions

1. Define the term '*actus reus*' and give three examples.
2. State the general rule in English law relating to omissions. Give four exceptions to this, quoting cases or statutes as appropriate.
3. Describe the two types of intention in English law.
4. What help should the judge now give the jury in cases of murder, where the accused is arguing that it was not his purpose to kill? Give three arguments in favour of the modified direction and three problems it may cause.
5. What is meant by the term 'recklessness'?
6. Define the two types of recklessness in English law with cases to substantiate your findings.
7. Give two examples where negligence will suffice for liability in criminal law.
8. Define a strict liability offence and state why the case of **B (a minor) v DPP 2000** is an important one.
9. Give five points in favour of retaining strict liability offences and five arguments against this.
10. How was sufficient criminal liability established in the cases of **Latimer 1886, Thabo Meli 1954, Fagan 1969** and **Le Brun 1991**?

Chapter 3

UNLAWFUL KILLING I: MURDER

3.1 Introduction

Having discovered the elements that are necessary before a crime is committed, it is now time to look at some of the most important crimes in more detail. These are known as substantive offences and in the following four chapters we shall be looking at offences against the person, starting with the most serious of these where a death results and then going on to look at non-fatal crimes, such as assault and rape.

It is very important to realize that you are not required to study every criminal offence. There are many thousands of these and it is obviously unrealistic, at this point in your studies, to expect you to have knowledge of them all. Indeed, very few barristers and solicitors would have such information; at best, they would know where to find detail on them, should this be necessary. Law courses, therefore, are selective in the choice of crimes to be studied. For example, the more general courses do not usually require knowledge of drug offences, or the more minor traffic ones. This book aims to cover the offences most commonly found in A Level and undergraduate courses.

3.2 General information on homicide

Firstly, it is important to realise that killing can be either lawful or unlawful. The diagram on the next page gives illustrations of each type.

3.2.1 The distinction between murder and manslaughter

Murder is the 'killing of a human being with malice aforethought'. This definition is examined in more detail below. People are said to be increasingly worried about the frequency of this crime but those who feel that it is no longer safe to walk the streets might take heart from the knowledge that London still has one of the lowest murder rates for capital cities. Statistics show that it is much safer than New York, Washington, Paris or Berlin.

Manslaughter can be voluntary or involuntary:

- Voluntary manslaughter arises where the definition of murder appears to have been satisfied but one of three possible defences granted by statute can be pleaded, which will reduce the offence from murder to manslaughter. These are diminished responsibility, provocation and the survivor of a suicide pact. This subject will be examined in Chapter 4.
- Involuntary manslaughter occurs where there is no malice aforethought but a death results because of an unlawful act or gross negligence. This type of manslaughter will be discussed in Chapter 5.

3.2.2 The *actus reus* and *mens rea* of these crimes

Murder and manslaughter share the same *actus reus*, which is the unlawful killing of a human being. The *mens rea* for murder and voluntary manslaughter is killing with malice aforethought. The *mens rea* for involuntary manslaughter varies, as will be noted later.

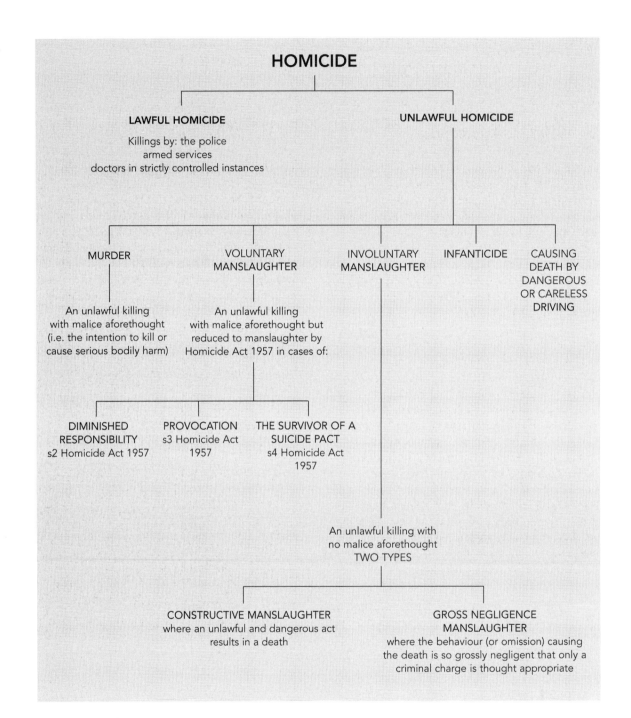

3.3 Murder

Murder is a common law offence, that is a crime developed by the judges, not one laid down by statute. It is one of the oldest and most reviled of crimes. In earlier times, a person convicted of murder was sentenced to death, i.e. to be hanged by the neck until dead. Once the foreman of the jury had announced that that the defendant was guilty of murder, the judge had no alternative but to don his black cap and deliver a sentence of death.

The death penalty was at first suspended and then abolished altogether by the **Murder (Abolition of Death Penalty) Act 1965.** Now, following a conviction for murder, the judge will impose a mandatory sentence of life imprisonment.

It should be noted that, while the mandatory life sentence remains, in most cases, the accused will be released on licence after a number of years in jail. The judge can help to influence the parole board in this respect by recommending that a minimum number of years be served before the defendant is considered for such release. In exceptional cases, he may urge that life should really mean life, as the following article shows.

Comment

There has been much criticism over the fact that the judges have no discretion as to the punishment to be imposed for murder. This can be unjust, because a sadistic serial killer and a mercy killer are both treated the same way and both will receive the mandatory punishment of life imprisonment. In English law, there are no degrees of murder as exist in other jurisdictions. The Criminal Law Revision Committee looked at this problem but decided not to recommend any change in the position.

In 1989, a Select Committee of the House of Lords also looked into the matter. This body believed that changes should be made but did not favour having different degrees of murder. Lord Nathan, who chaired the Committee, made the following comment:

To divide unlawful killing into categories is going the wrong route. You should give the judges discretion for the penalty.

Such a method also has its critics, especially among those who believe that some of the judges, when exercising their discretion, mete out sentences that are either too harsh or too lenient. This topic will be examined further in Chapter 4. At present, it is important to note that no change in the law has yet been effected and the mandatory life sentence remains for murder.

Judge's plea for 'whole life tariff' will test resolve

BY PHILIP JOHNSTON
HOME AFFAIRS EDITOR

THE judge's recommendation that Roy Whiting should remain in jail for the rest of his life [for the murder of Sarah Payne] would make him the 24th on a list of killers who will never leave prison.

Others include Myra Hindley and Ian Brady, the Moors Murderers; Peter Sutcliffe, the Yorkshire Ripper; Robert Black, murderer of three girls; and John Duffy, known as the Railway Killer.

By inviting the Home Secretary to impose a 'whole life tariff', Mr Justice Curtis has also prompted ministers to pursue the concept of indeterminate – or reviewable – sentences for paedophiles.

These have been promised for years without any action. In 1997, the Government suggested that paedophiles should be kept in jail until they were safe to release.

The pledge has been repeated on several occasions. There was even a formal statement in the Commons in February 1999, but nothing has happened. The matter is now being considered alongside a wider review of mental health laws.

Had such a law been in force when Whiting was first convicted of sex crimes, he might not have been released after serving only two and a half years of his four-year sentence.

Daily Telegraph, 13 December 2001

3.3.1 The original definition of murder

In Coke's Institute, an early work, the famous judge and former Lord Chief Justice of England laid down his definition of murder. This was said to arise where:

> a man of sound memory and the age of discretion unlawfully killed within any county of the realm any reasonable creature in *rerum natura* under the King's peace, with malice aforethought, either expressed by the party or implied by law, so that the party wounded or hurt etc. die of the wound or hurt etc. within a year and a day after the same.

You will be glad to discover that you are not required to learn this long definition because, over the years, modifications have been made to it.

The criminal liability of children has been extended

The term 'a man of sound memory and the age of discretion' covers people of either sex and includes all those who are not insane or allowed some other defence. The term also applies to children between the ages of 10 and 14. Until very recently, such children were presumed not to have criminal liability unless it could be proved that they knew that they were doing something seriously wrong. Since October 1998, this presumption has been removed and children of this age have the same liability as adults, although normally they will be treated differently in court and when sentenced. (There will be a fuller discussion on this in Chapter 10 on General Defences.)

The 'year and a day rule' has been abolished

Another very important change in Coke's definition was the removal in 1996 of what is called 'the year and a day rule'.

This ancient rule decreed that a charge of murder or manslaughter could not be brought if the victim survived for longer than a year and a day.

The rule was developed in earlier times to avoid the difficulties of proving whether the injury inflicted by the accused had caused the death or whether such a death had resulted from a later illness or accident. Now that medical science makes it easier to pinpoint the reason for the mortality, there have been repeated calls for the abolition of the rule.

In 1980, the Criminal Law Revision Committee looked at this question but rather surprisingly recommended the retention of the rule.

Its limitations can be seen in the sad case of **Dyson 1908**. The defendant assaulted his baby daughter on 13 November 1906 and again on 29 December 1907. She eventually died on 5 March 1908. At first instance, Dyson was convicted of manslaughter after the trial judge informed the jury that a conviction could be secured if the baby's death had resulted from either of these injuries.

On appeal, the conviction for manslaughter had to be quashed because of this misdirection by the trial judge of the 'year and a day rule'.

There was also injustice where victims of violent attacks survived for longer than a year and a day, sometimes for many years on life support machines, before eventually dying, and the offender could not be charged with murder.

Further calls for the rule to be reconsidered were made.

The Law Commission reopened the debate in its *Consultation Paper No. 136 (1994)*, in which it favoured abolishing the rule, so as to follow the lead given by other jurisdictions like Australia, South Africa and closer to home, Scotland. A bill was therefore drawn up by the Law Commission, and introduced into Parliament via a Private Member's Bill in December 1995. The Bill passed through all its later stages in one single day without opposition and emerged in June as the **Law Reform (Year and a Day Rule) Act 1996**.

3.3.2 The current definition of murder

After the modifications are taken into account, the current definition of murder can be said to be:

> the unlawful killing of a human being under the Queen's peace with malice aforethought.

This revised definition of murder now needs to be examined in more detail.

It has already been noted that for murder or manslaughter to be established, the killing must be unlawful, and we have seen that it is possible, in rare circumstances, for a killing to be given the approval of the State and therefore be rendered lawful.

Lawful killings
By an executioner

If the death penalty were to be returned, a defendant convicted of murder could be lawfully killed by the process agreed upon. In other jurisdictions, various methods have been adopted, including electrocution, gassing, shooting, hanging, administering a lethal injection and even beheading.

By the police or the armed forces

A soldier or policeman who kills in the lawful exercise of his duty will obviously not be guilty of murder. Should he exceed the powers given to him, however, he could face criminal proceedings, as is shown in the cases of **Clegg 1995** and other soldiers in Northern Ireland who were all originally convicted of murder. This subject is discussed more fully in Chapter 10, where the defences of self-defence and prevention of crime are explored.

By the medical profession

Doctors, too, may be allowed to shorten life in very limited circumstances. They have to be careful to operate within the current state of the law and are not normally permitted to accelerate the death of a patient without the judge's permission. The doctor may wish to end the suffering of a terminally ill patient but, if he intends to kill that person, his acts will come within the definition of murder and he could well face life imprisonment. He is accelerating the death of a human being and this is not allowed.

In **Adams 1957**, this fact was made clear to the jury by Devlin J who stated that:

> If life were cut short by weeks or months it was just as much murder as if it were cut short by years.

The judges have relaxed the strictness of this approach in very limited circumstances. One example is where the acceleration of the time of the death is minimal. Under what is called the '*de minimus* rule', a doctor would not face criminal proceedings if he gave an injection towards the very end of a patient's life, to ease his suffering, even if it was known that this might well accelerate the death by a very small degree. In the case of **Adams,** mentioned above, Devlin J did go on to qualify the statement that he made. He added:

> But that does not mean that a doctor aiding the sick or dying has to calculate in minutes or hours, or perhaps in days or weeks, the effect on a patient's life of the medicines he administers. If the first purpose of medicine – the restoration of health – can no longer be achieved, there is still much for the doctor to do, and he is entitled to do all that is proper and necessary to relieve pain and suffering even if measures he takes may incidentally shorten life.

A medical practitioner may also, in very limited circumstances, cease to provide treatment or food even though in other cases liability for gross negligence could arise, as shown in Chapter 2.

In the landmark case of **Airedale National Health Trust v Bland 1993**, the House of Lords decided that, provided that both doctors and close relatives agreed that it was futile to continue to treat and artificially feed a patient in a persistent vegetative state, the court could sanction the withholding of further treatment. The actual case concerned 17-year-old Tony Bland, who was crushed in the terrible Hillsborough disaster of 1989 and reduced to a persistent vegetative state. He was put onto a life support system but after a period of three years there was no sign that he would recover. The court gave permission to withhold further treatment but said that three conditions had to be satisfied before treatment and feeding could be withheld:

- The parties involved had to come to court to obtain a declaration.
- Before this could be granted, a full investigation into the case had to be undertaken, and an opportunity given to the Official Solicitor to obtain independent medical opinions and all the material necessary for the court hearing.
- The patient had to be in a persistent vegetative state with no hope of recovery.

The House of Lords decided that, if these steps were followed, the doctors would not then be liable for murder, even though the death was intended. Such action, or rather inaction, has thus been given the seal of approval by the courts and was followed by the Court of Appeal in the case of **Frenchay Healthcare NHS Trust v S 1994.**

The state of the law after these cases is that if the doctors administered a lethal injection to a patient in a persistent vegetative state or did some other positive act to end life, this would still be classed murder. If on the other hand, they chose not to continue to use artificial means to prolong life, this omission to act would not be criminal, provided that the guidelines formulated by the judges were clearly followed.

In **Re A (children) 2000**, lawful homicide by doctors was extended when this very unusual case came before the courts. Jodie and Mary, (not their real names), were conjoined twins. Mary's heart and lungs were too deficient to sustain life and if she had been born apart from Jodie, she would have died soon after birth. She stayed alive because a common artery enabled Jodie to circulate the blood for both of them. Jodie was in a healthier condition than Mary but the doctors believed that if she were not soon separated from Mary she too, would die. The doctors wished to perform the operation but faced a dilemma. If they went ahead with the operation, Mary would die and that arguably, could be seen as murder, following the principles laid down in **Woollin**, mentioned in the last chapter. If the doctors did nothing and allowed their patient Jodie to die, they could be guilty of gross negligence manslaughter. The hospital therefore, against the wishes of the parents, sought a declaration that the doctors would be acting lawfully if they proceeded. They were successful but the parents appealed.

The Court of Appeal decided that the doctors would not be acting unlawfully, although they faced some difficulty in arriving at this conclusion. First, they rejected the trial judge's arguments by which he had arrived at a similar answer. He had decided that the operation should not be classed as a positive act, but merely a withdrawal of Mary's blood supply. Secondly, he had taken the view that the operation that would result in her death was in her best interests. The Court of Appeal held that the operation must be seen as a positive act and as Ward L J accepted, one consisting of 'a number of invasions of Mary's body . . . before the positive step was taken of clamping the aorta and bringing about Mary's death'. Because of the decision in **Woollin**, therefore, the act would be murder, unless a suitable defence could be found. The doctors would know that even though it was not their purpose to kill Mary, her death would be a virtually certain consequence of their actions.

By a majority, the Court of Appeal used the defence of utilitarian necessity to decide that the doctors would not be acting unlawfully, although another defence called private defence was also argued. These issues will be returned to more fully in Chapter 11. The court made it clear that the judgment was to be restricted to similar cases, but after this decision, it can now be said that the circumstances in which a doctor will still be within the limits of lawful homicide have been increased. Professor Sir John Smith stated this new principle in his commentary on the case of **Re A**:

> *where A is, as the defendant knows, doomed to die in the near future but even the short continuation of his life will inevitably kill B as well, it is lawful to kill A, however free of fault he may be.*

It remains to be seen how such a principle will be used in future cases.

By other members of the public?

As stated earlier, euthanasia is not recognised in English law and those who are involved in such practices could well face prosecution. In November 2001, the House of Lords made it clear that the law is not ready to distinguish between 'willing victims' and unwilling ones, as can be seen in the article on the opposite page concerning the tragic case of Diane Pretty, who suffers from motor neurone disease. Lord Bingham clearly affirmed that 'Mercy killing is in law, killing'.

'Human beings'

In the old definition, this was said to be 'any reasonable creature in *rerum natura*'. This will usually be obvious but certain points need to be addressed.

- **The victim must be human**
  A person will not commit murder or manslaughter if he kills an animal intentionally, although he may well be liable for other offences. The term 'human' would, however, cover tragic cases where the newborn baby is hardly recognisable as a human being, as can occur after the mother's exposure to radiation or drug abuse. The baby might be anercephalic, i.e. without a head or brain, although a brain stem may exist. Some would argue strongly that it should not be regarded as murder if such a child were allowed to die. Current legal and medical opinion, however, appears to favour the view that any offspring of a human mother should be protected by the law, as was indicated in **Rance v Mid Downs Health Authority 1991.**

- **The courts must decide when life begins**
  Parliament has already decided that the killing of a child still in the womb, by either the mother herself or by another person is not homicide, although the guilty party could be convicted of abortion or child destruction, (see Chapter 5). In addition, as seen below, the attacker could be liable for manslaughter

if he injures a foetus which later emerges as a live child which then dies of its injuries.

For the offences of murder, manslaughter or infanticide to occur, the courts have decided that the foetus must have been expelled from the mother's womb and have an independent existence, a view affirmed by the Criminal Law Revision Committee. In **Rance v Mid-Downs Health Authority** it was stated that a baby is capable of being born alive if it can breathe through its own lungs.

What has been settled by the courts is that a child who is injured in the womb, then born alive and who later dies of the injuries inflicted before the birth occurred does come under the category of a human being. This would make the perpetrator of the injury liable for homicide in the form of murder or manslaughter, depending on whether or not he had the intention to injure the actual foetus. This view was stated in the early case of **West 1848** and appears to have been supported by the House of Lords in **Attorney General's Reference (No. 3 of 1994) (1996)**, a case mentioned in Chapter 2 under transferred malice.

The defendant had stabbed his girlfriend in the stomach, despite the fact that he knew of her pregnancy. The unborn child was affected because the knife had penetrated the uterus and entered the abdomen of the foetus, although this fact was not discovered until later.

The woman made a good recovery but later gave birth prematurely. The baby was born alive but died four months later. The accused was found guilty of grievous bodily harm in relation to the mother but the trial judge decided that, as a matter of law, he could not be convicted of the murder or manslaughter of the baby.

The Attorney General required the opinion of the appeal courts as to whether this statement was correct. The matter eventually reached the House of Lords. Their Lordships decided that a

Lords refuse woman's wish to end her life

By Roger Pearson

DIANE PRETTY today lost the last round of her battle for the right to let her husband help her to die.

Five Law Lords dismissed her appeal against the High Court's refusal to allow the terminally-ill motor neurone disease sufferer end her life.

Mrs Pretty, 43, had argued that the Human Rights Act entitled her to die with dignity. But the senior judges backed the decision that the Human Rights Act only protected the right to live with dignity.

While suicide was no longer a crime, it was not lawful for someone to help a person to kill themselves.

Senior Law Lord Lord Bingham said the criminal law did not distinguish between "willing victims" and others. "Mercy killing is, in law, killing," he ruled.

He sympathised with the plight of Mrs Pretty, who had challenged the Director of Public Prosecutions' refusal to offer her husband Brian immunity from prosecution if he assisted her.

"No one of ordinary sensitivity could be unmoved by the frightening ordeal facing her," Lord Bingham said.

He said questions of whether the terminally ill, or others, should be free to seek assistance in taking their own lives, and in what circumstances and subject to what safeguards, were of great social, ethical and religious significance. Widely differing beliefs and views were held, often strongly.

However, he said the Law Lords were not a legislative body and could not "act as a moral or ethical arbiter". They had to apply the law as it stood.

The Human Rights Act could not be interpreted as "conferring a right to die or to enlist the aid of another in bringing about one's own death".

Lord Bingham said the Government was under no obligation to ensure that a terminally ill person who was unable to take her own life should be legally able to seek assistance.

Philip Havers QC, for Mrs Pretty, had told the lords: "She is profoundly frightened by the thought of the distressing and undignified death she will inevitably have to endure, and very strongly wishes to control how and when she dies."

However, Lord Bingham said assisted suicide and consensual killing were unlawful in all EC countries except the Netherlands.

Mrs Pretty had also claimed that she was being discriminated against because the law was preventing her from taking her life. But Lord Bingham said the law conferred no right to commit suicide.

Evening Standard, 29 October 2001

murder charge could not be sustained if the defendant had not intended to kill or seriously injure the foetus itself. In this case, therefore, because the intention to injure the unborn child had not been proved, it was decided that the defendant did not have the necessary *mens rea* for the murder of the baby. It was however decided that a case of manslaughter could be brought in such circumstances.

Despite this conclusion, Lord Hope, in his judgment expressed the view that the fact that a child is not yet born did not prevent the *actus reus* for both murder and manslaughter being established. He stated:

> for the foetus life lay in the future; it could carry with it the effect of things done to it before birth which after birth might prove to be harmful.

◀ Comment

Professor Sir John Smith argues that the defendant, even where he intends to harm the foetus, is not intending to harm a person in being so therefore would not satisfy the *mens rea* for murder. He believes that, in such a case only a manslaughter charge is sustainable. The offender has committed an unlawful act and a death has resulted, therefore the elements constructive manslaughter are satisfied. Such crimes will be looked at in Chapter 5.

- **The courts must decide when death occurs**
  The old medical view was that death occurred when the heart stopped beating and breathing ceased. In 1976, the concept of brain death was adopted by the world of medicine and a person was pronounced dead where irremediable structural brain damage was shown.

The courts have not expressly adopted this test. In **Malcherek and Steel 1981**, however, the Court of Appeal accepted that:

> there is a body of opinion in the medical profession that there is only one true test of death and this is irreversible death of the brain stem, which controls the basic functions of the body such as breathing.

Such a definition of death would protect a doctor who removed an organ from a patient in such a state to sustain the life of another. On the other hand, criminal liability would arise if the patient was in an irreversible coma but was not yet classified as brain dead.

Activity

Topsy went into a hospital ward and switched off a life support machine connected to her friend, Tim, because she could not bear to see him in this state any longer.

Discuss her possible liability. Would your answer be any different if a serial killer had crept into the ward and switched off all the machines?

'Under the Queen's peace'

Most victims would come under this umbrella, including prisoners of war. The phrase would not, however, cover enemy aliens who are killed in the process of warfare.

'With malice aforethought'

This is a very archaic expression and has been criticised as being misleading in its present context. The word 'malice' seems to suggest that some sort of illwill must exist but this is not necessary. The expression 'malice aforethought' merely means that the accused must have the intention to cause death or grievous bodily harm. The latter was defined in **DPP v Smith 1961** as meaning really serious harm but in cases since then as, for example,

Saunders 1985, it has also been stated that the word 'really' need not be added. Currently, therefore, the phrase 'malice aforethought' merely means the intention to cause death or serious injury. Before 1982, there was some doubt as to whether the intention to cause grievous bodily harm was sufficient intention for murder or whether an intention to cause death had to be proved. In **Cunningham 1982**, the House of Lords made it clear that the intention to cause serious harm was enough.

The accused attacked his victim in a pub, hitting him many times with a chair. The victim subsequently died of the injuries inflected. The accused appealed, stating that the judge had misdirected the jury by saying that the defendant was guilty of murder if he intended to cause serious harm.

The Court of Appeal dismissed the appeal and a further appeal was made to the House of Lords. The defendant relied on certain statements made by two of the Law Lords in the case of **Hyam 1975**, stating that the intention to cause serious harm was not sufficient to constitute the *mens rea* of murder. In that case, two other Law Lords thought that sufficient *mens rea* did exist if this was established and the other was not prepared to give a conclusive opinion.

In **Cunningham 1982** the House of Lords was unanimous in its opinion that the intention to

FIVE KEY FACTS ON MURDER

- Murder is the most serious form of unlawful homicide. Less serious forms of homicide are voluntary and involuntary manslaughter and infanticide, which are dealt with in subsequent chapters.
- The current definition of murder is the unlawful killing of a human being with malice aforethought, i.e. with intent to cause death (express malice), or grievous bodily harm (implied malice) (**Cunningham 1982**). Constructive malice was abolished by **s1 Homicide Act 1957** and the 'year and a day rule' by the **Law Reform (Year and a Day Rule) Act 1996**.
- Certain killings can be lawful as, for example those sanctioned by the state or by the judges (**Airedale NHS Trust v Bland 1993**), and **Re A (children) 2000**, or where a full defence is possible. In other killings the charge may be reduced to manslaughter (see Chapter 4).
- A victim is considered to be a human being when he has an existence independent of his mother. It is not certain whether he must have drawn breath, although this would be the medical view. A victim is probably considered to be dead when he is brain dead.
- It appears that there could be an injury to a human being, even if this injury occurred before birth, if the baby was born alive but subsequently died (**AG's Reference [No. 3 of 1994] 1996**). It is not clear whether liability for murder would arise if the accused intended to harm the foetus. It is clear that the offender could be charged with involuntary manslaughter, if there had been an unlawful act against the mother, a live birth and then the subsequent death of the baby.

cause grievous bodily harm constitutes enough blameworthiness to amount to malice aforethought.

The different types of malice

The word 'malice' needs to be examined further. If a person intends to kill another human being, he is said to have express malice. If, however, he merely intends to cause serious harm he has implied malice. Before the **Homicide Act 1957**, a third category of malice existed, which was known as 'constructive malice'. Under this head, a person could be found guilty of murder if he killed in the furtherance of a felony (i.e. in the furtherance of a serious crime, such as rape or burglary), provided that he had the intention to commit the lesser crime. A murder charge was also possible if the defendant killed while intending to prevent a lawful arrest (either his own or that of another person), or to escape from lawful arrest or custody. The prosecution did not need to prove that he possessed the extra *mens rea* of intending to kill or cause grievous bodily harm.

S1 Homicide Act 1957 abolished liability for murder in these situations although the defendant would almost certainly face other charges, such as involuntary manslaughter, as discussed in Chapter 5.

3.4 Possible reform

The *Draft Criminal Code Bill*, prepared by the Law Commission in 1989, suggests that the *mens rea* of murder should be reformed. It states in *Clause 54* that the mental element should only be present in cases where a person kills intending to cause death or intending to cause serious harm and being aware that it may cause death.

If this were enacted, it would narrow the liability for murder as a person could only be convicted if he caused serious harm with the

knowledge that death might result. Under current law, there is no requirement that the defendant must have a foresight of death occurring; it is enough that he intends to cause grievous bodily harm.

3.5 The chain of causation

Before we leave the subject of murder, it is important to stress that the death must have been caused by the unlawful act of the defendant. It will be seen, however, that, in some cases, the defendant might not have been directly responsible for the final act which caused the death but will still be liable for the homicide because he set in motion the chain of events which led to it. This subject of causation is also applicable to other offences but will be examined in this chapter because many of the cases on causation have involved fatal offences against the person, in the form of murder or manslaughter.

3.5.1 Establishing the chain of causation

There are no rules laid down by statute concerning the problems of causation; instead, various principles have been established by case law, as problem areas have come before the courts.

In most cases, it is not difficult to discover whether the defendant's conduct caused the death in question although the jury, of course, has to be convinced of this beyond reasonable doubt. In some trials however, the defendant will be arguing that someone else caused the death, or at least contributed to it, or that the death was the victim's own fault in some way and these matters need to be explored. When ascertaining whether the defendant is the person on whom to fix liability, the courts will look at two issues:

- Did the conduct of the accused cause the resulting harm and, if so
- Was the defendant also liable in law?

It will be the jury's task to look at the facts of the case but when deciding on the second question, the jurors will have to apply the legal principles explained to them by the judge. Both these issues will be examined further in the following paragraphs.

3.5.2 The factual cause of death

It should first be noted that the defendant would only be criminally liable if his conduct made a significant contribution to the death. This was not established in the case of **White 1910.**

The accused had intended to murder his mother; he had poison in a glass ready for her but she suddenly died, instead, of heart failure. The accused was liable for attempted murder but it is clear that he had not caused her death, however much he had desired it to happen. He could not, therefore, be found guilty of murder.

The 'but for' test

When deciding on the factual cause of death, the courts use the 'but for' test, i.e. but for the act of the defendant, the death would not have occurred. It can be seen in the above case that this test was not satisfied, as the mother would have died anyway; the defendant's act had made no difference to the outcome.

A more difficult case for the jury was the early case of **Dalloway 1847.** A driver of a cart was not using his reins as he proceeded along a road. A three-year-old child then ran into the path of the cart and was killed.

It could have been argued that, but for the driver travelling along this road, the child's death would not have happened. The courts required the passing of a more stringent test, i.e. had the prosecution established that, but for the driver's

negligence in failing to use his reins, the death would not have happened. As the answer was 'no', the charge could not be sustained.

3.5.3 The legal cause of death

As mentioned earlier, the judge's task is to explain the legal principles to the jurors and they must then decide, after applying these principles to the facts with which they are presented, whether the prosecution has established the guilt of the accused beyond reasonable doubt.

After satisfying the test for factual causation, therefore, it still needs to be shown that the defendant's act was a substantial cause of the death and that no intervening act had broken the chain of causation.

The defendant's act must be a significant cause of the death

Many would argue that the defendant should only be liable if he makes a major contribution to the victim's death and, indeed, in earlier cases it was stated that the act of the accused had to be substantial. Cases like **Benge**, discussed below, support this.

The current view, however, is that liability might arise where the defendant has made a significant contribution to the death.

This point was confirmed in **Cato 1976**, a view which was later supported in the case of **Malcherek**, discussed below. In **Kinsey 1971**, it was not considered to be a misdirection by the trial judge when he stated that the contribution must merely be something more than 'a slight or trifling link'.

An example of such 'a slight or trifling link' would be where two mountaineers were roped together and one fell over a cliff. If the other were to cut the rope to save himself from a similar fate, he would certainly be accelerating the death of the other mountaineer but this would only be by a fractional period of time. It would not be significant enough to make him criminally liable for the other's death.

Similarly, a doctor administering painkilling drugs at the end of a patient's life might well accelerate the patient's death to a small degree but would also be protected.

The contribution must therefore be significant enough to contribute to the victim's death. In addition, nothing later must have occurred to break the chain of causation. This leads us on to the next point:

A *novus actus interveniens* must not have arisen

This means that no intervening act must have arisen to break the chain of causation leading from the defendant's act to the actual death. The defendant would be able to escape liability if he could prove that some other act had caused the death, not his own act of violence or his own omission. In the following wide range of situations, the defendants have tried to argue such a point, nearly always unsuccessfully.

Cases on causation

1. **Where the death is not directly caused by the accused**

   It might seem reasonable to a layman that if the actual death had been caused by some other event, such as an act of nature or by another person's act, the first person involved in the chain should escape liability. Very often, however, this is not the position. The courts have decided that the supervening act must be something unforeseeable in order to remove the liability of the first party. If the defendant knocked the victim unconscious and then left him on the seashore near to the water's edge so that he was later drowned by the incoming tide, such an event should have

been anticipated by the assailant and his liability would remain.

A more controversial situation occurred in **Pagett 1983**, where the defendant's conviction for manslaughter was upheld, even though the shot that killed the victim was fired, not by him, but by the police seeking to detain him.

The accused was being pursued by the police and had forcibly taken his pregnant girlfriend from her home to a block of flats, after injuring her mother and stepfather. He later came out of one of the flats, using his girlfriend as a human shield. He then fired his shotgun at two officers.

The policemen fired back instinctively and the girl was killed in the crossfire.

The defendant was found guilty of her manslaughter but appealed against this, arguing that the judge had misdirected the jury by stating that he had been the cause of the victim's death, not the police officers who had fired the bullets.

The Court of Appeal found that there was no misdirection. Goff L J compared the situation to one where the victim acts in self preservation but his attempt fails and, instead, causes or contributes to his death, as in the case of **Pitts**, discussed below. He went on to say:

> Now one form of self preservation is self-defence; for present purposes, we can see no distinction in principle between an attempt to escape the consequences of the accused's act and a response which takes the form of self-defence. Furthermore, in our judgment, if a reasonable act of self-defence against the act of the accused causes the death of a third party, we can see no reason in principle why the act of self-defence, being an involuntary act caused

by the act of the accused, should relieve the accused from criminal responsibility for the death of the third party.

The conviction was upheld.

2. **Where the victim has tried to escape and has caused himself harm**

In some cases a death has occurred because the victim has tried to escape from the violent actions of the accused. Once again, the defendant will find it difficult to escape liability if he put in motion the chain of events which led to the accused having to take evasive action through fear for his safety. A *novus actus interveniens* would only arise if the reaction of the victim was considered to be something totally unexpected, or, as stated in **Roberts 1971**, discussed below, something so 'daft', when compared to how a reasonable man in the same situation might have acted.

The victim's reaction was considered to have been reasonable in **Pitts 1842**, when he jumped into a river to escape further violent assaults. The defendant was held to be responsible for his death.

In **Mackie 1973**, a manslaughter conviction was upheld when a father frightened his three-year-old son so severely that the boy fell down the stairs and was killed.

In **Roberts 1971**, an assault case, described more fully in Chapter 6, the victim jumped from a moving car to escape the sexual advances of the defendant. The Court of Appeal decided that her reaction to the threat was a reasonable one and that the defendant was responsible for her injuries.

In **DPP v Daley 1980**, Lord Keith stated that, in cases such as these, the prosecution had to establish that the victim was in fear of being hurt physically and this fear had caused him to try to escape and thereby meet his death. The conduct of the

accused had to be unlawful and of a type which any reasonable and sober person would recognise as likely to subject the victim to at least the risk of some harm resulting from it, albeit not serious harm.

In **Williams 1992**, the defendants were luckier than most and their conviction for manslaughter was quashed because not enough direction had been given to the jury.

The prosecution claimed that the deceased had jumped from a moving car because he was in fear of being robbed. To support this contention, it was alleged that his wallet had flown into the air as he had jumped. The victim had been travelling to a festival in Glastonbury and had 'hitched' a lift from the defendants. He had jumped out five miles further on and been killed. The occupants were originally held to be liable for his death but appealed.

The Court of Appeal stressed that the conduct of the victim had to be proportionate to the threat of harm and:

> *within the ambit of reasonableness and not so daft as to make his own voluntary act one which amounted to a novus actus interveniens and consequently broke the chain of causation.*

The conviction was quashed because the trial judge had not directed the jury in this fashion. The Court of Appeal did, however, go on to state that:

> *It should of course be borne in mind that a victim may in the agony of the moment do the wrong thing . . . and . . . may act without thought or deliberation.*

3. **Where others apart from the accused, are involved in the death**

In some situations there may be more than one party involved in the chain of events;

others may well have contributed to the outcome. Nevertheless, the party starting the action will usually retain his liability, provided that, as mentioned before, his act was a significant factor in causing the death.

In **Benge 1865**, a foreman plate-layer had misread a timetable so that the track had not been re-laid by the time a train arrived. The defendant had also failed to put any fog signals into place and had positioned a flagman only 540 yards away, instead of the required 1000 yards. The driver of the train failed to stop and an accident occurred causing many deaths. The foreman was charged with manslaughter.

His defence tried to argue that the accident would not have occurred without the contributory negligence of the other people who were also involved.

The judge ruled that, provided that the defendant's negligence had been the main or a substantial cause of the accident, it was no defence to state that the deaths might have been avoided if the others had played their part correctly.

In **Towers 1874**, a young girl screamed very loudly when she was assaulted by the accused. At the time of the attack, she was holding a young baby in her arms who was so frightened by the screams that she went black in the face, had convulsions from that moment on and died four weeks later. It was decided that the girl's attacker could be charged with the manslaughter of the baby.

In **Malcherek and Steel 1981**, the two appellants had stabbed and injured their victims so severely that they had to be put on life support machines. When these machines were switched off by doctors, the defendants tried to argue that this action constituted a *novus actus interveniens*.

Their appeals failed. The Lord Chief Justice stated that where the medical treatment is given by:

> *competent and careful medical practitioners, then evidence will not be admissible to show that the treatment would not have been administered in the same way by other medical practitioners.*

In these two cases, there was no doubt that the original injuries inflicted by the stab wounds were still operating and were still the substantial cause of the deaths. The convictions for murder were upheld. Cases like **Cheshire** and **McKechnie**, mentioned below, are more controversial.

4. **Where the victim has a pre-existing medical condition**

In both criminal law and in the law of tort, there is a rule that the perpetrator of an act must 'take his victim as he finds him'. This is also known as the 'eggshell skull' rule. The courts will not allow the defendant to escape liability just because the victim is more susceptible to harm than the normal person or is unusually sensitive in some other way.

If, therefore, the victim already has a pre-existing medical condition that makes the likelihood of harm more acute, the accused cannot use this in his defence, provided that he set in motion the chain of events leading to the harm and his actions were still an operating cause of it. The following case illustrates this.

In **Hayward 1908**, the defendant had indicated that he was going to harm his wife. An argument developed and the woman ran into the road, followed by her husband who was still making threats against her. The woman then collapsed and died. She had a condition affecting her thyrus gland that would not normally have caused problems but the unusual physical exertion and the fright caused by her husband's treatment had caused her to collapse.

The husband was held to be liable for her death because her demise had been accelerated by his actions.

5. **Where the victim aggravates his condition or refuses medical treatment**
This overlaps in some measure with the above rule that the defendant must take his victim as he finds him. The defendant will not escape liability just because the victim takes an ill-advised course of action to relieve his pain or refuses to undergo the treatment suggested for his injuries, either through fear or because of religious objections.

In **Wall's Case 1802**, the Governor of Goree had inflicted an illegal flogging of 800 lashes on the deceased and was charged with his murder. He tried to argue that the victim had aggravated his condition by consuming strong alcohol to deaden the pain of the punishment. The judge refused to entertain such a notion.

Another early case, this time illustrating the victim's reluctance to undergo further treatment, is that of **Holland 1841**. The victim's hand had been severely cut by Holland, who had attacked him with an iron bar. Blood poisoning had then set in. The victim was advised to have his finger amputated but he refused to entertain the idea; lockjaw then set in and he died. Despite an assertion by a surgeon that the amputation would probably have saved the victim's life, the defendant was found guilty of his murder.

A more recent case illustrating the same point was **Blaue 1975**. The victim had been stabbed by the defendant, but, because of her religious beliefs as a Jehovah's Witness, she refused to have a blood transfusion which would probably have saved her life.

The Court of Appeal upheld Blaue's conviction for manslaughter on the grounds of diminished responsibility, even though the Crown had conceded that the girl may well have survived if the transfusion had been permitted.

Lawton L J stated:

> It has long been the policy of the law that those who use violence on other people must take their victims as they find them. This in our judgment means the whole man, not just the physical man. It does not lie in the mouth of the assailant to say that his victim's religious beliefs which inhibited him from accepting certain kinds of treatment were unreasonable. The question for decision is what caused her death. The answer is the stab wound. The fact that the victim refused to stop this end coming about did not break the causal connection between the act and the death.

The Court of Appeal upheld the principles stated in **Blaue** in the cases of **McKechnie 1992** and **Dear 1996**. In the first case the victim was in hospital after a very severe attack on him by the defendant and while there was discovered to have an ulcer. Because of his serious condition caused by the attack, the ulcer could not be operated upon. It burst and the victim died. As the jury had been correctly directed about the issues, the conviction was upheld.

In the second case, the victim indecently assaulted Dear's 12-year-old daughter and the defendant later attacked him, slashing him with a Stanley knife. The victim died two days later from the wounds but apparently had done nothing to staunch the flow of blood. It was suggested that he had actually reopened the wounds himself. Despite this, the defendant's conviction was upheld. The Court of Appeal stressed that the question to be asked of the jury was 'whether the injuries inflicted by the defendant were an operating and significant cause of the death'. If the jury believed that this was the case, they were entitled to find the defendant guilty whether or not the victim had neglected the wounds or had even deliberately made them worse.

6. Where the medical treatment given is inadequate

In the cases just discussed, medical treatment was actually refused by the victim or considered to be unwise by the doctors. In the following cases, treatment was given but was either wrong or, at best, given in a very negligent way. The courts had to decide whether this was enough to break the chain of causation. In line with the situations already examined, it will be noted that the courts are very reluctant to allow this to happen and, in most cases, the liability of the person starting the injuries leading to the death will remain.

The law on this subject is complicated by the case of **Jordan 1956**, which took a contrary approach, but, although this decision has not been overruled, it appears that it will not be followed in the future, unless the new circumstances are very similar to those in that case.

The victim had been stabbed. He was admitted to hospital but died eight days later. The defendant was convicted of murder. Later, evidence came to light that the medical treatment had been 'palpably wrong' and the defendant successfully appealed against his conviction.

The new evidence showed that the victim had been given terramycin, to which he had proved allergic. It had then been withdrawn but inadvertently reintroduced later by another doctor. Large quantities of liquid had also been given intravenously and broncho-pneumonia had set in. On the other hand, at the time of his death, the stab wounds had nearly healed.

The conviction, therefore, was quashed, Hallett J stated:

> Not only one feature but two separate and independent features of treatment were, in the opinion of the doctors, palpably wrong and these produced the symptoms discovered at the post-mortem examination which were the direct and immediate cause of death . . .

The court did, however, take pains to point out that in cases where normal treatment was given, the original injury would be considered to have caused the death.

The decision in **Jordan** caused concern among members of the medical profession who felt that wrongdoers might escape liability if it could be shown that any treatment given to try to save the victim was abnormal in some way.

The doctors need not have worried. The case of **Jordan** was later distinguished in **Smith 1959**, although, in this case too, the treatment given left a lot to be desired.

The victim had been stabbed twice in a barrack room fight between soldiers of different regiments. While being carried to the medical reception centre, the injured man was dropped twice. When he reached his destination, the doctor on duty failed to realise the seriousness of his injuries and administered treatment which was said at the trial to be 'thoroughly bad and might well have affected his chances of recovery'. An hour later, the victim died.

The defendant was still found guilty of murder and this was upheld by the Courts-Martial Appeal Court. It was stated that provided that the original wound was still an operating and substantial cause at the time of the death, the defendant would still be liable for the death even though some other cause of death was also operating. Lord Parker went on to say:

> Only if it can be said that the original wound is merely the setting in which another cause operates can it be said that the death did not result from the wound.

In the case of **Malcherek**, mentioned above, the judges of the Court of Appeal believed that the decision in **Smith** was preferable to that in **Jordan,** but decided that there was no need to make such a choice because of the different facts which indicated that **Jordan** had not been wrongly decided.

The matter was raised again in the case of **Cheshire 1991**, where the statements made in **Smith 1959**, appear to have been taken a step further.

The victim was shot in the stomach and the leg by the accused, during an argument in a fish and chip shop. He was operated upon but later developed breathing difficulties and had to have a tracheotomy tube inserted. He died two months later. It was discovered that his windpipe had narrowed and this had caused the severe breathing difficulties that he was experiencing at the time of his death. It was argued that this was due to the negligence of the hospital when the tracheotomy tube was fitted and that this, therefore, had broken the chain of causation. The trial judge directed the jury that a *novus actus interveniens* would only have occurred if the doctors had acted recklessly and the defendant was found guilty. He appealed against his conviction.

The Court of Appeal criticised the trial judge's reference to recklessness but still

upheld the conviction. The court came to this conclusion despite the fact that the immediate cause of the victim's death was due to the possible negligence of the doctors, not from the gunshot wounds inflicted by Cheshire. The court stated that this would not excuse the defendant from liability unless the negligent treatment:

> . . . was so independent of his acts, and in itself so potent in causing death, that they regard the contribution made by his acts as insignificant.

The principles developed in **Smith** and **Cheshire** were reinforced in **Mellor 1996**, another case where the victim did not receive the right medical treatment. He had been beaten by the defendant, resulting in bruising round his eyes, a painful shoulder and chest pain. He developed broncho-pneumonia and died two days later. The defendant tried to argue that he would not have died if he had been given sufficient oxygen and evidence given by experts supported this. Despite this, he was found guilty of murder and the conviction was upheld. Once again, the Court of Appeal stressed that if the attack had made a significant contribution to the death it was immaterial whether 'incompetence or mistake in treatment . . . may have also contributed significantly to the death'.

Comment

It has been shown from the many cases on this subject, that an offender is going to find it very difficult to prove that the chain of causation has been broken, even in cases where the intervening act appears to be substantial and the negligence of a third party is of a high degree. Some would argue that this view is to be commended because the victim would not have met his death or other fate if the accused had not put in motion the chain of events leading to the death. Others would argue that in some instances, particularly those involving gross negligence by medical staff, where it is clearly shown that the original wounds are healing well, it could be unjust to hold the original attacker liable for the full extent of the injuries.

FIVE KEY FACTS ON CAUSATION

- There is no legislation on this subject, only case law. When deciding on the factual cause of death, the courts use the 'but for' test, i.e. but for the defendant's act, the death would not have happened (**Dalloway 1847, White 1910**).
- When deciding upon the legal cause of death two further issues are examined, i.e. did the act of the defendant play a significant part in causing the death of the victim? (the term significant means more than a minimal role), and has any other event occurred to break the chain of causation?
- It has been decided that an event breaking the chain of causation must be something completely unforeseeable.
- It is not considered unforeseeable that the police might return the fire of a gunman (**Pagett 1983**), or that the victim might try to escape (**Pitts 1842, Roberts 1971, Mackie 1973, DPP v Daley 1980** and **Williams 1992**). It is foreseeable that others might be involved in the death (**Benge 1849, Towers 1874**), that the victims might already have a pre-existing medical condition (**Hayward 1908**), might refuse treatment (**Holland 1841** and **Blaue 1975**) or that they themselves might aggravate their injuries (**Wall's Case 1802**). It is also possible that doctors might have to switch off life support machines (**Malcherek and Steel 1981**), or refuse to operate because of the dangers involved (**McKechnie 1992**). Lastly, it is not unforeseeable that, on some occasions, the medical treatment might be negligently given or even be thoroughly bad (**Smith 1959, Cheshire 1991** and **Mellor 1996**).
- It will only be an accepted as a *novus actus interveniens* if the new act is completely independent and in itself 'so potent in causing death' that the original defendant's acts are insignificant (**Cheshire 1991**). The case of **Jordan 1956** provided an example of this but such cases are rare.

Activity

- In group discussion or in essay form, decide whether the rules of causation are now weighted too far against the interests of the defendant.
- Bart made an unprovoked attack on Homer during half-time at a football match and seriously injured him. Homer's friends took him to the first aid centre in the ground to receive attention but, because of the crush, they twice dropped him on the way. The centre was crowded with other people needing attention and Homer was not treated until two hours' later because the paramedic had not believed that his condition was life-threatening. In fact, Homer was a haemophiliac and was bleeding to death and, when this was discovered, it was too late to save him.

Advise Bart who has been charged with Homer's murder.

Self-Assessment Questions

1. What is the *actus reus* of the crime of murder?
2. Define the *mens rea* and show how this is established.
3. Describe the 'year and a day rule' and explain what has happened to it.
4. Using cases or examples to illustrate your answer, describe three situations where a doctor may lawfully kill a patient.
5. What is the definition of a human being? When does his life end?
6. With reference to decided cases, describe the 'but for' test.
7. What is the meaning of the expressions:
   a) *novus actus interveniens*
   b) the 'eggshell-skull rule'.
8. Why were the convictions upheld in the cases of **Pagett, Roberts, Pitts** and **Mackie**, even though the defendants had not physically committed the harm?
9. Describe the principles laid down in the cases of **Blaue, McKechnie** and **Dear**.
10. Giving cases to support your findings, explain the attitude the courts take when the defendant claims that the negligent medical treatment was responsible for the death, rather than his own actions.

Chapter 4

UNLAWFUL KILLING II: VOLUNTARY MANSLAUGHTER

4.1 Introduction

There have always been problems associated with this area of law. Lord Atkin made the following comment in the case of **Andrews v DPP 1937**:

> . . . of all crimes manslaughter appears to afford most difficulties of definition, for it concerns homicide in so many and so varying conditions.

The crime of manslaughter covers situations where it is obvious that the defendant intended to cause the death of the victim. It also encompasses other situations where it is clear that nothing could have been further from his mind, but due to a momentary lapse, albeit a very serious one, the accused has brought about the death of another person.

In this chapter, we are concerned with intentional killings but ones where the law has decreed that the person will escape liability for murder because certain conditions exist. These crimes come under the heading of voluntary manslaughter. Non-intentional killings, but ones in which the defendant is still considered to be blameworthy, will be dealt with in Chapter 5.

4.2 The crime of voluntary manslaughter

This crime is similar to murder in that an unlawful homicide has taken place, with the requisite malice aforethought on the defendant's part, but here special

circumstances exist which permit the less serious verdict of manslaughter to be brought in, with more discretion allowed to the judge on sentencing. The maximum sentence he can bestow is life imprisonment, the minimum is an absolute discharge.

The law on voluntary manslaughter is a mixture of common law rules and statutory additions. At common law only one type of voluntary manslaughter existed, that of provocation, but two further defences were added by the **Homicide Act 1957.** Voluntary manslaughter can now also be pleaded where the defendant is suffering from diminished responsibility or is the survivor of a suicide pact. If one of these three defences is successfully established, the crime will be reduced from murder to voluntary manslaughter. These three defences are illustrated in the following diagram:

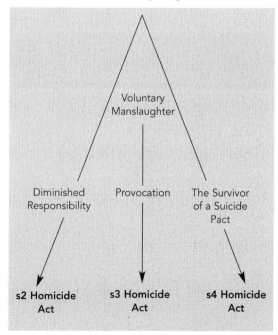

It is very important to realise that the defences are only applicable to the crime of murder, and to appreciate that they only reduce the offence from murder to manslaughter. **S2, 3,** and **4 Homicide Act 1957** cannot be used as defences for lesser crimes.

These special defences now need to be examined in turn, to ascertain precisely what has to be established for the defence to succeed.

4.3 Diminished responsibility

S2 Homicide Act 1957 states that a person may be found guilty of the lesser offence of voluntary manslaughter, rather than murder, if he was suffering from an abnormality of mind, caused by an inside source, that substantially affected his responsibility for his actions.

The precise wording is to be found in **s2(1)**. This states:

> *Where a person kills or is a party to the killing of another, he shall not be convicted of murder if he was suffering from such abnormality of mind (whether arising from a condition of arrested or retarded development of mind or any inherent causes or induced by disease or injury) as substantially impaired his mental responsibility for his acts and omissions in doing or being a party to the killing.*

S2(2) puts the burden of proof on the defendant; he will have to prove his abnormality of mind on a balance of probabilities and generally he must be the one to raise the defence. If, however, the accused is charged with murder and he pleads not guilty by reason of insanity, the prosecutor might, instead, show evidence of diminished responsibility. If the defendant relies on another defence, such as provocation, and

during the trial evidence of diminished responsibility comes to light, the judge is only under an obligation to draw the attention of the jury to the possibility of this other defence. Should the defendant plead guilty to a killing but put up diminished responsibility as a defence, the judge might be prepared to accept this without the case going to a jury, as seen overleaf.

If the defendant pleads not guilty, but his version of events is not believed by the jury and he is convicted, he will only be allowed to introduce the defence of diminished responsibility on appeal in rare cases. An example where this was successful was **Borthwick 1998.**

The body of a man who had been strangled was discovered in Borthwick's flat, with the latter's dressing gown cord around his throat. There was evidence that Borthwick had underlying personality problems, but he refused analysis of this or of his history and relationships and made the decision to plead not guilty. He maintained that someone else had been in the flat and had slept with the accused. The jury did not believe his story and convicted him of murder. He later admitted the killing to a psychiatrist, alleging that the death was accidental and had been caused by a bungled bondage session. This same doctor found that he was suffering from a form of mental illness, which could amount to paranoid schizophrenia and affect the sufferer's understanding, judgement and perception.

The Crown argued that it was the defendant's own fault that such evidence was not available at the trial. The Court of Appeal rejected this line of reasoning. The court decided that, if there was overwhelming evidence that a plea of diminished responsibility would have succeeded and it was the mental illness itself that caused the defence not to be put forward, then either a retrial or a substitution of a manslaughter verdict should be considered.

Sunbathing girl's killer sent to secure hospital

BY NICK BRITTEN

A MAN who killed a 16-year-old girl as she sunbathed in a city centre plaza was ordered to be detained indefinitely yesterday.

Inderjit Kainth, 44, carried a kitchen knife with him for a month because he believed that the only way to save himself from "agents" of Birmingham Education Authority was to kill a woman.

Birmingham Crown Court heard that Kainth at first thought that he had to kill a policewoman and was seen several times loitering outside the police training college in Edgbaston. He was scared off by a resident who believed he was going to burgle his home.

The unemployed electrician spent the next month carrying a knife hidden in a sheath made out of shampoo bottle and wrapped in a black bin liner in his pocket, looking for a victim.

At 1pm on May 12, one of the hottest days of the year, Rosie Ross and a friend had been shopping and decided to take a break in Birmingham's Centenary Square, which was packed with shoppers and sunbathers.

She was lying on a wall when Kainth, looking "oddly out of place" in a leather jacket, sat next to her before plunging the knife – which he later described as his "dagger of revenge" – into her stomach.

Kainth fled, pursued by three boys who caught him after he threw the knife into a canal. Two off-duty doctors tried to help Rosie, but she died later that afternoon in hospital. A few days later her parents Sean, 42, and Karen, 40, from Aldridge, West Midlands, found their daughter's will, which said that she was "in paradise" and urged them not to be upset.

The court heard that Kainth, 44, an "obsessive" marathon runner who had competed in more than 150 races, was suffering from paranoid schizophrenia.

The father of five admitted manslaughter on the grounds of diminished responsibility. The court was told he had been suffering from the mental illness since the mid-1980s, when he visited North America to trace a girl he had been obsessed with at school.

Kainth told psychiatrists that he would win the girl back if he killed a woman. After killing Rosie, the court heard he was "calm, somewhat relieved".

Sending Kainth to a maximum security hospital, Mr Justice Eady said Kainth was, and was likely to remain, a serious danger to the public.

Daily Telegraph, 11 December 2001

Similarly in **Martin 2001**, as shown in the accompanying newspaper report, the Court of Appeal allowed the Norfolk farmer's appeal against a murder conviction on the grounds of diminished responsibility, after accepting fresh evidence that the defendant had a paranoid personality disorder. This case caused great controversy over the extent to which a person could go in order to protect his home from burglars. The appeal court agreed with the jury that Martin had gone further than what was reasonable to do this but decided that, because of his state of mind, he was only guilty of manslaughter, not murder. The matter will be discussed more fully in Chapter 11.

Farmer who shot burglar dead could be free in year

By Lewis Smith

TONY MARTIN, the farmer who shot dead a burglar at his remote Norfolk home, is likely to be freed from prison next year after his conviction for murder was reduced to manslaughter by the Court of Appeal yesterday.

Martin was told that his life sentence would be reduced to five years and that, as he had served 18 months in jail, he would be eligible for parole next autumn after completing half his sentence.

He showed no emotion as the judges gave their reasons for reducing the sentence. Later, through his solicitor, James Saunders, he said that he was relieved no longer to be branded a murderer.

"There is light at the end of the tunnel," he told his solicitor. "I'm pleased the appeal has shown I'm not a liar and I'm relieved not to be called a murderer, but I still want to clear my name."

Mr Saunders indicated that Martin would take his case to the Lords. The Appeal Court ruling left it unclear how far a householder could go in defending his property, he said.

"No one really knows now what you can and can't do. That's the dilemma. When you are confronted by burglars, if you don't act it may be too late," Mr Saunders said.

Martin, 55, was convicted in April last year of murdering Fred Barras, 16, and wounding Brendan Fearon, 33, with an illegally held pump-action shotgun when they broke into his ramshackle home at Emneth Hungate, Norfolk, in August 1999. He was sentenced to life for murder and ten years in prison for wounding with intent.

The Lord Chief Justice, Lord Woolf, sitting with Mr Justice Wright and Mr Justice Grigson, yesterday accepted his appeal against the murder conviction on the ground of diminished responsibility.

Lord Woolf said he was satisfied that fresh evidence presented during the appeal showing that Martin had a paranoid personality disorder would have led to the original trial jury finding him guilty of manslaughter by reason of diminished responsibility. He added that a jail term had to be imposed because Martin was wrong to shoot the burglars, even though he had had previous break-ins and had little faith in the police.

Lord Woolf ruled: "Mr Martin was entitled to use reasonable force to protect himself and his home, but the jury were surely correct in coming to their judgment that Mr Martin was not acting reasonably in shooting one of the intruders dead and seriously injuring the other. We must make it clear that an extremely dangerous weapon cannot be used in the manner in which it was used by Mr Martin that night."

The judges rejected the farmer's other grounds for appeal, including that he acted in self-defence and failed to get a fair trial because of tactical blunders by his defence team.

Martin's counsel, Michael Wolkind, QC, had presented evidence to counter the prosecution's claim that Martin lay in wait on the ground floor of his home before firing on the burglars. Mr Wolkind said new tests showed the fatal shot had been fired as Martin came down the staircase, supporting the farmer's testimony.

He said psychiatric evidence showed he

had acted in self-defence because he was in fear of his life and that being sexually abused as a child meant he would react more violently than most people to threats.

The judges cut Martin's ten-year sentence

for wounding Mr Fearon to three years. A 12-month term for possessing an uncertified shotgun remains unchanged.

The Times, 31 October 2001

The differences between diminished responsibility and insanity

It will be seen that the defence of diminished responsibility is wider in the range of abnormal states of mind it covers, than is allowed under the general defence of insanity under the **M'Naghten** rules, which are examined in Chapter 10. On the other hand the defence under **s2** is more limited in that it is only available as a defence to a charge of murder. Even so, it is more popular with defendants who prefer not to face the stigma of insanity.

The elements of diminished responsibility

- There has to be an abnormality of mind.
- This must arise from an inside source, such as mental illness or handicap or other diseases of the mind.
- It must substantially affect the defendant's mental responsibility for his actions.

These three points need looking at in more detail.

4.3.1 An abnormality of mind

This is a state of mind a reasonable man would find abnormal. It is the task of the jury to decide this, not the medical experts, although the jury will obviously take notice of medical opinion. The jurors will also be influenced by the summing up of the judge. It is therefore vital that this gives the correct statement of the law.

This was not held to be the case in **Byrne 1960** and the defendant was successful in his appeal against a murder conviction.

Byrne strangled a young girl living in a YWCA hostel and then carried out horrific mutilations on her body. He claimed that he was suffering from diminished responsibility and had killed the girl while in the grip of an irresistible impulse caused by his perverted sexual desires. Three medical experts had testified that he was, indeed, a sexual psychopath. The judge told the jury that **s2** was not there to give protection 'where there is nothing else than what is vicious and depraved' and had earlier given the impression that a difficulty or even inability of the defendant to control his acts would not amount to an abnormality of mind. The jury then convicted him of murder.

The Court of Appeal quashed the murder conviction, believing that, if properly directed, the jury would certainly have found that the defence of diminished responsibility had been made out. Lord Parker stated that the term 'abnormality of mind' included a lack of ability to form a rational judgement or exercise the necessary willpower to control one's acts. He said that the term was:

> wide enough to cover the mind's activities in all its aspects, not only the perception of physical acts and matters and the ability to form a rational judgement whether an act is right or wrong, but also the ability to exercise willpower to control physical acts in accordance with that rational judgement.

The appeal against the murder conviction was allowed and a verdict of manslaughter substituted. The sentence of life imprisonment was not, however, disturbed.

It has been noted that the defence of **s2** covers 'the mind's activities in all its aspects'. In **Hobson 1997**, the Court of Appeal held that the cumulative effects of 'battered woman's syndrome' could lead to an abnormality of mind, thus affording a defence to a charge of murder if the abused woman turned on her tormentor and killed him.

Evidence of diminished responsibility in respect of such physical abuse was accepted in the retrials of two battered wives, **Ahluwalia** and **Thornton**. These cases will be discussed more fully under provocation.

4.3.2 Caused by an inside source

The second element of the defence of diminished responsibility states that the abnormality must be caused by 'arrested or retarded development of mind or any inherent causes or induced by disease or injury'. This means that the abnormality must have been caused by an inside source, i.e. some malfunctioning of the mind. Evidence, therefore, of mere intoxication, caused by drinking or drug taking (i.e. outside sources), cannot be put forward for this defence, unless the drinking or drug taking has actually damaged the mind itself, or where there was such a craving for drink or drugs that it could not be controlled.

In **Tandy 1989** the female defendant was an alcoholic who, on the day in question, drank almost a whole bottle of vodka. Her normal drink was said to be Cinzano, which is less potent. She then strangled her 11-year-old daughter after the latter claimed that she had been sexually interfered with by the defendant's husband and wanted to go to live with her grandmother. The accused made the significant admission that her drinking was not totally involuntary and that she did initially have some control over her choice of drink and the time she started drinking. The judge, therefore, withdrew the defence of diminished responsibility from the jury and she was convicted of murder. The Court of Appeal upheld the conviction stating that, for the defence to succeed, it was necessary for the abnormality of mind to be induced by the alcoholism. This would only have arisen if the defendant's mind had been damaged or there was evidence that she had no control over her drinking at the outset.

Similarly, in **Egan 1992**, the defendant was not allowed the defence of diminished responsibility when he killed a woman of 79 years after drinking an abnormally large quantity of alcohol (15 pints of beer and several gins and tonics). He was not an alcoholic but there was evidence that he suffered from retarded development and, possibly, a psychopathic disorder. The jury was told to disregard his drinking and to decide whether he would have killed without this. The jury obviously believed that his mental abnormality was not great enough on its own to substantially affect his mental responsibility and convicted him of murder. The Court of Appeal upheld the decision.

In **O'Connell 1997**, the Court of Appeal took a similar approach in relation to a prescribed drug called Halcion, which was alleged to have adversely affected the mind of the defendant. The court noted that the drug was absorbed very rapidly into the system and also that its effects wear off very quickly. They therefore took the view that its effect was similar to that induced by alcohol and decided that it could not therefore come under the definition of an abnormality of mind 'induced by disease or injury'. It will be seen that a different decision was arrived at in **Sanderson 1994**, mentioned below, because the Court of Appeal believed that the mental illness might well have existed before the sustained cocaine abuse.

While intoxication temporarily affecting the mind will not amount to an abnormality in this context, it should be clearly noted that the defendant does not have to be insane to use the defence. Lord Parker's comment that he thought that the phrase 'diminished responsibility' meant something bordering on insanity was later criticised by the Court of Appeal in **Seers 1984**. The defence has been allowed for someone who killed while in a fit of jealousy (**Miller 1972**) and for women suffering from post menstrual tension (**Smith 1982** and **Reynolds 1988)**. Chronic depression may also suffice, as was the case in **Seers** and **Gittens 1984.**

In the latter case, the defendant, after a violent quarrel, killed his wife by clubbing her to death and then raped and killed his stepdaughter. He claimed that he was suffering from chronic depression although he had also acted under the effects of drink and drugs. The Court of Appeal allowed his appeal against a conviction for murder on the grounds of a misdirection by the trial judge, although as in **Byrne**, mentioned above, the sentence of life imprisonment remained.

The court also agreed that the jury had been misdirected in **Sanderson 1994**, and again substituted a conviction for manslaughter rather than murder. As in **Gittens**, there was evidence of both mental illness and drug abuse and it needed to be decided if the former had existed before the latter. The Court of Appeal felt that in most cases, it would not be helpful to quote the whole of **s2** to the jury as this could cause confusion. Instead, the trial judge should 'tailor his directions to suit the facts of the particular case'. As an obiter statement, the court also made it clear that the words 'disease or injury' mentioned in **s2** did not, as such, cover mental injury but decided that this type of illness was covered by the earlier phrase 'any inherent cause'.

4.3.3 Which substantially affected his mental responsibility

The difficulty which the defendant faces here, is that his abnormality of mind must have been substantially greater than would have been experienced be an ordinary person. The impairment need not be total but must be more than trivial, as stated in **Simcox 1964**. There should be medical evidence to support this contention. Generally, the jury will accept such evidence, but it need not if there is other evidence available to suggest a more calculated killing.

In **Sanders 1991**, the defendant's conviction for the murder of his long-standing mistress was upheld by the Court of Appeal, despite the fact that two psychiatrists had testified that the accused was suffering from reactive depression amounting to an abnormality of mind. The jury convicted him despite such evidence, because it was shown that he had written letters to others stating that he was going to commit suicide but had not written to his mistress, nor included her in his will.

In **Campbell 1997**, the defendant did succeed in pleading diminished responsibility at his second appeal. He picked up a female hitchhiker and attacked her when she refused his advances. When he discovered that she was not dead, he tried to strangle her and eventually hit her across the throat with his hockey stick. He maintained that he was suffering from diminished responsibility caused by his epilepsy and frontal lobe damage and at his second appeal the court heard the evidence of two eminent psychiatrists in this field. Lord Bingham C J stated:

Having studied the available evidence of what the appellant did and said at the time, both doctors were of the clear opinion that at the time of the killing the appellant had been suffering an abnormality of mind of such significance as seriously to diminish his responsibility for the act he carried out.

A retrial was therefore ordered, although it was made clear that this could not lead to an acquittal, only a possible reduction of the murder conviction to manslaughter.

FIVE KEY FACTS ON DIMINISHED RESPONSIBILITY

- The defence is to be found in **s2 Homicide Act 1957**. It is only a partial defence, reducing the conviction from murder to manslaughter. In cases of homicide, it has largely replaced the general defence of insanity, which will be discussed in Chapter 10.
- Three elements have to be proved before the defence will succeed: an abnormality of mind, caused by an inside source, which substantially impairs the defendant's mental responsibility for his actions.
- The term 'abnormality of mind' encompasses a greater variety of situations than the general defence of insanity. It covers a person's inability to distinguish right from wrong but also includes the 'irresistible impulse' situation, where the defendant is unable to exercise the necessary will power to control his physical acts, as in **Byrne 1960**.
- The abnormality must derive from the mind itself, although the accused need not be insane (**Seers 1984, Sanderson 1994, Martin 2001**). Those suffering from alcoholism which is shown to have affected the mind, battered woman's syndrome (**Ahluwahlia 1992, Thornton (No. 2) 1995, Hobson 1997**), depression (**Seers, Gittens**, both **1984**), epilepsy (**Campbell 1997**), fits of jealousy (**Miller 1972**), and pre-menstrual tension (**Smith 1982, Reynolds 1988**), have all been able to use the defence. Those suffering from temporary intoxication cannot (**Tandy 1988, Egan 1992**).
- The abnormality must be great enough to substantially reduce the defendant's mental responsibility for his acts and the jury will be the body to decide this after listening to the evidence of doctors (**Sanders 1991** and **Campbell 1997**).

Comment

Some critics argue that the defence dilutes the seriousness of intentional killing. Women's groups claim that it is too readily available for defendants who kill their partners then produce medical evidence of long-term depression caused by emotional problems.

On the other hand, there is equally good evidence to indicate that the defence is not reaching some of those who need its help. Statistics show that successful diminished responsibility pleas are falling, rather than rising. As noted by R D Mackay, Professor of Criminal Policy and Mental Health, at De Montfort University, in the *Criminal Law Review* 1999 page 117, there were only 49 such pleas in 1996, compared to 78 in 1992. In contrast, there were 253 murder convictions. Professor Mackay states:

> One possible explanation for these complementary findings could be that the diminished responsibility plea is being looked at more sceptically by psychiatrists, the prosecution and juries.

We have already noted that there is a marked reluctance to allow the defence if the abnormal behaviour is wholly or partly caused by alcohol or drug taking. Professor Mackay reminds us that this view has prevailed even when the drug was taken on prescription, as was the case with regard to the sleeping pills used by O'Connell. This might be seen as unfair.

Women's groups and sections of the media have argued that the defence of diminished responsibility was less readily available for women. There have been some advances in this, as can be seen by the courts' recognition that severe pre-menstrual tension might result in an abnormality of mind. They have also accepted that mental and physical abuse over a long period, a condition known as 'battered woman syndrome', might reduce a woman's mental responsibility and cause her to kill her abuser.

It appears that the defence may, in rare instances, be refused on the grounds of public policy. There was obviously some sort of abnormality in the mind of Peter Sutcliffe, the notorious 'Yorkshire Ripper' and counsel for both sides wished to introduce the defence. The judge refused and Sutcliffe was found guilty of murder, a result that was welcomed by the public and relations of the victims. He has, however, spent most of his sentence in solitary confinement in a mental institution.

4.3.4 Possible reform of diminished responsibility

The *Draft Criminal Code* wishes to alter the wording of this defence to 'Such mental abnormality as would be substantial enough to reduce the charge of murder to manslaughter'. To date, there are no immediate plans to put this change into effect.

Activity

Max has a severe persecution complex, which has been made worse by alcohol and the regular taking of ecstasy tablets. He is convinced that his science teacher is a reincarnation of the Devil, come temporarily to Earth to ensure that Max fails his exams. On receiving an 'E' grade for a project that he believed was excellent, Max put poison in the teacher's coffee, causing the other to suffer an agonising death. Max has been charged with murder but wishes to use the defence of diminished responsibility. Advise him, quoting relevant cases to support your answer.

4.4 Provocation

The defence at common law

It has been suggested that as many as 45 per cent of all killings are committed by people who lose their temper. The defence of provocation may sometimes exist if this loss of control is caused by the provocative act of the other party.

The defence has existed for many years, at least for men. It was recognised by the common law where the defendant had been provoked after being subjected to a violent physical attack. Provocation was also allowed for a man who discovered his wife committing adultery, as in **Maddy 1671**, and killed her or the lover or both. Blackstone's early Commentaries (iv 192) stated that such a crime was of 'the lowest degree of manslaughter', a view to which not all would subscribe! The defence was at first limited to husbands but, as the cases of **Larkin 1943** and **Gauthier** of the same year illustrate, it was extended to men killing their mistresses in similar circumstances. In **Fisher 1837**, a father who killed a man he discovered in the act of sodomy with his son was also entitled to the defence. It can be seen from these circumstances that, at common law, there had to be a provocative act of some sort; mere words were not enough. In **Lesbini 1914**, the defence was not available for a man who shot and killed a girl in charge of a firing range in an amusement arcade, after she had made derogatory remarks about him. In **Holmes v DPP 1946**, the House of Lords held that the defence could not be used by a husband who killed his wife after hearing her verbal confession of adultery. This can be contrasted with the current position as seen in **Parnham 2002**, where the jury accepted a manslaughter verdict when a teacher killed after his wife threatened to leave him.

The defence under s3 Homicide Act

The restrictive nature of the common law defence was lifted in 1957. Under **s3 Homicide Act 1957** it states:

> *Where, on a charge of murder, there is evidence on which the jury can find that the person charged was provoked (whether by things done or by things said or by both together) to lose his self-control, the question whether the provocation was enough to make a reasonable man do as he did shall be left to be determined by the jury.*

This section of the **Homicide Act** clearly recognises and builds upon the common law defence of provocation. There has to be evidence of provocation but it now clearly states that this can arise from 'things said' in addition to 'things done'. It also reaffirms the position that it is the jury who will decide the issue, by measuring the conduct of the accused by the standard of the reasonable man, a concept first introduced in this context at common law in the case of **Welsh 1869**.

Under the **Homicide Act 1957**, therefore, the revised defence of provocation has three elements to it which have to be satisfied:

- There has to be evidence that the defendant was provoked.
- The accused must then have lost his self-control.
- The jury must be satisfied that a reasonable man might have acted in a similar way.

These three elements need to be looked at in turn.

4.4.1 There has to be evidence of provocation

Initially, it is the judge who will decide whether there is enough evidence of provocation to be put before the jury. As mentioned earlier, the provocation can, under **s3 Homicide Act**, arise from either things done or things said. In addition, the words or actions do not need to have come from the deceased, as was the case at common law, nor need they be directed at the defendant. In **Davies 1975**, the action of the wife's lover, of walking towards her place of work to meet her, was taken into account when the husband lost control and killed his wife. In **Doughty 1986**, the Court of Appeal held that even the continuous crying of a very young baby should have been considered by the jury as a possible provoking event, even though it was obviously not directed at the accused. Similarly, in **Pearson 1992**, the ill-treatment meted out over a period of eight years by the victim, had not been principally directed at the defendant but towards his brother. The Court of Appeal decided that this was still an act of provocation, which the accused could use in his defence when he killed his father by attacking him with a sledgehammer.

Self-induced provocation

To stop the possibility of a later appeal therefore, the accused should usually be given the benefit of the doubt. This even includes cases where the accused himself has started the trouble, which in law is known as 'self-induced provocation'. A case illustrating this is **Johnson 1989**. The accused started an argument in a night club, during which he made threats against the victim and his woman friend. A fight developed in the course of which the victim was fatally stabbed. The accused alleged that he was provoked by the fear of being 'glassed' by the victim but the judge declined to put this matter before the jury.

The Court of Appeal allowed the defendant's appeal, despite the fact that he had been the one who had started the trouble and even though he had been armed with a knife and the other only had a broken glass. Watkins L J, for the Court of Appeal stated:

> In view of the express wording of **s3** . . . we find it impossible to accept that the mere fact that a defendant caused a reaction in others, which in turn led him to lose his self-control, should result in the issue of provocation being kept outside a jury's consideration.

In **Baille 1995**, a similar appeal was successful. The defendant went to the house of a drug dealer armed with a sawn-off shotgun and a cut-throat razor, after serious threats were made by the dealer to the defendant's three sons. They were addicts who had been among his customers.

The father, who was strongly opposed to the taking of drugs, violently attacked the drug dealer with the razor and seriously injured him. When the victim tried to escape, the defendant fired the shotgun after him. The drug dealer was killed by particles of pellets blasted towards him from a wire mesh fence by the force of the shots.

The defendant tried to plead provocation, arguing that he suffered a temporary loss of control after his son told him about the threats and that this had lasted up to the time of the shooting. In the alternative, he also tried to claim that he lost his self-control when the victim tried to wrestle the gun from him, i.e. that this was self-induced provocation. The judge allowed the latter defence to be put before the jury but not the first issue, deciding that the loss of self-control must have ceased by the time the killing took place.

The appeal court followed an earlier decision in **Cambridge 1994** and held that the failure to put the issue of possible provocation to the jury was a material misdirection. The murder conviction was therefore quashed and one of manslaughter substituted.

The moral seems to be that if there is anything that could amount to provocation, it is better for the judge to 'play safe' and put the issue to the jury.

Other provoking events

In **Dhillon 1997**, the prosecution claimed that the accused deliberately ran over the victim in his car during a heated quarrel. The defendant, on the other hand, argued that the death was caused accidentally while he was trying to escape from another man, who was using a hockey stick as a weapon. There was enough conflicting evidence to support both versions of events. The defence of provocation was obviously inappropriate if the defendant's story was thought to be true and after consultation with both sides, the judge withdrew the issue from the jury. This body went on to find the defendant guilty of murder, obviously preferring the prosecution's account of what had happened. The defendant then appealed.

The Court of Appeal held this was a misdirection and decided that *both* issues should have been presented to the jury. The court therefore substituted a manslaughter verdict.

From the cases just discussed, it can be seen that almost anything can amount to evidence of provocation. There are limitations, however. From the wording of **s3**, it has been seen that the provocation must have been something done or something said, which would exclude naturally occurring acts. For example, if a landowner lost his self control and killed his gardener after discovering that his gardens had been destroyed by a terrible storm, he would not be able to plead provocation. Similarly in **Acott 1997**, the House of Lords decided that there was no evidence of any provoking words or conduct by another party, even though the savagery of the attack on the victim might have

indicated that the perpetrator had lost his self control for some reason. The defendant claimed that his mother's death was an accident caused by a fall but, on his conviction for murder, he appealed, arguing that the defence of provocation should have been put to the jury. Neither of the appeal courts found evidence of any provoking act and the man's conviction for murder was upheld by the House of Lords.

4.4.2 The defendant must have lost his self-control

It is not enough for the defendant to show that he has been provoked. He must then show that the provocation affected him so strongly that he then lost his self-control. This is obviously is a subjective test.

The classic definition of provocation was uttered by Lord Devlin in the case of **Duffy 1949** and, despite the changes made by **s3 Homicide Act**, the latter part of his direction still appears to be an authoritative statement of the law. It has been firmly upheld in later cases, as, for example by the House of Lords in **Baille 1995**, mentioned earlier.

The definition in **Duffy** allows the defence of provocation to be used where it has caused:

> *a sudden and temporary loss of self-control rendering the accused so subject to passion as to make him or her, for the moment, not master of his mind.*

In **Richens 1993**, the Court of Appeal stated that these words should not be extended to mean that there had to be a complete loss of control to the extent that the person did not know what he was doing, simply that the defendant had been provoked to lose his self control and had killed.

The definition of provocation was not satisfied in the case of **Cocker 1989**, where the defendant killed his incurably ill wife, after she repeatedly asked him to end her suffering. At the time of the killing, she had continually attacked him during the night both mentally and physically, for not honouring his promise to kill her. The defendant then suffocated her with a pillow. Although he tried to argue that the actions that night were 'the last straw', the defendant's appeal on the grounds that he had lost his self control was not accepted.

A cooling-off period?

The words 'sudden and temporary loss of self control' have also caused problems in cases where the accused has waited some time before acting. The jury (and the Court of Appeal) are less inclined to believe that a person has lost his self control if he or she has had time for a 'cooling-off' period and has then gone on to commit the offence.

This was the position in **Duffy 1949**, **Thornton 1992** and **Ahluwahlia 1992**, all cases concerning 'battered wives'.

In **Duffy 1949**, an abused wife, after a quarrel, left the room, changed her clothes and then returned with a hammer and a hatchet when her husband was in bed and killed him. Lord Devlin gave the now famous direction and decided that the woman's actions did not fall within it. Her conviction for murder, therefore, was upheld.

In the case of **Thornton 1992**, the couple had a very stormy relationship. Both of them drank heavily and in this state, the husband sometimes became violent and assaulted his wife.

On the night in question, after a serious quarrel, Mrs Thornton went into the kitchen, allegedly to find a truncheon to protect herself, and when she could not find it, sharpened a kitchen knife instead and returned to where her drunken husband was sleeping on a sofa. She asked him to come to bed but he refused and, after a further acrimonious exchange, she slowly plunged the knife into his stomach and killed him.

The defence relied on the plea of diminished responsibility at the trial but the trial judge also introduced the possible defence of provocation. Both pleas were unsuccessful and the jury convicted her of murder. The issue of provocation was again raised on her first appeal but this, too, was unsuccessful because it was felt that her actions of obtaining a knife and sharpening it did not indicate a loss of self-control. After several years in prison, another appeal was allowed and, at this, a retrial was ordered. At Oxford Crown Court, the defence of provocation was again dismissed but the alternative plea of diminished responsibility was accepted by the jury and a verdict of manslaughter substituted for murder. A sentence of six years imprisonment was given, which in view of the time already served, meant that Thornton could walk free from the court.

In **Ahluwalia 1992**, the defendant, who had been subjected to an arranged marriage, had suffered serious physical abuse by her unfaithful husband over a number of years. At the time of the killing, she had been threatened with a further beating in the morning. She therefore waited until her husband was asleep and then poured petrol over the bed and set fire to it. The victim later died of his injuries. Once again, it was difficult for the defence to show a sudden loss of self control and Ahluwalia was convicted of murder. After a strenuous campaign to free her, the murder conviction was changed to one of manslaughter but only because the defence of diminished responsibility, caused by what has become known as 'battered woman syndrome', and 'learned helplessness', was accepted. The Court of Appeal was prepared to accept that acts of provocation could take place over a period of time, a 'slow burn' effect but Lord Taylor, the Lord Chief Justice at that time still reiterated that the actual loss of self control at the end of the period had to be a sudden one.

He said that 'the longer the delay and the stronger the evidence of deliberation on the part of the defendant, the more likely it will be that the prosecution will negative provocation'.

In the case of **Duffy**, mentioned previously, the judge had followed his classic statement with the following comment:

> circumstances which induce a desire for revenge are inconsistent with provocation, since the conscious formulation of a desire for revenge means that a person has had time to think, to reflect, and that would negative a sudden temporary loss of self control, which is of the essence of provocation.

Revenge, rather than provocation, was said to be the reason for the crime in the case of **Ibrams and Gregory 1981.** The defendants had been terrorised and bullied by the victim. They and another woman involved in the case had failed to obtain satisfactory police protection so decided to take matters into their own hands. A few days later, therefore, they devised a plan for the woman to lure the man to bed, whereupon the defendants would burst in, attack him and break his arms and legs. Instead, the victim was killed and the defendants were found guilty of murder.

The Court of Appeal upheld the conviction, deciding that the formulation of a plan indicated that there was no sudden loss of self control and therefore no defence.

Comment

These cases show that a person who has been ill-treated in some way, whether physically or mentally, but who fails to retaliate immediately, either through fear or through a delayed reaction to the events, faces great difficulty in English law. The defence of provocation will not be open to such a person if there has been enough time for a cooling-off period. He will have to rely on the more limited defence of diminished responsibility and try to show that his mind has been badly affected by the cumulative effect of the abuse he has suffered.

4.4.3 A reasonable man must have acted in a similar way

This last point involves examining the behaviour of the accused and assessing the extent of his reaction to the provocation. After this, the jury will decide whether a reasonable man might have acted in the same way.

In **Phillips 1969**, Lord Diplock, for the Privy Council, stated:

> The test of provocation is two-fold. The first, which has always been a question of fact for the jury, assuming that there is any evidence upon which they can so find, is 'Was the defendant provoked into losing his self control?' The second, which is one not of fact but of opinion, is 'Would a reasonable man have reacted to the same provocation in the same way as the defendant did?'

He went on to say that the trial judge's summing up, where he made it clear to the jurors that it was their responsibility, not his, to decide upon this matter, was 'an impeccable direction'.

In **Brown 1972**, a married couple had a violent quarrel after the husband suspected that his wife was being unfaithful to him. The wife attacked the defendant with a knife but not seriously, merely scratching his neck. He then attacked her with a poker and cut her throat with a razor. His conviction for murder was upheld because the jury believed that a reasonable man would not have reacted in such an extreme way.

Before the leading case of **Camplin 1978**, the view of a reasonable man was decided by an objective test. This was applied in the case of **Bedder v DPP 1954**. The accused had tried, in vain, to have intercourse, a prostitute. He claimed that she struck him and taunted him about his impotence and he lost his temper and killed her.

The House of Lords dismissed his appeal against the conviction for murder, stating that a reasonable man would not have lost control in this way. No allowance was made for the special circumstances of the man's impotency.

Changes made after *Camplin*

The purely objective test was modified by the House of Lords in **DPP v Camplin 1978**. Their Lordships felt that a better test should be: 'Would a reasonable man with the same characteristics as the accused have acted in this way?'

In this case, Camplin, a 15-year-old boy had been drinking and went with a middle-aged man to the latter's house, where the boy was forcibly subjected to a homosexual assault. When he expressed shame at what had happened, the older man was alleged to have laughed and taunted him. The boy then attacked him with a heavy chipatti pan and killed him. He was convicted of murder after a direction from the judge about the qualities of a reasonable man.

His appeal eventually reached the House of Lords, where it was decided that, while certain of the boy's characteristics should not be taken into account for policy reasons, such as his drunkenness and excitability, other characteristics, such as his young age, could be. The question for the jury, therefore, was whether a reasonable youth of 15, in similar circumstances, would have acted as he did. Because this was a possibility, the appeal against the murder conviction was allowed.

Unfortunately, the use of the word 'characteristics', and the question of which of these may or may not be taken into account, has caused confusion among both judges and juries, leading, inevitably to further appeals.

In **Newell 1980**, the accused killed the victim by hitting him with a heavy ashtray, after the friend made homosexual advances to him. The defendant was an alcoholic who, at the time of the attack, was recovering from a drug overdose. He was in a bad emotional state because his girlfriend had recently left him.

The Court of Appeal held that, when looking at the characteristics of the accused, the jury should only take into account permanent ones and ones that actually relate to the provocation. Therefore the effects of his drinking and drug taking could not be considered. It was decided that alcoholism could be a permanent factor, which in some situations could be taken into account, but not in this case because it was unrelated to the actual attack. The appeal against the murder conviction was therefore unsuccessful.

Mental characteristics

Even though the appeal was unsuccessful, this case seemed to mark a turning point where a greater range of factors could be classed as characteristics that could be attributed to the reasonable man. The Court of Appeal had relied on a New Zealand authority, that of **McGregor 1962** and decided that certain mental characteristics could also be taken into account.

In **Humphreys 1995**, a young girl had been convicted of murder when she stabbed to death the man with whom she was living.

Humphreys, brought up by an alcoholic mother and stepfather, developed severe anti-social behaviour, often culminating in suicide attempts. She became a prostitute at the age of 16 and later moved in with the deceased, a much older man. The latter was of a violent disposition and unfaithful to her.

On the night of the stabbing, the deceased, in a pub with the accused and several others, made remarks about the possibility of a 'gang bang' later that night. Humphreys alleged that, on their return to his house, he started to undress and she feared that he was about to rape her. She had earlier made an unsuccessful effort to slash her wrists and he jeered at her about this failed suicide attempt. She stated that she then lost control and stabbed him.

At her trial, she tried unsuccessfully to plead provocation, stating that the sneering remarks about her failed suicide attempts, coupled with her past history and the earlier events that evening had caused her 'to snap'. Despite this, the jury found her guilty of murder.

As in the cases of **Thornton** and **Ahluwalia**, a campaign was mounted to secure her release, and her case was eventually referred back to the Court of Appeal. A manslaughter verdict was then substituted in place of the murder conviction because of two misdirections by the trial judge. Firstly, he had told the jury that they should consider the effect of the taunts on a reasonable woman in the same situation as Humphreys, not a woman with a distorted and explosive personality. Secondly, he had failed to give them full details of her history and the events leading up to the stabbing.

The Court of Appeal decided that the girl's characteristics of immaturity and attention-seeking could be likened to an illness like anorexia. They could be seen as part of a psychological illness and were sufficiently permanent characteristics to be attributed to the reasonable young woman.

The court also stated that, in a complex case such as this, the jury should have been given a more detailed analysis of the possible areas of provocation and not have been left without guidance simply to make its own decision. The appeal was allowed.

As stated earlier, **Ahluwalia** and **Thornton** were also the beneficiaries of this more liberal approach to the subject of characteristics which could be held by the reasonable man. While their retrials succeeded on the issue of diminished responsibility, the Court of Appeal, in an obiter statement in **Ahluwalia 1992** stated that post traumatic stress disorder and battered woman syndrome could come under the heading of characteristics for the purposes of the defence of provocation. This view was supported in **Thornton (No 2) 1996**, even though, as in the previous case, diminished responsibility rather than provocation, was accepted as the more relevant defence.

In **Dryden 1995**, the defendant's 'eccentric and obsessional personality traits' were considered, on appeal, to be mental characteristics which should have been pointed out to the jury.

Dryden had been ordered to demolish his bungalow, built without relevant permission. Instead, he shot and killed one of the planning officers who came to enforce the order.

At his trial, he put forward the defences of both diminished responsibility and provocation but was convicted of murder. With regard to diminished responsibility, the doctors had disagreed as to whether his abnormality of mind was sufficient to substantially impair his mental responsibility for his acts. He then appealed.

The Court of Appeal decided that when the defence of provocation was being explained to the jury, the judge should have discussed the possessiveness and eccentricity of the defendant which distinguished him from others. The court held that these factors amounted to characteristics of sufficient permanence to be attributed to the reasonable man. Despite the misdirection, however, the appeal failed because it was felt that no jury would have believed that a reasonable man, even one possessing the qualities of the accused, would have acted in a similar way.

In **Morhall 1995**, the defendant was taunted about his addiction to glue-sniffing several times on the day in question. He was involved in a fight with the victim, which was broken up. The victim then followed the defendant up to his room and was stabbed seven times. Morhall was convicted of murder, a decision that was upheld by the Court of Appeal. The court refused to consider glue-sniffing as a characteristic to be taken into account, likening it to drunkenness or drug-taking, which were felt to be repugnant to the idea of a reasonable man. The House of Lords, however, reversed the decision and substituted a conviction for manslaughter.

Their Lordships decided that a distinction had to be made between cases where the accused is taunted about an addiction he possesses, such as drug addiction, alcoholism or being a glue-sniffer, who then loses his self control, and cases where, because of his drugged state or his drunkenness, he loses that self control more readily. In the first type of situation, provocation could be pleaded but, in the latter case, it is felt that a reasonable man, or ordinary man as the House of Lords now chose to call him, would not have been drunk or drugged.

The House of Lords approved of the reasoning in **DPP v Camplin** mentioned earlier, but decided that, since that case, too much

emphasis had been placed on the word 'characteristic' and attempts to decide which of these could or could not be taken into account.

They decided that, instead of being asked to look at various characteristics of the accused, the jury should be asked to look at 'the entire factual situation'. This could include other factors that might be relevant to the provocation, in addition to the characteristics of the accused. These could include various addictions if they had been the subject of the provocation, as was the case here.

Retraction!

Lord Goff, while appearing to widen the ambit of provocation in this respect, did, however, add a note of caution. He stated that, in cases such as **Newell** and those following it, too much reliance had been put on dicta in the New Zealand case of **McGregor 1962**, a point he returned to in the case of **Luc Thiet Thuan 1996**, where a more restrictive approach was favoured.

This concerned an appeal made to the Privy Council from Hong Kong. The defendant claimed that he had killed his ex-girlfriend after tying her up and forcing her to reveal her bank code number, because she had taunted him about his inferior sexual prowess compared to that of her new boyfriend. There was medical evidence to show that he suffered from organic brain damage that made it difficult for him to control his impulses. The trial judge had directed the jury on this matter when dealing with the defence of diminished responsibility, but had not mentioned it in connection with provocation.

The case reached the Privy Council, which rejected the appeal. The court of five judges decided, four to one, that factors like mental instability which have reduced the defendant's powers of self control cannot be attributed to the reasonable man.

Lord Goff stated that the English Court of Appeal had, in the case of **Newell 1980**, taken a wrong turning regarding provocation and the characteristics to be attributed to the reasonable man, after it had adopted, 'without analysis', statements made in the New Zealand case of **McGregor 1962**. That case had allowed 'purely mental peculiarities' to be included as characteristics in the defence of provocation, which Lord Goff believed was wrong. He pointed out that New Zealand does not have a separate defence of diminished responsibility and therefore needed to take its own steps to rectify this shortcoming, as was discussed later in another New Zealand case, that of **McCarthy 1992**. English law, however, does have two separate defences, so he felt that such an approach should not have been adopted here.

He declared that the possible use of the defence of provocation in the cases of **Ahluwahlia** (post traumatic stress disorder or battered woman syndrome), **Dryden** (eccentric and obsessional personality traits), and **Humphreys** (abnormal immaturity and attention-seeking) would have been decided differently if the case of **McCarthy** had been brought to the Court of Appeal's attention. If this had been done, he argued, such mental characteristics would not have been considered. He stated that it was necessary to look at the law as stated in **Camplin**, although argued that the case of **Morhall** (in which Lord Goff himself gave the main judgment!), was 'in no way inconsistent' with it. Factors concerning mental infirmity, however, were not consistent with **Camplin** and should not be permitted.

Expansion!

Be that as it may, the Court of Appeal was not prepared to admit it was wrong. Under the doctrine of precedent, earlier decisions of the Court of Appeal are normally binding on the Court of Appeal in later cases, whereas decisions of the Privy Council are only persuasive. In **Campbell 1997**, therefore,

mentioned earlier under diminished responsibility, the Court of Appeal stated that it would still abide by its own earlier decisions until such time as it was ordered not to do so by the House of Lords.

Matters came to a head in the case of **Smith 1998**. The defendant and the victim, James McCullagh were both alcoholics and long-standing drinking partners and, during an argument over an alleged theft of his tools, Smith became increasingly furious at the other's denial of involvement. He then seized a kitchen knife and stabbed his friend to death. At his trial, he put forward the defences of both diminished responsibility and provocation. He claimed that medical evidence would show that he was suffering from a depressive illness that had damaged substantially his capacity for self control. The trial judge, however, directed the jury that, with regard to **s3**, the characteristics of mental impairment could only be brought forward when deciding on the gravity of the provocation; they were not relevant to the reasonable man's loss of self control. The accused was subsequently found guilty of murder.

The Court of Appeal disagreed with the Crown Court decision and substituted a verdict of manslaughter. On a further appeal to the House of Lords, the latter court upheld the wider view of provocation already accepted by the Court of Appeal. Their Lordships decided that the trial judge had erred by telling the jury that the effect of the defendant's depression on his powers of self-control was not material. In answer to the certified question, therefore, i.e. 'whether characteristics other than age or sex attributable to a reasonable man for the purposes of **s3 Homicide Act** are relevant not only to the gravity of the provocation but also to the standard of self-control to be expected?', the House of Lords decided that the answer was 'yes'.

The current state of the law, therefore is the same as that stated by the Court of Appeal in

Campbell. In **Smith**, their Lordships, (but only on a three to two majority) decided that the main rules relating to provocation are to be found in the cases of **Camplin** and **Morhall**. When looking at the characteristics possessed by a reasonable man however, they have decided that the jury is now allowed to take certain mental characteristics of the accused into account, not only with regard to the gravity of the provocation but also when seeking to assess the degree of self control to be expected of the reasonable man.

◀ Comment

There has been much comment over this expansion of the defence of provocation, most of it adverse. For example, it is abundantly clear that Smith does not like Smith! Professor Sir John Smith forcibly argues that the majority of the House of Lords has got the law wrong and has misinterpreted the statements made by their predecessors in **Camplin** and **Morhall**. He states that in **Camplin**, the House of Lords accepted that certain characteristics, peculiar to the defendant, could be taken into account, but argues that it is clear from the judgment that these statements were only made in relation to the gravity of the provocation. When assessing this, it has now been accepted that mental, as well as physical characteristics can be taken into account. He goes on to say however, that the passages in **Camplin** have nothing to say about the relevance of mental characteristics on the powers of self-restraint, which was the point of issue in **Smith**. He quotes Lord Diplock's view in **Camplin** of the reasonable man as being 'an ordinary person of either sex, not exceptionally excitable or pugnacious, but possessed of such powers of self control as everyone is entitled to expect that his fellow citizens will exercise in society as it is today'.

He then wonders how the defendant in question, 'whose ability to control his actions is substantially injured, who is disinhibited and who loses his self-control and inflicts fatal wounds with a knife simply because his friend will not admit to an accusation of stealing his property, could possibly fit such a description'.

Our leading academic lawyer approves of the decision in **Luc Thiet Thuan**, which he states was rightly determined under **s2**, not **s3**, and argues that the case of **Smith** is 'indistinguishable' from this earlier one.

Smith is not alone in his condemnation of the expansion of the defence of provocation. He reminds us that other academics like Professor Ashworth and Professor Glanville Williams have also argued that the characteristics of the accused 'must relate to the provocation'. John Gardner, Professor of Jurisprudence, University of Oxford and Timothy Macklem, Lecturer in Law at King's College London, argue in the *Criminal Law Review* 2001, page 623, that the decision in **Smith** was wrong in at least nine respects. They believe that it would not cause injustice to relate all questions of individual psychological make-up to the defence of diminished responsibility in **s2**. They state that they would be 'hard pressed' to imagine that, after the expansion of **s2**, there are still people who would fall into a crack between the two defences.

With regard to the argument that defendants would prefer to plead the defence of provocation to that of diminished responsibility, they argue that the proposed expansion of the former defence makes 'provocation itself the very defence of mental abnormality that self-respecting defendants would rather not plead'. They call **Smith** 'a triumph of spin-doctoring'.

The decision of the House of Lords in **Smith** has certainly meant that the lines between the defences of provocation and diminished responsibility have become increasingly blurred. Professor Sir John Smith states that, as a result of the changes made to provocation, it might now be possible for someone like Byrne, mentioned earlier, to argue provocation, in the form of 'a young woman flaunting her charms in sight of a sexual psychopath'. A worrying thought! The changes have certainly made life more difficult for the trial judge. It is far from certain as to how he must now direct the jury. In addition, the jury itself now has a more difficult task. The House of Lords has clearly affirmed that the decision as to whether there is sufficient provocation is one for that body to make. These lay personnel must now try to take into account the relevant characteristics of the accused in relation to the gravity of the provocation and also come to an opinion on the effect of these characteristics on his degree of self control. A daunting task!

Activity

Decide whether the defence of provocation is available for Darby and Joan in the following unrelated circumstances:

- Darby was often ill-treated by his domineering wife. He brooded about this for several months, but then crept into her bedroom and smothered her with a pillow.
- Joan is an alcoholic who also suffers from a long term depressive illness. She killed her partner by battering him with her chip pan, after he taunted her about her weight gain.

KEY FACTS ON PROVOCATION

- The law is to be found in the common law and in **s3 Homicide Act 1957**. The aforementioned Act extended provocation to things said as well as things done.
- The provoking words or action need not be directed at the accused (**Doughty 1983, Pearson 1997**), nor need they come from the victim (**Davies 1975**), but they do need to be something said or something done. It appears that if there is any possible evidence of provocation, the jury should be advised of this, even if it is felt that the plea would not succeed (**Doughty 1983, Baille 1995 and Dhillon 1997**). It has also been made clear that the defendant can use the defence of provocation, even if he started the trouble, as in **Johnson 1989**, and **Baille 1995**. This is known as self-induced provocation.
- Three elements have to be established before the defence can be used: as stated, there has to be evidence of provocation, the accused must have lost his self control and the jury must be convinced that the provocation was enough to make a reasonable man act in the same way.
- When looking at whether the defendant has lost his self control, the direction in **Duffy 1949** is still approved of, although a complete loss of control is not necessary (**Richens 1993**). As the law currently stands, the loss of control can now

come after a 'slow burn' (**Ahluwalia 1992**) or some delay (**Baille 1995**), but there still must be a final 'snapping' of the self control (**Cocker 1989**). Evidence of any premeditation will normally be fatal to a successful plea (**Ibrams and Gregory 1981**).

- The concept of the reasonable man, first laid down in **Welsh 1869**, has now changed to that of the 'ordinary' man (**Morhall 1995**). The question of whether such an ordinary man would have acted the same way, is decided by the jury.

- In the past, a purely objective approach was used, as in **Bedder v DPP 1954**. This was changed in **DPP v Camplin** to whether a reasonable person, sharing the same characteristics of the accused would have acted in the same way. In **Morhall 1995**, it was suggested that the whole factual situation needed to be looked at.

- Drunkenness or drug taking which might accelerate a person's loss of control were not characteristics that could be taken into account, although, if the defendant was an alcoholic, drug addict or glue sniffer, taunts actually relating to such factors could be considered (**Morhall 1995**).

- The Court of Appeal became prepared to attribute certain mental characteristics to the reasonable man, such as learned helplessness caused by long-term abuse, as in **Ahluwalia 1992**, eccentric and obsessional personality traits (**Dryden 1995**), abnormal immaturity and attention-seeking, as in **Humphreys 1995**, and a severe depressive illness as in **Smith 1998**.

- In **Luc Thiet Thuan 1996**, the Privy Council disapproved of this extension of provocation and stated that the courts should return to the law as laid down in **DPP v Camplin 1978** and applied in **Morhall 1995**. There was therefore a conflict between this court and the Court of Appeal, which stated in **Campbell 1997** that it would abide by its own earlier decisions unless the House of Lords decreed otherwise.

- This conflict was resolved by the House of Lords in **Smith 2000**, which approved of the direction taken by the Court of Appeal. The Law Lords, but only on a three to two majority, decided that characteristics of the accused other than age or sex could also be taken into account, not the gravity of the provocation but also when considering the degree of self control only when considering what is to be expected of the reasonable man.

Mercy for the twin who survived suicide pact

By Nigel Bunyan

IDENTICAL twin brothers embarked on a suicide pact after their parents tried to end their reclusive existence in a city centre housing estate, a court heard yesterday.

Kevin and Paul Dane shunned the company of their closest relatives and chose to leave their locked bedrooms only at night.

They decided to hang themselves on the day their parents set as a deadline for them to venture into the world and sign on for unemployment benefit.

Kevin succeeded in hanging himself in the bedroom he regarded as his "prison cell".

Paul, who had helped prepare the noose, did not. He was found by his father, Alan, trembling and distraught beneath his brother's body as it hung from a beam.

In a police interview, Paul Dane said his brother smiled at him moments before he died. When asked whether he thought he had done something wrong, he replied: "Sort of."

Yesterday a judge at Carlisle Crown Court sentenced Dane, now 21, to a three-year rehabilitation order after he admitted aiding and abetting his brother's suicide in the city's Lowry Hill Estate last October.

Passing sentence, Judge John Phillips described the case as "tragic, difficult and to some extent inexplicable."

Daily Telegraph, 8 September 2001

4.5 The survivor of a suicide pact

Until the **Suicide Act 1961** was passed, suicide was a crime and the person faced prosecution if he survived. In addition, if another was involved in a plan to commit suicide and he survived, he would be charged with murder. Suicide is no longer a crime and the law has decided that aiders and abettors in suicide pacts should be treated more leniently if they do not die along with the other.

Under **s4(1) Homicide Act 1957**, should two or more people enter into a suicide pact and one of them survive, that survivor would be charged with manslaughter, not murder. The burden of proving such a pact, should the accused have originally been charged with murder, will be on the defendant, **s4(2)**. Under **s4(3)** of the Act, a suicide pact is defined as:

an agreement between two or more persons which has as its objects the death of all parties to it.

The defendant therefore must have had a settled intention of dying. We noted in Chapter 3 that **s4** will not be of assistance to those who are asked to assist in another's suicide attempt but do not intend to die themselves. This matter was highlighted in the Diane Pretty case. The terminally ill woman wished to 'die with dignity' and wanted her husband to assist her. She claimed that the refusal of the Director of Public Prosecutions to state that Mr Pretty would not be prosecuted breached her human rights. As noted in the newspaper article, the House of Lords rejected this argument. A person assisting another to commit suicide could therefore face a murder charge.

Self-Assessment Questions

1. Define voluntary manslaughter and state where the law is to be found.
2. What is meant by the term 'diminished responsibility'?
3. Why were the defendants in **Borthwick** and **Martin** allowed to bring up the defence of diminished responsibility in their appeals?
4. Giving clear explanations and case examples to illustrate your answer, describe the three elements of the defence of diminished responsibility.
5. Give three criticisms that have been made of this defence.
6. Why did the appeals concerning provocation succeed in the cases of **Doughty, Baille** and **Johnson**?
7. Describe the definition laid down in **Duffy** and state why this caused problems in the cases of **Cocker, Ibrams, Ahluwalia** and **Thornton**? How were the last two cases eventually decided?
8. Why were the cases of **Camplin** and **Morhall** important in the law on provocation?
9. Which conflict did the House of Lords eventually resolve in **Smith**? Why has this decision been criticised?
10. What defence exists by virtue of **s4(1) Homicide Act**? Why would this defence as it stands, be of no avail in a mercy killing?

Chapter 5

UNLAWFUL KILLING III: INVOLUNTARY MANSLAUGHTER AND OTHER UNLAWFUL DEATHS

5.1 Involuntary manslaughter

With both murder and voluntary manslaughter, an intention to kill or cause grievous bodily harm has to be proved. With involuntary manslaughter, no such intention is necessary. It is enough that the defendant either has committed an unlawful and dangerous act and from that act a death has resulted or that the accused has been so grossly negligent that someone has died. These two types of involuntary manslaughter have been given the names of constructive manslaughter and manslaughter by gross negligence and will be discussed in more detail on the following pages. A third category of involuntary manslaughter has also been recognised over the years, that of reckless manslaughter, but at the present time it appears that this type of manslaughter has been merged with killings as a result of gross negligence. The rise and fall of this type of involuntary manslaughter will also be investigated. At the end of the chapter, other unlawful killings will be examined.

5.2 Constructive manslaughter

Constructive manslaughter is also known as unlawful act manslaughter because it is committed where the defendant has caused the death of a person by an unlawful and dangerous act. The distinction between this type of manslaughter and that of gross negligence manslaughter was clearly stated by Humphreys J in the case of **Larkin 1943**.

> If a person is engaged in doing a lawful act, and in the course of doing that lawful act behaves so negligently as to cause the death of some other person, then it is for the jury to say, upon a consideration of the whole of the facts of the case, whether the negligence proved against the accused person amounts to manslaughter, and it is the duty of the presiding judge to tell them that it will not amount to manslaughter unless the negligence is of a very high degree [. . .] That is where the act is lawful. Where the act which a person is engaged in performing is unlawful, then if at the same time it is a dangerous act, that is an act which is likely to injure another person, and quite inadvertently he causes the death of that other person by that act, then he is guilty of manslaughter.

There are three elements which have to be established before a person is liable for constructive manslaughter.

- There must have been an unlawful act.
- This act must have caused the death.
- The unlawful act must have been a dangerous one.

These three points now need to be examined in more detail.

5.2.1 There must be an unlawful act

In **Fenton 1830**, it was held that a person could be liable for unlawful act manslaughter when he committed a civil wrong, in this case the tort of trespass. The accused had thrown stones down a mineshaft and this act had caused the scaffolding to collapse, which resulted in the death of miners in the shaft. The act of the accused was enough to create liability for constructive manslaughter.

In the later case of **Franklin 1883**, however, this view was not sustained. The defendant had thrown a box belonging to a stall holder in Brighton, into the sea, where it had struck a swimmer and caused his death. The judge, Field J stated: '. . . the mere fact of a civil wrong committed by one person against another ought not to be used as an incident which is a necessary step in a criminal case.'

Such a defendant could, of course, be convicted on the grounds of manslaughter by gross negligence if it was felt that the degree of negligence was very high and, in the event, this is what happened.

When a person is charged with constructive manslaughter, the unlawful act often consists of an assault. It will not be a viable defence for the defendant to argue that he did not intend to injure the person who was actually harmed, provided that the assault itself has been established.

In the case of **Larkin**, the accused had discovered his mistress in the company of another man, had brooded about this for a while and had returned with an open razor. He alleged that he had only meant to frighten the man but that his mistress, who had been drinking, staggered into the path of the razor and cut her throat on it. Despite this claim, the conviction for unlawful act manslaughter was upheld because an assault had been committed and this assault had caused the death in question.

Difficulties in finding an unlawful act

For liability to arise, the prosecution has the task of establishing that an unlawful act has taken place. This was not proved in the following two cases.

In **Lamb 1961**, the accused and his friend had been playing with a revolver. This had two bullets in it, neither of which was opposite the barrel. Believing that this meant that the gun was safe, the defendant pointed it at his friend and pulled the trigger. It was established that he did not intend to harm the friend and the latter was not in fear of his acts. Unfortunately, the gun fired a live bullet and the friend was killed.

The Court of Appeal quashed the manslaughter conviction because it was decided that there had not been an unlawful act. It will be noted later, when looking at non-fatal offences against the person, that the crime of assault requires the victim to be put in fear that a battery will be inflicted upon him. In this case, no such fear existed.

In **Ariobeke 1988**, there was certainly fear on the victim's part but the actions of the defendant did not amount to criminal acts. There had been evidence of bad relations between the two men and the accused had been peering into the carriages of a train apparently looking for the victim. The latter appeared to have panicked and ran across a live railway line to try to escape. He was then electrocuted when he stepped on a live rail. Ariobeke was convicted of manslaughter but the Court of Appeal quashed the conviction on the grounds that an assault had not been established.

A similar approach was taken in **Scarlett 1993**. A publican ejected a drunken customer and the latter fell, hit his head and died. The Court of Appeal quashed the conviction, deciding that an unlawful act had not been clearly established. There was insufficient evidence that the publican had intentionally or recklessly used excessive force to remove the victim.

Stretching the rules

In two earlier cases, **DPP v Newbury and Jones 1977** and **Cato 1976**, the appeal courts had no trouble in upholding the convictions for constructive manslaughter, although they did not specify precisely what constituted the unlawful act. In the first case, two young boys had thrown a slab of paving stone from a bridge into the path of a passing train. This entered the window of the cab and killed the guard. The *mens rea* of assault requires that the accused must have foreseen that his act would cause harm and the boys claimed that they had not foreseen the possibility that anyone would have been injured by their actions. Despite this allegation, the House of Lords upheld the conviction for unlawful act manslaughter, a decision that has been questioned by legal writers. Their Lordships merely accepted that an unlawful act had been committed and proceeded to answer the point of law put forward on that basis.

Similar problems about establishing an unlawful act occurred in **Cato 1976**. The defendant and the person who died were drug users. They agreed to give each other their 'fixes'. The defendant injected the victim several times during the night with a mixture of heroin and water, although the victim himself actually prepared the mixture. The amount taken proved to be fatal and the defendant was charged with both manslaughter and with administering a noxious thing, contrary to the **Offences Against the Person Act 1861**. The jury found him guilty on both counts. Cato then appealed.

He argued that, while it is an offence to possess or supply heroin under the **Misuse of**

Drugs Act 1971, it is not an offence under that act merely to take a mixture, already prepared by another person and then just give it to him. The Court of Appeal decided that there was no need to refer to the **Misuse of Drugs Act**, because the unlawful act had been established by the other charge, i.e. the defendant had administered a noxious thing contrary to the **Offences Against the Person Act 1861**. An unlawful act had therefore been committed. Despite this, Lord Widgery C J decided to deal with the point raised by the defence. He stated:

> But since he [the defence counsel], went to such trouble with the argument, and in respect for it, we think we ought to say that had it not been possible to rely on the charge under **s23** of the **1861 Act**, we think that there would have been an unlawful act here, and we think the unlawful act would be described as injecting the deceased . . . with a mixture of heroin and water which at the time of the injection Cato had unlawfully taken into his possession.

This reasoning, rather than that in **Dalby**, mentioned below, was followed in **Kennedy 1999**. In this case it was the drug dealer who prepared the solution of heroin and water but the victim actually injected the solution into himself. The dose proved to be fatal and the dealer was convicted of manslaughter.

Once again the Court of Appeal upheld the conviction, despite the fact that there were problems with causation, as mentioned below, and it could be argued that the dealer did not actually cause the victim's death. The court affirmed that the unlawful act was established either by using **s23 Offences Against the Person Act 1861**, as in **Cato**, or by the victim's act of taking possession of heroin and injecting it. Kennedy had wilfully encouraged this unlawful and dangerous act because he must have known of the risks involved.

5.2.2 The unlawful act must have caused the death

As noted in Chapter 3, the unlawful act of the accused must be closely connected to the death that has resulted, and a *novus actus interveniens* (a new intervening act) must not have arisen to break the chain of causation. The unlawful act need not however, be the sole cause of the death, provided that it made a significant contribution to it.

It was originally decided by the courts that the unlawful act had to be directed at a human being, even if the wrong person actually died, as occurred in **Latimer**. The Court of Appeal upheld this view, and in fact went further than this, in the case of **Dalby 1982**, where it stated that the unlawful act must be directed at the victim. The defendant and the victim were drug users but, unlike **Cato**, the defendant in **Dalby** had not injected the other person with drugs. He obtained a drug called diconal lawfully on prescription, but then gave some of the tablets to his friend and they injected themselves intravenously before going to a discotheque. While they were out, the friends parted company and there was evidence that another person also injected the victim at least twice more with unspecified drugs. The latter died the following day.

Dalby was charged with supplying drugs and also with the offence of constructive manslaughter and was found guilty on both counts. One of the questions the jurors were asked to consider was whether the supply of the diconal was a substantial cause of the victim's death. They were told that it did not have to be the only cause, but that it had to be a substantial cause, i.e. one which was not merely trivial. The jury found him guilty of manslaughter.

The Court of Appeal quashed the manslaughter conviction, stating that:

> *The difficulty in the present case is that the act of supplying a controlled drug was not an act which caused direct harm. It was an act which made it possible, or even likely, that harm would occur subsequently, particularly if the drug was supplied to someone who was on drugs. In all the reported cases, the physical act has been one which inevitably would subject the other person to the risk of some harm from the act itself.*

The Court of Appeal then went on to state categorically that:

> *In the judgment of this court, where the charge of manslaughter is based on an unlawful and dangerous act, it must be an act directed at the victim and likely to cause immediate injury, however slight.*

The acceptance of indirect acts

Later cases have modified the strong statements made in **Dalby**. In the case of **Mitchell 1983**, it was decided that an act intended for another person could, under the doctrine of transferred malice, be classed as being directed at the victim.

In this case, the defendant had tried to 'jump the queue' in a busy post office and a 70-year-old man had remonstrated with him. The accused hit him in the mouth and then either hit him again or pushed him backwards so that he fell against others in the queue, including an even older woman who suffered a broken leg. As a result of this, she had to have an operation to have a hip joint replaced. At first she appeared to be recuperating well but then died suddenly.

The defendant was convicted of manslaughter but appealed. The Court of Appeal had to decide whether the person at whom the act is aimed must also be the person whose death is caused. Staughton J stated:

> We can see no reason of policy for holding that an act calculated to harm A cannot be manslaughter if it in fact kills B. The criminality of the doer of the act is precisely the same whether it is A or B who dies.

After this case, therefore, it was the law that, while the unlawful act must still be directed at someone, it need not be at the person who dies. In **Goodfellow 1986**, the Court of Appeal went further and decided that the accused could also be liable when he did not direct his unlawful act at a person at all.

The accused was being harassed by two other men and wanted to move from his council accommodation, but knew that his chances of a transfer were slight. He therefore decided to take matters into his own hands and set fire to his house, making it look as if it had been petrol-bombed, hoping that this would lead to him being re-housed. Unfortunately, the intensity of the fire was greater than was planned and Goodfellow's wife, son and his son's girlfriend all died in the blaze. The Court of Appeal upheld his conviction for manslaughter even though the unlawful act of arson was not directed at the people who died. The court held that the accused could have been liable for both reckless manslaughter, which existed at that time and for unlawful act manslaughter. With regard to the latter charge, the court held that it had to be shown that the act was committed intentionally, that it was an unlawful one, that reasonable people would recognise that it was likely to cause harm and that a death had resulted. The Court of Appeal felt that all these points had been established and the conviction was upheld.

Comment

This decision and the ones in **Cato** and **Kennedy**, indicate that the Court of Appeal is unlikely to disturb the convictions in such cases even if the existing rules have to be stretched to accommodate the facts.

5.2.3 The act must also be dangerous

The third element that needs to be established for constructive manslaughter is that the act must be a dangerous one. The act, therefore, has to be both unlawful and dangerous, which in this context means an unlawful act that is also likely to injure another person. This two-fold approach was clearly stated in **Larkin 1943**, mentioned earlier.

Whether the act is considered a dangerous one is decided objectively, i.e. it must be an act that a sober and reasonable man would regard as dangerous.

This was affirmed in the case of **Church 1966**. The Court of Criminal Appeal, as it was then, stated:

> An unlawful act causing the death of another cannot, simply because it is an unlawful act, render a manslaughter verdict inevitable. For such a verdict inexorably to follow, the unlawful act must be such as all sober and reasonable people would inevitably recognise must subject the other person to, at least, the risk of some harm resulting therefrom, albeit not serious harm.

The defendant panicked after hitting a woman who mocked his inability to satisfy her. Believing her to be dead, he threw her into a river, where she drowned. His conviction for manslaughter was upheld.

In **DPP v Newbury and Jones 1977**, the House of Lords specifically approved of the dicta in **Church** and decided that an act of throwing a paving slab in front of a passing train was one which all reasonable people would look upon as dangerous.

Similarly, in **Ball 1989**, the defendant's argument that he believed that the cartridge in his gun was merely a blank, and so should not be liable, was rejected by the Court of Appeal.

A great deal of ill feeling existed between the accused and the victim. The woman climbed over a wall, accompanied by two men and was shot by the defendant. The latter alleged that he was in great fear of them and therefore grabbed a gun and a handful of cartridges in order to frighten them. He claimed that he kept both live and blank cartridges in the pocket of his overall but believed that a blank was in the gun. He argued that when the question of whether a reasonable man would believe that his actions were dangerous was looked at, this mythical person should consider the fact that the accused believed the gun was harmless.

The appeal court refused to accept this, stating:

> . . . the question whether the act is a dangerous one is to be judged not by the appellant's appreciation but by that of the sober and reasonable man, and it is impossible to impute into his appreciation the mistaken belief of the appellant that what he was doing was not dangerous because he thought he had a blank cartridge in the chamber. At that stage the appellant's intention, foresight or knowledge is irrelevant.

Ball's counsel had tried to use the earlier case of **Dawson 1985** to support his argument, where the defendant had been luckier and his appeal allowed. Dawson and masked accomplices had attempted to rob a garage. They threatened the 60-year-old garage

Comment

The Court of Appeal obviously felt that it had no choice but to quash the conviction in **Dawson** because of the misdirection. It is submitted that the ruling is not laying down a more general proposition that a defendant could never be liable in such a situation. It is interesting to speculate on the possible decision of the jury if the correct explanation of the law had been given. It should be remembered that the ruling in **Church** was as follows:

> the unlawful act must be such as all sober and reasonable people would inevitably recognise must subject the other person to, at least, the risk of some harm resulting therefrom, albeit not serious harm.

It is not inconceivable that a sober and reasonable man might well have decided that waving a pickaxe, plus a gun not known at that time to be a replica at a victim might subject that person to the risk of harm. It can be seen, however, that the direction in **Church** is strongly phrased, using the words 'inevitably' and 'must'.

attendant with a pickaxe and an imitation gun. After he pressed the alarm, however, they fled empty-handed. The attendant, who suffered from a heart disease, had a fatal heart attack shortly after the police arrived on the scene. Dawson was convicted of unlawful act manslaughter.

The Court of Appeal quashed the conviction because the trial judge had told the jurors that they must decide whether the act of the robbers was a dangerous one and that they should approach this from the point of view of a reasonable man 'who knew the facts that you know'. The jury, however, had knowledge of the victim's heart condition, whereas a

FIVE KEY FACTS ON CONSTRUCTIVE MANSLAUGHTER

- Constructive manslaughter occurs where there is an unlawful and dangerous act and, as a result the victim dies; it is also known as unlawful act manslaughter.
- The *actus reus* is the death resulting from the unlawful act. The *mens rea* will be that which is required by the unlawful act.

  In the case of assault and battery, an intention to commit the assault or battery will need to be proved or **Cunningham**-style recklessness, i.e. subjective recklessness. There is no requirement to prove an intention to cause the death of the victim, nor to prove recklessness that such a death might occur.
- Three elements have to be established for constructive manslaughter: an unlawful act, which is also dangerous, which has brought about the death of the victim.
- The unlawful act must be a criminal wrong, not merely a civil one (**Franklin 1883**), and must be clearly established. In **Lamb 1961**, **Ariobeke 1988** and **Scarlett 1993**, it was decided, on appeal, that the alleged assaults had not been proved. In **DPP v Newbury and Jones 1977**, **Cato 1976** and **Kennedy 1999**, the unlawfulness of the acts was upheld, perhaps for reasons of public policy. The unlawful act must have been a substantial cause of the victim's death, although it need not be the only cause. Despite the dicta of the Court of Appeal in **Dalby 1982**, it now appears that the unlawful act need not be directed at the victim nor, indeed, at a human being at all (**Mitchell 1983** and **Goodfellow 1986**).
- A dangerous act is one which carries with it the risk of some harm resulting, although not necessarily serious harm (**Church 1966**). Whether the act is dangerous is to be assessed objectively, i.e. by the view of a sober and reasonable person (**Larkin 1943** and **Church 1966**). When deciding whether the act is dangerous, these sober and reasonable people will look at the situation encountered by the defendant (**Dawson 1985**), but may not accept his claim that his mistaken belief frees him from liability (**Ball 1989**). They may also expect him to become aware of the vulnerability of his victim (**Watson 1989**).

reasonable man, at the time of the attack, would not have known this fact. He therefore might not have assumed that the acts of the defendant might cause the victim injury: fear, perhaps but not physical harm.

Dawson was distinguished in the case of **Watson 1989**. The latter and an accomplice threw a brick through the window of the victim's house and disturbed the 87-year-old resident. They then fled without taking anything. The elderly man died shortly afterwards from a heart attack.

The Court of Appeal held that the defendant should have become aware of the great age and frailty of the victim during the course of the burglary. In the event, the defendant's conviction was quashed because it could not be satisfactorily established whether the burglary had caused the attack or the entry of the police workmen afterwards. The dicta of the Court of Appeal, however, could ensure that liability might arise in future.

◀ Comment

It may well act as a deterrent to make potential defendants aware that they 'take their victims as they find them' and a strict approach by the courts may help to reduce crimes directed at the old and frail. Society surely has a duty to protect vulnerable members of society, particularly the very old and the very young. With regard to the latter, we should try to ensure that the horrible deaths like those suffered by Lauren Wright and Victoria Climbie do not happen again. It is little consolation to note that long prison sentences are at last being meted out for such crimes but this does at least reflect society's revulsion against such horrible acts.

Activity

While waiting on the edge of the platform for a train to take them to college, Bill and Ben started to argue loudly about the merits of two pop groups currently in the charts. Their heated discussion turned into anger and they began to throw punches at each other. Bill's second punch sent Ben reeling. He was pushed against Daisy, who fell in front of the incoming train and was killed.

Advise Bill, who has been charged with the manslaughter of Daisy.

5.3 Manslaughter by gross negligence

In the preceding paragraphs, we have been looking at defendants who have committed criminal acts that have resulted in a death. There may also be other situations in which it is felt that the defendant should face a manslaughter charge, even though he may not have been involved in any criminal activity. Under this second form of involuntary manslaughter he may be charged because his behaviour has been so grossly negligent that it has brought about the death of another person.

In **Adomako 1994**, Lord Mackay decided that liability for this type of manslaughter will arise where the jury decides that:

> *having regard to the risk of death involved, the conduct of the defendant was so bad in all the circumstances as to amount in their judgment to a criminal act or omission.*

- The *actus reus* of the offence is the death which has resulted from the negligent act.
- The *mens rea* of the offence is the defendant's grossly negligent behaviour.

Manslaughter by gross negligence has had a chequered history and, before the above case, it seemed to have virtually disappeared and to have been overtaken by reckless manslaughter. The position now appears to have come full circle and there is serious doubt as to whether reckless manslaughter continues to exist. In **Adomako**, it was firmly decided by the House of Lords that the gross negligence test is the correct one to use in all cases where a duty of care has been broken. It may also be the test to use for all cases of manslaughter where there is no unlawful act. See below for details of this case.

5.3.1 The development of gross negligence manslaughter

The leading cases on gross negligence manslaughter are **Bateman 1925**, **Andrews 1937** and **Adomako 1994**.

In **Bateman 1925**, the accused took away part of a woman's uterus during childbirth and did not remove her to hospital until five days later, where she subsequently died. Bateman's conviction for manslaughter was quashed because it was felt that he had been carrying out normal procedures which were approved by the medical profession. The procedure itself had been at fault.

The Court of Appeal stated that manslaughter by gross negligence should not be found lightly. It would only arise where:

> in the opinion of the jury, the negligence of the accused went beyond a mere matter of compensation between subjects and showed such disregard for the life and safety of others as to amount to a crime against the State and conduct deserving punishment.

In **Andrews v DPP 1937** the defendant was charged with manslaughter after a pedestrian was killed by his dangerous driving. Andrews was sent by his employers to deal with a broken-down bus. On his way to the scene, he drove above the speed limit, overtook a car and was on the wrong side of the road, when he struck a pedestrian. The victim was carried along the road on the bonnet of the defendant's van, then thrown from this and run over. The defendant did not stop. He was later convicted of manslaughter but appealed.

The House of Lords stated that manslaughter caused by bad driving was to be treated in the same way as other cases of homicide caused by the defendant's negligence, and went on to state that a person would only be criminally liable if his behaviour was very bad. Their Lordships laid down the following test:

> Simple lack of care which will constitute civil liability is not enough. For the purposes of the criminal law there are degrees of negligence and a very high degree of negligence is required to be proved.

The appeal had been based on a possible misdirection by the trial judge and their Lordships admitted that some parts of his summing up were open to criticism. On balance, however, they felt that there had been a proper direction about the high degree of negligence that needed to be established for this type of manslaughter and the conviction was upheld.

5.3.2 The rise of reckless manslaughter

The development of gross negligence manslaughter came to a halt for a while after the case of **Seymour 1983**. In this case, the House of Lords followed the cases of **Caldwell** and **Lawrence**, mentioned in Chapter 2 and decided that this type of involuntary manslaughter should be redefined as reckless manslaughter.

The defendant and his woman friend quarrelled and her car and his lorry were involved in a collision. The woman got out of her car and went towards the accused. The latter then drove his lorry at the car. He later claimed that he only intended to push it away but the woman was crushed between the lorry and her own vehicle. She died later of her injuries and the defendant was found guilty of manslaughter. The House of Lords stated that the ingredients for causing death by reckless driving (now replaced by dangerous driving), and the type of involuntary manslaughter which did not come within the definition of constructive manslaughter, were identical. From this case, and later cases modifying the principle to some extent, it appeared that criminal liability would arise if the defendant's conduct caused an obvious and serious risk of some personal injury and, as a result, someone died.

The Privy Council supported this approach in the case of **Kong Cheuk Kwan 1985**, a case concerning the collision of two hydrofoils near Hong Kong, and denied that a separate category of manslaughter by gross negligence was still appropriate.

By 1993, therefore, it appeared that the concept of gross negligence manslaughter had given way to **Caldwell**-style reckless manslaughter. Enough doubts remained, however, to make it inevitable that the matter would be reopened.

5.3.3 The re-emergence of gross negligence manslaughter

This occurred in the case of **Prentice and Others 1994**, when the Court of Appeal resurrected manslaughter by gross negligence for cases where there was a breach of duty of care by the defendant.

In **Prentice and Others**, three separate appeals were heard together by the Court of Appeal to decide on the correct test to be used in involuntary manslaughter cases, other than those of constructive manslaughter. These three appeals concerned the cases of **Prentice and Sullman, Holloway** and **Adomako**, and only in the last case was the conviction upheld.

The case of **Prentice and Sullman** concerned two junior hospital doctors. Prentice, the most inexperienced, had wrongly injected a drug directly into the spine of a patient suffering from leukaemia. This very serious error was compounded by the wrong action being taken when the mistake was discovered. The result was damage to the patient's brain and spinal cord which ultimately caused his death.

Prentice had been supervised by Sullman and had assumed that the latter was overseeing of the whole procedure. Sullman, on the other hand, believed that he was only supervising the actual injection.

The trial judge had felt bound by the case of **Seymour** and had therefore directed the jury on the lines of **Caldwell**-style recklessness. There was an obvious and serious risk of harm and the patient had died, so the defendants were originally found guilty.

In **Holloway**, a qualified and experienced electrician had installed a new domestic central heating system and afterwards family members began to get electric shocks. The electrician checked his work and found no faults in the wiring but, when the trouble continued, he made arrangements to replace the heating programmer. Before this new part could be obtained, a member of the family received a fatal electric shock.

It was discovered that some of the wires were 'live' and that the circuit breaker, which should have afforded protection, was ineffective. The electrician was charged with manslaughter and found guilty after the judge, as in **Prentice**, directed the jury on the lines of reckless manslaughter.

In both cases, the Court of Appeal quashed the convictions, stating that the correct test to use in these cases, where a duty of care was owed to the victim, was not that of recklessness but that of gross negligence manslaughter.

In **Adomako 1995**, the last of the three cases, the manslaughter conviction was upheld. The defendant was an anaesthetist in a hospital who had been left in sole charge after the senior anaesthetist was called away. Adomako had failed to notice that a tube leading from the patient to the ventilator had become disconnected. When the alarm sounded, his first thought was that the machine itself was faulty and he therefore took the wrong action. By the time the mistake was discovered, the patient had died.

Rather surprisingly in this case, the jury had been directed on the issue of gross negligence, rather than recklessness, despite the fact that gross negligence manslaughter was currently in decline. The defendant was convicted by a majority of ten to one. Adomako based his appeal on the issue that the jury should have been directed with regard to recklessness.

The Court of Appeal was satisfied that the jury had, in fact, been properly directed and upheld the conviction for manslaughter. A duty of care had been owed (in this case by the anaesthetist to the patient), and this duty had been broken by the high degree of negligence of the defendant.

As stated earlier, the Court of Appeal looked at these three appeals together to decide on the correct test to use in such cases. Lord Taylor, the former Lord Chief Justice, decided that manslaughter by gross negligence should be revived and should be classed as the proper test to use in all cases where a breach of duty had arisen. He decided that only cases of motor manslaughter should be treated differently, where the test of reckless manslaughter (**Caldwell**-style) should be retained. (The Court of Appeal felt obliged to make this distinction because in motor manslaughter cases it was bound by the House of Lords' decision in **Seymour**.)

There was a further appeal in the **Adomako** case to the House of Lords. Their Lordships agreed with the revival of the gross negligence test set out by the Court of Appeal with regard to criminal negligence involving a breach of duty and approved of the cases of **Bateman and Andrews**, cited in that court. Lord Mackay

stressed that it was no longer appropriate to refer to the detailed definition of recklessness stated in **Lawrence** and said that the test in cases such as this should be one which is clear to an ordinary member of the jury with no particular knowledge of the law. He felt that complicated definitions that the jury could not later remember, gave 'no service to the cause of justice'. He did, however, agree that, in some circumstances, it would not be a misdirection for a judge to use the word 'reckless' in its ordinary sense, if this was felt to be necessary to indicate the seriousness of the behaviour.

In addition to agreeing with the Court of Appeal's new direction in **Prentice and Others**, their Lordships went further and stated that motor manslaughter should not be put into a separate category. It was clearly stated that the gross negligence test was the one to be used in all forms of involuntary manslaughter where no unlawful act was found.

When deciding whether a person is criminally liable, therefore, the House of Lords agreed with the Court of Appeal that ordinary principles of negligence should be adopted to see if the defendant had broken a duty of care to the victim and this breach had caused his death. If the answer was in the affirmative, then the jury should be given the task of deciding whether the negligence was so gross that it should be considered to be a crime. Lord Mackay put it succinctly:

> The essence of the matter, which is supremely a jury question, is whether, having regard to the risk of death involved, the conduct of the defendant was so bad in all the circumstances as to amount in their judgment to a criminal act or omission.

The very vagueness of this test is bound to cause further discussion and possible appeals.

Recent cases on gross negligent manslaughter

In **Kite 1996**, the Court of Appeal rejected the defendant's appeal against his conviction for gross negligence manslaughter. He was the managing director of the St Albans Activities Centre and had allowed an 'ill-conceived and poorly executed' canoe trip in adverse weather conditions to take place. What was meant to be a mere two-hour paddle by students and their teachers to Charmouth in Dorset, ended with the canoes being swamped and the occupants being forced into the water for hours. This led to the deaths of four of the sixth-formers and Kite's subsequent conviction.

In **Litchfield 1997**, the Court of Appeal also upheld the conviction of the owner and captain of a square-rigged schooner, which had foundered on the rocks off the Cornish coast. He had steered too closely to the shore and had also used contaminated fuel, causing the engines to fail. Three members of the crew of 14 had died. The court decided that the principles laid down in **Adomako** had been correctly applied and the defendant had been rightly convicted of being grossly negligent.

Two years later, the Court of Appeal decided that it is not always necessary to take the defendant's state of mind into account before gaining a conviction. An **Attorney General's Reference (No 2 of 1999)(2000)** was brought after the collapse of a manslaughter case brought after the Southall rail crash.

In 1997, a high-speed train from Swansea had crashed into a freight train at Southall, killing seven people and injuring many others. The operator was charged later with gross negligence manslaughter but the trial judge stopped the trial. He stated that it was necessary in this type of manslaughter, to prove a guilty mind. He took the view therefore, that where a non-human defendant was prosecuted, that body could only be convicted via the guilt of a human being with whom it could be

identified. As a result, the company was only sentenced for failures under the **Health & Safety at Work etc. Act 1974**. The Attorney General brought this matter to the attention of the Court of Appeal, asking two questions:

1. Can a defendant be convicted of gross negligence manslaughter in the absence of evidence as to the defendant's state of mind?
2. Can a non-human defendant be convicted of the crime of gross negligence manslaughter in the absence of any evidence establishing the guilt of an identified human being for the same crime?

The answers revealed a partial victory. The Court of Appeal answered 'yes' to the first question and 'no' to the second. As noted below and in Chapter 14, it has proved very difficult to obtain manslaughter convictions against larger companies. The affirmative answer to question 1 may help in cases where a human defendant can also be identified. It may ensure that some companies can be penalised for their gross negligence, while everyone waits for Parliament to take more radical action to see that this happens more easily. The negative answer to the second point will be discussed further in Chapter 14. It illlustrates that changes to the law are very necessary.

The next case shows that the relatives of victims killed by the gross negligence of companies are fighting back. In **R v DPP ex p Jones (Timothy) 2000**, a brother of the victim sought judicial review of the decision of the DPP not to prosecute the company in question. The victim, on his first day of working for the company, was involved in unloading bags of cobblestones from the load of a ship. A crane holding a grab bucket was being utilised for this purpose and the victim, who was standing beneath it, was decapitated when it closed suddenly.

The DPP had decided that there was insufficient evidence on which to bring a manslaughter prosecution. He claimed that he had used the

Adomako guidelines to reach this decision but the victim's brother successfully challenged the decision not to press charges. The High Court decided that while the DPP had correctly identified the requirements necessary for such a prosecution, as laid down in the above case, it had not acted rationally when making the actual decision that the evidence was insufficient to bring a successful case.

The tragic consequences of gross negligence can be seen in **Edwards 2001.** Gareth Edwards and his wife Amanda were found guilty of this form of manslaughter after failing to prevent their children and two of their friends playing on a railway line while they sat looking at the sea. The two boys managed to jump to safety when a train suddenly appeared but the two girls, the couple's daughter and her eight-year-old friend, Kimberley were mown down and killed.

Cases uncannily reminiscent of **Adomako** and **Kite** appeared on the same day in a national newspaper, the first concerning the trial of a surgeon in Truro and the other relating a canoeing disaster in Switzerland, which is reproduced below.

Wall of water hit us, says canyon girl

By Fiona Fleck in Geneva

A SURVIVOR of the Swiss canyoning disaster in which 21 people, including three British tourists, were killed said yesterday that she and her group were swept away by a wall of water "as high as the gorge".

Rachel O'Brien, 22, from Australia, the only survivor called as a witness in the manslaughter trial of eight guides and managers from a Swiss sports company, said they had only two seconds to grab a handhold.

It had been obvious that a storm was brewing as they set off from base camp, Miss O'Brien told a court in the Swiss Alpine town of Interlaken.

It was pouring with rain and there was thunder and lightning when the party arrived at the top of Saxet gorge.

The group, clad in wetsuits and helmets, had completed three jumps, canyoning or body surfing down rapids without rafts. As they were preparing to make their fourth jump the water became murky.

"We were all standing together holding hands because the water was so high," Miss O'Brien said. "Suddenly the last person in the group, Briana Smith, yelled that a wave was coming.

"We all looked behind us and we saw the wave of water, which would have been as high as the canyon, coming toward us. We had probably two seconds to react.

"The guides told us to hold on to something. There was a rope going into the water for the jump. We grasped that. Then the water hit and the force pushed all of the first people off on to us and then slowly I lost grip of the rope."

Miss O'Brien said she was swept away but managed to grab on to a rock and pull herself out, suffering only minor cuts and bruises.

She had to wait for an hour before being rescued by a helicopter.

Her best friend, Kylie Morrow, and 19-year-old Miss Smith, were swept to their deaths. Only three of the 11 tourists in the group survived the accident in July 1999. Miss O'Brien said that she had to have psychological counselling for a year afterwards.

"After the accident I had trouble getting back to normal life and dealing with the accident and the death of my best friend," she told the court. "I felt guilty, depressed. But I had to get on with life."

The defendants, five guides and three board members of the now bankrupt Adventure World, have denied responsibility for the accident.

They insisted that the wave of water was "a freak of nature" which could not have been foreseen or avoided. The local fire chief, Markus Gerber, described seeing bodies washed downstream.

He told the court that the gorge flooded every year. It was common knowledge that storms caused flooding in the area.

He said that a year or two before the tragedy he had warned the managers of Adventure World that the Saxet brook could be very dangerous.

A verdict is expected on Tuesday. If convicted, the defendants could face up to a year in prison or a heavy fine.

Daily Telegraph, 8 December 2001

FIVE KEY FACTS ON GROSS NEGLIGENCE MANSLAUGHTER

- This form of manslaughter is to be used in all cases where there is no unlawful act but where a death has arisen because of the high degree of negligence of the defendant (**Adomako 1994**). Reckless manslaughter, in the form of the detailed direction in **Lawrence 1982**, seems to have disappeared and should no longer be used.
- The cases of **Bateman 1925** and **Andrews 1937** on gross negligent manslaughter have been specifically approved by the House of Lords.
- The *actus reus* of gross negligence manslaughter is a death arising from the negligent act of the accused. The *mens rea* is the gross negligence of the accused.
- The jury will decide this, after considering whether, having regard to the risk of death involved, the defendant's conduct was so bad that it should be classed as criminal.
- At present, the maximum punishment for this type of involuntary manslaughter is life imprisonment.

The punishment for gross negligence manslaughter

As with all other types of manslaughter, there is a maximum sentence of life imprisonment for this offence but no minimum. Because the circumstances are often so varied, such

discretion is felt to be very necessary. Despite this freedom, the judges often face difficulty in sentencing for gross negligence manslaughter. If they are too lenient, the relatives of the victims are rightly outraged. If they sentence too harshly, this could be seen as unfair on someone who obviously had no intention to kill and may well be full of remorse and already have had his life dramatically altered because of the tragic events. Such a sentence might also lead to a costly appeal, as seen in the case of **Kite 1996**, mentioned above. While Kite was unsuccessful in getting the verdict changed, he did get the sentence reduced from three years to two. Kite's counsel had argued that the longest prison sentence passed for a similar offence had been 21 months.

In some cases, the defendants may not face prison at all, as shown in the case of **Edwards**, discussed earlier. The judge took the view that the couple's surviving children would be the ones to suffer most if their parents were sent to jail. Their sentences of 12 months' imprisonment were therefore suspended.

Corporate manslaughter

As stated above, there has been great difficulty in imposing criminal liability on larger companies, even where it is very apparent that gross negligence has been present. This subject and the proposals for dealing with this in a more satisfactory way, are dealt with in Chapter 14 and should be read in conjunction with this chapter.

Activity

- In **Adomako**, Lord Mackay made the following comment: 'I entirely agree with the view that the circumstances to which a charge of involuntary manslaughter may apply are so various that it is unwise to attempt to categorise or detail specimen directions'.

In group discussion or in essay form, discuss whether this is the correct approach for the law to take or whether you feel that it puts too much responsibility onto the jury.

- Rachel was the director of a company running weekend adventure courses in Snowdonia. She

was left short-staffed after two of her experienced guides left to take up positions elsewhere, after criticising the lack of instruction being given on basic safety procedures. Rachel then engaged two teenagers on a part-time basis, hoping that they would gain experience 'on the job'.

Monica and Joey were among those attending a course on a very cold weekend in November. They were sent off to climb Mount Snowdon, in the company of one of the new part-timers. Rachel was informed of the likelihood of adverse weather conditions but decided to ignore them, hoping that the reports were an exaggeration. In fact, the temperature dropped sharply and it started to snow. Monica, who was only wearing ordinary trainers, slipped and fell down a crevasse. She was roped to Joey but the latter managed to cut the rope just before he, too, would have been pulled over. The part-time instructor did not have enough expertise to effect a rescue herself and Monica died before more expert help arrived.

Discuss the possible liability of Rachel and Joey.

5.4 Reform of involuntary manslaughter

The state of the law on involuntary manslaughter has been widely criticised over the years. Some have argued that constructive manslaughter is unfair to the accused and should be reformed or abolished together; Professor Smith, for example, declared in the *Criminal Law Review* in 1986, when discussing the case of **Goodfellow**, that the law in this area was in 'a discreditable state of uncertainty'. Other commentators have disapproved of the constant changes regarding reckless and gross negligence manslaughter.

The Law Commission considered the matter and published a report on the subject (*Law Com No 237, Involuntary Manslaughter 1996*). It recommended the complete abolition of constructive manslaughter and suggested modifications to the law on gross negligence manslaughter.

In more detail, the Commission suggested the creation of two new offences, that of reckless killing and killing by gross carelessness.

- Reckless killing would be committed where the accused is aware of a risk that his conduct will cause death or serious injury and it is considered unreasonable for him to have taken that risk. When considering the latter, all the circumstances known or believed by him to exist will be taken into account.

The maximum sentence for this would be life imprisonment.

- The second new offence would be killing by gross carelessness. The offence will be committed where a person's careless conduct has caused a death and it would have been obvious to a reasonable person in the defendant's position that this would happen. The defendant will only be liable if he was capable of appreciating such a risk and it is established either that his conduct had fallen far below the standard expected or that he had intended by his conduct to cause injury or was aware of the risk that this might occur.

This offence is not considered so blameworthy as that of reckless killing and this is reflected in a maximum sentence of ten years.

Comment

The proposed abolition of unlawful act manslaughter is no surprise and is a logical step forward. In earlier times, any unlawful act causing death would have resulted in a murder charge. This came to be seen as unjust where there was obviously no intention to kill or cause serious injury to the victim. Taken further, it could be argued that, in similar circumstances, a person should not face a manslaughter charge either. Others would argue that those who are guilty of unlawful or grossly negligent acts should incur criminal liability in order to deter others. It remains to be seen whether the new offences, if ever enacted, will afford this. If the unlawful act is considered a manifestly reckless way to act, the defendant could be charged with the new offence of reckless manslaughter. It should be remembered, however, that a more subjective approach is taken here when establishing possible liability so there are bound to be people who would not be found guilty under reckless killing who would have been liable for constructive manslaughter.

It is also interesting to note that the Law Commission proposes to revive the concept of recklessness with regard to homicide, after its recent curtailment by the House of Lords, although this is similar in form to **Cunningham** recklessness, and subjective in approach, a move which brings the new offence in line with other offences against the person.

With regard to the second offence, the change from the word 'negligence' to that of 'carelessness' shows an intention to move away from civil law concepts of liability which, some have argued, have no place in criminal law. It will also solve the problem of having to establish whether a duty of care exists. Under the new offence, the defendant will be *prima facie* liable if the conduct causing the death falls far below that which is expected and he knows this.

5.5 Other unlawful homicides

5.5.1. Causing death by dangerous driving

This was changed from causing death by reckless driving by the **Road Traffic Act 1991**, which amended **s1 Road Traffic Act 1988** after the North Report, in 1988, favoured such a move.

S1 Road Traffic Act 1988, as amended, states that:

A person who causes the death of another person by driving a mechanically propelled vehicle dangerously on a road or other public place is guilty of an offence.

The amended offence carries a maximum punishment of ten years' imprisonment and a possible fine.

A person is held to drive dangerously if his driving falls below the standard expected of a competent and careful driver and it would be obvious that driving in this way would be dangerous. In **AG's Reference (No 4 of 2000) 2001**, the Court of Appeal made it clear that the test for dangerous driving is an objective one and that it is not necessary to establish a specific intention to drive dangerously. A person would also be criminally liable if his vehicle is in a dangerous state.

The offence is now extended to 'any mechanically propelled vehicle', not just motor vehicles. It can be committed on a road or other public place.

S3A Road Traffic Act 1988, as amended, also creates a new offence of causing death by careless or inconsiderate driving when under the influence of drink or drugs. The courts have made it clear that normally a substantial custodial sentence will be given, seen in the five year term for Gary Hart. He was alleged to have fallen asleep while driving. His Land Rover ran off the motorway on to a railway track just as the London-bound express approached at 125 mph. The collision derailed the train and threw it into the path of an on-coming freight train. Ten people were killed and 76 injured.

5.5.2 Infanticide

The law is in **s1(1) Infanticide Act 1938**. It is available to a woman who 'by any wilful act or omission' causes the death of a child of hers under 12 months but does so because the balance of her mind is disturbed because she has not fully recovered from the effect of giving birth or from breast feeding the baby. In such a case she will be guilty of infanticide instead of murder and will normally be dealt with more leniently.

5.5.3 Abortion

This is an offence under **s58 Offences Against the Person Act 1861** where it states that it is an offence to procure a miscarriage. The offence can be committed by the woman herself or by another, by use of 'a poison or other noxious thing' or by 'an instrument or any other means.'

There is no requirement to show that there has actually been a miscarriage as a result. To commit the crime, however, the woman herself must actually be pregnant whereas with others who try to procure the miscarriage this is not necessary. Where others are involved the woman could be charged with aiding and abetting the bringing about of a miscarriage, or be charged with conspiracy to procure her miscarriage. In practice such charges are rarely brought.

The word 'poison' refers to a recognised poison and the administrators of it would be guilty however small the amount as laid down in **Cramp 1880**.

The words 'noxious thing' covers things that are harmful in the quantity given, even if harmless in small doses *(Marcus 1981).*

Lawful Abortions

By **s1(1) Abortion Act 1967** (as amended in 1990), there is no offence if the pregnancy is terminated by a registered medical practitioner, provided that the correct procedures are laid down.

5.5.4 Child destruction

It is an offence under **s1(1) Infant Life Preservation Act 1929** for any person, intending to destroy the life of a child capable of being born alive, to wilfully cause the child to die before it has an existence of its own.

There is a defence if the act was done in good faith to save the mother's life and in **Bourne 1939**, this was held to cover a doctor who carried out an abortion on a 14-year-old girl who had been raped.

In **Rance v Mid-Downs Health Authority 1991**, it was held that a child is capable of being born alive if it is able to exist as a living child breathing through its own lungs alone.

Self-Assessment Questions

1. State the other name for unlawful act manslaughter.
2. Describe the three elements that have to be proved for this offence.
3. Why was the crime established in **Larkin** but not in **Lamb** and **Ariobeke**?
4. Why have the cases of **Cato, Newbury & Jones** and **Kennedy** caused problems for the courts and how were these difficulties resolved?
5. Why were the convictions quashed in the cases of **Dalby** and **Dawson** but upheld in **Mitchell** and **Goodfellow**?
6. With regard to unlawful act manslaughter, what is the definition of a dangerous act and where is the law?
7. Why was the conviction for gross negligence manslaughter confirmed in the case of **Andrews** but quashed in **Bateman**?
8. Why were the convictions quashed in **Prentice** and **Holloway** but not in **Adomako**? What test was laid down by the House of Lords in the latter case?
9. What is the punishment for involuntary manslaughter?
10. Briefly define two other types of unlawful homicide and state where the law is to be found.

Chapter 6

NON-FATAL OFFENCES AGAINST THE PERSON

6.1 Introduction

This chapter deals with non-fatal offences against the person. Not all such offences will be dealt with; only the ones most commonly found in examination specifications. These include common assault, battery, actual bodily harm and grievous bodily harm in its two forms, laid down in **s18** and **s20 Offences Against the Person Act 1861**.

In addition, there will be a brief mention of certain offences against the police, indecent assault and rape.

It can be seen by its date that the **Offences Against the Person Act** (not, as one student delightfully described it, the Offensive Person's Act!), is an ancient one, which contains some very archaic terms. In addition, it will also be discovered that, although in English law, the words 'assault' and 'battery' have very different meanings, the two terms are often confused, not only by laymen but also by the judges and the draftsmen of the statutes relating to this area of law. In many cases, the word assault is used to encompass both an assault and a battery or, indeed, either one of these. It will come as no surprise, therefore, to learn that there have been strong calls for the urgent reform of this whole area of law.

6.2 Assault

An assault (or common assault as it is sometimes called) is committed when the accused intentionally or recklessly causes the victim to apprehend immediate and unlawful violence. The House of Lords recently confirmed this definition in the case of **Ireland**

1997. A battery, on the other hand, is a separate offence and concerns the actual infliction of the force.

The two separate crimes were created by the common law but were classified as indictable offences under **s47 Offences Against the Person Act 1861** (noted in future as **OAPA 1861**), which also laid down the punishment. This part of **s47** has been repealed and now **s39 Criminal Justice Act 1988** decrees that the offences of common assault and battery are to be treated as summary offences. The same section also lays down a maximum sentence of six months' imprisonment and a fine not exceeding level 5.

It was generally believed that the two crimes remained as common law offences, despite the fact that certain procedural information, such as the provisions just mentioned, were put into statutory form. In **DPP v Taylor, DPP v Little 1992**, however, the Divisional Court stated that common assault and battery had been classed as statutory offences since the enactment of **s47 OAPA 1861**! A prosecutor, therefore, should now charge the defendant with either assault or battery under the amended law, i.e. under **s39 Criminal Justice Act 1988**.

6.2.1 The *actus reus* of assault

The *actus reus* of assault occurs when the defendant causes the victim to apprehend immediate and unlawful violence.

It can be seen that no force need actually be applied to constitute this offence. The victim need only apprehend personal injury. Examples of such apprehension would include raising a fist or pointing a gun at the victim. The latter must, however, be aware that violence might be enacted. In **Lamb 1967**, mentioned in Chapter 5 under constructive manslaughter, the victim at whom the gun was pointed did not fear the possible infliction of violence because neither he nor his friend believed that the gun with which they were playing would fire. No assault, therefore, had taken place. Conversely, an assault would have been committed if an imitation weapon had been used but the victim believed it to be real.

Can words alone constitute an assault?

It has been clearly decided that conduct causing the victim to believe that harm might be inflicted may amount to an assault but there was, until very recently, far less certainty as to whether words alone could do this. Earlier dicta suggested that they could not. In **Meade and Belt 1823**, the judge stated that 'no words or singing are equivalent to an assault'.

Over the years, however, the judges have changed their opinion on this. In the case of **Wilson 1955**, Lord Goddard stated, *obiter*, that the words 'get out the knives' would, on their own, be sufficient to constitute an assault. Similarly, in the civil case of **Ansell v Thomas 1974**, a verbal threat to eject the plaintiff was considered to be a civil assault. The most important landmark has occurred very recently, when the Court of Appeal in **Constanza 1997** stated categorically that an assault could arise from words alone and held that older authorities stating otherwise rested on 'a dubious foundation'. It will also be seen, when looking at the case of **Ireland 1997**, under actual bodily harm, that the House of Lords has also upheld that in certain circumstances, even silence can amount to an assault, as where the defendant terrorised women with silent phone calls.

Words might prevent an assault

What was established much earlier was that words could prevent an action from being an assault. In the very early case of **Tuberville v Savage 1669**, the accused put his hand on his sword and said 'if it were not assize time I would not take such language from you'. The act of putting his hand on his sword was threatening but this had to be weighed against his words, which clearly implied that no physical action would be taken because the judges were in the vicinity!

How immediate must the threat be?

When looking at the the *actus reus* of assault, it will be seen that the victim must believe that immediate violence will be inflicted upon him. The courts, however, have adopted a liberal interpretation of the word 'immediate', in order to give justice to the victim.

It was stated in **Smith v Chief Superintendent of Woking Police Station, 1983** that 'When one is in a state of terror, one is very often unable to analyse precisely what one is frightened of as likely to happen next'.

In this case, the victim, who was in her nightclothes, was badly frightened by the accused, who had trespassed onto private property and was staring in at her through the windows of her ground floor bedsitting room.

The Divisional Court upheld the defendant's conviction for being on enclosed premises for an unlawful purpose (i.e. an assault). The defence tried to argue that the accused could not have committed an immediate assault because the windows and doors were all locked. The appeal court held that it was enough that the woman believed that she was in danger of having immediate violence inflicted on her. Her fear did not have to be rationalised.

The issue of whether a threat needs to be an immediate one was also addressed in the case of **DPP v Ramos 2000**. The defendant was actually charged under **s4 Public Order Act 1986** and **s3 Crime and Disorder Act 1998** for distributing letters containing writings that were threatening, abusive or insulting, with intent to cause that person to believe that immediate unlawful violence would be used against him. He had sent two letters to an organisation offering advice to the Asian community in West London, alleging that a bombing campaign was being arranged and that the recipient of the letters would also be killed. The District Judge (magistrates' courts) decided that, as no time had been mentioned for the proposed attack, this lacked the immediacy required by the statutes and the defendant had been acquitted.

The prosecution appealed on this point of law and the Divisional Court decided that the important matter was the victim's state of mind, rather than the statistical risk of violence occurring within a short space of time. Provided therefore, that the victim believed that something nasty could happen at any time, the defendant could be convicted. The matter was therefore referred back to the magistrate with a direction to continue with the case.

It will be seen, when looking at cases on actual bodily harm that a similar approach was taken by the Court of Appeal in the case of **Constanza 1997**.

6.2.2 The *mens rea* of assault

The *mens rea* of assault is satisfied when the defendant intends to cause the victim to apprehend immediate physical violence or does this recklessly.

The Court of Appeal stated in the case of **Venna 1976** that:

We see no reason in logic or in law why a person who recklessly applies physical force to the person of another should be outside the criminal law of assault.

The defendant was actually convicted of assault occasioning actual bodily harm but the principles laid down relate also to assault and battery.

It will be remembered that there are two types of recklessness in English law, **Cunningham** recklessness and **Caldwell** recklessness. In **Venna**, **Cunningham**-style recklessness, i.e. subjective recklessness, was applied but after the decision in **Caldwell 1981** it was for a short while assumed that it would be sufficient to establish the more objective type of recklessness in all criminal offences where recklessness was part of the *mens rea*. **Caldwell**-style recklessness was therefore accepted by the Divisional Court in **DPP v K 1990**. As noted in Chapter 2, this change in the accepted position did not last long with regard to offences other than criminal damage. **DPP v K** was overruled by the Court of Appeal in **Spratt 1991** and, although that case was itself overruled on another point, this stricter approach to the *mens rea* of assault and battery was affirmed by the same court in **Parmenter**, also in 1991. When the latter case went to the House of Lords, this point was not directly discussed but *obiter dicta* by Lord Ackner appears to support the Court of Appeal's view. **Cunningham** recklessness, therefore, must be established for the offences of assault and battery.

6.3 Battery

This consists of an act by which the defendant intentionally or recklessly applies unlawful physical force to another person, as affirmed by the House of Lords in **Ireland 1997**.

The difference between assault and battery, therefore, is as follows:

- an assault is committed where the victim believes that he is likely to be subjected to some sort of harm
- a battery does not take place until the force is applied.

While the latter offence is known by the term 'battery', however, it is not usual to state that the defendant has battered the victim. Instead, to the great confusion of all, the word 'assault' is used in its wider layman's form.

With regard to a battery, the law takes the view that an individual has a right to be protected from molestation. Blackstone, the eminent jurist, stated in his early Commentaries that:

the law cannot draw the line between different degrees of violence and therefore totally prohibits the first and lowest stage of it; every man's person being sacred and no other having a right to meddle with it, in any the slightest manner.

In the case of **Collins v Wilcock 1984**, described below, Goff L J affirmed this approach. He declared that 'The fundamental principle, plain and incontestable is that every person's body is inviolate'. He went on to quote with approval, the statement in **Cole v Turner 1704**, that 'the least touching of another in anger is a battery.'

It can be seen from these quotations that the degree of physical force need not be high. In **Collins v Wilcock**, it was considered that a battery had been inflicted when a policewoman took hold of the arm of the defendant she believed to be soliciting in order to detain her but without the intention to effect an arrest.

The Divisional Court of the Queen's Bench Division decided that the action of the policewoman amounted to an unlawful battery and quashed the defendant's conviction for the assault she had inflicted.

This decision followed a succession of cases

where the police were held to be acting unlawfully in detaining suspects. They should not, therefore, try to prevent a suspect leaving unless they wish to arrest him and this was not the position in **Kenlin v Gardner 1967** and **Ludlow v Burgess 1971**, so the detentions were unlawful. In **Donnelly v Jackman 1970**, however, the court held that the officer in question did not commit a battery when he merely tapped on the other's shoulder to attract his attention.

A similar view was taken in **Smith v DPP 2000**. The police had been summoned via a 999 call and found the defendant outside the house, shouting and banging on the door. One of the officers took his arm, not to arrest him but to lead him away from the door so that the 999 call could be investigated. The defendant resisted this and lashed out at the officers. He was charged with assaulting the police officers but appealed, claiming that the policemen had exceeded their duty by taking his arm.

The Divisional Court rejected the appeal, deciding that a person interfering with a right of entry could be required by reasonable force to move away from the entrance in question.

The courts have decided that touching the clothing of a person amounts to touching the person himself, provided, of course that the defendant has the necessary *mens rea* of battery. In the case of **Day 1845** the defendant slashed the victim's clothes while in **Thomas 1985**, even though the actual offence was not made out, the rubbing of a girl's skirt was held to amount to a battery.

Naturally, not all touching will have this effect. In **Collins v Wilcock**, Goff went on to state that:

most of the physical contacts of ordinary life are not actionable because they are impliedly consented to by all who move in society and so expose themselves to the risk of bodily contact. So nobody can complain of the jostling which is inevitable from his presence in, for example, a supermarket, an underground station or a busy street; nor can a person who attends a party complain if his hand is seized in friendship, or even if his back is (within reason) slapped.

Indirect batteries

The courts have long since decided that the battery need not be directly inflicted on the victim. In **Scott v Shepherd 1773**, a civil case, the court held that the defendant had committed a battery when he threw a live squib into a market place and, after two people had picked it up and thrown it further away, it injured a third party. In **Martin 1881**, an even more serious offence was committed when the defendant placed an iron bar across an exit in a theatre, turned out the lights and shouted 'fire!' In the ensuing panic, several people were injured as they rushed out of the theatre. The defendant's conviction for grievous bodily harm was upheld. More recently, this view was supported in the case of **Fagan v Metropolitan Police Commissioner 1969**, mentioned earlier in Chapter 2. It will be remembered that a police officer had ordered the defendant to park his car close to the kerb, and Fagan had reluctantly complied. In doing so, he drove the car onto the policeman's foot. This was done accidentally but, when asked by the policeman to remove the car, he said 'F . . . you, you can wait' and proceeded to turn off the ignition.

He unsuccessfully tried to argue on appeal that no offence had been committed. The Divisional Court disagreed, stating: 'it matters not, in our judgment, whether the battery is inflicted directly by the body of the offender or through the medium of some weapon or instrument controlled by the action of the offender . . .'

This point was taken further in **Haystead 2000** where the defendant punched a woman in the face causing her baby to fall out of her arms and hit his head on the floor. The Divisional Court of QBD rejected his contention that his

conviction was wrong because there had been no direct force against the baby.

The court decided that the woman's action in dropping her baby was a direct and immediate result of the defendant's action in punching her. The judges felt that there was no difference between what had occurred and the use of a weapon to cause the baby to fall to the floor and that it was right for the offence of assault to be charged.

6.3.1 The *actus reus* of battery

This consists of the application of unlawful physical force on another, as confirmed by **Ireland 1997**. It will be seen, when discussing actual bodily harm, that the House of Lords decided in the latter case that the causing of psychiatric injury by silent telephone calls will not constitute a battery, though such an action may well be an assault.

6.3.2 The *mens rea* of battery

This is satisfied where the defendant intends to do such an act or is reckless about whether such force will be applied.

As with assault, this is **Cunningham**-style recklessness, as laid down in **Venna 1976**. It is necessary, therefore, to prove that the accused himself was aware that he was acting recklessly.

A battery may start off as an innocent, accidental act but may later become a battery during a sequence of events among which the *mens rea* of the offence is formed. This was the position in the case of **Fagan**, mentioned above.

The defendant had also argued that he did not have the necessary *mens rea* for the offence. The Divisional Court held that 'there was an act constituting a battery which at its inception was not criminal because there was no element of intention, but which became criminal from the moment the intention was formed'. The conviction, therefore, was upheld.

6.4 The defence of consent

General defences, which can be put forward in response to many different types of crime including offences against the person, will be examined in Chapters 10 and 11, but the defence of consent, which is of special relevance to offences against the person, will be examined in this chapter. The courts have decided that if the alleged victim has given a valid consent to the assault and/or battery inflicted upon him, no offence will have been committed. This position was clearly affirmed by Lord Lane, a former Lord Chief Justice in **Attorney General's Reference (No 6 of 1980) 1981.** He stated that as a general starting point:

> *it is an essential element of an assault that the act is done contrary to the will and without the consent of the victim . . .*

Should the defence of consent be accepted it will be a complete defence and the defendant will be acquitted.

As one would expect however, strong restrictions have been put upon this general proposition. It was stated in the same case that 'It is not in the public interest that people should try to cause, or should cause, each other bodily harm for no reason'. The court therefore decided that the defence of consent could not be used when a fist fight in the street took place, even though the parties wanted to settle their differences in this way. This followed an early decision in **Coney 1882**, where the courts held that a prize fight conducted with bare fists was unlawful, despite the agreement of the parties. In **Leach 1969**, the defendants were unable to argue that the

victim consented to his injuries even though he had asked to be crucified on Hampstead Heath! Fortunately, in this case, the misguided victim lived but it should also be noted that it is not possible for a person to give someone else permission to kill him, no matter how strongly the first party wishes to die, as was seen in the **Diane Pretty** case. Consent may, however, be available in limited circumstances for the less serious offences against the person. These circumstances were described in **AG's Reference (No 6 of 1980)1981** as 'properly conducted games and sports, lawful chastisement or correction, reasonable surgical interference, dangerous exhibitions, etc.' In addition, practical joking and consent to minor harm in sexual activities have also been tolerated.

Properly conducted games and sports

With many games and sports there is always a risk of some bodily harm occurring. The most obvious and perhaps difficult case to justify is

But the judges tell us such manly diversions are good for you!

boxing, where, by the very nature of the sport, the participants intend to cause harm to the other. Despite this, it was clearly affirmed by the House of Lords in **Brown 1994**, that the sport of boxing is a lawful activity. 'Cudgels, foils and wrestling' were other examples which came under the heading of 'manly diversions' which were said 'to give strength, skill and activity, and may fit people for defence, public as well as personal, in time of need'. This early view was quoted with approval in **Donovan 1934**.

With regard to these 'manly diversions', which include related sports like football, rugby and hockey, the victim is said to consent to harm that occurs within the rules of the game, provided the defendant did not intend to cause serious injury. If he did have such an intention, then it would, of course, be immaterial that he was playing within the rules. Bramwell L J made this point clear in **Bradshaw 1878**, where the victim died during a game of football. Similarly, the defence would not be available to someone who deliberately broke the rules, as the newspaper article below illustrates.

Lawful chastisement

Parents have always been allowed to use reasonable force to chastise their children and after the decision in **Watkins 2001**, it appears that teachers, too, can use reasonable force to restrain unruly pupils. Punishment, however, cannot be inflicted 'for the gratification of passion or rage or if it be immoderate or excessive in its nature or degree'. This view was

Public school boy locked up for rugby kick that broke jaw

A FATHER lashed out today after his son was put behind bars for smashing an opponent's jaw during a rugby match at his public school.

Civil engineer Chris Calton, 50, said outside court: "It seems to me to be ridiculous that an incident on a rugby pitch should end up in court."

David Calton, 19, now a tourism student at Sheffield Hallam University, was given a 12-month youth custody sentence at Sheffield Crown Court for kicking another boy with such force that one spectator said the impact "sounded like a gunshot".

The court heard how Calton, while a pupil at Mount St Mary's Catholic College, Spinkhill, near Sheffield, was playing "a hard fought and closely contested game" at Pocklington School, East Yorkshire, when he attacked 16-year-old Andrew Wilson late in the game. Mr Mark Bury, prosecuting, said:

"The victim was knocked out with a kick to the head which broke his jaw while he was getting up from a ruck.

"There was a crowd at the game and Pocklington headmaster David Grey said the kick was levelled with all his might." The victim was taken to York District Hospital and underwent surgery.

The court heard how, since the incident in January, the boy had been left with throbbing pains in his jaw which makes "cracking sounds" when he eats.

Calton told police that Wilson had been aggressive towards him during the game, which was abandoned with the score at Pocklington 12, Mount St Mary's 17. But he admitted kicking out at him.

Taken from an article in the *Evening Standard*, 28 September 1998 taken in the case of **Hopley 1860** and currently, there is much less tolerance of such physical punishment. In June 2001, a man who punished his stepson so severely that he was left with permanent injuries, was jailed for two years.

Reasonable surgical interference

A person may consent to the infliction of bodily harm for good medical reasons, even in some cases where the risk is substantial, such as an operation with only a small chance of success. The matter is not so clear cut in situations where the operation or other process has little medical advantage. It is believed, however that the act is acceptable if it has some therapeutic value to the person requesting it. The defence of consent, therefore, could normally be raised by those performing operations such as cosmetic surgery, ear-piercing or tattooing, (though not tattooing of a minor as this is forbidden by legislation). Legal attitudes are constantly changing in this area to keep abreast of advances in medical science. Circumcision of males, as required in some religions, has long been accepted as lawful although female circumcision is banned by statute. Sterilisation, sex change operations and organ transplants have been added more recently, provided that they are conducted properly and are not for an unlawful purpose. In **Richardson 1998** patients were held by the Court of Appeal to have consented to their dental treatment, even though they might have been less willing to undergo this if they had known that the woman had been struck off by the General Dental Council!

Dangerous exhibitions etc.

Within the field of entertainment, the law allows a person to consent to the possibility of some harm arising, as, for example where a person allows knives to be thrown at him or a cigarette shot from his mouth. It is, however, uncertain how much licence the law will permit, in either civil or criminal law.

Horseplay

In addition to the categories mentioned in **AG's Reference (No 6 of 1980) 1981**, other exceptions where a person may be held to have consented to an assault or battery have, over the years, been recognised. These include what the judges have called horseplay and some forms of sexual activity.

From time immemorial people have been prone to play jokes upon each other. The law might become involved where the joke has backfired and someone has been harmed.

In **Jones 1987**, two young schoolboys were injured after being tossed in the air by the defendants but the Court of Appeal quashed the convictions for grievous bodily harm. The judges decided that the boys' consent to such 'rough and undisciplined play' could provide a defence.

In **Aitken and Others 1992**, the practical jokes engaged in by RAF officers were even more potentially dangerous. The defendants set fire to the victim's supposedly fire resistant suit but the joke backfired and the victim received severe burns. The Court of Appeal held that it was a misdirection to state that such an activity could never be lawful and the convictions were set aside.

Consent to harmful sexual activity

The extent to which a person can consent to be harmed when indulging in sexual activity has also caused problems for the courts, with different approaches being taken by different judges. A controversial early example was the case of **Clarence 1888**, where the defendant escaped liability for both assault and rape because his wife had consented to the actual act of intercourse. She unsuccessfully contended that she would not have given this consent if she had been made aware of the fact that her husband was suffering from venereal disease which was then communicated to her.

In an important Canadian case, **Cuerrier 1998**, the defendant was eventually convicted in a similar type of case. He had unprotected sex with two women, knowing he was HIV positive. This new 'doctrine of informed consent' has not yet become part of English law.

The defendant may also be held liable, despite the other's consent, if the harm inflicted is more than trivial and is directly inflicted on the victim, as in **Nichol 1807**, where the defendant harmed a 13-year-old pupil. In **Donovan 1934**, a young girl of 17 was beaten on her buttocks with a cane merely to give sexual gratification to the defendant, and in **Boyea 1992**, the victim was held to have consented to the sexual intercourse but not to the harm that this caused. In the latter case, the defendant was aware of his actions. In **Slingsby 1995**, there was no liability after vigorous sexual activity had taken place because the defendant had not committed any direct harm. He had been charged with unlawful act manslaughter because the woman had died from blood poisoning when internal cuts caused by the defendant's signet ring became infected but the case was dismissed.

Sado-masochism – the courts' approach

The position becomes more difficult where the participants actually desire the infliction of pain.

The House of Lords dealt with this issue in **Brown and Others 1993 1994**. The case attracted a great deal of publicity because it involved the sexual activities of a group of homosexual males who took part in sado-masochistic activities, apparently enjoyed by all concerned. They burnt each other with matches and metal wires, beat each other with whips and indulged in unusual and painful forms of genital torture. Their activities came to light when the police found a video detailing them, which was passed to group members. The instruments were sterilised and the wounds dressed so none of the men suffered

permanent injuries. Nevertheless, they were convicted of offences under **ss47 and 20 OAPA 1861** and were sentenced to terms of imprisonment ranging from two to four and a half years. The House of Lords upheld the convictions by a majority of three to two.

For the majority, Lord Templeman stated that in cases where no actual bodily harm is caused, the consent of the person affected precludes him from complaining, thereby recognising the defence of consent in relation to common assault and battery. He also added that Parliament, under the **Sexual Offences Act 1967** had permitted homosexual sexual activities in private between consenting adults. He refused, however, to accept the contention of the defendants that their sexual appetites could only be satisfied by the infliction of bodily harm because, as he pointed out:

> sado-masochism is not only concerned with sex. Sado-masochism is also concerned with violence. The evidence discloses that the practices of the appellants were unpredictably dangerous and degrading to body and mind and were developed with increasing barbarity and taught to persons whose consents were dubious or worthless.

He ended with a very clear message, stating that 'I am not prepared to invent a defence of consent for sado-masochistic encounters which breed and glorify cruelty and result in offences under sections 47 and 20 of the Act of 1861.'

Lord Jauncey discounted the argument that there needed to be hostility, as laymen understood the word, on the part of the person inflicting the bodily harm. He decided that if the act was unlawful, it was also a hostile one under the legal meaning of the word. He went on to stress the dangers to health inherent in these activities and the possible corruption of younger participants and decided that if such acts were to be rendered lawful it was up to Parliament to do this.

Lord Lowry stated that 'Sado-masochistic homosexual activity cannot be regarded as conducive to the enhancement or enjoyment of family life or conducive to the welfare of society'.

Lord Mustill, in one of the two dissenting judgments, took a more liberal view. He stated that the state should intervene 'no more than is necessary to ensure a proper balance between the special interests of the individual and the general interests of the individuals who together comprise the populace at large.' He believed that the acts indulged in by the group were not, at present, criminal ones and was not prepared to create a new offence to make them so. He argued that this was Parliament's role, if it was deemed to be necessary.

Suggestions for reform

The Law Commission issued a Consultation Paper (No. 139), entitled 'Consent in the Criminal Law 1995', asking for opinions on the proposition that 'the intentional causing of any injury to another person other than a serious disabling injury should not be criminal if, at the time of the act or omission causing the injury, the other person consented'.

The current position

This was only a consultation paper so it is important to keep track of the current state of the law. Despite their differences on other points, all five Law Lords in **Brown 1993** appeared to accept that consent could be a complete defence to common assault and battery. The majority, however, went on to decide that consent is not a defence to actual bodily harm or grievous bodily harm unless it comes within one of the recognised exceptions. In **Wilson 1997**, the Court of Appeal was prepared to include 'bottom branding' in the recognised categories of tattooing and ear piercing.

A doctor had discovered that Wilson's wife had scars on her buttocks in the form of the initials A and W and reported the matter to the

police. They discovered that her husband, at her request, had burnt his initials onto her buttocks with a hot knife. Wilson was charged with assault occasioning actual bodily harm under **s47 OAPA 1861**. Unsurprisingly, the judge decided that he was bound by the cases of **Donovan** and **Brown** and directed the jury to convict.

The Court of Appeal quashed the conviction and expressed its disquiet that the prosecuting authority should have thought it necessary to bring the proceedings, which, it claimed served no useful purpose and yet involved considerable public expense. The court decided that **Brown** did not lay down a proposition that consent was never a defence to actual bodily harm, deliberately inflicted, as all five Law Lords had recognised that there were exceptions to the general rule.

The court also decided that it was preferable for the law to develop on a case by case basis. It believed that the current case was vastly different to the cases of **Donovan** and **Brown**. It felt that the first case involved aggression on the part of the defendant and the second physical torture that carried risks of serious physical injury and blood infection. The court felt that in the current case, there was no aggression and the act was more akin to a desire for physical adornment. It was therefore decided that the public interest did not demand that the defendant's activities should be treated as criminal.

Comment

There are many problems concerning the defence of consent. The following are examples:

- The current position, involving as it does a possible disagreement between the House of Lords and the Court of Appeal as to the extent to which consent can be a defence for the more serious cases of bodily harm leaves a lot to be desired. The House of Lords appears to have decided that the defence of consent to actual or grievous bodily harm is not available unless it comes within one of the recognised exceptions. It could be argued that the Court of Appeal is taking a different approach and stating that the defence of consent is available unless this is felt to be against public policy.

- Some would argue that the defence should not be available for 'horseplay', so that the participants in such activities would know that they cannot rely on the law to help them if the joke goes tragically wrong. This approach has been taken in civil law and has helped to curtail some of the more harmful practical jokes and rituals, particularly in the field of employment.
- While it is accepted that attitudes change and the law should, in most cases, keep abreast of prevailing attitudes, the adoption of a 'case by case approach', as suggested by the Court of Appeal in **Wilson**, renders the law uncertain, which is both undesirable and unfair.
- There also appears to be a fundamental disagreement among the judiciary about how to treat cases of bodily harm inflicted at the request of the victim. Some argue that the prevention of such activities is an interference with the liberty of the subject and is too paternalistic in approach. Increasingly, it is considered that what consenting adults do in the privacy of their homes is their own concern and the State should not intervene.
- Critics of this view would argue that any intentional infliction of pain degrades both the aggressor and the victim and can lead to an escalation of the violence. As stated earlier, Lord Templeman subscribed to this view. The horrific case of Frederick and Rose West illustrates the lengths to which such cruelty can go, although in this case the poor victims were obviously not consenting.
- These critics believe that, even in these more permissive days, society has a duty to draw the line somewhere and state the limits of what is acceptable. If the participants then wish to continue and hope that they will not be discovered, then that is their affair. One has some sympathy for those who can only obtain sexual gratification in such a fashion and, in many cases, their activities would never come before the courts. If they did, and the circumstances were not too excessive this could be reflected in the sentence. The State, however, by retaining the general rule that such behaviour comes under the heading of unacceptable violence, is not then being seen to condone such acts.
- In **Laskey and Others v United Kingdom 1997**, the European Court of Human Rights refused to uphold a complaint by the men in **Brown** that their convictions were an unjustifiable interference with their right to respect for private life. Even that famously liberal court decided that their prosecutions were necessary in a democratic society for the protection of health.
- It is also maintained that the young may well be corrupted by such actions. In the case of **Brown**, the 'victims' were young men and the perpetrators of the violence were middle-aged. There was also some evidence that a youth had been initiated into what were known as 'bondage affairs' at the age of 15.
- It can be argued that, even in the less extreme situation in **Wilson**, a doctor was obviously concerned enough about the degree of harm to report the matter to the police. Why then should not the law take the matter seriously?
- The law makes a distinction between actual consent and mere submission but, in

practice, the two states may be confused. It was clear in **Wilson** that the wife desired to be branded but there could be other cases where a partner merely submitted to the infliction of harm, through fear, perhaps or for love of the partner. The decision in **Wilson**, which apparently sets the law's seal of approval on some violent acts, may make it more difficult for the victim to protest. It is submitted that a better approach in cases like **Wilson** would be not to prosecute or to take all the circumstances into account when sentencing.

In conclusion, it appears from the cases that Parliament badly needs to take the initiative in this matter and lay down clear guidelines on the use of consent as a defence.

TEN KEY FACTS ON ASSAULT AND BATTERY

- Assault and battery are two distinct offences, although the word 'assault' is often used as a verb to cover both types of offence. Both offences were created at common law but are now held to be statutory offences under **s39 Criminal Justice Act 1988 (DPP v Taylor, DPP v Little 1992)**. The maximum sentence for either offence is six months' imprisonment, coupled with a fine.

- The definition of an assault is where the accused intentionally or recklessly causes the victim to apprehend immediate and unlawful violence.

- The *actus reus* of assault is causing the victim to apprehend immediate and unlawful violence (**Ireland 1997**), although the word 'apprehend' can cover states of mind which are less acute that than real fear. Anxiety would probably be sufficient. The *mens rea* of assault is satisfied where such apprehension is caused either intentionally or recklessly (**Venna 1976**). The type of recklessness to be proved is **Cunningham**-style recklessness (**Parmenter 1991**).

- The Court of Appeal, in **Constanza 1997**, decided that words alone could, in some circumstances, be enough to constitute an assault. The House of Lords went even further in **Ireland 1997** and held that even silent telephone calls could, if the *mens rea* of the defendant was established, amount to an assault. The court decided, however, that a battery could not be committed in such a fashion.

- The victim must apprehend immediate violence but the courts will not inquire too deeply into the rationality of the fear, provided that it is a genuinely held belief (**Smith 1983, Ireland 1997, Ramos 2000**).

- A battery occurs where the defendant intentionally or recklessly applies unlawful physical force to the victim. Psychiatric injury caused by silent telephone calls will not suffice (**Ireland 1997**). The force applied need only be minimal, provided that it is unlawful (**Cole v Turner 1704, Collins v Wilcock 1984**). The slashing and even touching of someone's clothes could be included (**Day 1845, Thomas 1985**), although there is implied consent to a certain amount of touching in everyday life, even by the police (**Collins v Wilcock 1984, Smith v DPP 2001**). There is no requirement that the force must be directly inflicted (**Scott v Shepherd 1773, Martin 1881, Fagan v Metropolitan Police Commissioner 1969, Haystead 2000**).

- The *actus reus* of a battery is the application of physical force on the victim (**Ireland 1997**). The *mens rea* is doing this intentionally or recklessly. Like assault, **Cunningham** or subjective recklessness must be proved (**Venna 1976**). The *mens rea* may be formed at a later time provided that the sequence of events is continuing (**Fagan v Metropolitan Police Commissioner 1969**).

- Consent by the victim may be a defence to assault and battery (**Attorney General's Reference (No 6 of 1980) 1981, Brown and Others 1994**), provided that the activity comes within one of the recognised categories. Included are properly conducted sports like boxing, football, rugby and similar games (**Bradshaw 1878, Brown 1994**). Prize fights with bare knuckles and fist fights in the street are not (**Coney 1882, Donovan 1934**).

- Consent can also be given expressly or impliedly for lawful chastisement (which was not the case in **Hopley 1860**), for lawful surgical operations and other procedures if there is some benefit in the activity, for dangerous exhibitions and for horseplay which goes wrong (**Jones 1987, Aitken 1992**).

- Consent will not be a defence where actual bodily harm is inflicted during the course of sexual activities (**Nichol 1807, Donovan 1934, Boyea 1992** and **Brown and Others 1994**), although the Court of Appeal appears to have made an exception to this with regard to 'bottom branding', likening this to a mere tattoo (**Wilson 1997**).

Activity

Using the cases of **Brown** and **Wilson** as a basis for your arguments, decide whether the defence of consent should be extended, curtailed or remain as it is.

6.5 Actual bodily harm

This offence is found under **s47 Offences Against the Person Act 1861**. It concerns an aggravated assault. It was stated, rather confusingly, by Hobhouse L J in **Chan-Fook 1994** that the offence 'must be an assault which besides being an assault (or assault and battery) causes to the victim some injury.'

There is no definition in the act itself as to what constitutes actual bodily harm, although case law has provided assistance, as seen below. The offence of occasioning actual bodily harm was created at common law and **s47** merely describes the penalty. In the case of **Courtie 1984**, however, the House of Lords decided that the offence of actual bodily harm should be treated as a statutory offence, despite the fact that the section merely states that:

> whosoever shall be convicted on indictment of any assault occasioning actual bodily harm shall be liable to imprisonment for not more than five years.

The offence has since been made a triable either way offence and the section lays down a maximum sentence of five years for when the offence is tried in the Crown Court. If the magistrates agree, however, the offence can be dealt with summarily, with a maximum prison sentence of only six months.

As mentioned earlier, actual bodily harm is a form of aggravated assault so before it is decided that the victim has suffered such harm, it is first necessary to establish that he has been subjected to either an assault or a battery. It is therefore very important to remember the constituents of these offences.

In the case of **Constanza 1997**, the Court of Appeal upheld a conviction under **s47** after deciding that an assault had been established and this assault had caused actual bodily harm.

The defendant, a former work colleague, had subjected the victim to a sustained campaign of harassment. This included numerous telephone calls, over 800 letters, following the victim, daubing offensive words on her door and making other unsolicited visits. As a result, the woman became clinically depressed and, after receiving two further letters, of the belief that the man was going to harm her physically.

The Court of Appeal stated that there was sufficient evidence that the victim was in fear of immediate violence because it might have

occurred at any time, particularly as the defendant lived quite close to the victim.

The court also decided that there was no actual rule that an assault could not be committed by words alone and said that earlier authorities on this which stated otherwise rested on a dubious foundation.

In **Ireland 1997,** another case concerning harassment, the House of Lords upheld the view that repeated silent telephone calls could constitute an assault.

The court decided, however, that a battery could not be committed in this way, because this offence required proof that unlawful force had been applied.

6.5.1 The definition of actual bodily harm

In **Miller 1954**, the definition was said to include 'any hurt or injury calculated to interfere with the health or comfort of the victim'.

In **Chan-Fook 1994** the Court of Appeal stated that the words 'actual bodily harm':

> are three words of the English language which require no elaboration and in the ordinary course should not receive any. The word 'harm' is a synonym for 'injury'. The word 'actual' indicates that the injury (although there is no need for it to be permanent) should not be so trivial as to be wholly insignificant . . . The body of the victim includes all parts of his body, including his organs, his nervous system and his brain. Bodily injury therefore may include injury to any of those parts of his body responsible for his mental and other faculties.

In this case, the Court of Appeal held that the judge had misdirected the jury when he said that it was enough to amount to actual bodily harm if the victim had been put in 'a nervous, maybe hysterical condition'. She had been questioned roughly by the defendant and locked in a room, after being suspected of stealing an engagement ring.

From this it is apparent that, while actual bodily harm encompasses physical harm, psychiatric injury and other identifiable clinical conditions, it does not cover emotions like fear, distress or panic. There may well have been a common assault and even a battery if the victim was manhandled but the more serious offence under **s47** would not exist.

6.5.2 The *actus reus* of actual bodily harm

This is simply an assault (with the word used in its wider sense), causing actual bodily harm. As with a battery, it appears that the bodily harm need not be directly applied. In **DPP v K (a minor) 1990**, a 15-year-old boy left his chemistry class alleging that he needed to wash acid from his hand. He took a boiling tube of concentrated sulphuric acid with him to the lavatory block in order to conduct some tests of his own. While he was experimenting with the acid, he heard footsteps and, in his panic, poured the remaining acid into a hot air hand and face dryer. The footsteps then receded but the boy left the acid in the dryer and returned to class, intending to deal with the problem at a later time. Unfortunately for him and the victim, the latter went into the block before this and his face was permanently scarred after he turned on the dryer and the acid was ejected. K's conviction for actual bodily harm was upheld by the Divisional Court.

6.5.3 The *mens rea* of actual bodily harm

Originally, there was a great deal of confusion over the *mens rea* for this offence but in **Savage and Parmenter 1992**, the House of Lords clearly stated that the *mens rea* is the

same as that required for common assault and battery. This means that all the prosecution has to show is that the accused intended or was reckless about putting the victim in the state of apprehending immediate physical violence or intended or was reckless about touching the victim unlawfully. There is no requirement to go further and prove that he intended or was reckless about causing actual bodily harm.

This restated the position laid down in the case of **Roberts 1971**. Following this case there had been confusion over the subject in the Court of Appeal. In **Roberts**, the victim had jumped out of a car travelling between 20 and 40 miles per hour, after the driver, who was giving her a lift to a party, had told her to undress and had grabbed her coat. He had claimed earlier that he had beaten up other girls who had refused his advances.

The Court of Appeal upheld his conviction for actual bodily harm because, although he had not directly inflicted the injuries, he was responsible for them. The defendant had inflicted a battery on the girl and her action of jumping out of the car was one which could reasonably have been foreseen as a consequence of this. The court stated that the matter would have been different if the girl had done something 'so "daft" . . . or so unexpected . . . that no reasonable man could be expected to foresee it'.

This view prevailed until the case of **Spratt 1991**. The Court of Appeal, without referring to **Roberts**, suddenly decided that subjective recklessness about causing, not just a battery, but actual bodily harm itself, was required. This new view of the law was later followed in the case of **Parmenter**.

By a strange and embarrassing coincidence, however, in the case of **Savage**, decided on the same day as **Spratt**, the original view of the law had been upheld by another sitting of the Court of Appeal! The defendant had thrown a glass of beer over a former girlfriend of her husband. While attacking her rival, the beer glass had also left her hand (she claimed this was an accident), and had broken and cut the victim's wrist. The conviction for grievous bodily harm was quashed but the defendant was found guilty of the lesser crime of actual bodily harm. With regard to the *mens rea* required for this latter offence, the Court of Appeal restated the position in **Roberts**, although, once again, the name of that case was not mentioned.

There were therefore two conflicting views as to the *mens rea* required for actual bodily harm and, as stated, the House of Lords was called upon to decide the matter in the joint appeals of **Savage and Parmenter 1991**.

The House of Lords decided that the law was correctly decided in **Roberts**.

The *mens rea* for actual bodily harm therefore is the same as for common assault and battery. If actual bodily harm results as a consequence of either putting the person in fear of a battery intentionally or recklessly, or intentionally or recklessly touching the victim unlawfully, then the greater crime under **s47** has been committed. There is no extra requirement to prove that the defendant intended to cause actual bodily harm itself or had been reckless about whether this would happen.

It should be remembered that, when recklessness is alleged, **Cunningham**-style recklessness must be proved, as was clearly affirmed by the Court of Appeal in the case of **Venna 1976**.

FIVE KEY FACTS ON ACTUAL BODILY HARM

- Actual bodily harm is an aggravated assault, details of which appear under **s47 OAPA**. The offence is a statutory one (**Courtie 1984**), for which the maximum punishment is five years' imprisonment.
- The prosecution must first establish the existence of an assault or a battery (**Constanza 1997**). If fear of immediate harm is present, an assault may arise from harassment caused by words alone or even by silent telephone calls (**Constanza 1997, Ireland 1997**). A battery, however, cannot be committed this way; it requires unlawful force (**Ireland 1997**). Such force can, however, be inflicted indirectly, as in **DPP v K (a minor) 1990**.
- The word 'actual' means more than trivial, the word 'harm' means some injury and the words 'bodily harm', include psychiatric injury. The words do not cover mere emotions like distress, fear and panic (**Chan-Fook 1994**).
- The *actus reus* of s47 is an assault causing actual bodily harm. The *mens rea* is the same as for an assault or a battery, i.e. the defendant has intentionally or recklessly caused the victim to apprehend that a battery might be inflicted upon him (assault) or has intentionally or recklessly unlawfully touched the victim (a battery). There is no further requirement to show that the defendant intended to cause actual bodily harm (**Roberts 1971, Savage and Parmenter 1992**).
- The recklessness must be subjectively proved, as with all non-fatal offences against the person (**Cunningham 1957, Venna 1976**).

Before we leave this offence, it should be noted that a person charged with wounding under **s20** may, instead, be convicted of the lesser offence of actual bodily harm.

It is not, however, possible for a person charged under **s47** to be convicted, in the alternative of common assault or battery, if he has not been charged with those offences. Assault and battery are summary offences only.

6.6 Malicious wounding or grievous bodily harm under s20 OAPA 1861

S20 states that: 'whosoever shall unlawfully and maliciously wound or inflict any grievous bodily harm upon any person, either with or without any weapon or instrument shall be guilty of an offence'.

The maximum punishment for this offence is, surprisingly, the same as for actual bodily harm, i.e. imprisonment for five years.

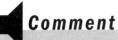

Comment

The **Offences Against the Person Act 1861** was merely a consolidating act and made no attempt to rationalise the law which came from several different sources. **S20**, however, has always been thought of as the more serious offence and it appears very strange to a layman that it attracts the same maximum penalty as actual bodily harm. It is one more reason why reform in this area of law is long overdue.

It can be seen from the definition of **s20** that the offence has two aspects to it, the malicious wounding of another or the malicious infliction of grievous bodily harm. It is important for the prosecution to make a correct charge, as otherwise the defendant could escape liability. This unfortunate state of affairs occurred in **C (a minor) v Eisenhower 1984**, where pellets from the defendant's air gun had caused injury to the victim's eye. There was bruising under his eye and rupturing of the internal blood vessels surrounding it but, crucially, no breaking of the skin. The Divisional Court held that no wounding had taken place. It was decided that there must be 'a break in the continuity of the whole skin'. It was, however, pointed out that the term 'skin' may also include the skin of an internal cavity where it is continuous with the outer skin. It is also important to realise that if there is proof of a wounding, the actual injury need not be severe; any breaking of the skin will suffice.

Comment

The latter fact has also been criticised. Many people would be puzzled to learn that the degree of harm needed for malicious wounding need not be as high as that required for the second aspect of the defence, i.e. the infliction of grievous bodily harm. To the non-legal eye, the infliction of a minor wound would equate more easily to the offence of actual bodily harm. On the other hand, the law takes the view that the use of a weapon to cause any sort of wound is a serious matter, however small the actual harm.

With regard to the second part of the offence, it has to be established that the defendant has unlawfully and maliciously inflicted grievous bodily harm upon the victim. In the case of **DPP v Smith 1961**, the House of Lords held that the words 'grievous bodily harm' simply mean really serious harm. In **Saunders 1985**, it was also decided that it would not be a misdirection to leave out the word 'really'; the words 'serious harm' would suffice.

6.6.1 The *actus reus* of the offence under s20

This consists of an unlawful wounding or the unlawful infliction of grievous bodily harm.

The word 'inflict' in **s20** has caused problems. It will be seen that, in **s18 OAPA**, where the offence of grievous bodily harm with intent is laid down, the word 'caused' is used, rather than 'inflict'. The courts have therefore been faced with the problem of whether the words cause and inflict are synonymous or should be interpreted differently. If the latter approach is taken, it has to be decided whether the word 'inflict' in **s20** means that any harm done to the victim has to be directly inflicted upon him. Until the House of Lords' decision in **Burstow 1997**, there seemed to be conflicting authorities on this. One strain of cases suggested that the word 'inflict' should be interpreted narrowly and only apply if the defendant had caused direct harm. An example of this approach was the early case of **Clarence 1888**, noted earlier in the chapter relating to the issue of consent. The defendant was not held to have inflicted grievous bodily harm on his wife by infecting her with venereal disease because he had not made a direct assault upon her. She had consented to the sexual intercourse, even though she would not have done so if she had known the full facts.

Indirect harm included

The other line of cases treated the word 'inflict' in the same way as the word 'cause'. The judges took the view that the defendant could be convicted if the harm was caused in a more indirect way. The case of **Martin 1881**, mentioned above, is an example, where the defendant was convicted under **s20** when he placed a wire across the gangway in a theatre,

because he had indirectly caused the injuries. Similarly, in **Halliday 1889**, a man was convicted of grievous bodily harm when he so frightened the victim that the latter jumped through a window and sustained serious injuries. In **Lewis 1970**, a husband was equally liable when his wife broke her legs in her efforts to escape him.

In **Wilson 1984**, the House of Lords looked at this conflict and preferred the latter approach. The law, therefore, is that there may be liability under **s20**, even though there was no direct assault. Their Lordships relied on an Australian case, that of **Salisbury 1976**, to support their contention, although certain exceptions were detailed in that case.

In **Burstow 1997**, a similar view was taken. The defendant had refused to acknowledge that a relationship was over and had subjected the victim to a campaign of harassment. He sent letters and photographs, made telephone calls, followed the woman, stole her washing and planted offensive items in her garden. He refused to stop his campaign even though he had been warned about his behaviour, had been prosecuted and even imprisoned. As a result of this obsessive attention, the woman had suffered a severe depressive illness amounting to grievous harm of a psychological nature.

The Court of Appeal, and subsequently the House of Lords, stated that there could be liability for grievous bodily harm without any direct or indirect application of physical violence.

Comment

The decisions in **Constanza, Ireland** and **Burstow**, show a willingness on the part of the judges to take a liberal approach to the wording in the ancient **OAPA**, and are, therefore, to be welcomed. It has been officially recognised that cases on stalking are on the increase and, at a time when there was no specific legislation to deal with this problem, the courts needed to be flexible to avoid injustice.

The position has been partially rectified by the **Protection from Harassment Act 1997**, which creates two new offences.

- The less serious summary offence is committed where the defendant pursues a course of conduct that amounts to harassment of the victim. It requires harassment on at least two occasions. It is specifically laid down in **s7** that the word 'conduct' can include words alone. The maximum punishment is six months' imprisonment and a fine on level 5 of the scale.
- The more serious offence, of putting a person in fear of violence appears in **s4**. Once again, there must be conduct causing such fear on at least two occasions and the defendant must have known or should have been aware that his conduct would cause such fear.

This offence is a triable either way offence and, if tried on indictment, the maximum punishment is five years' imprisonment.

The creation of these new offences means that the judges will no longer have to strain the meaning of existing words in the **OAPA**. It also gives out a clear statement that the State is not prepared to tolerate stalking and other obsessive behaviour. Burstow, for example, shows little sign of giving up his

campaign of harassment. In January 1999, he was given a fourth term of imprisonment by Bracknell magistrates.

Unfortunately, this very necessary act is attracting a large number of appeals due to its deficient drafting. There have been calls for its provisions to be more clearly stated, particularly in relation to what constitutes a course of conduct, and what is meant by the word 'violence' in relation to the more serious offence in **s4**. There have been instances where the obviously guilty have successfully exploited these weaknesses. The defendants in **C (Sean Peter) 2001** and **R (A child) v DPP 2001** were not so fortunate. The first defendant tried to argue that he had only committed the offences because of his schizophrenia and that, taking this into account, his behaviour had been reasonable! The second appellant argued that the requisite two threats against the victim had not been made out because while the first had been made against the woman, the second threat of violence was made against her dog! Once again, the appeal was dismissed.

6.6.2 The *mens rea* of the offence under s20

It can be seen from the definition of the offence, that the wounding or infliction of grievous bodily harm must be done 'maliciously'. This word requires explanation. It was decided in the case of **Cunningham 1957**, discussed earlier in Chapter 3 in relation to the subject of murder, that the word has a very precise meaning in law and should not be equated with wickedness. Use of the word in law means that the defendant must be shown to have intended to inflict harm or have been reckless as to whether such harm would occur.

It was decided that the defendant would only be liable if he had actually foreseen that his actions would cause grievous bodily harm, i.e. really serious harm. Currently, the defendant can be convicted more easily. It was decided by the Court of Appeal in **Mowatt 1968**, that foresight of such a high degree of harm need not be proved. It is enough for the prosecution to show that the accused must have foreseen that *some* harm would result. The House of Lords, in **Savage and Parmenter 1992**, approved of this diluting of the *mens rea* for grievous bodily harm under **s20**.

In **DPP v A 2000**, the magistrates originally dismissed a charge of malicious wounding under **s20**. The defendant and his friend had been playing a game with air pistols, aiming to shoot each other below the knees. Somehow, the defendant had managed to shoot his friend in the eye instead! There was no suggestion that the defendant had intended to do this and the magistrates dismissed the charge of malicious wounding under **s20**. The prosecution appealed by way of case stated, arguing that the magistrates had applied the wrong meaning to the word 'maliciously'.

The Divisional Court agreed, stating that the correct test to apply when judging the extent of foresight necessary for a conviction was whether the defendant had foreseen that the harm that might be done and had then gone on to take the risk. The appeal therefore was allowed.

In **Savage and Parmenter**, mentioned above, the House of Lords affirmed that it is possible for a defendant charged under **s20** to be convicted, instead, of actual bodily harm, provided that the jury has been properly directed about this.

6.7 Malicious wounding or grievous bodily harm under s18 OAPA 1861

This is the most serious form of assault other than homicide.

S18 OAPA 1861, as amended by the **Criminal Law Act 1967**, states:

Whosoever shall unlawfully and maliciously by any means whatsoever wound or cause any grievous bodily harm to any person . . . with intent to do some grievous bodily harm . . . or with the intent to resist or prevent the lawful apprehension or detainer of any person, shall be guilty of an offence.

At first glance, this seems to be very similar to the offence under **s20** and the words 'wounding' and 'grievous bodily harm' have similar meanings. There are, however, important distinctions to be made between the offences. First, the maximum sentence for a **s18** offence is life imprisonment, as opposed to five years for a **s20** offence – secondly, the **s18** offence arises where the accused 'causes' grievous bodily harm, rather than 'inflicting' it, as in **s20**. The offence is therefore wider than **s20**.

As was noted earlier, the **s18** offence is committed when the accused has 'caused' grievous bodily harm to another. Taken literally, therefore, the offence is wider than **s20** and there is no requirement that the wounding or bodily harm must be directly inflicted. The section also uses the words 'by any means whatsoever' which reinforces this.

In **Mandair 1994**, the House of Lords decided that a charge of grievous bodily harm under **s18** is wide enough to cover an allegation of 'inflicting' grievous bodily harm under **s20** in a case where the full requirements of the **s18**

FIVE KEY FACTS ON GRIEVOUS BODILY HARM

- There are two offences describing these crimes laid down in **s18** and **s20 OAPA 1861**. Both offences have two aspects to the *actus reus*, malicious wounding and grievous bodily harm.

- To constitute a wounding, there must be a breaking of the whole skin (**C (a minor) v Eisenhower 1984**), but the injury itself need not be a severe one.

- The word 'inflict' in **s20** is to be interpreted in the same way as the word 'cause' in **s18** (**Wilson 1984, Burstow 1997**). This approach enables a conviction to be obtained in cases of psychiatric harm caused by stalking and other obsessive behaviour (**Constanza 1997, Ireland 1997, Burstow 1997**), although the creation of the two new offences under the **Protection From Harassment Act 1997** will lessen the need for this.

- To decide on the *mens rea* of **s20**, the word 'malicious' needs to be examined. It now means intending to wound or inflict some harm on the victim or being reckless about this. The earlier requirement that the defendant must have intended to inflict serious harm has been changed (**Mowatt 1968, Savage and Parmenter 1992**). **Cunningham**-style recklessness is required.

- It is possible for the defendant to be convicted of the lesser offence under **s47**, if a **s20** offence cannot be proved (**Savage and Parmenter 1992**).

- The offence under **s18 OAPA** is, apart from rape, the most serious of the non-fatal offences against the person. The maximum sentence is life imprisonment.

- The *actus reus* occurs where the defendant wounds or causes grievous bodily harm by any means whatsoever. *Prima facie*, it is therefore wider than **s20**.

- The *mens rea* will only be established if it can be proved that the defendant intended to cause grievous bodily harm or intended to resist or prevent an arrest.

- The word 'intention' has the same meaning as for murder. The prosecution must, as a minimum, show that the defendant foresaw as a virtually certain consequence that his actions would cause serious harm.

- If this cannot be proved, the word 'cause' has been held to be wide enough to allow, in the alternative, a conviction under **s20**.

offence cannot be made out. This approach allows the defendant to be convicted on the lesser charge, even though he has not been charged with it.

The House of Lords also used this opportunity to overrule the Court of Appeal decision in **Field 1993** where the wrong drafting of a **s20** offence was considered fatal.

6.7.1 The *actus reus* of the offence under s18

The *actus reus* of **s18** is committed when the accused unlawfully and maliciously wounds another or causes him grievous bodily harm by any means whatsoever.

6.7.2 The *mens rea* of the offence under s18

It is very important to realise that recklessness will not suffice for liability under **s18**. The wounding or grievous bodily harm must be done maliciously but also with a further intention to either cause grievous bodily harm or with intention to resist or prevent a lawful arrest or detention.

The word 'intention' has the same meaning as required for the crime of murder. The prosecution must therefore prove that it was the defendant's purpose to cause grievous bodily harm or to resist arrest or that he foresaw this as a virtually certain consequence of his actions. If the latter is shown, then the jury may find that he had the necessary intention, just as in the murder cases looked at earlier in this book.

Activity

- Evaluate the following statement:

  'The state of the law concerning non-fatal offences against the person is uncertain, unjust and badly in need of reform.'

- Describe the offences which might, (or might not), have been committed in the following scenario:

  Tony Corleone and Michael Soprano were the leaders of two notorious London gangs, the Jets and the Comets. They agreed to merge the two gangs and to have a fist fight to decide who should be in overall charge. During the fight, Tony's eye was badly bruised by the knuckle-duster used by Michael and there were signs of internal bleeding. Tony then landed a heavy punch on Michael, which broke the latter's collarbone. While trying to deflect further blows from Tony, Michael was outraged to hear the abuse being heaped upon him by Al, a member of the opposing gang. Michael shouted, menacingly, 'If I were not so busy right now, I would not take such language from you!'

  Mrs Malone, a bystander, was jeered at as she tried to pass by and, although she wasn't hurt, she was jostled and pushed by a member of the gang and her skirt was grabbed.

  Meanwhile, Moll, Tony's ex-girlfriend has complained to the police about his obsessive behaviour. She said that he is refusing to accept that their relationship is over, is following her everywhere and has made so many silent telephone calls to her that she is in a state of mental collapse.

6.8 Possible reform of non-fatal offences against the person

A Draft Bill from the Law Commission in 1993 attached to the Report (Law Com No 218), *Legislating the Criminal Code: Offences Against the Person and General Principles*, sought to sweep away the old-fashioned wording of these offences and provide more modern and sensible definitions. This Bill was never brought to Parliament's attention, an omission attracting much criticism. In 1998 therefore, the Home Office produced a consultation document on the same subject, accompanied by a Draft Bill incorporating the changes suggested by the Law Commission. Under the Offences Against the Person Bill, the offences of assault and battery, actual bodily harm under **s47**, grievous bodily harm under **s20** and grievous bodily harm under **s18** would be changed to the following:

- Assault
- Intentional or reckless injury
- Reckless serious injury
- Intentional serious injury

It can be seen that assault or battery would be combined into one new offence simply called 'assault'. This would be committed if a person intentionally or recklessly applied force to or caused an impact on the body of another without his consent or, where the act was intended to cause injury, with or without the consent of the other. It would also be committed where the defendant intentionally or recklessly, without the consent of the other, caused the victim to believe that any such force or impact was imminent.

Clause 4(2) states that no offence would be committed if the assault merely comprises the touchings experienced in the normal course of daily life if the defendant does not appreciate that such an action is unacceptable to the other party.

With regard to the more serious offences, the current word 'harm' would be changed to the word 'injury'. This would include both physical and mental injury. The word 'serious' is not defined.

Comment

The creation of the new offences would be a vast improvement on the present position. One can only hope therefore, that the Bill will be given the chance to become law in the not too distant future.

The combining of the offences of assault and battery is a good move, doing away with the confusion that currently exists. The sensible, ordinary wording of the more serious offences is also to be welcomed. The phrases 'malicious wounding' and 'grievous bodily harm' can then be consigned to the history books where they rightly belong.

6.9 Other offences

6.9.1 Obstructing a police officer in the execution of his duty

A person who resists or wilfully obstructs a police officer in the execution of his duty or someone helping the police officer in his duty, will be guilty of an offence under the **Police Act 1996.** This offence carries a maximum penalty of one months' imprisonment and a fine not exceeding level 3 on the standard scale.

6.9.2 Assaulting a police officer in the execution of his duty

This offence is also found in the **Police Act 1996** and is obviously more serious. To reflect this, it has a maximum punishment of six months' imprisonment and a fine not exceeding level 5.

One of the most difficult aspects of these offences is to decide exactly when the officer is acting in the execution of his duty. If the courts are not convinced of this, the conviction will be quashed.

6.9.3 Indecent assault

Under **ss14** and **15 Sexual Offences Act 1956,** as amended, it is an offence for a person to make an indecent assault on either a woman or a man. The maximum penalty is 10 years' imprisonment.

In **Court 1989,** the House of Lords stated that there were three requirements for this offence:

- An intentional assault on the victim.
- An assault which was considered by 'right-

minded persons' to be indecent.
- A further intention to commit an indecent act.

This offence covers a wide range of cases, including those where the crime of rape cannot be established, as where the victim is forced to engage in oral sex or as in **Court 1989,** where the defendant admitted putting a girl of 12 across his knee and spanking her.

In **Tabassum 2000**, the Court of Appeal dismissed the defendant's appeal and found that the offence of indecent assault had been made out. It distinguished the case of **Clarence**, mentioned earlier under the defence of consent. The accused had posed as a doctor and had then intimately examined several women. The court took the sensible view that the women had only agreed to such action for medical reasons.

6.9.4 Rape

The offence of rape is defined in **s1(1) Sexual Offences Act 1956**, as amended by the **Criminal Justice & Public Order Act 1994**. The amended section states that it is an offence for a man to rape a woman or another man. Under **s1(2)**, a rape is committed if the man has sexual intercourse, either vaginal or anal, with someone who does not consent, and at the time, the man knows that the other does not consent or is reckless as to whether the person has consented.

Under **s44** of the Act, the act of sexual intercourse need not be completed, proof of penetration will be enough. The man need not ejaculate, nor need the woman's hymen be ruptured. The offence is also committed if the man refuses to withdraw after being asked to do so, as in **Kaitamaki 1985**.

Lack of consent

One of the essential elements of the offence is that the woman (or man) does not consent to sexual intercourse. The word is not defined but, over the years, the cases have established that

a woman is not consenting when she is asleep, unconscious, mentally backward, too young to give a proper consent, as in the case of **Howard 1966**, or senseless through drink or drugs, as in **Malone 1998**. The burden of proof is on the prosecution to show a lack of consent. This was established in **Harling 1938**, where a girl of 13 was shown to have a weak intellect and was therefore not held to be capable of giving a valid consent.

The victim in **Flattery 1877**, was not held to have consented when she thought the intercourse was part of a medical examination, nor was the woman in **Williams 1923**, when she was told that the act was being performed in order to improve her singing! In **Olugboja 1982**, the Court of Appeal stressed the difference between an active assent and a mere submission through fear. The court decided that the young girl in question had not consented because, although actual violence had not been used against her, the man had threatened to keep her all night in a bungalow if she did not submit.

As mentioned earlier in this chapter, the wife in **Clarence 1888** was held to have consented to the act of sexual intercourse even though she would not have done so if she had known the man had a venereal disease. Presumably, the same principle would still apply to a man with the HIV virus, although the decisions in **Burstow** and **Ireland** would suggest that he could now be convicted of grievous bodily harm. Perhaps less seriously, it was held in **Linekar 1994**, that a prostitute had given a valid consent even though she would not done so if she had known that she was not going to be paid.

Under **s1(2) Sexual Offences (Amendment) Act 1976**, it is stated that an honest belief in the woman's consent will mean that the offence has not been committed. This put into statutory form the decision in **DPP v Morgan 1976**, where the House of Lords also decided that an honest but unreasonable belief in the other's consent could afford a defence.

This view has been criticised so the amended section goes on to say that the fact as to whether the man has reasonable grounds for his belief is a matter to be taken into account with all the other evidence to see whether the belief is honest.

Rape within marriage – the changing law

Until 1994, when further amendments were made to the **Sexual Offences (Amendment) Act 1976**, the definition of rape included the word 'unlawful'. The view prevailed, therefore, that sexual intercourse within marriage, even without the woman's consent, could not be termed unlawful. In 1736, a quote by Hale, an eminent jurist, illustrated a view of marriage that has persisted until very recent times. He stated that a man 'could not be guilty of a rape committed by himself upon his lawful wife for by their mutual matrimonial consent and contract, the wife hath given herself as in this kind unto her husband which she cannot retract'.

Fortunately for women, the position gradually changed. In **Miller 1954**, it was decided that whereas a husband could not be convicted of rape within marriage, he could be found guilty of actual bodily harm. In **O'Brien 1974**, a husband was found guilty of raping his wife when the parties had already obtained a decree nisi for divorce. In **Steele 1976**, a husband was convicted when he disobeyed an undertaking he had given not to molest his wife and in **Roberts 1986**, a husband was found guilty when he raped his wife when a formal separation agreement was in existence.

The Law Commission was busily preparing a report on this subject when, in 1992, in the case of **R**, the House of Lords finally decided that a husband could commit the offence of rape within marriage even when these situations did not exist.

Self-Assessment Questions

1. Where is the law to be found on assault and battery? Define the *actus reus* and the *mens rea* of these offences.
2. Giving cases to support your findings decide whether words can ever constitute an assault. Why was no assault found in the case of **Tuberville v Savage**?
3. How did the courts decide that the threat of assault was an immediate one in **Smith, Constanza** and **Ramos**?
4. Illustrating your answer with decided cases, decide whether a battery is indirectly inflicted.
5. Why were the police held to be acting unlawfully in **Collins v Wilcock** and **Kenlin v Gardner** but lawfully in **Donnelly v Jackman** and **Smith v DPP**?
6. Describe four situations where the defendant can consent to being harmed and two instances when he cannot.
7. Describe the *actus reus* and *mens rea* of actual bodily harm, giving cases to back up the points made and state where the law is to be found.
8. Apart from the difference in the *mens rea*, state three other differences between the offences under s20 and s18 **Offences Against the Person Act 1861**.
9. Why was the conviction for malicious wounding quashed in **C (a minor) v Eisenhower**?
10. State the *mens rea* required for a) s20 and b) s18.

Chapter 7

PROPERTY OFFENCES I: THEFT AND RELATED OFFENCES

7.1 Introduction

This chapter deals with the offences of theft, robbery, burglary and blackmail under **ss1, 8, 9,** and **21** of the **Theft Act 1968**. The crime of blackmail only needs to be studied by post-A Level students.

7.2 Theft

Stealing from others has always been considered a reprehensible crime and nearly every jurisdiction has some sort of sanction against stealing. In the UK, the law is to be found in the **Theft Act 1968**. This Act was passed after the Criminal Law Revision Committee looked at this topic and decided that the time was right for 'a new law of theft and related offences . . . embodied in a modern statute.' The idea was to replace old-fashioned terms like larceny and, instead, to try to make the law more understandable and more easily accessible.

Theft is a triable either way offence. Originally, the maximum penalty was ten years'

imprisonment if tried on indictment. Now, under **s7**, as amended by the **Criminal Justice Act 1991**, the maximum sentence has been reduced to seven years.

Where is the law of theft?

The first point to note is that the whole of the law of theft is to be found in just seven sections of the **Theft Act 1968**. **S1** contains the complete definition of theft, and **ss2–6** give further information on this. It will be seen in the table that **s2** and **s6** contain further detail on the *mens rea* of theft and that **ss3, 4** and **5** elaborate on the *actus reus*. As noted above, **s7** lays down the punishment.

The definition, under **s1 Theft Act 1968**, states that a person is guilty of theft if he 'dishonestly appropriates property belonging to another with the intention of permanently depriving the other of it'.

The *actus reus* is appropriating property belonging to another. The offender will have the necessary *mens rea* if he does this in a dishonest way, intending to permanently deprive the true owner of it. This can be seen more easily in Figure 7.1.

Theft		
Section No	**Word or phrase**	**Actus reus or mens rea?**
1	whole definition	both
2	dishonestly	mens rea
3	appropriates	actus reus
4	property	actus reus
5	belonging to another	actus reus
6	with the intention of depriving the other of it	mens rea

Figure 7.1 The elements of theft

7.2.1 The *actus reus* of theft

It has been noted that the *actus reus* of theft is committed when a person 'appropriates property belonging to another'.

These words need to be looked at more fully.

Appropriates (s3)

This part of the definition of theft has caused the greatest problems for the courts. The word is described in **s3** of the Act and the current major authorities on its interpretation are found in the cases of **Lawrence 1972**, **Gomez 1993** and **Hinks 2000**.

S3 Theft Act states that:

> any assumption by a person of the rights of an owner amounts to be an appropriation, and this includes, where he has come by the property (innocently or not) without stealing it, any later assumption of a right to it by keeping or dealing with it as owner.

A person appropriates property, therefore, when he assumes the rights of the true owner. In the case of **Pitham and Hehl 1977**, the Court of Appeal decided that a man who invited the two defendants into his friend's house while the latter was in prison and then sold them some of his furniture, had been assuming the rights of the owner. He was therefore held to have appropriated the property and this decision meant that the defendants' conviction for handling stolen goods could be upheld.

In **Williams 2000**, the Court of Appeal decided that the accused had appropriated property belonging to another when he presented certain cheques for payment after defrauding the victims. When the cheques were honoured, this caused a diminution of their credit balances and the assumption by Williams of their rights.

At first sight, the explanation of appropriation in **s3** appears to be straightforward but, unfortunately for the student, over the years since the passing of the Act, various problems have arisen with it. These problems are addressed under the headings listed below.

Does the thief have to assume all the rights of the real owner?

This question was addressed by the House of Lords, in **Morris, Anderton v Burnside 1984**. Lord Roskill stated clearly that it is enough for the prosecution to prove that any of the rights of the owner have been assumed. The House of Lords later affirmed this view of the law in the case of **Gomez 1993**.

In **Morris**, mentioned above, the defendant had taken some goods from a supermarket shelf and substituted lower price labels for the ones currently on the goods. He then went to the checkout desk and paid the lower price and was subsequently arrested.

In **Anderton**, a shopper had removed the price label from a joint of pork and replaced it with a much lower price from another item. He reached the checkout but was arrested before he had attempted to pay for the goods.

Both offenders were appealing against their convictions for theft. Their contention was that they had not appropriated property belonging to another, because they had not assumed all the rights of the real owner. Both appeals were dismissed. The House of Lords decided that they had assumed at least one of the rights of the real owners of the store by switching the labels on the goods and this action was sufficient to amount to an appropriation.

At what time does the appropriation take place?

In **Gomez 1993**, Lord Keith refused to follow another statement by Lord Roskill that the appropriation only occurred when the labels were switched and the goods were placed into a supermarket basket. Lord Keith decided that the appropriation took place earlier than this. He stated that:

> the switching of the price labels on the article is in itself an assumption of one of the rights of the owner, whether or not it is accompanied by some other act such as removing the article from the shelf and placing it in a basket or trolley. No one but the owner has the right to remove the price label from an article or to place a price label on it.

He dealt with the possible problem of a practical joker being convicted of theft by arguing that such a person would not have the *mens rea* for the offence because he would not be dishonest and would not have intended to permanently deprive the owner of the goods. He would, however, have committed the *actus reus* of theft because he had appropriated property belonging to another.

It can be seen, therefore, that **Gomez** has decided that an appropriation takes place the moment that the offender assumes any of the rights of the real owner. Cases such as **Skipp 1975** and **Fritschy 1985**, where the courts had decided that an appropriation did not take place until the defendant had done something that he had not been authorised to do, were overruled.

This new view of the law meant that the convictions of the defendants in **Atakpu and Abrahams 1994** could not be sustained. The offenders had devised a plan to hire expensive cars abroad and then to bring them to England to sell them. Suspicions were aroused, however, when the men reached Dover and they were arrested. The case came to trial before the decision in **Gomez** and it was decided at first instance that the men were guilty of conspiracy to steal. The state of the law at that time decreed that the theft would have taken place in England, i.e. when the cars had been retained after the hire period had

expired. By the time the case reached the Court of Appeal, however, **Gomez** had been heard by the House of Lords and it was reluctantly decided that the offenders had, instead, appropriated the property when they had, with dishonest intent, hired the cars in Brussels and Frankfurt. The men, therefore, could not be said to have been conspiring to steal in England and the convictions had to be quashed. The Court of Appeal was prepared to recognise that an appropriation could be a continuing act while the act of stealing was taking place, but would not stretch this to include actions taken days after the cars had been obtained.

Can an appropriation exist where the owner has given his consent to the taking?

The answer to this question is now a definite 'yes'. Lord Roskill, in **Morris**, believed that, for an appropriation to arise, there had to be an adverse interference or a usurpation of the rights of the real owner. This statement, however, seemed to be in direct contradiction with an earlier House of Lords' decision, made in **Lawrence v Metropolitan Police Commissioner 1972**. In that case it had been decided that an appropriation had taken place, and a theft committed, when the real owner had apparently agreed to the taking of the money.

An Italian student had arrived at Victoria Station in London on his first visit to England. Mr Occhi spoke little English but showed a taxi driver a piece of paper on which was written an address in Ladbroke Grove. The taxi driver falsely indicated that the journey was a long and expensive one and, when offered a £1 note, took a further £6 from the student's open wallet.

The driver was convicted of the theft of the £6 but appealed on the grounds that the owner had consented to the taking. The case eventually reached the House of Lords, where their Lordships decided that there could be an appropriation 'even though the owner has permitted or consented to the property being taken'.

Until the case of **Gomez 1993**, therefore, there were two conflicting House of Lords' decisions on this subject. In the civil case of **Dobson v General Accident Fire and Life Assurance Corp 1990**, the Court of Appeal made it clear that it preferred the decision in **Lawrence**. The court stated that 'whatever **R v Morris** did decide it cannot be regarded as having overruled the very plain decision in **Lawrence's** case that appropriation can occur even if the owner consents . . .'

The House of Lords upheld this view of the law in the case of **Gomez 1993**. The defendant was employed as assistant manager at a store selling electrical goods and agreed with an acquaintance to supply goods to him in return for two stolen, unsigned building society cheques, amounting to £17,200.

The manager of the shop was presented with a list of goods to the value of the first of the stolen cheques, told that it was a genuine order and asked for his authorisation for the payment to be made by cheque. He requested that the bank be contacted to confirm that the cheque was a valid one. The defendant pretended that he had taken this step and declared that he had been informed that the cheque was 'as good as cash'.

The goods were duly delivered to the accomplice, with the defendant helping to load up his van.

A similar procedure was taken with regard to the second cheque, and this time the manager merely accepted the position. Some time later, the cheques were returned bearing the words 'Orders not to pay. Stolen cheque'.

Gomez, together with another employee and the man posing as the genuine buyer, was arrested and subsequently sentenced to two years' imprisonment. He claimed that he could not be said to have appropriated the property in question because the manager had authorised the sale. The Court of Appeal accepted this defence and quashed the conviction.

A point of law of general public importance was, however, certified for the attention of the House of Lords. The question asked took the following form:

> when theft is alleged and that which is alleged to be stolen passes to the defendant with the consent of the owner, but that consent has been obtained by a false representation, has (a) an appropriation within the meaning of **s1(1)** of the **Theft Act 1968** taken place, or (b) must such a passing of property necessarily involve an element of adverse interference with or usurpation of some right of the owner?

Lord Keith gave the main judgment. He decided that **Lawrence** was right and **Morris** was wrong and was, in addition, only *obiter dicta*. He stated that:

> The decision in **Lawrence** was a clear decision of this House upon the construction of the word 'appropriates' in **s1(1)** of the **1968 Act**, which has stood for 12 years when doubt was thrown upon it by the obiter dicta in **Morris. Lawrence** must be regarded as authoritative and correct, and there is no question of it now being right to depart from it.

The conviction for theft was reinstated.

It is now clearly the law, therefore, that there may still be an appropriation of property even if the owner appears to have consented to the taking. The House of Lords clearly affirmed this in **Hinks 2000**, discussed below. Earlier company cases, such as **McHugh 1993**, in which the Court of Appeal had stated that 'An act done with the authority of the company

that, while it was possible for some cases of deception to also come within the definition of theft, it would not be theft where the owner obtained ownership of the goods.

Comment

The actual point of law in **Gomez** was quite a narrow one, concerning as it did a case where the consent was only given after a false representation had been made. The judges of the House of Lords, however, did not confine their reasoning solely to this type of situation, so therefore the implications of the decision are far wider. Smith and Hogan state that 'the effect is to create an extraordinarily wide offence, embracing many acts which would more naturally be regarded as merely preparatory acts'. It also means that every case of obtaining property by deception under **s15** (to be discussed in the next chapter) will also be theft.

cannot in general amount to an appropriation', are no longer good law. After **Gomez**, directors or others holding a majority share holding in a company who appropriate company property for their own use, can be found guilty of theft. This view was affirmed in an unsuccessful action for judicial review in **R (on the Application of A) v Snaresbrook Crown Court 2001**.

In **Gomez**, Lords Jauncey, Browne-Wilkinson and Slynn agreed with Lord Keith's judgment. Lord Lowry, however, made a powerful dissenting speech and stated firmly that cases such as **Gomez** should be dealt with under **s15** of the **Theft Act**, i.e. by charging the offender with obtaining property by deception, not with theft. He was the only judge to refer back to the Eighth Report of the Criminal Law Revision Committee that preceded the **Theft Act**. (Lord Keith had decided that this would serve no useful purpose!) This Report had clearly stated

Does there have to be a taking of property to constitute an appropriation?

We have seen that the House of Lords, in **Gomez**, implied that the answer to this question was 'no' because it decided that an appropriation occurs the moment that the defendant assumes any of the rights of the owner, whether or not he goes on to take the property. (It would, of course, be more difficult to establish the *mens rea* of theft at such a point because it would have to be shown that the defendant was acting dishonestly and had an intention to permanently deprive the owner of the goods.)

The Court of Appeal, however, appeared to come to a different decision in **Gallasso 1993**, decided on the same day as **Gomez**. The accused was a nurse in charge of a house for people with severe learning difficulties and was authorised to deposit and withdraw money from the patients' accounts to meet their daily needs.

One of the residents received three cheques, one for £4,250, another for £4,000 and the third for £1,800.32 but, instead of depositing the money in the existing account, Gallasso opened other accounts in the patient's name and withdrew some of this money for her own use. She was charged with various counts of theft but disputed that a theft had occurred by the opening of the separate accounts in the resident's name.

The Court of Appeal quashed the conviction for theft on this count and decided that, although **Gomez** had laid down that an appropriation could take place even though the real owner appears to have given his consent, it was still necessary to have a taking. In this situation, while the nurse had obviously intended to commit criminal acts, it was felt that, at this stage, there had not been any appropriation of the resident's property.

This decision does not sit easily with the case of **Gomez** and is felt by many to be wrongly decided. The defendant was certainly assuming some of the rights of the owner by the opening of other accounts and **Gomez** has decided that this is enough to amount to appropriation.

What approach should be taken when criminal law and civil law rules conflict?

This matter came to the attention of the Court of Appeal in the case of **Mazo 1996.** A maid was appealing against a conviction for the theft of large sums of money from her employer, an elderly woman whose mental faculties were weakening. The maid alleged that the money was a gift from a grateful employer and this point seemed to be made out because the employer had authorised the cashing of the cheques after the bank had made inquiries

about them. The Court of Appeal decided, therefore, that a valid gift of the money might well have been made and held that, in such a situation, there could not be a conviction for theft. The Court of Appeal did pay lip service to the decision in **Gomez**, by stating that the act would have been theft, even though the owner had apparently consented to the taking, *if that consent had been secured by deception.* The court, therefore, was recognising the narrowest ratio of the House of Lords in **Gomez**. In the present case, however, the judges felt that no such deception existed, the jury had been misdirected on the issues and therefore the defendant should be given the benefit of the doubt.

It was argued that this result did not stand easily with the judgment in **Gomez**. Those in favour of it pointed out that it appeared that the defendant had acquired 'an absolute, indefeasible right to the property' and that any conviction for theft would therefore conflict with established civil law principles. In the case of **Hinks 2000**, the House of Lords showed scant respect for this line of reasoning; instead their Lordships actually extended the principles in **Gomez**.

Hinks had befriended a 53-year-old man of limited intelligence and between April and November 1996 had persuaded him to give her a television set and, much more seriously, to withdraw sums of money amounting to £60,000 from his building society, which were then deposited in the defendant's account. Hinks argued that the money and goods were either loans or gifts and therefore had not been appropriated by her but despite this, was convicted.

The Court of Appeal upheld the conviction but allowed an appeal to the House of Lords on the question of whether the acquisition of an indefeasible title to property could still be classed as amounting to an appropriation of property belonging to another.

On a three-to-two decision, the House of Lords decided that it could. The court decided that the word 'appropriation' was not to be too narrowly construed; it was a natural word which comprehended any assumption of the owner's rights. Therefore, the acquisition of an indefeasible title to property by accepting a gift from a vulnerable and trusting person was capable of amounting to an appropriation under the **Theft Act 1968**. There had been a very strong prosecution case, which had been accepted by the jury after a fair and balanced summing up. The conviction was therefore declared safe, the precedents in **Lawrence** and **Gomez** upheld and the law on appropriation widened still further.

The current state of the law on appropriation

After the decisions in **Lawrence**, **Morris**, **Gomez** and **Hinks**, the law on appropriation is as follows: there can be an appropriation of property if just one of the rights of the owner is assumed (**Morris**). An appropriation can occur even though the owner appears to consent to the taking (**Lawrence**, **Gomez**), and even where the defendant has acquired a good title to the property in question (**Hinks**). It also appears that every case of obtaining property by deception under **s15 Theft Act 1968** will also be theft under **s1**.

In the earlier case of **Kendrick and Hopkins 1997**, the Court of Appeal did not face the difficulties encountered in **Hinks** because no valid gift had ever been made. The defendants were in charge of a residential home and had taken over management of the affairs of a 99-year-old resident. They had obtained a power of attorney, cashed her investments and had also persuaded her to make a new will naming them as beneficiaries. They were convicted of conspiring to steal and the Court of Appeal upheld the decision. The judges distinguished **Mazo**, arguing that in the current case, the elderly resident did not have the mental capacity to make a valid gift and therefore the

ownership of the property had not passed to the defendants. The jury was therefore entitled to conclude that dishonesty had been present.

Before leaving the subject of appropriation, it should be noted that a person who obtains property in good faith, which later turns out to have been stolen, would not be guilty of theft for assuming the rights of the true owner. This is stated in **s3(2)**.

Comment

The following observations can be made after these decisions on the meaning of the word 'appropriation'.

- It is unfortunate that in **Hinks**, there is yet another disagreement by the House of Lords on an important issue in criminal law. Lord Hobhouse and Lord Hutton gave dissenting judgments, which obviously weaken the authority.
- Professor Sir John Smith strongly disapproves of these decisions. In his commentary on **Hinks**, he states: 'No reader of these commentaries over the years is likely to expect the decision of the majority to receive a warm welcome here'. He adds wearily that 'those who make the decisions seem to turn a blind eye and a deaf ear' to any criticisms but nevertheless goes on to mention some of these, hoping that other jurisdictions may heed them. He believes that the House of Lords went astray back in the cases of **Lawrence** concerning consent and in **Morris**, in deciding that the words 'any assumption by a person of the rights of an owner' also includes the assumption of just one of those rights. He argues that the decision in **Hinks** is against common sense because it allows a person to be convicted of stealing something that is his already and also creates a conflict with

civil law principles. He strongly asserts that the criminal courts should take the law ' – all of it – as they find it'.

- Other academics also condemn the decision, including Professor Glanville Williams. Simester & Sullivan in *Criminal Law Theory and Doctrine* state forcefully that '**Hinks** must be undone . . . This decision is both impossible and absurd'.

It appears that we have not heard the last on the subject of appropriation!

Activity

Read the preceding information on appropriation and decide whether the judgments of the House of Lords in **Lawrence**, **Gomez** and **Hinks** have widened liability for theft in an unacceptable way.

Property (s4)

The word 'property' is widely defined in **s4(1)** to include:

> money and all other property, real and personal, including things in action and other intangible property.

It can be seen, therefore, that nearly every type of property may be stolen. The definition includes both real and personal property, although, under **s4(2)**, this is qualified to some extent. This section states that a person cannot steal land, or things forming part of the land, except in the circumstances specified. These include situations where a trustee or personal representative disposes of the land under his control in an unauthorised way, where a person not in possession of the land severs something from it or where a tenant misappropriates fixtures which should have remained attached to the land.

Blood and urine samples can be classed as property, allowing the defendant in **Welsh 1974** to be convicted when he removed the urine sample he had provided for the analysis by the police! Similarly, body parts preserved for scientific examination can also be stolen, as confirmed in **Kelly 1998**.

'Things in action', mentioned in the definition, are known in civil law as choses in action, and consist of intangible property like patents, copyrights, shares, debts and insurance policies. The courts have had to decide how far the term 'things in action and other intangible property' will extend.

In **Oxford v Moss 1978**, an engineering student at Liverpool University acquired the proof of an examination paper, intending to read its contents and then return it.

It was clear that the student had no intention to steal the actual paper, which was obviously the property of the university. The point of law sent by the prosecutors to the Divisional Court to decide upon, therefore, was whether the information contained in the examination paper could amount to property within the meaning of the **Theft Act 1968**. The Court decided that the right to confidential information was not in the category of intangible property laid down in **s4(1)** of the Act. The student, therefore, could not be convicted of theft.

The term 'other intangible property' widens the definition of property to encompass things like quotas allowed for the export of textiles. This enabled the director of a company in **AG of Hong Kong v Chang Nai-Keung 1987** to be convicted of stealing his company's property when, without authorisation, he sold his company's excess quota for a grossly reduced price to another company in which he had an interest.

'Other intangible property' has also been held to include things like gas stored in a container, but, owing to difficulties under the previous law, the dishonest abstraction of electricity has been made a separate offence under **s13 Theft Act 1968**, punishable by a maximum term of imprisonment of five years.

Sections 4(3) and 4(4)

S4(3) and **s4(4)** are easy to understand. They deal with wild flowers, plants and animals. Under **s4(3)** no offence is committed if a person picks mushrooms which are growing wild, or wild flowers, fruit or foliage, provided that this is not done for a commercial purpose. **S4(4)** lays down that a person will not commit theft if he captures a wild animal which has not been tamed or reduced to captivity.

Activity

Decide whether the following people have stolen property. Give clear authority for your answers:

- Anthony took the manuscript of Joanna's new novel and published it under his own name.
- Jane picked a quantity of bluebells from Austen Wood and sold the blooms in her local market.
- Charlotte, a student at Bronte University, discovered the whereabouts of the English examination paper, memorised the questions and returned it to the filing cabinet.
- Anna captured a wild pony on Sewell Moor, tamed it and kept it for her own use.
- William was given notice to quit Hathaway Cottage and, in a fit of temper dismantled and took with him all the fitted bookcases.

Belonging to another (s5)

These words are given a wide meaning under **s5(1)**, which states that:

> property shall be regarded as belonging to any person having possession or control of it, or having in it any proprietary right or interest . . .

S5(1) People in possession or control

It can be seen, therefore, that the property can belong, not only to the actual owners of it, but also to those who are currently in possession of it or have some sort of right over it.

This can mean that it is possible, in certain circumstances, for a person to be convicted of stealing his own property, if others have gained rights over it.

This point is illustrated in the case of **Turner (No 2) 1971**. The defendant put in his car for repairs but then returned after the repairs had been carried out and took away the car from the road in which it had been put without informing the garage owner and without paying for the repairs. His conviction for theft was upheld. Lord Parker stated that:

> This court is quite satisfied that there is no ground whatever for qualifying the words 'possession or control' in any way. It is sufficient if it is found that the person from whom the property is taken, or to use the words of the Act, appropriated, was at the time in fact in possession or control.

In **Meredith 1973**, however, it was decided that the police did not have rights over the defendant's car which had been impounded for causing an obstruction while the owner was at a football match, only the right to enforce the statutory charge. It was therefore decided that the accused had no case to answer in theft when, as in **Turner**, he removed the car, plus a police Krooklok immobilising it, without authority.

S5(1) People with a proprietary interest in the property

When looking at the term 'proprietary interest', it should be noted that the Crown has such an interest in 'treasure', discovered on land. Until the **Treasure Act 1996**, this was known as 'treasure trove'. 'Treasure' now consists of items of predominantly gold or silver, mainly over 300 years old, where the true owner is unknown. In **Hancock 1990**, the defendant had been charged with stealing from the Crown some Celtic silver coins, which he had discovered with the aid of a metal detector and had not disclosed to the authorities.

The Court of Appeal decided that the mere fact that an item may later be classed as treasure would not, at that point in time, be an established proprietary interest. It was therefore necessary for the jury to decide on this point before a conviction for theft could be sustained. The passing of the **Treasure Act 1996** will make it easier to establish this as, unlike the previous law, it is no longer necessary to prove that the find has been deliberately hidden. It has also been made a criminal offence not to report such a find within 14 days.

Waverley Borough Council v Fletcher 1995, a civil case, established that, if an item is not classed as 'treasure', the owner of the land will have a better claim to the article than the finder, provided that the article is attached to the land or found within it. If the find is not attached to the land, the owner will only have a better right if he has exercised some clear form of control over the land and what is on it. In the early civil case of **Bridges v Hawksworth 1851**, the finder of some bank notes on the floor of a shop was held to have a better title than the shopkeeper.

Ss 5(2) and **(3)** deal with situations where the defendant has acquired ownership or control of property, so that, in law, it would normally be taken as belonging to him, but special circumstances exist to prevent him doing as he likes with the property.

S5(2) Trust property

With the vast majority of trusts, there are identifiable beneficiaries and if their interests are adversely affected they can take action under **s5(1)** as being the holders of a proprietary interest. **S5(2)** plugs a possible loophole where there are no ascertainable beneficiaries. It states that where the property in question is the subject of a trust, the property shall be taken as belonging to any of the people who have rights under the trust. Accordingly, if the person is in charge of a charitable trust which, as yet, has no ascertainable beneficiaries, and absconds with the proceeds, action can be taken against him. The property over which he has control would be deemed to belong to another and, provided that the other elements of theft are established, he could be convicted.

S5(3) People holding money for a particular purpose

This section covers situations where a person receives property under the obligation to deal with it or the proceeds of the property in a special way. Once again, the property will be held to 'belong to another' if he does anything unauthorised with it.

An illustration of this is the case of **Davidge v Bennett 1984**, where the defendant was given money by her fellow flat-sharers to pay the communal gas bill. When she spent the money on Christmas presents instead, she was held to be guilty of theft.

The facts were somewhat similar in the case of **Floyd v DPP 1999**, but in this case a third party was taking action against the wrongdoer. The defendant had collected weekly premiums from her colleagues at work, in order to purchase food hampers. She failed to pass all of the money on to the supplier but then tried to correct the deficit by giving the company various cheques. These cheques were dishonoured and the defendant was convicted of theft. The defendant claimed that the cash belonged to her colleagues, not to the hamper company and that no obligation to pay the company existed until all the goods had been delivered. The appeal reached the Divisional Court.

This court decided that, under **s5(3) Theft Act 1968** the defendant was under an obligation to hand over the money collected to Home Farm Hampers.

◀ Comment

It has been suggested that the reasoning in this case was wrong, although arguably, there could have been a conviction using other arguments. The agreement to look after the money for the purchase of the hampers was made between the defendant and her fellow workers, not between Floyd and the company and it was therefore these colleagues who were the victims of theft, not the company. The court could have used the arguments put forward in **Wain 1995**, i.e. that a trust had been created and that Floyd therefore was also under an obligation to the company, as Wain had been to the charity in question. Such an argument, however, was not put forward. In future, there is likely to be less difficulty in such cases because the **Contracts (Rights of Third Parties) Act 1999** now allows a third party to take action when an agreement made between two other parties 'is purported to confer a benefit on that third party'.

There can be other difficulties with this subsection. It was stated in **Hall 1972**, that 'each case turns on its own facts'. One example, where the holder of money must deal with property in a particular way, is where the public puts money into special collecting tins; the collector cannot use the money for his own purposes. Another such example is where a builder is given money specifically to purchase supplies; he, too, cannot use the money advanced for other purposes. Other situations where most laymen would assume that the subsection would apply, do not appear to be covered. In **Hall 1972**, a travel agent took deposits from customers, among them teachers paying a lump sum on behalf of their pupils for air trips to America, and placed the money in the firm's general trading account. The firm subsequently foundered and the flights never materialised. Nor were any of the deposits returned. At first instance, Hall was convicted of theft but the Court of Appeal reluctantly decided that the partner was not, in these circumstances, under an obligation to deal with the customers' money in a particular way. While the defendant was undoubtedly dishonest in his dealings and his conduct held to be 'scandalous', he was not appropriating property belonging to another.

The question appears to turn on whether there is a clearly agreed obligation to deal with the money or proceeds in a particular way. Usually, this will arise where there is a stipulation that the money or proceeds should be kept in a separate fund but, in special circumstances, liability might continue even when permission has been given for the money to be transferred to another fund, as in **Wain 1995**.

The defendant had raised over £2,000 for charity in a 'telethon' organised by Yorkshire Television and paid it into a separate bank account. He made several excuses for not sending it to the television company and was eventually allowed to pay the money into his own account and to send a cheque drawn on that account. The cheque was subsequently dishonoured and Wain was convicted of theft. His appeal against this was rejected. McCowan L J stated:

*It seems to us that by virtue of **s5(3)**, the appellant was plainly under an obligation to retain, if not the actual notes and coins, at least their proceeds, that is to say the money credited in the bank account which he opened for the trust with the actual property. When he took the money credited to that account and moved it over to his own bank account, it was still the proceeds of the notes and coins donated which he proceeded to use for his own purposes, thereby appropriating them . . .*

People generously sponsoring the deeds of others for charity will be heartened to note that the Court of Appeal took the opportunity to disapprove of the earlier case of **Lewis v Lethbridge 1987**. In that case the Divisional Court had decided that a competitor in the London Marathon was not under a specific obligation to account to the charity for the actual sponsorship money or its proceeds; he was merely a debtor who had to account for the amount he had collected.

Similarly in **Klineberg 1998**, although the appeal succeeded in part, the Court of Appeal affirmed that where a party (in this case buying a time-sharing property) is induced to contract on the understanding that his money would be protected by a trusteeship, there was a legal obligation under **s5(3)** to deal with the money in a particular way.

The question of the property being protected by a trusteeship was crucial to the decision in **Re Kumar 1999**. Like **Hall**, mentioned earlier, the case also concerned the proprietor of a travel agency, this time a company called ARG. Unlike **Hall** however, this defendant's conviction was upheld. Kumar was permitted to sell passenger flight tickets on behalf of IATA but as part of the arrangement he agreed a trustee relationship under which, after he had deducted his own 15% commission, he was to transfer the balance by direct debit to IATA. ARG had no credit facility with its own bank so the transfers could only be honoured if there were sufficient funds in ARG's account at the relevant time. The prosecution alleged that the company had continued to trade, knowing that it had debts and therefore could not pay the direct debits due to IATA in the first three months of the year in question. The defendant tried to argue that the trustee relationship had not clearly been defined and that therefore he had the right to treat the money from the ticket sales as his own.

The Divisional Court of Queen's Bench Division refused to accept this. The court decided that

in a simple case of breach of trust, where the full terms of the trust are not to be found in the written document creating it, the obligations of the trustee are not complex. From the time that a trustee holds money on behalf of a beneficiary he is not, without more, entitled to treat the money as his own. For the purposes of the law of theft, it is only necessary to have regard to **s5(3)**. In the case in question, the terms on which the parties dealt were sufficiently expressed to include the requirement to 'deal with the property in a particular way', i.e. by retaining enough money in the bank account to meet the direct debit payments and this had not been done.

S5(4)

This deals with circumstances where a person receives property by mistake. In such a case, he is under an obligation to restore the property to its rightful owner. If he fails to do this, he will be classed as intending to deprive the other of it.

As under **s5(3)**, the obligation imposed on the current owner of the property, in this case to restore the property to another, is felt to be a legal, rather than merely a moral obligation. It might well be argued, therefore, that an overpayment of a gambling win would not be recoverable, as any agreements relating to wagering or gaming are generally unenforceable in law. The court will have to use other means to gain a conviction.

In **Gilks**, the defendant had visited one of Ladbrokes' betting shops and bet on a horse called Fighting Scot. This horse was not placed but, by a strange coincidence, another horse called Fighting Taffy won! By mistake, the defendant was paid out a sum of over £100 as if he had won on this latter horse. He was convicted of theft when he failed to disclose the mistake and, as stated, his appeal against this conviction was dismissed.

The court did however, clarify the boundaries of **s5(4)**. Cairns L J stated:

An alternative ground on which the trial judge held that the money should be regarded as belonging to Ladbrokes was that 'obligation' in s5(4) meant an obligation whether a legal one or not. In the opinion of this court that was an incorrect ruling. In a criminal statute, where a person's criminal liability is made dependant on his having an obligation, it would be quite wrong to construe that word so as to cover a moral or social obligation as distinct from a legal one . . .

S5(4) is often invoked where employees have been overpaid and have failed to return the money. The following point of law came to the attention of the Court of Appeal in **AG's Reference (No 1 of 1983) 1985:**

whether a person who receives an overpayment of a debt due to him . . . by way of a credit to his bank account through the 'direct debit' system . . . and who knowing of that overpayment intentionally fails to repay the amount . . . may be guilty of theft. [The answer was said to be 'yes'.]

In this case, a policewoman had been paid an additional sum of £74.74, had discovered this fact but had failed to inform her employer. The trial judge had ordered an acquittal. The Court of Appeal decided in the *Reference* that, on the wording of **s5(4)**, a person should be found guilty of theft even though he had not touched the money and had merely left it in an account. It would, of course, be a different matter if the employee really believed that he was entitled to the money or was genuinely unaware of the overpayment.

The position in equity regarding mistake

S5(4) applies in law where the ownership of goods has passed to the alleged thief but where he is held, in special circumstances, to be under an obligation to restore the property or risk being convicted of theft. It has been argued that the subsection may be superfluous because the wrongdoer may also be under a fiduciary duty to restore such property to the original owner because that person still retains an equitable interest in it. This is known as the Chase Manhattan principle, after the case of **Chase Manhattan Bank NA v Israel-British Bank (London) Ltd 1981**. In this case, it was decided that the bank in question, which by mistake, had paid over £2 million to a third party, was entitled under equitable principles to have the whole amount restored to it, after the third party had gone into liquidation.

This principle was used in **Shadrokh-Cigari 1988**, another banking case. A mistake had been made whereby a child's account had been credited with the amount of £286,000, instead of a mere £286! The child's guardian had arranged for the child to authorise bank drafts using this money and, when the guardian was arrested, only £21,000 remained.

The Court of Appeal upheld the guardian's conviction for theft, deciding that the bank had retained an equitable interest in the property and that, therefore, the defendant had appropriated property belonging to another under **s5(1)**.

Activity

Decide whether the defendants in the following circumstances have appropriated property 'belonging to another'. Give full legal reasons for your answers:

- Del booked a holiday in the Carribean with Peckham Travel and forwarded a large deposit. The travel agent, Rodney, used Del's money on other ventures and did not arrange the holiday, as promised. The firm then went into liquidation and Rodney was arrested.
- Edina obtained sponsorship money of £5,000 for abseiling down the White Cliffs of Dover. The money was given to help a children's charity but Edina spent it on clothes.

- Patsy put her grandfather clock into the local antique shop for repair and, after the work had been effected, she entered the shop while the owner was unloading his van and removed the clock without his knowledge.
- Ant, a traffic warden, discovered that he had been credited twice with his monthly salary. He decided to keep silent about this.
- Dec was paid an amount of £2,000 because of a mistake made by his local bookmaker. The correct amount should have been £200 but Dec decided to keep the money in the belief that the bookmaker could afford the loss!

7.2.2 The *mens rea* of theft

As stated earlier, the *mens rea* of theft requires that the accused should 'dishonestly' appropriate property 'with the intention of permanently depriving the other of it'. These two terms need to be examined.

Dishonestly (s2)

The drafters of the **Theft Act** preferred to use the word 'dishonestly' to the word 'fraudulently' which was used in the old law on larceny, because it was believed that a jury would find it easier to understand this new word. There is no actual definition of dishonesty under **s2** of the Act and it is the jury that has to decide the matter. What the Act does, instead, is to describe three situations in **s2(1)** where a person is not to be classed as dishonest and two situations in **s1(2)** and **s2(2)** where he would be.

S2(1)(a)

S2(1)(a) states that a person will not be regarded as dishonest if he appropriates property, for himself or a third party, believing that he has a right in law to deprive the other of it. It appears from the case of **Holden 1991**, that it is not necessary for the accused to prove that his belief is a reasonable one, providing that it is genuinely held. The defendant must,

believe, however erroneously, that he has a legal, as opposed to a moral right to the property.

The defendant had been accused of stealing scrap tyres from Kwik-Fit, a previous employer. His defence was that he knew that others had taken the tyres with the permission of a supervisor. On the other hand, the depot manager gave evidence that the taking of the tyres was disciplinary offence, meriting dismissal. The jury was directed that the question to be asked was whether the defendant had a reasonable belief that he had a right to take the tyres.

This was held, on appeal, to be a misdirection. The Court of Appeal held that a person was not dishonest if he had an honest belief that he had a right to take the property. Obviously, however, if the belief is a very unreasonably held one, the jury is less likely to believe that it is an honest one.

S2(1)(b)

Under **s2(1)(b)**, a person will not be considered dishonest if he takes property believing that the other would consent to this course of action if he knew about it. An example would be borrowing a fellow student's law books while that person was away, in the belief that he would approve of this course of action.

S2(1)(c)

The last exception is more controversial. Under **s2(1)(c)** a person will not be dishonest if he appropriates property belonging to another believing that the person to whom it belongs cannot be discovered by taking reasonable steps. This section helps to protect a finder of property from a conviction for theft, who would otherwise satisfy the *actus reus* of theft; this sub-section prevents him having the *mens rea*, provided that he fits the criteria.

In **Small 1988**, the defendant claimed that a car he had appropriated had been abandoned by its owner. It had been left in one place for over a week with the keys in the ignition. The jury obviously did not believe his story but the Court of Appeal decided that his conviction ought to be quashed if he had honestly believed that this was the case.

The sub-section specifically excludes trustees and personal representatives, so they may well be dishonest in the circumstances laid down. It is believed that such people should not become entitled to the property of others in such circumstances because, if the beneficiaries cannot be found, the property would revert to the Crown.

Sections 1(2) and 2(2)

The paragraphs mentioned above provide defences to a charge of theft. Conversely, **s1(2)** decides that a person may still be convicted of theft despite the fact that his appropriation of property is not made with a view to gain, or for his own benefit and **s2(2)** states that he may still be classed as dishonest even if he is willing to pay for the property.

It will still be theft, therefore, for a Robin Hood type figure to steal from the rich and give to the poor. It is also theft if property is merely removed for spite and is just destroyed or thrown away.

The basic test for dishonesty

This has changed over the years. There were differing opinions as to whether the test for dishonesty ought to be decided in an objective way or according to the defendant's own belief, i.e. subjectively. In **McIvor 1982**, the Court of Appeal sought to reconcile these differences, deciding, rather strangely, that a subjective approach should be taken where the charge was conspiracy to defraud, but that the question of dishonesty in theft should be decided objectively. A little later, in the case of

Ghosh 1982, the Court of Appeal re-thought the matter and rejected this distinction. Currently, therefore, the same test is to be used for both these offences and for the crime of obtaining property by deception, contrary to **s15 Theft Act 1968**. The test, however, has been altered and is now a mixture of an objective and subjective approach. The rather complicated twofold test asks the jury to decide upon the following matters:

- whether according to the ordinary standards of reasonable and honest people what was done was dishonest. If the jury decides that it was not, that is the end of the matter.
- If, however, the jurors decide that it was dishonest, they should then consider whether the defendant himself realised that what he was doing was by those standards dishonest.

The accused can only be convicted if the answer to both questions is 'yes', but in **Price 1989** Lord Lane stated that there was no requirement for the judge to give the **Ghosh** direction in the vast majority of cases. It was only necessary in cases where the defendant appeared to believe that his actions were not dishonest but there was some doubt about whether he really thought that others would share this view.

For example, the test would be applicable where the defendant was accused of stealing from the rich to give to the poor and argued that he honestly believed that ordinary reasonable people would not think he was doing wrong. In such a case, using the **Ghosh** test, he could not be said to be acting dishonestly.

If, however, the accused merely liked to think of himself as a latter-day Robin Hood but knew that others would think that he was acting wrongly, he would be considered dishonest.

Comment

The **Ghosh** test is not an easy one for juries, and indeed students, to understand. It has been subjected to a great deal of criticism, with some opponents of it calling, instead, for a statutory definition of dishonesty. In the earlier Australian case of **Salvo 1980**, the judge felt that it was not always the case that a citizen 'knows dishonesty if he sees it', and that further help was needed in some cases. At present, however, **Ghosh** does represent the law on the subject until there is an intervention by either the House of Lords or Parliament.

With the intention of permanently depriving the other of it (s6)

Edmund Davies L J in **Warner 1970** made it clear that, as with the word 'dishonestly', there is no definition of the phrase 'intention of permanently depriving the other of it' in the **Theft Act 1968**. The Criminal Law Revision Committee had believed that the term required no further explanation but made it clear that mere borrowing, even dishonest borrowing, was not normally meant to be included. **S6**, however, was added later and, while said by J R Spencer in the *Criminal Law Review* in 1977 to sprout 'obscurities at every phrase', gives extra illustrations of where such an intention to permanently deprive can be assumed even when it is argued that there is no such intention. Summarising these instances, **s6(1)** provides that a person will be taken as permanently depriving the other of property if he intends to treat the property as his own to dispose of regardless of the real owner's rights and states that this may sometimes occur even in cases where the offender is claiming that he has only borrowed the goods.

The full, rather obscure wording of **s6(1)** is as follows:

A person appropriating property belonging to another without meaning the other permanently to lose the thing itself is nevertheless to be regarded as having the intention of permanently depriving the other of it if his intention is to treat the thing as his own to dispose of regardless of the other's rights; and a borrowing or lending of it may amount to so treating it if, but only if, the borrowing or lending is for a period and in circumstances making it equivalent to an outright taking or disposal.

Borrowings

This would cover situations where a person borrows property without intending to return it or takes the property of another intending to sell or otherwise dispose of it. In **Downes 1983**, the Court of Appeal upheld a conviction for theft when the defendant sold some tax vouchers, made out to him but belonging to the Inland Revenue, to others so that they could obtain tax advantages. The same court also refused to quash the conviction in **Velumyl 1989**. The defendant took over £1,000 from his employer's safe in breach of company rules and was convicted of theft. He was unsuccessful in his allegation that he had not committed the crime of theft because he had intended to repay the money after the weekend break and, therefore, had no intention permanently to deprive the employer of his property. The Court of Appeal showed scant sympathy for this argument and upheld the conviction on the grounds that he could not have intended to pay back the exact notes and coins he had taken.

In the earlier case of **Lloyd, Bhuee and Ali 1985**, the defendants had been luckier. Lloyd was chief projectionist at the Odeon Cinema in Barking and over a period of months had temporarily removed films from the cinema in order that his accomplices could take illegal copies of them and sell the pirate videos at a substantial profit. The films were only taken for a few hours and then returned but the defendants had been caught red-handed while making a copy. It had to be decided whether the defendants had committed the offence of theft. The Court of Appeal decided that there were circumstances where there could be an intention to permanently deprive even though the goods were actually returned, but stated that this would be in cases where the value of the item stolen was affected. Here, it was decided that 'the goodness, the virtue, the practical value of the films to the owners has not gone out of the article . . . The borrowing, it seems to us, was not for a period, or in such circumstances, as to make it equivalent to an outright taking or disposal'.

In **Bagshaw 1988**, the defendant's conviction had to be quashed because these matters had not been properly explained to the jury. Bagshaw had been charged with the theft of some glass cylinders but alleged that he had only borrowed them. The trial judge had failed to explain to the jury that he could only be convicted in such a case if he had intended to keep the cylinders until all the 'goodness' in them had been utilised. His appeal against his conviction on the grounds of this misdirection was therefore upheld.

From these decisions it can be seen that a person would be permanently depriving the other of property if he took an article like a season ticket, used it until it had expired and then returned it. The value (or goodness or virtue) in the article would have been removed. A person would also be held to be permanently depriving the other if he took the property and then put conditions on its return. Here, it may be safely assumed that if the conditions were not met, the property would not go back to the rightful owner. Lord Lane has quoted the example of an offender taking a valuable painting and refusing to return it until a large sum of money had been paid.

An examination of the cases shows that people steal the oddest things. In **DPP v Lavender 1994**, the alleged theft concerned two doors! The defendant had removed these from property being renovated by the local council and used them to replace two damaged doors in his girlfriend's residence. Despite the

difficulties caused by the fact that this property, too, was owned by the local authority, the defendant was classed by the Divisional Court as treating the doors as his own to dispose of and this, it was felt, was enough. This appears to widen the law and sits uneasily with the view of the Court of Appeal in **Cahill 1993**, that there had to be more than a mere intention to use the thing as one's own because of the inclusion of the words 'to dispose of'. Hopefully, there will be a further discussion of this issue in the future.

Unsuccessful thefts

A last point regarding **s6(1)** which needs examination is whether an offender can be classed as permanently depriving the other of goods, and so be guilty of attempted theft, when he is trying to assess whether there is anything worth stealing. An example would be where he breaks into a car in order to see if it contains a radio or, as in **Easom 1971**, rifles through a handbag to see if the contents are worth stealing and then returns it when nothing of value is found. In this case, the handbag had been attached, by a string, to the wrist of a policewoman and, despite the fact that the bag had been returned to her, the defendant was convicted of the theft of the bag and its contents. The Court of Appeal quashed the conviction stating that 'a conditional appropriation will not do' and this view of the law was upheld in **Husseyn 1977**, where the article in question was a holdall containing valuable sub-aqua equipment. In **AG's References (Nos 1 and 2 of 1979) 1980**, however, the Court of Appeal decided that this would only be a problem in cases where the indictment specifically mentioned a particular article. In other cases, there could be a conviction for theft.

S6(2) states that person may be regarded as treating the property of another as his own in cases where he parts with possession of it 'under a condition as to its return which he may not be able to perform'. An example would be where he pawned the goods in question, knowing that it might not be possible to redeem them.

TEN KEY FACTS ON THEFT

- The law on theft is to be found in **ss1–7 Theft Act 1968**. The full definition of theft is laid down in **s1**, which states that a person is guilty of theft if 'he dishonestly appropriates property belonging to another with the intention of permanently depriving the other of it'. **Ss2–6** give further detail of the words in the definition and **s7** lays down the maximum punishment of seven years.

- The *mens rea* of theft is appropriating property 'dishonestly', as seen in **s2** and with 'the intention to permanently deprive the other of it' (**s6**).

- There is no definition in the Act of what is meant by the word 'dishonesty' and it will be up to the jury to decide this. Normally no direction on this will be needed (**Price 1989**), but in cases where the defendant is disputing the claim of dishonesty, the **Ghosh** direction should be given. This states that the jury should first decide whether according to the standards of reasonable and honest people what was done was dishonest and, if so, whether the defendant realised this (**Ghosh 1982**).

- **S1(2)** and **s2(2)** give two examples where the defendant will still be acting dishonestly. The first will arise when he argues that he has not appropriated the goods for gain or for his own benefit and the second when he alleges that he intended to pay for the property. On the other hand, **s2(1)** lays down three special circumstances where a person will not be classed as dishonest. The first is where he believes that he has a right in law to the goods, even if this belief is not reasonably held, as in **Holden 1991**. The second instance is where he believes that the victim would have consented to the taking and the third is where he believes that the real owner cannot be discovered by the taking of reasonable steps to do this.

- There is no clear definition of the phrase 'intending to permanently deprive the other of the property' (**Warner 1970**), but **s6** states that this will occur when the defendant treats the property as his own to dispose of. **S6** also describes situations where this state of mind will be presumed, as noted in cases like **Downes 1983, Velumyl 1989** and **Lavender 1994**. If the accused uses the property of another but then returns it, he will only be permanently depriving the other of it if the value in the property has been used up (**Lloyd 1985, Bagshaw 1988**). Conversely, provided that the indictment is correctly worded, the defendant can be found guilty of attempted theft where he searches property to see if there is anything worth stealing and then discards the item, as noted in **AG's References Nos 1 & 2 of 1979**.

- The *actus reus* of theft arises where the defendant 'appropriates property belonging to another'. Explanations and further detail on these terms are found in **ss3, 4 and 5.**

- The word 'appropriates' means to assume the rights of the owner (**s3**). The House of Lords decided in **Morris 1984** that the definition will be satisfied if just one of the rights of the owner is assumed. This court also decided in **Gomez 1993** that such an appropriation takes place the first time any of the rights of the owner are assumed.

- The cases of **Lawrence 1972, Gomez 1993** and **Hinks 2000**, all House of Lords' decisions, have firmly established that there can be an appropriation of property even though the victim appears to be consenting to the taking. **Gomez** also established that there is no necessity for an actual taking to establish the *actus reus*, although it was recognised that it might then be more difficult to prove the *mens rea*. The Court of Appeal decision in **Gallasso 1993** appears to be wrongly decided. In **Hinks 2000**, the House of Lords decided that the word 'appropriation' was not to be too narrowly construed. On a three-to-two majority, their Lordships decided that there could even be an appropriation of property belonging to another in a case where the defendant had acquired an indefeasible title to the property in question, if such a gift had come from a vulnerable and trusting person and the evidence of wrongdoing appeared strong.

- The word 'property' is widely defined in **s4** to include most types of tangible and intangible property. It does not however include confidential information, if the papers on which this is contained are returned (**Oxford v Moss 1978**), nor land, unless something is severed from it, a trust is involved or a fixture removed from it. Wild animals, fungi, fruit, flowers and foliage also cannot be stolen unless taken for profit but 'treasure' belongs to the Crown. Other finds belong to the owner of the land, if attached to it or under the owner's control, but to the finder in other cases.

- The property stolen must, under **s5**, belong to another but it can be taken as belonging to another if that other has temporary possession or control of it, as in **Turner No 2 1971** or where it is given to the defendant to deal with in a particular way (**s5(3), Davidge v Bennett 1984, Wain 1995, Floyd v DPP 1999** and **Re Kumar 1999**). No such obligation was found in **Hall 1973**. Under **s5(4)**, the defendant will be liable if he obtains property by mistake and fails to return it when there is a legal obligation for him to do so (**AG's Reference No 1 of 1983**). He may also be liable to restore the property where the other party has an equitable interest in the goods and the **Chase Manhattan** principle is invoked, as in **Shadrokh-Cigari 1988**.

In conclusion, it can be seen that the law of theft has grown quite complex, mainly because of the uncertainty generated by changing decisions on the interpretation of various words and phrases making up the definition of theft in **s1** and the explanations provided in **ss2–6**. It is very important, therefore, to know these sections well and to be fully conversant with the latest case law on the subject.

Activity

Decide whether Dennis has the *mens rea* for theft in the following situations. Quote section numbers and supporting cases where relevant:

- He removed several mattresses from a large furniture store without paying for them, in order to distribute them to people 'sleeping rough' in London doorways.
- He borrowed a book from the library and gave it to his cousin for a Christmas present.
- He saw a bicycle resting against the railings in the town centre, which was identical to the one he had lost in that same place the previous week, and took it home. In fact, the bicycle belonged to the local postman.
- He found a gold watch in the railway station. He took it to the lost property office but, finding this closed, decided to keep it.
- He was suddenly invited to a 'black tie' event at a local hotel, so decided to wear a dinner jacket belonging to his absent flatmate. The friends often 'swapped' clothes. Would your answer be different if Dennis had taken £30 from the till of his employer in order to pay for the hire of such a jacket, with the intention of returning the money after the weekend?
- On the dance floor at the hotel, he found two expensive tickets for the musical 'Miss Peking' and pocketed them. He took his girlfriend to see the show a few days later and later returned the ticket stubs to the hotel.

Now that the elements making up the offence of theft are known, it is appropriate to look at certain other offences, not involving deception, for which most examination boards require knowledge and which are also to be found in the **Theft Act 1968**. These are robbery, burglary, aggravated burglary and blackmail.

7.3 Robbery

S8 Theft Act 1968 defines this. It states:

A person is guilty of robbery if he steals and immediately before or at the time of doing so and in order to do so, he uses force on any person or seeks to put them in fear of being then and there subjected to force.

S8(2) Theft Act 1968 provides that the maximum sentence is life imprisonment.

Under **s2** of the controversial **Crime (Sentences) Act 1997** (the provisions of which are now in the **Powers of the Criminal Courts Act 2000)**, a second serious offence of robbery could attract an automatic life sentence. There is a possible defence against such an imposition in exceptional circumstances. This is generating many appeals such as the one in **Williams 2000**, where the defendant told a shop assistant that he had a gun and demanded a bottle of whisky. In reality, the carrier bag only contained another bottle. The defendant had numerous convictions, mainly caused by a drink problem, including a previous one of carrying an imitation firearm with intent. He was therefore given a life sentence, despite the fact that he had not actually been violent in either case. He appealed on the grounds of exceptional circumstances but was unsuccessful.

The Court of Appeal decided, that it was not sufficient merely to establish that exceptional circumstances existed. The court must also be satisfied that the offender no longer posed a danger to the public and this was not held to

'Perfect mum' terrified cashier in office raid

Playgroup leader was desperate for money, reports **Thomas Penny**

A PLAYGROUP leader and chorister who made a living as a romantic novelist has been convicted of robbery after her picture as "the perfect mum" appeared in a national newspaper.

A court heard that 36-year-old Mary Dalton, who helped with the local toy library and had a reputation as a devoted mother, stole hundreds of pounds after telling a terrified cashier she had an armed accomplice outside.

The mother of two, who looked the picture of respectability as she attended court carrying a wicker basket, made off with more than £1,500 from the office of a financial adviser in a raid in October last year. But when she tried to rob the same office again two months later she was refused the money and fled empty-handed.

She went back home and continued her respectable life running the village playgroup, singing in the church choir, taking her two daughters to school and mingling with other mothers.

A few weeks after the failed raid she disappeared and, because it was so out of character for the devoted mother to desert her children, an appeal for information was issued through national newspapers.

A *Daily Mail* story, with photographs, said that the "perfect mum" had mysteriously vanished. Her family, including her father, a retired Oxford University music lecturer, made an anguished plea for her to contact them.

Police were amazed when they received a call from cashier Rosa Bullion in January saying that she recognised the missing single mother as the woman who had robbed her.

Eloise Marshall, prosecuting, told Reading Crown Court on Thursday that in the first raid on the financial advice centre in Caversham, Reading, Dalton disguised herself with "Jackie Onassis-style" sunglasses and handed Mrs Bullion a note saying she was carrying out a robbery, to remain calm and to fill a shopping bag with cash.

The note added that an accomplice was waiting outside with a gun, so the cashier followed her instructions. Two months later, on Dec 22, when Dalton, from Wheatley, Oxon, walked into the same firm, Mrs Bullion recognised her and refused to hand over any cash.

Dalton fled empty-handed after saying, "Please, I'm desperate", but without making any further threats.

The court heard that a navy blue suit found at Dalton's home was the one she wore on the first robbery and the coat she wore to court was the one she had worn on the second attempt.

Three days after the successful robbery, Dalton deposited £803 into her bank account, including £18 in £1 coins.

Miss Marshall told the court that Dalton was "a robber in an Alice band, not your typical robber".

She added: "The newspaper article portrayed her as a perfect mother who, to all intents and purposes, was a typical middle-class member of the community. You may be confused as to how it is that someone like Mary Dalton committed a robbery."

She said Dalton carried out the robbery because banks were concerned about her overdraft and she had taken out a loan for the deposit and rent on her new home.

Dalton told the jury the money she deposited in her account had come from the sale of jewellery she had inherited from her grandmother.

She also said that she did not have money worries and had taken out the loan only to tide her over until her housing benefit cheque arrived in January.

After she went missing, police found her in Wiltshire. She said she could not remember what had happened to her since she left home.

The court heard that she was placed in a psychiatric hospital for three weeks and assessed to have had a black-out triggered by stress.

Dalton, now living in Bath, denied robbery and attempted theft but was found guilty of both charges.

The case was adjourned for sentence until Jan 19. Dalton was released on bail.

Daily Telegraph, 16th December 2000

be the case here. The life sentence therefore was upheld. Professor Sir John Smith calls the decision 'yet another illustration of the bizarre workings of the **Crime (Sentences) Act**'.

It can be seen by the definition that robbery is aggravated theft so it is very important to realise that, firstly, theft, with all the elements discussed earlier in this chapter, must be established. There must, therefore, be a dishonest appropriation of property belonging to another with the intention to permanently deprive the other of it. In addition, the theft must be accompanied by the use of force or the threat that immediate force may be used.

Cases on robbery

The elements of theft were not established in the case of **Robinson 1977**. The defendant ran a clothing club and was owed money by the victim's wife. A fight took place and in the course of this a £5 note fell from the victim's pocket which the defendant appropriated. He further claimed that he was still owed £2.

The Court of Appeal quashed the conviction for robbery. The defendant had an honest belief that he was entitled to the money so could not be held to have stolen it. He could, of course, have been charged with other crimes, such as actual bodily harm but should not have been convicted of burglary.

The additional elements required before a robbery is committed would also not be made out in cases where the force is used first and the wrongdoer then goes on to steal. This could occur, for example, where the offender attacked another who made derogatory comments about him and when his victim was lying unconscious, stole his wallet. It would also not be robbery where a theft took place and violence was used when the getaway was prevented. In these situations, the force is not being used or threatened 'in order to' steal and is not taking place 'before or at the time of' the theft. The courts, however, take a pragmatic approach to these words and have decided that a theft can be a continuing affair, as in **Hale 1978**.

The defendant and an accomplice, wearing stocking masks, forced their way into the victim's house, put a hand over her mouth to stop her screaming and later tied her up. Meanwhile, the accomplice had stolen a jewellery box from the rooms upstairs. They were later convicted of robbery but appealed, arguing that the theft was over when the force took place. The court refused to accept this claiming that 'the act of appropriation does not suddenly cease. It is a continuous act and it is a matter for the jury to decide whether or not the act of appropriation has finished'.

The court was also prepared, in the alternative, to accept that the act of putting a hand over the victim's mouth was also using force and this, too was done to facilitate the theft.

The Criminal Law Revision Committee, when devising this section, made it clear that there had to be more than a mere snatching of property from an unresisting owner before it could be held to be a robbery. The courts, however, have decided that it is enough that there is some resistance to the taking. In **Clouden 1987**, for example, the defendant's conviction for robbery was upheld when he used both hands to wrench a shopping bag from the victim and ran off with it. In the earlier case of **Dawson 1976**, jostling the victim was also held to be enough force. Lawton L J stated that 'Force is a word in ordinary use. It is a word which juries understand'. He decided, therefore, that the jurors 'were entitled to the view that force was used'. In **Corcoran v Anderton 1980**, it was held to be immaterial that the robbery had not been effected. This case concerned another bag-snatching attempt, of the type that has become so commonplace in recent times. The attack had been planned and the victim was pushed from behind and her handbag snatched from her. She then screamed and fell and the two youths ran away without taking the bag. The Divisional Court was asked to decide whether 'the tugging at the handbag, accompanied by force, amounted to robbery, notwithstanding the fact that the co-accused did not have sole control of the bag at any time'.

The Divisional Court decided that 'there cannot possibly be, save for the instance where a handbag is carried away from the scene . . . a clearer instance of robbery than that which these justices found was committed.' They held that the forcible tugging of the handbag was a sufficient exercise of control by the accused.

Activity

Grant has borne a grudge against members of the acting profession ever since he was rejected for a part in a popular soap opera. Decide whether he has committed robbery in the following instances:

- He visited a film premiere and, as Peggy was going into the cinema, pulled one of her diamond earrings from her ear.
- He had a fight with Beppe and knocked him out. While Beppe was on the floor, Grant decided to steal his Rolex watch.
- He forced his way into Sharon's house and stole the contents of her safe. He then tied her to a chair and made his escape.
- He wrestled with Pat as the latter was leaving a film set and snatched her camera. Pat then started to fight back so Grant dropped the camera and ran away.

7.4 Burglary

S9 Theft Act 1968 lays down a rather complicated definition of burglary. To summarise this, **s9(1)(a)** states that:

Burglary is committed where the defendant enters a building or part of one as a trespasser, with the intent to steal, to inflict grievous bodily harm or to rape therein or to do unlawful damage to the building or anything inside it.

S9(1)(b) provides that it is also committed when a person steals or inflicts grievous bodily harm on another, after he has entered as a trespasser, or attempts to do either of these things.

The maximum sentence for this offence is laid down in **s9(3)** and is 14 years' imprisonment.

It can be seen that one difference between these two sections is that, in subsection (a), the offender must intend to steal or commit the other offences laid down at the time he trespasses, but in subsection (b) the intent to steal can be formed after the trespass. Another difference is that the offence under **s9(1)(b)** only applies to theft and grievous bodily harm, but, unlike **s9(1)(a)**, also includes attempts to do either of these things.

The words 'entry', 'trespasser' and 'building' have caused problems and need looking at further.

Entry

The first point to note is that the entry must have been effective. In earlier cases it was decided that the entry had to be both substantial and effective, as held in **Collins 1973** but this is no longer necessary, as the cases of **Brown 1985** and **Ryan 1996** illustrate.

Collins is a case known to nearly every law student because of its peculiar facts.

The defendant, who was 19, had seen the girl in question when he worked near her house and after drinking a considerable amount had decided to visit the premises. He saw a light in her bedroom and fetched a ladder to reach the room. He then saw the girl naked and asleep in a bed very near the window. He descended the ladder, took off all his clothes except his socks, and then re-climbed the ladder and reached the window sill. He alleged that as he was pulling himself into the room the girl awoke. She got up, knelt by the bed, embraced him and appeared to pull him towards it. They then had sexual intercourse.

The girl argued that she had awoken at about 3.30am and seen a vague form with blond hair in the open window. She was unable to say categorically whether the person was on the outside part of the window sill or actually inside of the room. She firmly believed at that point that her boyfriend had come to make a nocturnal visit but later, during the intercourse, started to have doubts about this! She then turned on the light, discovered that her fears

were justified and slapped the defendant's face. When she visited the bathroom, the defendant made his escape.

Collins was later convicted of burglary. The girl, not unnaturally, argued that she would not have agreed to the intercourse if she had known that the man in question was not her boyfriend. The defendant, on the other hand, claimed that he would not have entered the room if the girl had not beckoned him in. Despite this contention, he was convicted. He later appealed on the basis that he had not entered as a trespasser.

The Court of Appeal decided that, in a case such as this, three ingredients to the offence of burglary had to be proved. Firstly, there had to be an entry into the building. This point was soon proved. Secondly, the defendant needed to have entered as a trespasser, which was far more difficult to decide upon. Lastly, he had to have intended, at the time of entry, to commit rape.

The Court of Appeal decided that the judge had misdirected the jury on both of these points, particularly the second one. The court stated that 'Unless the jury were entirely satisfied that the appellant made an effective and substantial entry into the bedroom without the complainant doing or saying anything to cause him to believe that she was consenting to his entering it, he ought not to be convicted of the offence charged. The point is a narrow one, as narrow maybe as the window sill which is crucial to this case. But this is a criminal charge of gravity and, even though one may suspect that his intention was to commit the offence charged, unless the facts show with clarity that he in fact committed it he ought not to remain convicted'. The conviction, therefore, was quashed.

The fact that there must be a substantial and effective entry followed the earlier common law position but has since been disputed. In **Brown 1985**, the Court of Appeal upheld a conviction for burglary even though the defendant argued that his entry was ineffective because a major part of his body was still on the highway. He had been caught while leaning through a broken shop window and sorting through the goods. In **Ryan 1996**, the Court of Appeal went even further and refused to entertain the idea that there could not be an effective entry because the wrongdoer had got stuck trying to effect one! The defendant had got himself into this unfortunate position by trying to climb through a small window of a residential property in the dead of night. Eventually, the fire brigade had rescued him. At his trial, Ryan tried to argue that he was only attempting to recover his baseball hat, which his friend had thrown through the window. The jury refused to believe such a story and the Court of Appeal upheld his conviction for burglary, despite the fact that he was unable to go any further in his efforts to gain entry.

Now that's what I call an effective entry.

Trespasser

It is now necessary to examine the word 'trespasser'. Usually, it will be easy to show that the wrongdoer is trespassing but occasionally there are problems, as, for example, when the defendant claims that he has a right to be there. This was the case in **Jones and Smith 1976**. The defendants removed two television sets from the home of Smith's father during the night and were convicted of burglary. At the trial, however, the father had tried to protect his son by arguing that he was not a trespasser because he had unreserved permission to enter the house. The Court of Appeal was not prepared to accept this and decided that the word 'trespasser' also covered cases where a person acts in excess of the permission given. The court quoted with approval the civil case of **Hillen and Pettigrew v ICI 1936**, and particularly the comment that 'When you invite a person into your house to use the staircase you do not invite him to slide down the banisters.' The appeals, therefore, were dismissed. The court made it clear that a person is a trespasser if he enters premises of another knowing that he is entering in excess of the permission that has been given to him, or being reckless as to this fact.

Building

Lastly, the word 'building' needs investigation. There is no definition of this word in the Act but **s9(4)** states that the word includes an inhabited vehicle and a vessel, even if they are not inhabited at the time of the offence. In the early civil case of **Stevens v Gourley 1859** it was suggested that a building was 'a structure of considerable size and intended to be permanent, or at least endure for a considerable time'. In **B and S v Leathley 1979**, there appeared to be an extension of this definition because a locked freezer container, resting on sleepers and connected to the main electricity supply, was held to be a building. In **Norfolk Constabulary v Seekings and Gould 1986**, however, the courts were not prepared to widen the definition to include two lorry trailers; these remained as mere vehicles.

Burglary will also be committed where the trespasser enters 'any building or part of a building'. This point was at issue in the case of **Walkington 1979.** The defendant went up to the first floor in Debenham's department store, went behind one of the moveable counters and looked into the open drawer of the till. He discovered that it was empty, slammed it shut and tried to leave the store. He was arrested and later convicted of burglary. The Court of Appeal quoted from Professor Smith's book, *The Law of Theft*, in which it is stated:

> A licence to enter a building may extend to part of a building only. If so, the licensee will trespass if he enters some other part.

If the offender then intends to commit a crime in that other part, he will be guilty of burglary. The Court of Appeal also decided that such a person still commits the offence even if he only intends to steal on the condition he finds something worth stealing.

7.4.1 The *mens rea* of burglary

The offender must know that he is a trespasser or be reckless as regards this fact and then must have the intention to commit the ulterior offence.

7.5 Aggravated burglary

S10 Theft Act 1968 states that:

> A person will be guilty of aggravated burglary if he commits any burglary and at the time has with him any firearm or imitation firearm, any weapon of offence, or any explosive.

S10(2) states that the term 'firearm' also includes airguns and air pistols and 'imitation firearm' means 'anything which has the appearance of being a firearm, whether

capable of being discharged or not'. This obviously brings a wide range of real and imitation guns within the definition. The term 'weapon of offence' has caused some problems. It is defined as 'any article made or adapted for use for causing injury to or incapacitating a person or intended by the person having it with him for such use'.

It can be seen from these sections that the aggravated offence is established if the defendant possesses any of these articles at the time of the offence; he does not have to use them or even intend to do so. In **Stones 1989**, the defendant had a household knife in his possession but claimed that this was merely for self-defence because 'some lads from Blyth' were after him. The prosecution admitted that this was not an article 'made or adapted for use', etc. but decided that the person intended to use it for the causing of injury or to incapacitate someone. The Court of Appeal upheld the conviction on the grounds that it was not necessary to prove that the defendant intended to use the article in the burglary; it was enough that he had the article with him and intended to use it in any way.

In the earlier case of **O'Leary 1986**, the defendant had not been armed when he entered the house but took a knife from the kitchen upstairs with him. His conviction under **s10** was upheld as he had the weapon with him when he made the decision to steal.

7.6 Blackmail (Post-A Level only)

The crime of blackmail is now found under **s21 Theft Act**, which states that a person will be guilty of blackmail if:

> with a view to gain for himself or another or with intent to cause loss to another, he makes an unwarranted demand with menaces.

Gain and loss

The first thing to note is that, under **s34 Theft Act**, the words 'gain' and 'loss' only apply to gains or losses in money or other property, although this is normally what will be demanded. The words 'with a view to gain for himself' mean, however, that it would also be blackmail if the defendant demanded a superior job or better housing, if such a demand was unwarranted and was made with menaces, because extra money would be involved or better property.

In **Bevans 1987**, a man crippled with osteo-arthritis produced a gun and demanded a morphine injection from a doctor he had summoned. He threatened to shoot the doctor if he did not comply. The court decided that the morphine came under the heading of 'property' and his conviction for blackmail was upheld.

It would not, however, be blackmail if services were demanded with menaces. An example would be where sexual favours were demanded, accompanied by a threat to expose some unsavoury conduct of the victim should the service not be performed. In a case like this, there would be no gain or loss of money or other property.

Unwarranted

Next, to satisfy the definition, the demand must be 'unwarranted'. The Criminal Law Revision Committee held that two of the essential features of blackmail are that the defendant is demanding something to which he knows he has no right and, secondly, that he knows that the use of menaces is wrong. The approach, therefore, is subjective; it is not what the reasonable man believes but, instead, the defendant himself must know that he is not entitled to the property demanded or at least have knowledge that it is wrong to demand it in this way.

In **Harvey 1980**, the defendants tried to argue that they had a right to act as they did but the jury obviously did not agree and they were convicted. They had arranged to pay £20,000 to a person called Scott, in return for a large supply of cannabis. Scott supplied worthless goods and the enraged defendants then kidnapped his wife and child and demanded the repayment of their money. They were convicted of blackmail along with other offences but appealed.

The Court of Appeal acknowledged that the trial judge had failed to make it clear to the jurors that it was up to them to decide whether the defendants genuinely believed that they had reasonable grounds for making the demand. It was decided, however, that this misdirection would not have prejudiced the defendants. The appeal, therefore, was dismissed.

Demand

It is now necessary to look at the word 'demand'. This is the essence of the offence. The crime of blackmail will still exist even in cases where the defendant fails to receive what has been asked for, provided that a clear demand has been made. The courts have also decided that the demand can be implied from the circumstances, as well as being made in a more express way. In **Collister and Warhurst 1955**, the defendant was intended to overhear the comments of two police officers, suggesting that the charges might be dropped if a payment was made by the accused. This was held to constitute a demand. It also appears from the case of **Treacy v DPP 1971**, that, if the demand is made by post, it takes effect as soon as the letter is posted and it is immaterial whether the letter actually reaches the proposed victim.

Menaces

The word 'menaces' used only to cover threats of violence but has since widened. In **Thorne v Motor Trade Association 1937**, it was said to be 'an ordinary English word which any jury can be expected to understand'. In the same case it was held to include 'threats of action detrimental to or unpleasant to the person addressed'. The threat 'Unless you pay me within seven days . . . you will have to look over your shoulder before you step out of doors', had been made by roof repairer who had not been paid because the work was thought by the householder to be sub-standard. Later, other threatening words had been uttered and the defendant's conviction for blackmail was upheld.

In **Clear 1968**, the word was narrowed slightly when it was held that the menaces should be:

of such a nature and extent that the mind of an ordinary person of normal stability and courage might be influenced or made apprehensive.

There will be some cases, therefore, where the demand is not considered to be in this category. This view was taken in the case of **Harry 1974**, where a treasurer of a college rag committee sent letters to over 100 shopkeepers asking them to buy posters for charity. The poster was stated to protect the shopkeeper 'from any Rag Activity which could in any way cause you inconvenience'. A few of the people to whom the letter was addressed felt unhappy with the tone of the latter and, later, the prosecution agreed that it contained 'the clearest threat or menace however nicely it was couched'. Judge Petre of Chelmsford Crown Court (perhaps remembering his own student days!), did not agree. He stated 'Menaces is a strong word' and directed the jury to acquit.

TEN KEY FACTS ON ROBBERY, BURGLARY AND BLACKMAIL

- The crime of robbery is defined in **s8 Theft Act 1968**; the maximum sentence is life imprisonment **(s8(2))**. The elements of the crime of theft must first be established **(Robinson 1977)**. It then has to be proved that the defendant used force, or threatened to use it, immediately before or at the time of the crime, although the courts have been prepared to find that a robbery can be a protracted affair **(Hale 1978)**.

- A simple snatching of property would be theft rather than robbery but the latter may be established if the victim resists the attack **(Clouden 1987)** and maybe even where the victim has merely been jostled **(Dawson 1976)**. There is no requirement that the goods have to be taken **(Corcoran v Anderton 1980)**.

- Burglary is defined in **s9 Theft Act 1968** and can be committed in one of two ways. Both require a trespass by the defendant. Most trespasses will be obvious but a person will also be a trespasser if he acts in excess of any permission given to him **(Jones and Smith 1971)**. Under **s9(1)(a)** burglary is committed where the defendant enters a building or part of one intending to steal, to inflict grievous bodily harm (gbh), to rape or to cause criminal damage. It will also be burglary where the defendant steals or inflicts gbh after having entered as a trespasser **(s9(1)(b))**.

- The entry must be considered to be an effective one but the courts now take a broader view of this. There is no longer a requirement that the entry should be substantial **(Collins 1973, Brown 1985** and **Ryan 1996)**.

- A building is not defined in the Act but will include a vehicle or vessel which is inhabited. The courts have also included a freezer container with mains electricity attached in this category (**B and S v Leathley 1979**) but were not prepared to recognize two stationary lorry containers as such (**Norfolk Constabulary v Seekings and Gould 1986**).

- A person will become a trespasser if he enters a prohibited part of a building and commits one of the prescribed crimes there (**Walkington 1979**).

- Aggravated burglary is defined in **s10** and takes place where the burglar has a real or imitation firearm, other weapon or explosive with him at the time he commits the offence. He does not have to bring the weapon with him so long as he has it at the time of the crime (**O'Leary 1986**). The term 'other weapon' includes things made or adapted to cause injury or incapacitation (**s10(2)**) and it is immaterial that the burglar does not intend to use the article during the commission of the crime (**Stones 1989**).

- Blackmail is defined in **s21 Theft Act 1968** and takes place where the defendant makes an unwarranted demand with menaces with a view to obtaining a gain for himself or another of money or other property or a loss of the same to some other person. The unlawful obtaining of drugs, even those which have to be injected, will come under the definition of property (**Bevans 1987**).

- The demand can be made expressly or be implied from the circumstances (**Collister and Warhurst 1955**), and if posted, takes effect at the time of posting (**Treacy v DPP 1971**). It will be unwarranted when the defendant knows that he is demanding something to which he has no entitlement or when he knows that the use of menaces is wrong (**Harvey 1980**).

- The word 'menaces' is to be given its ordinary meaning, and there is now some doubt as to whether a threat to do something which is merely unpleasant would suffice (**Thorne v Motor Trade Association 1937, Clear 1968** and **Harry 1974**). In **Clear 1968**, it was decided that the threat must be such that it would influence an ordinary person of normal stability and courage.

Activity

Decide whether the following people have committed any offences under **ss9**, **10** and **21** of the **Theft Act 1968**:

- Jack fell asleep at the end of a working day. He awoke to find the building empty so decided to steal one of the computers from the office of his boss.
- Jill was desperate for money and planned to steal the silver candlesticks in her local church. She had just put her head through the window when the parish priest discovered her.
- Mary broke into a department store and then stole a knife from the kitchen department. She used this to force the security officer to give her the contents of the safe.
- Simon, a chocoholic, was waiting to be served in a sweet shop. Overcome with a longing for a Toblerone bar, he vaulted across the counter and snatched one from the shelf. He later claimed that he had every intention of paying for the goods.
- Tom was a member of a fanatical group of activists. He sent a demand to the management of Tessbury stating that all their cosmetic range, allegedly tested on animals, should be withdrawn from the shelves in all their stores. The letter stated that if this action were not taken, a bomb would be planted in one of their busiest branches.

Self-Assessment Questions

1. Define theft and state where the law is to be found. Decide which parts of the definition comprise the *actus reus* of the offence and which part the *mens rea*.
2. What is meant by the term 'appropriation' in **s2**? Explain why this word caused problems for the courts in the cases of **Morris, Lawrence, Gomez** and **Hinks** and describe how these issues were resolved.
3. Define the word 'property' under **s4** and explain why this caused difficulties in the case of **Oxford v Moss**.
4. Why were the defendants, in **Turner No 2, Davidge, Floyd, Wain** and **Kumar** held to have property 'belonging to another' but not **Hall**?
5. When will theft be committed under **s5(4)**?
6. Giving section numbers and cases to support your answer, decide how the issue of dishonesty is settled.
7. What is meant by the phrase 'with the intention to permanently deprive the other of it'? Why were the convictions in **Downes, Velumyl** and **Lavender** upheld but not those in **Lloyd** and **Bagshaw**?
8. Define the crime of robbery. Explain why the offence was not made out in **Robinson** but the convictions upheld in **Hale, Clouden** and **Corcoran**.
9. Describe the two different ways that burglary can be committed under **s9(1)(a)** and **s9(1)(b)** of the **Theft Act**. State why the conviction in **Collins** was quashed but the crime of burglary established in the cases of **Brown, Ryan, Jones and Smith** and **Walkington**.
10. What is meant by the term 'aggravated burglary'? Describe the effect of **s10(2)**.

Chapter 8

PROPERTY OFFENCES II: MAKING OFF WITHOUT PAYMENT AND DECEPTION OFFENCES

8.1 Introduction

In this chapter, the first offence to be looked at is that of making off without payment under **s3 Theft Act 1978**. After that, five offences involving deception will be examined. Some A Level students will be happy to discover that the deception offences are no longer included in their programme but knowledge of these is necessary for AQA, ILEX examinations and other post-A Level courses. Three of the deception offences are to be found in the **Theft Act 1968** and two more in the **Theft Act 1978**.

8.2 Making off without payment

As stated earlier, this offence is described in **s3 Theft Act 1978**. It was created to plug a loophole in the **Theft Act 1968** where people obtained goods without at that time deceiving the other party but later refused to pay for them. An example of this type of behaviour was shown in the case of **DPP v Ray 1974**, where a diner in a restaurant made off without paying for his meal. It was also intended to cover the passenger in a taxi who fails to pay the fare and the motorist who drives off after filling his tank with petrol.

S3 Theft Act 1978 states that:

> . . . a person who, knowing that payment on the spot for any goods supplied or service done is required or expected from him,

> dishonestly makes off without having paid as required or expected and with intent to avoid payment of the amount shall be guilty of an offence.

J R Spencer in an article in the *Criminal Law Review* in 1983 put forward the view that the term 'making off' means 'disappearing: leaving in a way that makes it difficult for the debtor to be traced', and the Oxford English Dictionary states that it means 'to depart suddenly'. Others would argue that the term merely means 'to leave'. Whatever interpretation is put on the phrase, the offender must be aware that payment on the spot for either goods or a service is expected from him before liability is incurred.

8.2.1 The *actus reus* of making off without payment

This arises in cases where the accused makes off without paying for the goods purchased or a service supplied. In **Aziz 1993**, two men asked a taxi driver to take them to a night-club, refused to pay the £15 requested when they arrived there and offered £4 instead. The taxi driver decided to drive them to a police station but on the journey, the men started to damage the taxi. The driver then went into a garage and asked for the police to be called. The two men ran off but one of them was caught and charged under **s3**.

The appellant tried to argue that he had not made off from the spot where payment was due. The Court of Appeal held that in journeys by taxi, payment on the spot could either be in the taxi or outside it and in this case the men were still inside it when payment was requested. The court went further and stated that it was enough that the requirement to pay the money had arisen; a particular location was not necessary.

For liability to arise, the payment must be 'required or expected'. In the case of **Troughton v Metropolitan Police Commissioner 1987**, the taxi driver had not completed the journey so was not held to have the right to demand payment. His passenger had asked to be taken to Highbury but had not specified the exact address. He was under the influence of drink and on the journey had quarrelled with the driver, accusing him of making an unnecessary deviation. The taxi driver was unable to get an address from the passenger so made a detour to take him to a police station to try to clarify matters. The defendant was later charged and convicted under **s3**.

The Court of Appeal quashed the conviction, deciding that, as the driver had not completed the contract, the defendant could not be required or expected to pay for the journey.

In a similar vein, payment cannot be demanded if the goods supplied or the service provided is contrary to law. This is made clear in **s3(3)** of the Act. A defendant who refused to pay a prostitute, therefore, would not incur liability under this section. He could, however, be charged under **s1 Theft Act 1978** for obtaining services by deception because, under this section, no such limitation is imposed.

The term 'making off' suggests that the defendant must have left the premises. Should he be prevented from doing this, it was stated in **McDavitt 1981** that the correct charge should be an attempt.

8.2.2 The *mens rea* of making off without payment

There are three elements to the *mens rea*:

- The defendant must know that payment on the spot is required or expected.
- He must then dishonestly make off without making such a payment.
- He must have the intention to avoid making it.

With regard to the first two elements, the defendant would not be liable in the restaurant type of situation if he genuinely but mistakenly believed that someone else was going to pay the bill.

In **Brooks and Brooks 1982**, the Court of Appeal held that this point had not been made clear to the jury and the daughter's conviction for obtaining a meal without paying for it was quashed, even though she had left the restaurant early in some haste.

In the same case, the court held that 'the words "dishonestly makes off" are words easily understandable by any jury which, in the majority of cases, require no elaboration in a summing up'. In the case of **Allen 1985**, however, the House of Lords was eventually called upon to decide whether the defendant had been dishonest and had also intended to avoid payment.

He had stayed for nearly a month at an hotel but then left without paying his bill. He contacted the hotel a few days later, explained that he was in financial difficulties but stated that he would leave his passport as security for the debt when he came to collect his belongings. Instead, the police were called and he was later convicted under **s3**.

The House of Lords quashed his conviction. Lord Hailsham agreed with the Court of Appeal that the words 'with intent to avoid payment' meant an intention to evade payment altogether, not just an intention to defer or delay payment. In this case, it was felt that the accused should be given the benefit of the doubt.

The defendant in **Vincent 2001** also had his conviction quashed in somewhat similar circumstances. He had stayed for two weeks at two different hotels in Windsor and left one without paying the bill at all and only part paying the other. When charged under **s3**, his defence was that he had made arrangements with the hoteliers to pay when he could and that therefore payment on the spot was not expected. He also claimed that he was not acting dishonestly and had no intention of avoiding the debts. The judge directed the jury that a dishonestly obtained agreement to postpone payment could not be relied on to negate the expectation of payment on the spot but did stress that the prosecution must prove the latter point. The defendant was convicted but appealed.

Activity

Decide if liability under **s3 Theft Act 1978** exists in the following situations:

- Jamie went into Gordon's restaurant and ordered the five-course set dinner. Jamie became increasingly annoyed about the high prices and large tips being left by some of the City workers so took the view that the owner had made enough money. He therefore ran out of the restaurant after completing his meal while his waiter, Ainsley, was serving another customer.
- Would your answer be any different if Jamie merely left early in the belief that his companion Gary would pay the bill?
- Nigella hailed a taxi to go to the television studios, five miles away. After travelling for five hundred yards, she noted that there was a solid traffic jam as far as the eye could see. Fearful of being late, she suddenly jumped out of the taxi and finished her journey by Tube.

FIVE KEY FACTS ON MAKING OFF WITHOUT PAYMENT

- This offence is found in **s3 Theft Act 1978** and the maximum sentence is two years' imprisonment (**s4**).
- The term 'making off' is not defined; it could mean merely 'to leave', or 'to depart suddenly' or, more precisely, 'to leave in a way that makes it difficult for the debtor to be found'.
- The *actus reus* exists when the defendant makes off without having paid as required or expected (**Aziz 1993**; contrast with **Troughton 1987**, where no liability was incurred).
- Should the offender be apprehended before he leaves the place where payment is due, the correct charge would be attempting to make off without payment (**McDavitt 1981**).
- The *mens rea* of **s3** consists of having knowledge that payment on the spot is required, being dishonest within the ordinary meaning of the word or under the Ghosh test, and having an intention to evade payment altogether (**Allen 1985**).

The Court of Appeal quashed the conviction, deciding that **s3** was intended to create a simple and straightforward offence and that it was not therefore necessary to analyse whether the agreement had been obtained by deception. The fact that the agreement to postpone the debt had been gained by dishonest means did not mean that **s3** could be resurrected. To gain a conviction therefore, the defendant should have been charged with another offence, i.e. **s2 Theft Act 1978** (see later).

8.3 Obtaining property by deception

This offence is found in **s15 Theft Act 1968**. **S15(1)** lays down both the definition and the maximum sentence. It states:

A person who by any deception dishonestly obtains property belonging to another, with the intention of permanently depriving the other of it shall on conviction on indictment be liable to imprisonment for a term not exceeding ten years.

It can be seen that the definition of this offence is very similar to that of theft, under **s1.** It should also be remembered that, since the case of **Gomez**, every time an offender satisfies the definition of obtaining property by deception, he also satisfies the definition of theft under **s1** and could be charged with this offence. In certain situations, this could make it easier for the prosecution to prove its case. There are, however, some important differences between the two crimes. The first is that, under **s15**, there is a need for a deception to have been practised so while anyone alleged to have obtained property by deception can also be found guilty of theft, the reverse is not true. Secondly, under **s15**, the word 'obtains' is used, rather than the word 'appropriates' in theft. The third difference is in the sentence; the maximum sentence for theft has been

shortened to seven years, whereas it is ten years for the **s15** offence.

- The *actus reus* of **s15** is satisfied where the defendant by any deception obtains property belonging to another.
- The *mens rea* exists when the accused does this dishonestly and with the intention of permanently depriving the other of it.

8.3.1 The *actus reus* of obtaining property by deception

The various components of the *actus reus* now need to be studied.

By any deception

This phrase is the key element of this offence. Obviously, there can be no liability under **s15** if the victim has not been deceived. It was stated in **Re London and Globe Finance Corporation 1903** that to deceive is 'to induce a man to believe that a thing is true which is false and which the person practising the deceit knows or believes to be false'. It can be seen from this that a person must be involved, it is not possible to deceive a machine. There would be no liability under **s15**, therefore, if an offender put worthless tokens in a machine to obtain something of value from it. Likewise, a deception would not operate where the buyer makes it clear that he was not influenced by the words or conduct of the other party. In **Laverty 1970**, the defendant had changed the registration and chassis number plates on a car and then sold it. His conviction under **s15** was quashed on appeal, as the court was not convinced that the buyer had bought the car solely as a result of this action.

S15(4) helps to clarify the word 'deception' by stating that it includes deliberate and reckless deception by either words or conduct. In addition, the courts have decided that the deception can be either expressed or implied.

There could, therefore, be liability where goods were paid for by cheque in circumstances where the drawer of the cheque knows that the bank would not honour it, provided that it can be shown that someone had been deceived. This could cause problems where a guarantee card accompanies the cheque because, in such circumstances, the retailer is relying upon the card and knows that the cheque will be honoured. It could be argued that he is not therefore concerned about the fact that there are no funds to meet it. The courts originally took a robust attitude towards the word 'deception' to ensure that cases like this were covered and the offender did not escape liability. This approach can be seen in the case of **Metropolitan Police Commissioner v Charles 1976**, a case which will be discussed more fully later. The House of Lords decided that the defendant's cheques had only been accepted because of the belief that he was acting properly. It followed, therefore, said Lord Edmund-Davies, that the victim was being deceived, even though he may not have been concerned about the deception and may not have incurred any loss.

A similar approach was also taken in **Lambie 1982**, regarding the misuse of a credit card. The defendant used her Barclaycard over 60 times after her credit limit had been exceeded, including a transaction at Mothercare. Lambie had been convicted of obtaining a pecuniary advantage by deception but, on appeal, the conviction had been quashed. The House of Lords then restored the conviction. Their Lordships decided that she had made a representation that she had actual authority to make a contract with Mothercare on the bank's behalf that the bank would honour the voucher on presentation. Lord Roskill also queried why the charge of obtaining property by deception had been rejected and decided that it would have been made out. He rejected the contention that it was necessary in every case to call the person on whom the fraud was first perpetrated, arguing that if this were so, the guilty would often go free.

These cases also illustrate that it is possible to practise a deception by conduct as well as by words.

In **Nabina 1999**, the defendant was luckier. At first instance he was convicted on 14 counts of obtaining property by deception. He then appealed, arguing that the judge had misdirected the jury. He admitted obtaining a number of credit cards by giving false information about his personal circumstances. He also agreed that he had later used those cards to obtain goods and, on one occasion travellers' cheques, from several different outlets but denied that he had done this dishonestly or by falsely representing that he was the legitimate holder of the cards.

The Court of Appeal quashed the conviction, doubting that a properly directed jury would have decided that deception of the outlets was a necessary inference from the facts. In these transactions there was nothing to suggest that the money would not be forthcoming. It appeared that the defendant did have actual authority to warrant that the transactions would be honoured by the issuers, and even if the issuers would have been entitled to revoke that authority because of the fraudulent claims, they had not done so. The facts therefore, differed to those in **Charles** and **Lambie** where no such authority existed because the respective credit limits of the card users had been exceeded. Professor Sir John Smith argues that the way the law stands at present it would be safer to charge the defendant with theft.

A deception was found in the case of **DPP v Stonehouse 1978**, where the extraordinary conduct of the MP John Stonehouse hit the headlines all over the world. His financial affairs were in chaos so he decided to fake his death while on a business trip to Miami. He gave the impression that he had drowned by leaving his clothes on the beach, and fled to Australia to start a new life with his mistress. He had earlier transferred his money to Australia so that his estate would be insolvent but, to provide for his wife after his 'death', had taken out insurance policies in her favour. Suspicions were aroused and he was discovered live and well in Australia. The press, of course, had a field day and the MP later returned to this country to face charges of attempting to obtain property by deception. The Court of Appeal upheld his conviction, deciding that 'the accused . . . had done all the physical acts lying within his power that were needed to enable Mrs Stonehouse to obtain the policy moneys if all had gone as he intended'.

Another cruel attempt to obtain property by deception was practised on an elderly widow in the case **King and Stockwell 1987.** The defendants pretended that they were from a reputable firm of tree surgeons and falsely told the victim that many of the trees in her garden were dangerous and needed to be removed. They then offered to do the work immediately for the sum of £470, if paid in cash. Their deception came to light when a sympathetic building society cashier noted the woman's distress as she attempted to withdraw the money for the work, and called the police. The Court of Appeal upheld the convictions of the two men. Neill L J stated 'there was ample evidence on which the jury could come to the conclusion that had the attempt succeeded the money would have been paid over by the victim as a result of the lies told to her by the appellants'.

Obtains

The word 'obtains' is explained under **s15(2)**, which states that a person is treated as obtaining property 'if he obtains ownership, possession or control of it'. He is also classed as doing this if the obtaining is for another person.

A gap in the law was disclosed in cases like **Collis-Smith 1971**, where the defendant obtained the property first and then practised a deception on the other party. Collis-Smith had filled up his car with petrol; therefore, at that moment, ownership in the property had passed

to him. He then falsely indicated that his company would pay for it. The conviction under **s15** was quashed because the property had not been obtained by the deception. Ownership had come earlier. It will be seen later in this chapter that this gap has been closed by the passing of the **Theft Act 1978** and that the defendant could now be charged with evading a liability by deception under **s2**.

Property

The word 'property' is not defined in **s15** but **s34** states that the definition of property in **s4(1)** will apply to all sections of the Act. The word therefore includes 'money and all other property, real or personal, including things in action and other intangible property'. The limitations under **s4(2)**, however, imposed with regard to the offence of theft, do not apply to **s15**. It would appear, therefore, that almost anything might be obtained by deception, including land. An example of this would be where an impostor claimed the estate of a deceased person.

Belonging to another

Under **s34**, this phrase, too, will be taken to have the same meaning as in theft. It is possible, therefore, to obtain by deception property that belongs to the offender but is in the temporary control of another.

8.3.2 The *mens rea* of obtaining property by deception

It will be remembered that the *mens rea* of this offence will be present when the defendant obtains the property 'dishonestly' and 'with the intention of permanently depriving the other of it'. In addition, he must have made the deception, discussed above, deliberately or recklessly. These points require further examination.

Dishonestly

It is very important to realise that, in addition to any deception, it is also necessary to prove a dishonest intent. This was clearly stated by the Criminal Law Revision Committee when the Bill was being drafted and is also obvious from the definition. To clinch matters, the Court of Appeal affirmed this position in **Feeny 1991**, when it was said that the offence could not be committed 'unless dishonesty is established as a separate and essential ingredient'.

When deciding whether the defendant is dishonest, the **Ghosh** test, mentioned under theft, will be used. The jury needs to be convinced of two things, first, that the defendant's behaviour was dishonest when judged against the standards of reasonable and honest people and secondly, that the defendant himself realised that he was doing wrong by those standards. As stated in **Price 1990**, however, on many occasions this will be obvious and, if so, it is not necessary for the trial judge to give the **Ghosh** direction.

In **Lightfoot 1993**, the defendant had obtained a Barclaycard issued in the name of Plummer, a fellow firefighter. Lightfoot had used the card to purchase goods to the value of £3,000. There was some doubt as to whether he had done this with the consent of the named person and Plummer strongly denied this. The direction of the trial judge did not follow exactly the words laid down in the **Ghosh** test but they were similar. The Court of Appeal held that this was good enough and upheld the conviction on the grounds that the defendant must have appreciated that he was doing wrong by the standards of reasonable and honest people.

With regard to dishonesty in theft, **s2(1)** lays down situations where a person is not classed as being dishonest; it is important to realise that there is no corresponding section with regard to obtaining property by deception.

With the intention of permanently depriving the other of it

S15(3) states that the extended definition of this phrase, laid down in **s6** concerning theft, also applies to **s15**. A person will commit the offence, therefore, if he treats the property as his own to dispose of, provided, of course, that the other elements of obtaining property by deception are present.

Whether deliberate or reckless

In addition to the two phrases within the definition of **s15(1)**, **s15(4)** also states, indirectly, that the deception must be practised deliberately or recklessly. In **Staines 1974**, the Court of Appeal held that the term 'recklessness' meant more than mere carelessness or negligence on the part of the defendant. It is also made clear by the cases that in all the deception offences, **Cunningham**-type recklessness must be proved.

Greenstein 1976 can be cited as a rare example of a reckless deception. The case concerned the very questionable activity of 'stagging', whereby large blocks of shares were applied for by the defendant, 'paid for' with a cheque for which funds were not available. This was done in the knowledge that the shares would be over-subscribed and only a proportion of the shares applied for would be issued. By using this method, the applicants would receive a higher allocation of shares than if they had only applied for shares to the amount that they could afford and had then been given a proportional allocation of this quantity. The practice of stagging was considered to be highly irregular and to try to combat it, the issuers of the shares would sometimes ask applicants to give an assurance that the cheque would be met on its first presentation. This was the position in this case and the defendants were charged with obtaining the shares by deception, when such a declaration was held to be a false one. The defendants tried to argue that they had not been dishonest because in the vast majority of cases where such a practice had been employed in the past, the cheques had almost always been honoured. The Court of Appeal decided that the cheques could only be met if the applicants were successful in their deception on the issuers of the shares. This deception was that their application was a genuine one. It could also be argued that the defendants were reckless because, while they hoped that their cheques would be met, there was always a chance that they would not be. They were aware that in 14 out of 136 transactions the return cheque had not been cleared in time to cover the amount needed for the first cheque.

8.4 Obtaining a money transfer by deception

The law on this is to be found in a new **s15A**, inserted into the **Theft Act 1968** by the **Theft (Amendment) Act 1996**. The very swift change in the law followed the controversial finding of the House of Lords in **Preddy 1996**, that no existing deception offence had been committed when the defendants had obtained mortgages by giving false information. Their Lordships had come to this conclusion because no property had passed from the payer to the payee; there had merely been a transfer of money between the two accounts.

S15A states:

A person is guilty of an offence if by any deception he dishonestly obtains a money transfer for himself or another.

Such an offence occurs where money is debited from one account and credited to another and

'the credit results from the debit or the debit results from the credit' (**s15A(2)**). The maximum punishment is laid down in **s15A(5)** and is ten years' imprisonment.

8.4.1 The *actus reus* of obtaining a money transfer by deception

The *actus reus* of this offence is satisfied when a person by any deception obtains a money transfer for himself or another.

8.4.2 The *mens rea* of obtaining a money transfer by deception

The *mens rea* occurs when the deception is deliberate or reckless (**s15B** states that the word is to have the same meaning as in **s15**), and the obtaining is done dishonestly.

8.5 Obtaining a pecuniary advantage by deception

The offence and the punishment for it are laid down in **s16(1) Theft Act 1968**, which states that:

a person who by any deception dishonestly obtains for himself or another any pecuniary advantage shall on conviction on indictment be liable to imprisonment for a term not exceeding five years.

S16(2) states the circumstances when such an offence will occur.

Under **s16(2)(b)**, a person unlawfully acquires a monetary advantage for himself if, by deception, he is permitted to become overdrawn, take out an annuity or insurance policy or to secure an improvement on the terms of any such transaction. An example would be where the wrongdoer falsely tells his bank that he needs an overdraft for repairs to his house but, in reality, intends to spend the money on a trip to the Bahamas.

Similarly, the defendant in **MPC v Charles 1977**, mentioned earlier in this chapter, also committed this offence. He visited a gaming club called the Golden Nugget and, in just one evening, used all the cheques in his book to purchase chips for gaming. Each of them was made out for the sum of £30 and covered by a cheque guarantee card so each cheque subsequently had to be honoured by the bank. The defendant tried to argue that the casino owner was not deceived, because he was unconcerned as to whether the defendant had the bank's authority to issue these cheques; he would be paid in any event. As noted previously, however, the House of Lords took a liberal approach to the question of deception and his conviction was upheld.

S16(2)(c) states that a person also commits this offence if, by his deception:

he is given the opportunity to earn remuneration or greater remuneration in an office or employment.

Such an offence would be committed if the defendant lied about his qualifications and thereby obtained a higher paid job, as shown in the case of **Steel 1998**, where a teacher was ordered to do 180 hours of community service and repay the money given as a result of such a deception.

In **Callender 1992**, the wording of **s16(2)(c)** was held to cover self-employed people as well as employees. The defendant had been engaged to prepare the accounts for several small businesses, had received payment for the work but had not performed his side of the bargain. It was discovered that he had lied about his professional qualifications and was not, as claimed, a qualified accountant. He was therefore charged under **s16**. In his defence, Callender tried to argue that he did not come under the definition of 'an office or employment'. The Court of Appeal decided that this term should be interpreted liberally and upheld his conviction.

The observant student might have noted that there has been no explanation of **s16(2)(a)**. This section was repealed after criticism of its ambiguous wording and the difficulty of obtaining convictions under it. In its place, **s2 Theft Act 1978** created a new offence of evading a liability by deception. A case illustrating the now defunct section is that of **DPP v Ray 1974**.

The defendant, together with his three friends, ordered a meal in a restaurant. The defendant did not have enough money to pay his share but an arrangement was made that the others would lend him the money. After the meal, however, they all decided not to pay, and, later, when the waiter was out of the room, they ran out of the restaurant.

The defendant was convicted of obtaining a pecuniary advantage by deception under **s16(2)(a)** but this was quashed, on appeal, by the Divisional Court. There was a further appeal to the House of Lords where the conviction was restored. Their Lordships decided that the defendant had evaded his debt by deceiving the waiter. This deception had been practised by the defendant remaining in the restaurant after finishing the main meal thereby giving the impression that he and his friends were 'ordinary honest customers'. In this way, they had encouraged the waiter to lower his guard and disappear into the kitchen.

8.5.1 The *actus reus* of obtaining a pecuniary advantage by deception

This takes place when a person by any deception obtains for himself or another a pecuniary advantage.

8.5.2 The *mens rea* of obtaining a pecuniary advantage by deception

The mental element of this offence is satisfied when the deception is practised deliberately or recklessly **(S16(3))**, and the obtaining is done dishonestly.

Ten years after the passing of the **Theft Act 1968**, the **Theft Act 1978** came into force to help remedy some of the shortcomings found in the earlier Act. Three new offences were created, two of them dealing with deception. The third offence, that of making off without payment has already been discussed under 8.2.

8.6 Obtaining services by deception

This offence is found in **s1 Theft Act 1978**, which states:

> *A person who by any deception dishonestly obtains services from another is guilty of an offence.*

S4 states that the maximum punishment for this offence is five years' imprisonment and **s5** states that deception is to have the same meaning as in **s15 Theft Act 1968**.

S1(2) gives further details on the obtaining of services. This occurs when the other party is induced to confer a benefit on the understanding that it will be paid for. Examples quoted by academics include car repairs, taxi rides and house painting, provided that these acts are done for gain. The benefit given by the other party includes doing an act or causing or permitting one to be done, so would also cover the provision of hotel accommodation or a seat at a theatre. This section, could, on occasion, overlap with the offence under **s15** of the **1968 Act**.

It is important to realise that, on the wording of **s1 Theft Act 1978**, the deception must occur before the services are obtained. Forms of deception are various; they could include paying for services with a worthless cheque, posing as a wealthy client so that payment is deferred or, as in **Rai 1999**, obtaining a grant for a downstairs bathroom for use by his elderly sick mother and failing to tell the council that she had died.

There was great consternation when it was decided by the Court of Appeal in **Halai 1983**, that a mortgage advance was not a service under this section and that the correct charge should have been one under **s15. Halai** was distinguished in **Widdowson 1985**, where the Court of Appeal decided that a hire-purchase agreement was not to be treated in the same way as a mortgage advance. The court announced that it was rejecting the suggestion 'that the obtaining of a hire-purchase agreement cannot amount to the obtaining of services'. The same court suggested in **Teong Sun Chuah 1991** that **Halai** was wrongly decided and overruled it in **Graham 1997**. At roughly the same time, Parliament also decided to deal with the problem. The **Theft (Amendment) Act 1996** inserted a new subsection into **s1 Theft Act 1978. S1(3)** now decides that a mortgage advance is to be treated as a service.

8.6.1 The *actus reus* of obtaining services by deception

This occurs where a person by any deception obtains services from another.

8.6.2 The *mens rea* of obtaining services by deception

The required mens rea exists when the offender deceives the other party deliberately or recklessly and obtains the service dishonestly. **S5** of the Act states that the word 'deception' is to have the same meaning as in **s15 Theft Act 1968**.

8.7 Evasion of liability by deception

This offence is to be found in **s2 Theft Act 1978**. It was designed to cover many different situations where the accused, by deception, has tried to avoid the payment of a debt so has three parts to it.

Section 2(1)(a)

Under **s2(1)(a)** a person commits an offence if, by any deception, he:

dishonestly secures the remission of the whole or part of any existing liability to make a payment, whether his own liability or another's.

This means that by deceiving the other party and by acting in a dishonest way, the defendant has managed to get all or part of his debt extinguished, or the debt of someone else extinguished.

For example, if a person dishonestly convinced his creditor that he (the debtor) was dying and thereby persuaded him not to enforce the debt, he would be liable under this subsection.

The offence was also committed in Jackson 1983, when the defendant paid for petrol with a stolen credit card. The court decided that he had an existing liability to pay for the petrol already poured into the tank of his motorbike and he had deceived the garage owner about the validity of the credit card.

The *actus reus* of this part of the offence is where the defendant secures the remission of his own or another's liability.

The *mens rea* of the offence is doing this dishonestly and by practising a deliberate or reckless deception. **S5(1)** states that the word 'deception' in all parts of **s2** is to have the same meaning as in **s15 Theft Act 1968**.

Section 2(1)(b)

Under **s2(1) (b)** a person evades liability if:

with intent to make permanent default in whole or in part on any existing liability to make a payment, or with intent to let another do so, [he] dishonestly induces the creditor or any person claiming payment on behalf of the creditor to wait for payment . . . or to forgo payment.

A person who writes a cheque or uses a credit card knowing that he is exceeding his authorisation to do this would be liable under this subsection, because **s2(3)** specifically provides for this.

A person who convinces the creditor that payment has already been made would also be liable.

In **Holt and Lee 1981**, the Court of Appeal decided that the defendants were rightly convicted of attempting to commit this offence. They were sitting in a pizza restaurant after having consumed a meal and devised a scheme that they would tell their waitress that payment had already been made to another member of staff. They then planned to leave when the coast was clear. Unbeknown to them,

TEN KEY FACTS ON DECEPTION OFFENCES

- Obtaining property by deception is an offence found under **s15 Theft Act 1968** and carries a maximum punishment of ten years. Since the case of **DPP v Gomez**, all those liable under **s15**, would also be guilty of theft under **s1**.
- The *actus reus* of **s15** is established when, by any deception the defendant obtains property belonging to another (**DPP v Stonehouse 1978, Lambie 1982, King and Stockwell 1987**). The *mens rea* is said to exist when the defendant does the obtaining in a dishonest way, intending to permanently deprive the other of the property and his deception is practised deliberately or recklessly (**s15(4), Greenstein 1976, Lightfoot 1993**).
- **S15A Theft Act 1968** creates a new offence of obtaining a money transfer by deception (**Theft (Amendment) Act 1996**). The punishment for this is ten years' imprisonment (**s15A(5)**). The *actus reus* exists when a person by any deception obtains a money transfer for himself or another (**s15A(1)**). The *mens rea* is established when the obtaining is dishonest and the deception is deliberately or recklessly practised (**s15A(1), s15B(2)**).
- **S16(1)** lays down the offence of obtaining a pecuniary advantage by deception and states that the maximum punishment is five years' imprisonment. **S16(2)(a)** has been repealed. **S16(2)(b)** states that the offence will occur when a person, by his deception is allowed to become overdrawn, to take out an annuity or insurance policy or to obtain an improvement on existing terms (**MPC v Charles 1976**). Under **s16(2)(c)** the offence is also committed when the offender deceives another in order to gain remuneration or a higher salary or other payment 'in an office or employment'.
- The case of **Callender 1992** decides that the term 'in an office or employment' is to be construed widely, so it will cover self-employment.
- The *mens rea* of the offence of obtaining a pecuniary advantage by deception is acting dishonestly (**s16(1)**) and deliberately or recklessly deceiving the other party (**s16(1), s16(3)**).
- The **Theft Act 1978** created two additional offences, obtaining services by deception under **s1** and evading a liability by deception in **s2**. **S4** decrees that the maximum punishment for both these offences is five years' imprisonment.
- **S1(2)** states that a service is obtained under **s1** when the other party 'is induced to confer a benefit by doing some act, or causing or permitting some act to be done on the understanding that the benefit has been or will be paid for'. Services provided free, therefore, will not be covered, even though a deception may have

been practised. Under **s1(3)**, the provision of mortgage advances now comes within the meaning of services, overruling **Halai 1983 (Theft (Amendment) Act 1996)**.

- The *actus reus* of **s1** occurs when a person by any deception obtains services from another. The *mens rea* is present when this is done dishonestly, and the deception is deliberately or recklessly practised (**s1(1), s5**).

- The offence of evading a liability by deception under **s2 Theft Act 1978** is in three parts. **S2(1)(a)** states that it will occur when the defendant, by any deception, dishonestly secures the remission of the whole or part of a debt. Payment by a stolen credit card would be an example (**Jackson 1983**). Under **s2(1)(b)**, the offence is also committed when the defendant, by any deception, dishonestly persuades the creditor to wait for payment or to forgo payment entirely with the intention never to pay. Pretending that the debt has already been paid would be covered here (**Holt and Lee 1981**). **S2(1)(c)** states that the offence will also arise where the defendant, by any deception, dishonestly gains exemption from liability (**Sibartie 1983, Firth 1991**). **S5** states that the deception must be made deliberately or recklessly. The courts have decided that it should be **Cunningham**-style recklessness.

however, their conversation had been overheard by another diner. He was an off-duty policeman who promptly proceeded to arrest them!

The *actus reus* of **s2(1)(b)** is satisfied if the defendant by deception, somehow induces a creditor to wait for his money or to forgo payment altogether.

The *mens rea* is present if this is done in a dishonest way, with a deliberate or reckless deception and is meant to be permanent. Temporary stalling devices by the debtor in order to obtain more time to pay would not be enough to incur liability.

Section 2(1)(c)

Under **s2(1)(c)** a person will also commit this offence if, by any deception, he:

dishonestly obtains any exemption from or abatement of liability to make a payment.

An example would be where a person deceives the Inland Revenue into giving him a lower tax assessment or wrongfully gains a rate rebate by making a false statement. It was also decided in **Sibartie 1983** that liability could also arise where the defendant by deception tries to prevent a debt from arising at all.

The defendant passed a ticket inspector and waved an invalid season ticket in his direction. The Court of Appeal decided that he had been correctly convicted of an attempt to commit this offence. He had tried to give the impression that he was the holder of a valid season ticket and was therefore under no liability to pay and, by these means, was trying to gain an exemption. It could be argued that he was also attempting to induce the other to forgo payment under **s2(1)(b)**.

It is possible to practise such a deception under **s2(1)(c)** by failing to reveal certain information in the knowledge that the other is being deceived by this omission. In **Firth 1990**, the defendant was a consultant gynaecologist/obstetrician who performed both National Health and private work. He failed to inform the hospital that two of his patients were private patients so was not billed for the services provided for them. The Court of Appeal upheld the conviction under this section because he had thereby gained an exemption from liability.

The *actus reus* of **s2(1)(c)** occurs if the defendant by any deception obtains any exemption from or abatement of liability to make a payment.

The *mens rea* occurs if the deception is effected deliberately or recklessly and the exemption is obtained dishonestly.

Activity

Discuss the possible liability of Sly in the following unrelated situations:

- He visits an upmarket tailor and purchases two designer suits, using a credit card to make payment. He had acquired this card by giving false information.
- He then attends a job interview with a leading firm of solicitors, pretends that he has passed his Legal Practice Course with Distinction and secures a training contract with a leading firm of solicitors.
- He falsifies information on a mortgage application form and acquires a substantial mortgage advance in order to purchase a riverside apartment.
- He joins a health club and starts his weight training programme in the knowledge that he cannot afford the yearly subscription.
- He tells the bookseller from whom he had purchased his law books on credit, that his father will be paying the debt in the near future. In fact, his father is in prison, having embezzled company funds. The bookseller believes Sly's tale and stops his demands for payment.

Self-Assessment Questions

1. Define the offence under **s3 Theft Act 1978** and separate the *actus reus* and *mens rea* of the offence.
2. Explain why the defendant's conviction was upheld in **Aziz** but not in **Troughton, Allen** and **Vincent**.
3. Where is the offence of obtaining property by deception to be found? Identify three differences between this offence and theft under **s1**.
4. Describe the *actus reus* and *mens rea* of obtaining money by deception.
5. Explain why the defendants were found guilty of this offence in **Charles** and **Lambie** but the conviction quashed in **Nabina**.
6. How is the question of dishonesty established in this offence?
7. Which new offence was created in **s15A**? Define the *actus reus* and the *mens rea*.
8. State the different points that have to be proved under **s16(2)(b)** and **s16(2)(c)**, giving examples to support your statements.
9. Describe the *actus reus* and *mens rea* of obtaining services by deception. How was the conflict caused by the decision in **Halai** resolved?
10. Analyse the three different components of the offence of evading a liability by deception, under **s2 Theft Act 1978**, giving examples of each.

Chapter 9

PROPERTY OFFENCES III: CRIMINAL DAMAGE

9.1 Introduction

You will be relieved to know that this is a comparatively easy area to learn, compared with the complications concerning theft and deception, particularly as some examination boards only require knowledge of the basic offence.

The law on criminal damage is in the **Criminal Damage Act 1971**. This Act was largely the work of the Law Commission and was designed to replace the archaic **Malicious Damage Act 1861**. The **Criminal Damage Act** now contains, in a more simplified form, most offences concerning damage to property.

S1 Criminal Damage Act creates three offences:

- The basic offence of criminal damage is laid down in **s1(1)**.
- Aggravated criminal damage is to be found in **s1(2)**.
- Criminal damage by the use of fire is in **s1(3)**.

S2 of the Act creates two offences:

- Threatening to destroy or damage property.
- Threatening to do so in a way that is likely to endanger life.

S3 makes it an offence to have possession or control of something intending to use it for either simple criminal damage or for criminal damage likely to endanger life.

9.2 The basic offence under s1(1)

A person will be guilty of the basic offence of criminal damage if he destroys or damages property belonging to another, either intentionally or recklessly.

A more precise definition is to be found in **s1(1)** of the Act, which states:

> *A person who without lawful excuse destroys or damages any property belonging to another intending to destroy or damage any such property or being reckless as to whether any such property would be destroyed or damaged shall be guilty of an offence.*

9.2.1 The *actus reus* and *mens rea* of criminal damage

The *actus reus* of the basic offence is destroying or damaging property belonging to another and the *mens rea* is doing this intentionally or recklessly.

9.2.2 The punishment

If the damage or destruction is above £5,000 in value, the offence comes into the category of a triable either way offence for which the maximum punishment is ten years' imprisonment.

For damage of £5,000 or less, the court must proceed as if the offence were triable only summarily as laid down in **s22 Magistrates' Courts Act 1980**, as amended by **s4 Criminal Justice and Public Order Act 1994**.

Party mob wrecks girl's home while parents are away

KEITH and Sarah Young have no idea what lies in store when they return from their holiday in Spain.

They know nothing of the ruined carpets, the smashed windows, the graffiti, the thefts and the broken furniture that await them when they come home to White Horse Cottages in Sutton Poyntz, Dorset.

The Youngs have yet to learn that twice on Saturday night police were summoned to this normally quiet village to evict an unruly mob of more than 100 drunken teenagers from their home.

The couple had agreed to let their daughter Caroline, 15, who was being cared for by an aunt, host a sleep-over party for 10 girl friends in the cottage.

They could not have imagined that the party would be gate-crashed by scores of alcohol fuelled teenagers, few of them older than 15, intent on causing mayhem.

At one point 10 police officers and a dog unit chased the youths through the village and surrounding fields.

Amid the chaos, an ambulance crew was attending to a girl who had collapsed beside the mill pond. She was taken to hospital to be treated for alcohol poisoning.

Peter Smith, the landlord of the Springhead public house, said yesterday: "I spent most of the night on the door stopping them from coming in – there must have been 150 or more roaming around the village.

"They brought lots of drink with them and they systematically wrecked the house. They must have done several thousand pounds worth of damage. Some of the neighbours tried to clear the house but this lot were going nowhere, so we called the police."

Officers from Weymouth, two miles away, were on the scene within minutes. Mr Smith said: "One minute there were 150 youngsters here and the next thing the place was deserted. They all ran off into the gardens and fields. The police cleared the house and locked it and took the girl back to her aunt's house."

But the youths returned shortly before midnight, breaking into the cottage to continue their party. "You could hear them smashing things up so I called the police," Mr Smith said. PC Rick O'Shea, one of the officers who attended the scene, said widespread and deliberate damage had been done to the Young's home.

He said that Caroline had issued a number of invitations for the sleep-over to close friends but one appeared to have fallen into the wrong hands, was copied and widely distributed.

"Some of the people who turned up were from three or four miles away and were not connected with her at all. The damage is malicious and quite deliberate. The electrical fittings have been pulled out, lights, windows and crockery smashed, alcohol poured over the carpets and CDs and tapes destroyed. Most of the youngsters were very drunk and just set about the place."

Taken from an article by Sean O'Neill in the *Daily Telegraph*.

In **Fennell 2000** however, the Court of Appeal made it clear that though 'low value' criminal damage required the magistrates to treat the case as if it were a summary one; it did not make the offence of criminal damage a summary one. In this case, the accused had been acquitted of racially aggravated criminal damage but convicted of the alternative offence of basic criminal damage. He tried to argue that because the criminal damage was less than £5,000, a jury should not have decided the case, unless this matter had been the subject of a separate charge.

The Court of Appeal dismissed this argument for the reasons stated above.

In **R (on the application of Abbott) v Colchester Magistrates' Court 2001**, the defendant was charged with causing criminal damage to experimental genetically modified maize. The prosecutor had intended to put the amount of damage as £3,250, £750 for the loss to the farmer and £2,500 for the producers of the seed. The defendant was seeking a jury trial, hoping that it would be more sympathetic because of the controversial issues involved and obtained a report from a scientist putting the loss to the Government at £13,900! The magistrates then had the task of deciding whether the case should be dealt with by them as if it were a summary one or be treated as a triable either way offence. The point of law on how the value was to be determined went to the Divisional Court of Queen's Bench.

This court decided that **Schedule 2** to the **Magistrates' Courts Act 1980** was directed simply and solely to identifying the value of the damage to the property itself and was not concerned with determining what, if any, consequential losses might have been sustained as a result of that damage.

9.2.3 Elements of the basic offence

The words 'destroying' and 'damaging' need to be analysed, as do the terms 'property' and 'belonging to another'.

Destroys or damages

Neither of these words is defined in the Act and the courts appear to have taken a common sense approach to their meaning.

The courts have decided that the word 'destroys' will cover rendering the property useless, in addition to total destruction.

The word 'damage' can be used where property is made imperfect or inoperative or if the harm affects its usefulness or value. A car would be damaged if an important part of it were to be uncoupled as, for example, a brake cable. In **Roper v Knott 1898**, beer was held to have been damaged after water had been added to it.

In **Samuel v Stubbs 1972**, it was stated that the word damage 'is sufficiently wide in its meaning to embrace injury, mischief or harm done to property'. It was also agreed that property would be damaged where it could no longer serve its normal purpose. It appears that a temporary cessation of its function will sometimes be sufficient. In this case, a policeman's cap had been trampled upon. The court held that the item had, in fact, been damaged, even though the headgear may well have been returned easily to its original state.

In **Hardman v Chief Constable of Avon and Somerset Constabulary 1986**, members of CND had been convicted of criminal damage and mounted an appeal against this. In order to mark the 40th anniversary of the dropping of the atomic bomb on Hiroshima, they had used watersoluble paint to draw silhouettes on a pavement illustrating vaporised human remains.

The defendants tried to argue that their actions did not amount to criminal damage because the harm done was only temporary. They claimed that the paintings would have been erased naturally, if left alone, by the footsteps of pedestrians and by the elements. Despite these submissions, the convictions were upheld because the local authority had been put to the expense of employing people to wash off the paintings with pressurised water jets.

Similarly, in **Roe v Kingerlee 1986**, the defendant had smeared mud over the walls of a police cell, which cost £7 to clean off. This was held to amount to criminal damage, even though no lasting damage had been done.

There is, however, a limit to liability. In **A (a juvenile) v R 1978**, spitting on a police officer's raincoat was not held to amount to criminal damage because the spittle could easily be removed with a damp cloth and no lasting damage had been done. A different decision may well have been made if the article had been stained and had needed dry cleaning.

In a similar vein, merely running over the land of another would not amount to damaging that land, as decided in **Eley v Lytle 1885**, a civil case, whereas the actual trampling down of grass could constitute liability (**Gayford v Choulder 1898**).

In **Lloyd v DPP 1992**, a person tried to turn the tables on those arguing that he was at fault by accusing the other party of effecting criminal damage to his car by wheel-clamping it.

He had parked in a prohibited place, despite notices warning that illegally parked cars would be clamped and had returned to discover that such action had been taken. He then refused to pay the amount of £25 demanded for the release of the clamp and, instead, had used a disc cutter to prise it off. He was later charged with effecting criminal damage to the clamp. In his defence, he tried to argue that the other party had been trespassing on his property by applying the wheel clamp in the first place and used some very old authority to support his findings. Despite his novel attempt to evade liability, such arguments were not accepted by the court and his conviction was upheld.

Grey areas

In some cases, the article itself may not be damaged but, instead, an item which helps it to operate. In **Cox v Riley 1986**, the defendant was found guilty of criminal damage after he had erased a programme from a plastic circuit card operating a saw to cut wood to specially programmed designs. The court decided that, while no damage had been caused to the saw itself, there had been damage to the card.

A similar approach was taken in **Whiteley 1991**. In this case, a computer hacker had infiltrated JANET, the Joint Academic Network, had altered and deleted files and changed some of the passwords. The computer had not been damaged by this misuse, but it had been rendered inoperable because of the damage to the magnetic particles on the disks.

The problem of computer misuse has now been recognised as a subject worthy of treatment in its own right and the passing of the **Computer Misuse Act 1990** has made it easier to obtain convictions for such offences. The Act is not only concerned about harm caused to the actual computer but also the harm caused by the unauthorised use of the material contained within. **S3** deals with this and creates an offence if a person intentionally does any act that causes any unauthorised modification of the contents of any computer. This has lessened the need to stretch the meaning of the word 'damage' under the **Criminal Damage Act.** If the matter had been left like this, however, it would have caused an overlap between the two Acts, which might have caused future problems. For example, the new offence only carries a maximum penalty of five years' imprisonment, whereas criminal damage attracts ten years. In addition, the new offence can only be committed intentionally, whereas offences under the **Criminal Damage Act** can also be committed recklessly.

S3(6) Computer Misuse Act, therefore, makes it clear that:

> *a modification of the contents of a computer shall not be regarded as damaging any computer or computer storage medium unless its effect on that computer or computer storage medium impairs its physical condition.*

Property

Under the **Criminal Damage Act 1971**, property encompasses all items of a tangible nature, including money and animals belonging to another person. Wild animals that have been tamed and/or kept in captivity will come into this category but wild mushrooms, flowers, fruit or foliage will not.

This definition of property appears very similar to the one in the **Theft Act 1968** but there are some important distinctions. While land, under the law of theft, cannot be stolen, it can, under the **Criminal Damage Act**, be damaged. Conversely, intangible property rights, such as patents and copyrights can be stolen but do not come within the definition of property under the **Criminal Damage Act**.

Belonging to another

Under the basic offence the property that is damaged or destroyed has to belong to someone else. It will be noted, later, that this is not the case for the more serious offences which may arise under **ss1(2), 1(3)**, nor for the offences under **ss2** and **3**.

Following on from this, it is obviously not an offence under **s1(1)** to damage or destroy one's own property and the person may also be protected if he honestly but mistakenly believes that the property was his, provided, of course, that the jury believes his version of the events.

In **Smith 1974**, a tenant of a ground floor flat gave notice to quit but asked that his brother might be allowed to stay on. The landlord refused to entertain the idea. The tenant then damaged floor boarding, roofing and wall panels in a conservatory. He claimed that this was done in order to remove some electric wiring which he and his brother had installed, with the permission of the landlord, so that they could use their stereo equipment more effectively. Damage totalling £130 was caused and the appellant was charged under **s1(1)**. He argued that he believed that the property belonged to him and that therefore he had a lawful excuse. In fact, the items had become fixtures that should not have been removed.

The trial judge declared in no uncertain terms that such an argument was unacceptable but the Court of Appeal held that this was a fundamental misdirection and the conviction was quashed. The appeal court was influenced by the law preceding that in the **Criminal Damage Act**. This made it clear that an offence would not be committed by a person who destroyed or damaged property belonging to another, if he had done this in the honest but mistaken belief that the property was his own, or had believed that he had a legal right to do the damage. This was illustrated in the early case of **Twose 1879**.

The Court of Appeal felt that the creators of the revised law on criminal damage did not intend to increase the liability when the Act was passed so decided that:

> *no offence is committed under this section (i.e. **s1(1)**), if a person destroys or causes damage to property belonging to another if he does so in the honest though mistaken belief that the property is his own, and, provided that the belief is honestly held, it is irrelevant to consider whether or not it is a justifiable belief.*

The term 'belonging to another' is given a wide meaning under **s10(2)**. Property is treated as belonging to another if that other has custody or control of it, a proprietary right in it, a charge over it, or a right under a trust.

It would be an offence, therefore, if the defendant caused damage to his own goods, if they had been lent to someone else. It is, however essential to prove that that the other had a proprietary right or interest in the goods. An insurer would not come into this category, so if a person destroyed or damaged his own property in order to claim from an insurance company, he would not be committing an offence under this section, as he would not be harming the goods of another.

Before leaving this subject, it should be noted that, if the damaged property belongs to a spouse, the consent of the Director of Public Prosecutions is needed before a charge can be brought. The restriction would not apply where the parties are no longer under a duty to cohabit.

9.2.4 The *mens rea* of the basic offence

As stated earlier, this is satisfied if the person unlawfully destroys or damages property belonging to another, either intentionally or recklessly. With regard to the word 'intention', it is quite clear that the defendant cannot be found guilty on this part of the count unless he possesses a clear intent to cause the damage. In addition, he must intend to act unlawfully and damage property belonging to another. If, therefore, he is under the mistaken impression that the property is his own, as in the case of **Smith 1974**, described above, he would lack the *mens rea* for the basic offence.

With regard to the word 'reckless', it should be remembered that this is **Caldwell**-style recklessness. As already discussed in Chapter 2, this is the more objective form of recklessness. Lord Diplock stated in **Metropolitan Police Commissioner v Caldwell 1982**, that a person

is reckless if 'he does an act which in fact creates an obvious risk that property will be damaged or destroyed and, when he does the act he either has not given any thought to the possibility of there being any such risk or has recognised that there was some risk involved, and has nonetheless gone on to take it.'

Comment

Caldwell was a House of Lords' decision and is, therefore, an authoritative statement of the law regarding recklessness in criminal damage, despite the fact that this type of recklessness was not originally envisaged by the Law Commission, when that body discussed the **Criminal Damage Act**. It is obvious, when looking at the report on the deliberations of the Commission, that a more subjective test as to the nature of the recklessness was planned. By 1982, however, the House of Lords had come to believe that this was no longer appropriate.

The possible loophole in Caldwell recklessness

In **Chief Constable of Avon and Somerset Constabulary v Shimmen 1986**, a case mentioned in Chapter 2, the defendant had aimed a kick at the window of a store and caused damage of £495 to the plate glass window. He tried to argue that he had given some thought to the possibility of there being a risk of damage to property but had decided that his skills in martial arts were so great that no damage would result. He therefore claimed that he fell outside the **Caldwell** definition of recklessness.

On an appeal by the prosecution to the Divisional Court, the judges decided that there was an obvious risk that property would be damaged; the defendant had recognised that there was such a risk, but had believed, wrongly, that he had taken sufficient steps to minimise it. He had then gone on to take the risk. The appeal court decided that this was not the same as the 'lacuna' situation put forward by academics, i.e. that the party had considered whether there was a risk and had decided, erroneously, that one did not exist. The appeal of the prosecution was, therefore, successful and a direction to convict the accused was given.

Until Parliament steps in to change the law, therefore, it is very important to remember that offences of criminal damage only require proof of **Caldwell** recklessness, not the more subjective recklessness, laid down in the case of **Cunningham**, which is needed for most other offences.

The judges of the Divisional Court adroitly managed to bring the situation in **Shimmen** within the definition in **Caldwell**, while not denying that a lacuna did still exist in very limited circumstances. In **Reid 1992**, in a now outdated reckless driving case, the House of Lords accepted the existence of a possible loophole in the **Caldwell** definition, but did not discuss this in relation to criminal damage. Their Lordships did, however, state that the term 'recklessness' might have different meanings in different contexts.

9.2.5 Defences to a charge of criminal damage

All the normal general defences, which are described more fully in Chapter 10, are *prima facie* available to a charge of criminal damage and the related offences in the Act. In addition to this, there is a special defence provided in the Act itself, the defence of lawful excuse. It is important to note that this special defence is not available for the aggravated offence of criminal damage.

Section 5(2) and section 5(3)

According to **s5(2) Criminal Damage Act 1971**, there are two situations where the defendant will be acting with lawful excuse in relation to the property which is alleged to have been damaged or destroyed. The first is where he believes that the other party would have consented to the damage. The second situation is where he destroys or damages the property of another in order to protect other property belonging to himself or another. In the latter type of situation, the defendant must have believed that the property in question was in immediate need of protection and the methods he adopted to do this must be considered reasonable in the circumstances. Should this be the case, **s5(3)** goes on to state that it does not matter if his belief is unjustified, provided that it is an honestly held one.

In **Chamberlain v Lindon 1998**, the defendant demolished a wall built by a neighbour because he believed that it threatened his own right of access. His defence of lawful excuse was accepted by both the trial judge and the Divisional Court. The latter decided that the defendant had an honest belief that his property was in need of immediate protection and, provided such a belief was honestly held, he was entitled to use the defence.

> *S5(3) states that it is immaterial whether a belief is justified or not provided it is honestly held.*

Cases on lawful excuse

The following case illustrates the width of this defence, which allows a defendant to escape liability when he would not be so successful when using the general defence of mistake.

In **Jaggard v Dickinson 1981**, the defendant was charged with basic criminal damage, after breaking into a house belonging to a stranger. She acted in the mistaken belief that the house belonged to her friend and that this friend would, if she had been aware of the situation, have consented to the damage! The magistrates stated that she could not rely on **s5(2)** because she was intoxicated and her drunkenness was self-induced. It will be noted in Chapter 10, that self-induced intoxication will not normally negative *mens rea* in basic intent crimes, such as criminal damage, so the general defence would not be available.

The Divisional Court refused to deny her the use of **s5**. Mustill J stated:

> . . . *Parliament has specifically isolated one subjective element, in the shape of honest belief, and has given it separate treatment and its own special gloss in* **s5(3)**. *This being so, there is nothing objectionable in giving it special treatment as regards drunkenness, in accordance with the natural meaning of the words.*

Another case illustrating **s5(2)(a)** and **s5(3)** is **Denton 1982**. The defendant started a fire at

his employer's mill. He claimed that his employer had encouraged him to take this action so that the employer could make a fraudulent claim against his insurance company. His honest belief that the employer had authority to order such an action was sufficient to afford him the defence of **s5**.

In **Appleyard 1985**, however, a managing director's claim that he could give himself such authority, by virtue of his position, was rejected by the Court of Appeal.

The case of **Blake v DPP 1993** was an unusual one in that the defendant tried to argue that God himself had consented to the vicar's acts of criminal damage! The vicar had used a marker in order to write passages from the Bible on a stone pillar near to the Houses of Parliament. He was protesting against the possible use of force in the 'run up' to the Gulf War.

He also invoked **s5(2)(b)** by arguing that he was taking this action to protect the property of people in the Gulf States who would be affected by such military action.

Unfortunately for him, the Divisional Court of Queen's Bench Division was not prepared to accept either of these arguments. The court stated that there was no authority concerning consent given by God and also felt that, when viewed objectively, there was nothing in his action that could effectively protect the property of people so far away from the scene.

A similar approach to **s5(2)(b)** was taken in the case of **Hunt 1977**. The defendant had claimed that he was concerned about the defective fire alarms in the block of old person's flats of which his wife was a deputy warden.

He claimed that he had set light to some bedding to draw attention to this deficiency, and that by his action, he was, in reality, seeking to protect the property. The court failed to be convinced of this.

The courts were similarly unmoved in the case of **Hill and Hall 1988**, where demonstrators were protesting against the presence of American military bases in this country. The defendants had gone to the site with equipment to cut the perimeter fences and tried to use **s5(2)(b)** in their defence. They argued that they were taking this action in order to protect property in the neighbourhood, which might otherwise be destroyed by a retaliatory attack if military action was undertaken from the base.

The Court of Appeal rejected this, despite the subjective nature of **s5(3).** The judges decided that, while the first point needing examination is what the defendant honestly believed, when deciding whether the property was actually in need of protection, a more objective approach should be taken. The jury should decide on this after an appropriate direction from the trial judge. Despite the genuine beliefs of the defendants, therefore, the convictions were upheld.

Comment

It is apparent that Parliament wanted to retain a subjective element in the special defence given under **s5(2)**, by the very precise nature of the wording in **s5(3)**, but it is equally clear that the courts are worried about the possible width of this and are seeking to curtail it. Some would argue that, if the courts did not take this approach, defendants would be able to escape the consequences of their actions by putting forward all sorts of odd beliefs and might then have to be given the benefit of the doubt.

FIVE KEY FACTS ON BASIC CRIMINAL DAMAGE

- The basic offence is under **s1 Criminal Damage Act 1971**. It is committed when a person destroys or damages property belonging to another, intending to do this or being reckless about it. The maximum punishment is ten years' imprisonment.
- Property is destroyed or damaged if it is totally destroyed, made imperfect or inoperative or where it no longer serves a useful purpose. The damage may well be far slighter than this (**Roper v Knott 1898, Samuel v Stubbs 1972, Hardman v C C of Avon 1986, Roe v Kingerlee**), and can cover plastic circuit cards and computer disks (**Cox v Riley 1986, Whiteley 1991**), but will not normally include spittle or simple trespassing (**A 1978, Eley v Lytle 1885**).
- The **Computer Misuse Act 1990** now helps with some forms of damage.
- Property will include most tangible things but not wild flowers, fruit, fungi and foliage.
- A person will have a defence if he mistakenly believes that the property is his (**Smith 1974**) or that the owner would have consented to the damage or that the damage was necessary; the belief does not have to be reasonably held (**Smith 1974**) and can be used even when the defendant is intoxicated (**Jaggard v Dickinson 1981**).

Activity

Decide whether the following have committed basic criminal damage and, if so, whether any defences in the **Criminal Damage Act** are available to them:

- Lenny, in retaliation for a practical joke played on him, decided to water down a crate of Billy's best malt whisky. To divert suspicion from himself, he also diluted two of his own best bottles of brandy.
- Jo knocked a policeman's hat from his head and it rolled into a puddle of water.
- Bob, a martial arts expert, was demonstrating his skills outside the leisure centre in which he worked. He aimed a kick at the glass door of the centre, intending to stop just short of this, but smashed into it instead and broke it. He strongly maintains that his skill is normally of such a high standard that he believed that there was no risk in taking the action that he did.
- Vic covered the wall of his local theatre with crayoned messages urging the public to support their local comedians. He claimed that the voice of Eric had come to him in a dream urging him to take such action.
- Jennifer missed the last train home after a lively Christmas party. She broke the lock and entered number 13 Railway Cuttings. Jennifer believed that the house belonged to her friend Dawn who would not object to her sleeping on the sofa. In fact, Dawn lived at number 15.

9.3 The aggravated offence under s1(2)

This offence is committed where a person destroys or damages property intending by the destruction or damage to endanger the life of another or being reckless about this.

It is not a requirement that someone's life must actually be put at risk; it is enough that a reasonable man would have believed that there was such a risk **(Sangha 1988)**.

The maximum punishment for this offence is life imprisonment.

It can be seen that the same *actus reus* and *mens rea* of the basic offence must be present, with the additional *mens rea* of intending to endanger life or being reckless about this.

9.3.1 Comparisons between s1(1) and s1(2)

- With the aggravated offence, the property destroyed or damaged does not have to belong to another.
- The special defence of lawful excuse permitted in **s5** does not apply to this more serious offence, although the more general defence of lawful excuse negativing *mens rea* in the first place could still be argued in appropriate circumstances.
- The *mens rea* for the part of the aggravated offence relating to recklessness is the same as for the basic offence.

It should be remembered that, in the case of **Metropolitan Police Commissioner v Caldwell 1982**, which has caused so much comment, the defendant was charged with offences under both **s1(1)** and **s1(2)** and that, while he was prepared to admit to the first count, he strongly argued that he should not be held liable under the second, because, in his drunken state, it had not crossed his mind that someone's life might be endangered. Unfortunately for him, as noted earlier, Lord Diplock in the House of Lords, decided that the test for recklessness in this context had a more objective element in it and his conviction was upheld.

It is also important to realise that, with the aggravated offence, the danger to life must come directly from the damage to property and not from some other source. This is graphically illustrated in the case of **Steer 1988**. In this case, the danger was coming from the rifle that Steer was firing, not from the slight damage to the window.

The defendant had quarrelled with his former business partner and, in the early hours of the morning had gone to his bungalow, armed with an automatic rifle. He rang the bell and woke up the occupants and, when they looked out of the window, he fired one shot in that direction, plus two further shots, one at another window and the other at the front door. Mr and Mrs Gregory were not injured and it was not suggested that Steer had deliberately fired at them.

The defendant was charged under **s1(1)** and **s1(2) Criminal Damage Act** and also with an offence under another act of possessing a firearm with intent to endanger life. He appealed against the conviction under **s1(2)**, stating that the judge had misdirected the jury about this. He argued that the danger to life in this case had been caused by the rifle shots, not by the damaged property. The case eventually reached the House of Lords. Their Lordships stated that the prosecution had to prove that the danger to life came from the destruction or damage of the property.

Steer's conviction for this offence, therefore, was not upheld.

9.4 Arson

The common law offence of arson was abolished by the Act and added to the offences of criminal damage. **S1(3)** states that if a person destroys or damages property by fire this will be charged as arson. The maximum penalty for arson is life imprisonment.

This was the sentence imposed initially in **Simmonds 2001.** The defendant had received a letter informing him that his wife was seeking a divorce. Despite an injunction prohibiting him from going near the matrimonial home, he had visited the house, poured petrol all round it and then set fire to it. The house was not

occupied at the time and the building and other houses in the terrace were saved. The contents, however, were completely destroyed.

The defendant had telephoned the police to tell them that he had not intended to hurt his wife but he also informed them that he had a shotgun which he was going to use against those who had hurt him in the past. He also stated that he would use this against the police if they tried to pursue him. When he was approached later by police officers, the weapon turned out to be a wooden-handled axe.

At first instance, Simmonds was sentenced to life imprisonment. The Court of Appeal, however, following guidelines laid down in the case of **McPhee 1998**, decided that while the defendant's conduct was very worrying, this did not justify an indeterminate sentence. This was therefore quashed and a sentence of six years was substituted in its place.

In **Miller 1983**, the House of Lords upheld the charge of arson when the defendant accidentally started a fire and failed to take the necessary steps to put it out. Using **Caldwell**-style recklessness, the risk was an obvious one and it was immaterial that the defendant may not have foreseen it.

This may lead to a harsh result, as was shown in the case of **Elliot v C (a minor) 1983**, mentioned earlier in Chapter 2. It will be recalled that an educationally sub-normal girl of fourteen was convicted of arson, despite the fact that she could not explain why she had poured white spirit over a carpet in a neighbouring shed and had set it alight. The Divisional Court reluctantly upheld the conviction but Goff L J stated: 'I would be lacking in candour if I were to conceal my unhappiness about the conclusion which I feel compelled to reach'.

Comment

When the Law Commission was debating the law on criminal damage, it recommended that arson should not be treated as a separate offence. Parliament, however, was not prepared to accept this and **s1(3)** was formulated. A person can be charged under this section, in addition to **s1(1)** or **s1(2)** if there is any damage caused by fire. It need not be great. The potential punishment, however, is very severe, i.e. life imprisonment and, as noted above, the court may well be prepared to sentence up to this maximum. This may well be necessary in extreme cases but, as mentioned in Chapter 2, it is disquieting to note that **Caldwell** recklessness suffices when establishing liability for aggravated criminal damage and for arson, whereas in most other serious offences, **Cunningham** recklessness must be proved.

9.5 Other offences

S2 makes it an offence where a person, without lawful excuse, makes a threat to another that he will destroy or damage his property, or that of a third party, intending that other to fear that he will carry out the threat, or threatens to destroy or damage his own property in a way which he knows is likely to endanger life.

S3 of the act states that a person will be guilty of an offence where he has something in his possession which he intends, without lawful excuse, to use to destroy or damage property belonging to another or to permit or cause someone else to do this, or has something in his possession which he intends to use for destroying or damaging his own property in a way which is likely to endanger the life of others.

Activity

Mariah, aged 16, had a quarrel over money with her wealthy employer Danny. She decided to teach him a lesson and, after seeing him leave for work in the morning, she entered his house, piled the silk cushions from the sofa into the middle of the room and set fire to them. She then emptied two bottles of Danny's best champagne over the blaze to put it out and left the premises. The dense smoke and fumes from the remains of the cushions reached Britney, in the next room. She had stayed the night with Danny, a fact not envisaged by Mariah, and she now had to spend three days in hospital.

Advise Mariah in relation to her liability for offences under the **Criminal Damage Act 1971.**

FIVE KEY FACTS ON OTHER OFFENCES OF CRIMINAL DAMAGE

- Aggravated criminal damage can be committed where the party destroys or damages property intending by that destruction or damage to endanger life or being reckless as to whether life is endangered, **s1(2)**. The maximum punishment is life imprisonment.
- The danger to life must be caused by the destruction or damage (**Steer 1988**).
- **S1(3)** states that if a person destroys or damages property by fire, this will be arson, for which the punishment is life imprisonment.
- The *mens rea* for these offences is intention or **Caldwell** recklessness (**MPC v Caldwell 1982, Miller 1983, Elliot v C (a minor) 1983**).
- **S2** makes it an offence, punishable by ten years' imprisonment, to make a threat to another, knowing that the other would fear that this will be carried out, to destroy or damage that other's property or to damage or destroy his own property in a way which he knows is likely to endanger life. **S3** imposes liability on a party who has something in his possession or control which he intends to use, or allow someone else to use, to damage or destroy property the property of another. The second part of the offence is committed where he has something in his possession or control which he intends to use to damage or destroy his own or another's property in a way which he knows is likely to endanger life. Once again, the maximum sentence is ten years.

Self-Assessment Questions

1. Where is the law on basic criminal damage? State the elements of the offence.
2. What principles did the appeal courts lay down in **Fennell 2000** and **R (on the application of Abbott) 2001**?
3. Why were the convictions in **Samuel, Hardman** and **Roe** confirmed but not that in **A (a juvenile)**?
4. Why did interference with computer programmes cause difficulties for the courts and how was this problem resolved?
5. Which of the following constitutes 'property' that could be damaged under the

Criminal Damage Act:
A blackberry bush
A farmer's field
A patent
A clump of wild mushrooms
A £20 pound note

6. Why was **Smith's** conviction overturned?
7. How is the *mens rea* of criminal damage established?
8. Using decided cases to illustrate your answer, decide when the defence of lawful excuse can be used.
9. What extra factor needs to be proved for aggravated criminal damage? Why was **Caldwell's** conviction upheld and that of **Steer** overturned?
10. What is arson and where is the law?

Chapter 10

GENERAL DEFENCES I

10.1 Introduction

We noted when discussing substantive offences, that, in some instances, special defences may be used by the accused in relation to the particular crime in question, such as the limited defences of provocation and diminished responsibility in murder and the full defence of consent in assault and battery. This chapter and Chapter 11 look at the more general defences, which may also be of great help to the defendant in specific instances. There are ten of these to examine and knowledge of some of them is required for all the major examination boards. You need to check carefully to see which defences are part of your particular course. The ten defences are listed below.

- Infancy (or lack of capacity)
- Insanity (or insane automatism)
- Non-insane automatism
- Intoxication
- Mistake
- Necessity (in very limited circumstances)
- Duress
- Duress of circumstances
- Marital coercion (rare)
- Public and private defence

Infancy, insanity, automatism and intoxication are looked at in Chapter 10 and the remaining defences are examined in Chapter 11.

10.2 Infancy or lack of capacity

The criminal law treats the matter of age rather differently and, until very recently, put the liability of children and young persons into three categories, those under the age of 10, those between the ages of 10 and 14 and

those of 14 and over. With regard to the first category, it is still comparatively rare for children of this age to be involved in serious criminal activity. It is not however, unknown and some very young children have been involved in horrific acts of violence. One example that resurfaced in recent years, when the question of payment for her life story hit the headlines, was the case of Mary Bell who, at the age of nine, murdered two very young children. There is also a disturbing increase of some types of criminal activity among the 10 to 14-year-old age group, mainly in relation to joy riding, criminal damage and minor theft. Fortunately, cases like the James Bulger affair still remain rare. This case, involving the abduction and killing of a two-year-old child by two 11-year-old boys attracted a great deal of publicity because of the brutality and lack of compassion displayed by the young offenders, Jon Venables and Robert Thompson. It was established that they knew that they had done something seriously wrong and they were found guilty of murder. The case attracted more headlines when the European Court of Human Rights declared that it had been wrong for the Home Secretary to fix a period of years during which the boys could not be released. This matter was one for the courts.

10.2.1 Children below the age of ten

It has been decided that, however awful the circumstances, criminal liability should not be imposed upon children under the age of 10. The Latin phrase 'doli incapax' is used, which means 'incapable of crime'. The law is to be found in **s50 Children and Young Persons Act 1933, as amended**.

It should be noted that, while such a young offender would not face a trial, the child could well be subject to care proceedings if the crime is a serious one. Where the most serious offences are concerned, the child will not be released back into the community until it is decided that he no longer poses a threat to society.

10.2.2 Children between the ages of ten and 14

The question of liability for children between the ages of ten and 14 has been the subject of much debate in recent times. The current position is stated in the **Crime and Disorder Act 1998**. This states that children of this age are now held to be criminally liable for their actions; the presumption that they are incapable of committing a crime, which had been affirmed by the House of Lords in **C (a minor) 1996**, has been removed.

Before this change in the law was effected, a presumption existed that a child between the ages of ten and 14 was not criminally liable for his actions. It was possible to rebut this presumption if the prosecution could establish that the child knew that he was doing something seriously wrong. The law called such knowledge 'a mischievous discretion'. The prosecution had to prove that the child knew that the act he was performing was wrong in law; mere 'naughtiness', as the law put it, was not enough. Such evidence could have been deduced from the child's background, his behaviour after the act, his mental capacity, the replies he made to police questioning or his attitude in court. The mere fact of running away was not in itself conclusive, because the child could have run away after non-criminal acts, if he thought he was likely to get into trouble. The age of the child was always an important factor because the courts rather naturally took the view that the older the child and the more serious the act, the more likely it was that he knew that he was doing something wrong.

Until the mid-1990s therefore, the law on this subject was clear; a presumption of lack of capacity for children between the ages of 10 and 14 existed and the prosecution had to rebut this. In the case of **C (a minor) v DPP 1996**, however, the Divisional Court threw the matter wide open by roundly declaring, that in these days of universal education, the presumption was outdated and should no longer form part of English law.

The case concerned a boy of 12, observed by the police on private property holding the handlebars of a Honda motor cycle while his friend tampered with the chain and padlock securing it. The boy ran away when challenged but was caught. He later appealed against his conviction on the grounds that the prosecution had not rebutted the presumption that he lacked criminal liability. The Divisional Court refused to entertain the appeal and made the provocative statements discussed above.

There was a further appeal to the House of Lords and this time it was successful. Their Lordships firmly upheld the existence of the presumption, deciding that it came from 'a long and uncontradicted line of authority'. Lord Lowry decided that the question of punishment for child offenders was a social and political matter as well as a legal one and believed, therefore, that if change were to be effected, this was a matter for Parliament.

The Divisional Court was obliged to follow the ruling of the House of Lords in this matter but in the following two cases, it took a robust attitude to the question of whether the young offenders knew they were doing something wrong.

In the case of **A v DPP 1997**, it decided that a 12-year-old boy had known he was doing wrong, despite the fact that he had remained silent during questioning and throughout his trial. The court found the evidence of this because he had forced the girl in question to have sex with him even though her distress was

Comment

It might be argued that the House of Lords was more concerned about the attack on its authority by the Divisional Court, than in regarding the appeal as an opportunity to look further at the question of liability of young offenders. The presumption that children between the ages of 10 and 14 lack the capacity to commit a crime was one which had been developed by the common law so the decision that only Parliament should deal with the matter was questionable to say the least. The presumption had been the subject of much criticism and the Ingleby Committee had already suggested that it should be abolished.

obvious and he had later run away from the scene.

In **DPP v K and C 1997**, two girls of 14 and 11 had threatened, falsely imprisoned and robbed another 14-year-old girl. A boy, who had not been traced, had also raped her. The girls were charged, among other things, with aiding and abetting this rape. The magistrates were of the opinion that they could not convict on this count so the Crown appealed on a point of law to the Divisional Court.

The boy allegedly committing the rape was said to be between 10 and 14 years of age but, because he had not been traced, the prosecution had not had a chance to rebut the presumption about his lack of criminal liability. The Divisional Court decided that this was not fatal to the possible liability of the two girls. A rape had been established, the girls were present when it took place, had desired that it should happen and had helped to procure the result. The court was therefore of the opinion that a conviction on this count was possible.

In the interim period, a provision removing the presumption that children of this age do not have liability for their criminal acts was being put into statutory form. It finally appeared in **s34 Crime and Disorder Act 1998**, which came into force in October 1998.

10.2.3 Children and young persons over the age of 14

A child aged 14 or over has always been considered to be 'as responsible for his actions entirely as if he were 40'. This comment was made in **Smith 1845**, and the position is still the same today with regard to his actual liability for his criminal acts. The courts may, however, recognise the youth of the offender when it comes to the choice of the court to be used for his trial and, when the case is over, in the matter of sentencing him if he has been found guilty.

10.3 Insanity

Most people would agree that someone suffering from insanity, who is completely unaware of his actions, should not be branded as a criminal. On the other hand, members of the public need reassurance that they will be protected from his violent acts. The criminal law therefore, has to strike a balance between these two principles and this section will examine how this is done.

The special verdict

The first point to note is that, if possible, such an offender should face trial. If it is then proved that he committed an unlawful act, he will not be found guilty; instead a special verdict will be recorded of 'not guilty by reason of insanity'. The public will normally be protected because the court then has the power to deal with the defendant. It possesses a range of special orders to impose upon him. Before 1991, there was only one such order at the court's disposal;

FIVE KEY FACTS ON INCAPACITY

- There is a conclusive presumption that children under the age of 10 are not criminally liable for their actions (**s50 Children and Young Persons Act 1933, as amended**).
- With children between the ages of 10 and 14, there used to be a rebuttable presumption that they were not criminally liable (**C (a minor) v DPP 1996**).
- The prosecution was then obliged to produce evidence that the child committed the act and also knew that the act was seriously wrong. Enough evidence of these two matters was shown in the cases of **A v DPP 1997** and **DPP v K and B 1997**, but not in **C (a minor) v DPP 1996**.
- The presumption has now been abolished and children between the ages of 10 and 14 are now criminally responsible for their actions (**s34 Crime and Disorder Act 1998**).
- Children of 14 or over also have full criminal responsibility (**Smith 1845**), but along with children of 10 and over, they may well be tried in a Youth Court and receive a different sentence to that given to an adult.

on a finding of insanity, the court was obliged to order that the defendant be admitted to a secure hospital without limitation of time. He could then only be released on the authority of the Home Secretary. In 1991, however, the **Criminal Procedure (Insanity and Unfitness to Plead) Act 1991** was passed, to amend **s5** of the **Criminal Procedure (Insanity) Act 1964**. Despite the complicated name, the purpose of this former Private Member's Bill is laudable. It permits a wider range of disposals to be made when the defendant is found to have committed the crime but is also found to be insane. If the crime is murder, there is still no choice about treatment and hospital order without limitation of time must be imposed. In other cases, however, the court is permitted to impose a hospital order, accompanied by a time limit, a guardianship order, a supervision and treatment order or even an absolute discharge.

It is now necessary to look at the question of insanity in more detail and, before this, the three periods of time when this state of mind might be relevant.

10.3.1 Insanity before the trial

If a person is in custody but is obviously insane, it may be considered unwise to bring him to trial, both because of the effect on his mental state and because the public needs to be protected. The Home Secretary, therefore, has the power to detain him immediately in a mental hospital provided that he has confirmation of the offender's state of mind from two doctors.

10.3.2 Unfitness to plead at the time of the trial

If, because of his mental or physical state, the defendant is unable to appreciate the significance of the criminal trial, he may be found unfit to plead. Such a decision is not taken lightly. The Royal Committee on Capital Punishment recommended that, where possible, the defendant should have the benefit of a full trial. In **Podola 1960**, therefore, even though the defendant could not remember anything at all about the crime with which he was charged because he was suffering from amnesia at the crucial time, the trial proceeded because, in all other respects, he was completely sane.

The question of unfitness to plead may be raised by the defence, the prosecution or by the judge himself. It may be claimed that the defendant is unable to understand the charges made against him, or is unable to appreciate the difference between the pleas of guilty or not guilty. Alternatively, he may be unable to instruct his defence. If the claims are felt to have merit, a special jury will be empanelled to decide upon the matter. This body is only permitted to find the defendant unfit to plead if reports from two doctors support this view and one of the doctors has been approved by the Home Secretary as having special expertise in the field of mental illness.

If matters were left like this, it could result in unfairness to the defendant because the case has not been proved against him. Amendments made to the **Criminal Procedure (Insanity) Act 1964** now provide that the jury must also decide whether, on the evidence available, the defendant actually committed the offence. If the jury agrees that he has done the act, then the judge will decide what should happen to the accused. We noted earlier, that under the **Criminal Procedure (Insanity) Act, as amended**, the judge, in all but murder cases, has a variety of orders from which to choose when deciding how best to deal with the offender. If the jury is not convinced that the defendant did the act, he must be acquitted and no further action will be taken against him. It is also possible for the defence to make the prosecution put its case forward before the issue of unfitness to plead is brought up. If the case is weak and the judge rules that there is no case to answer, the matter of the defendant's unfitness to plead will not be examined at all.

In the case of **Antoine 2000**, a special jury, after hearing psychiatric evidence, had decided that the defendant was unfit to plead because of insanity. Another jury was then called upon to decide whether the accused had done the act that he was charged with. The question then came up as to whether he could put forward the defence of diminished responsibility under **s2 Homicide Act 1957**. The trial judge decided that he could not and proceeded to make an order that the defendant be admitted to hospital without a time limit. The defendant appealed and the case reached the House of Lords.

Their Lordships agreed with both the trial judge and the Court of Appeal that the defence of diminished responsibility could not be brought up in such circumstances is not there to judge on the mental element of the offence. The defence of diminished responsibility is only available as a limited defence where the defendant faces being found liable for murder. In a case of unfitness to plead, the first jury has decided that a trial for murder cannot go ahead, therefore the defendant does not face such a fate. If the second jury then goes on to find that the defendant did do the act charged against him, this finding is not classed as a conviction. The House of Lords did however decide that when deciding on whether the defendant committed the *actus reus* of the crime, the defences of mistake, accident, self-defence or involuntariness (i.e. non-insane automatism), could be brought up.

10.3.3 Insanity at the time the crime was committed

This is a completely different issue. In this situation the defendant is considered fit to plead, but either the defence, the prosecution or, on rare occasions, the judge, is claiming that he was insane at the time he committed the act in question. In such a case, the question of whether or not he is insane is determined by reference to the rules laid down by the House of Lords after the case of **M'Naghten** in 1843.

If the defence of insanity is successful, an amended **s2** of the offensively named **Trial of Lunatics Act 1883**, provides that a special verdict has to be recorded, stating that the defendant 'is not guilty by reason of insanity'. Once this finding has been given, one of the orders mentioned above will then be put into force. If the crime is murder, then the judge is required to commit the defendant to a mental hospital at the discretion of the Home Secretary.

In practice, the defence of insanity is rarely used, although the changes made concerning treatment may alter this position. When the crime is homicide, most defendants prefer to use the limited defence of diminished responsibility, which, as noted in Chapter 4, reduces the offence from murder to manslaughter. Even if the defence is unsuccessful and the accused is sentenced to life imprisonment for murder, he may well be released on licence after serving a period of years in prison. If the defence of diminished responsibility is made out, the period of imprisonment may be considerably shorter. In both cases, prison is often felt to be a more acceptable alternative than incarceration in a mental hospital, and being labelled insane. It should be remembered that, with either diminished responsibility or insanity, the judge has the power to send the defendant to a secure mental hospital if the circumstances seem to warrant this, as seen in the following article.

'Deal with Jesus' led to bomber's hate campaign

By Nigel Bunyan

A PARANOID schizophrenic who claimed Jesus had told him to send a series of parcel bombs across Britain was sent indefinitely to a secure hospital yesterday.

Glynn Harding, 27, agreed to "a deal" in which he would post 100 of the bombs in return for his stillborn baby being allowed to leave Hell and enter Heaven.

Harding, an animal rights sympathiser who searched the internet for information on how to make parcel bombs, had posted 15 by the time police arrested him near his home in Crewe, Cheshire, last February.

In the three months of his campaign he left one middle-aged woman disfigured and blinded in one eye, and transformed an outgoing six-year-old girl into a child who often cries when she is left at school.

Judge Elgin Edwards, the Recorder of Chester, told Harding he had admitted to crimes of "pure evil". Were it not for his illness, he would have been jailed for life.

Judge Edwards said that only the Home Secretary could authorise his release and added: "I am bound to say . . . that I do not think you will be released for many, many years."

Harding, a father of two, began his campaign last December. One of his first victims was Leah Cain, six, whose father, Michael, runs a pest control business in Cheshire. The child heard what she described as a "sissing" sound as she began to open a parcel sent to her home. Alarmed, she dropped it a split second before it exploded. She suffered cuts and burns to her lower body.

Janet Blyth, 46, who worked for an agricultural agent, was blinded in one eye when she opened one of the packages in Patrington, Humberside.

Duncan Bould, prosecuting at Chester Crown Court, said Harding had designed a series of "relatively straightforward" bombs. One was a pipe bomb, the rest nail bombs loaded with ballbearings and cut-down panel pins.

Harding paid for the components out of his state benefits money. In every case, the bombs were targeted at people whose jobs were loosely connected with animals. These included those working in agriculture and, in one case, a fish and chip shop. The suspicion that Harding was linked to animal rights protesters was fostered by his scrawling of the initials ARM (Animal Rights Militia) on two of the packages police intercepted. But he was not a member of any group.

The last bomb to reach its target went to a British Heart Foundation shop in Lytham St Anne's, Lancs. Inscribed within it was the message: "Please find enclosed my donation to your fund."

At the home he shared with his common-law wife, Teresa Done, and their children, Chelsea and Jake, detectives found numerous bomb-making components. They also found the names of seven future targets. Among them was an MP, whose identity has not been disclosed.

The court heard how the bomber attributed the start of his campaign to the stillbirth of his baby in March 2000 and its burial inside a jam jar.

In the weeks that followed, said Mr Bould, he heard "the voice of Jesus" instructing him to send 100 bombs "to ensure that the baby was allowed to go from Hell to Heaven".

Simon Mills, defending, said Harding, whose partner still regards him as "a perfect father", began to suffer from mental illness as an adolescent.

Mr Mills added: "Throughout the campaign he knew that what he was doing was wrong."

Daily Telegraph, 22 September 2001

10.3.4 The defence of insanity under the M'Naghten rules

As mentioned earlier, the rules relating to insanity were laid down after the case of **M'Naghten 1843.**

The accused, Daniel M'Naghten, tried to kill the Prime Minister at that time, Sir Robert Peel, but instead, shot and killed the Prime Minister's Secretary, Edward Drummond. M'Naghten was found not guilty of murder on the grounds that he was insane. This caused such an outcry that, after the case, the House of Lords consulted with all the judges and, from the responses to a series of questions, the **M'Naghten Rules** were formulated.

The **M'Naghten Rules** state that the jury should be informed that a person is presumed to be sane and responsible for his crimes unless it can be proved that, at the time of the offence:

> *he was labouring under such a defect of reason, from disease of the mind, as not to know the nature and quality of the act he was doing, or if he did know it, that he did not know he was doing what was wrong.*

The burden of proof is on the defendant, who must prove his own insanity on the balance of probabilities. (This is the only general defence where the burden is not on the prosecution to disprove it, once it has been raised.)

It can be seen that there are three stages in proving the defence of insanity:

- The defendant must prove that he was suffering from a defect of reason.
- The defect must have been caused by a disease of the mind.
- The defect has meant that the defendant did not know what he was doing or, if he did, he did not know that his act was wrong.

A defect of reason

The courts have decided that this means a complete loss of the power of reasoning, not mere confusion or absentmindedness.

In **Clarke 1972**, the accused was charged with the theft of: a jar of coffee, a packet of butter and a jar of mincemeat, which she had transferred from the wire basket to her bag. Her defence rested on the fact of her forgetfulness, which, she claimed, had been caused by depression. The trial judge decided that this raised the issue of insanity. The woman quickly changed her plea to one of guilty but then appealed against the judge's finding.

The Court of Appeal held that her behaviour 'fell very far short of showing that she suffered from a defect of reason'. The court decided that the rules are not meant to apply 'to those who retain the power of reasoning but who in moments of confusion or absent-mindedness fail to use their powers to the full'. Her conviction, therefore, was quashed because of the misdirection.

Caused by disease of the mind

It is important to realise that it is the judges who have made the decision as to what constitutes a disease of the mind. It is not a medical decision, although conditions such as schizophrenia are obviously covered. Over the years, it has been decided that the term 'disease of the mind' is not merely confined to diseases of the brain alone; any malfunctioning of the mind caused by an inside source will be included.

This position was made clear in **Kemp 1957**, where the Court of Appeal clearly stated that the law:

is not concerned with the brain but with the mind, in the sense that 'mind' is ordinarily used, the mental faculties of reason, memory and understanding.

In this case, the accused inflicted grievous bodily harm on his wife with a hammer for no apparent reason. Evidence had been brought to show that he was normally a mild-tempered man and a devoted husband. He claimed that he had lost consciousness because he was suffering from arteriosclerosis, which had caused a congestion of blood in his brain. The prosecution argued that the defect of reason had been caused by a physical illness, not a mental one and was not, therefore, within the definition of the **M'Naghten Rules.** Devlin did not agree with this view and upheld the trial judge's finding of insanity.

In addition, it might cause surprise and concern to learn that epilepsy, diabetes and the effects of a brain tumour can also lead to a finding of legal insanity. This will occur if it is shown that these diseases have caused a defect of reason resulting in the commission of a crime. Such a condition can be a temporary illness as well as a permanent one, a curable one in addition to an incurable one.

In **Bratty v Attorney General for Northern Ireland 1963**, Lord Denning affirmed that the question of insanity could be raised by the prosecution or the judge, in addition to the defence. He also agreed that conditions such as epilepsy and cerebral tumours could come under the definition of diseases of the mind, thus disapproving of the earlier case of **Charlson 1955**, where a contrary statement was made. Lord Denning went on to state firmly that:

any mental disorder which has manifested itself in violence and is prone to recur is a disease of the mind.

In **Sullivan 1984,** the House of Lords addressed the issue with regard to epilepsy.

In this case, the accused had kicked and injured an 80-year old man during an attack of psychomotor epilepsy and was charged with grievous bodily harm. The medical evidence showed that the defendant had committed the offence during the third stage of his epileptic fit when he unaware of what was happening. The judge decided that he would have to direct the jury on the issue of insanity. The accused, therefore, changed his plea to guilty of actual bodily harm and was sentenced to three years' probation. He then appealed against the judge's direction.

The House of Lords, although expressing sympathy for the defendant, nevertheless dismissed his appeal. The statements made in **Kemp** were approved of. Their Lordships decided that it was not important whether the impairment of the defendant was organic, as in epilepsy, or functional, or permanent or transient and intermittent, provided that the disease existed at the time of the act.

The difference between hyperglycaemia and hypoglycaemia

If the accused is alleging that he only committed the crime because he was suffering from the effects of diabetes, the courts have made a distinction between two different states. In this illness the blood sugar level has to be controlled by insulin. If not, the person may suffer from disorientation and aggression, which could end in loss of consciousness, a coma or even death. If the sufferer forgets to take his insulin, this can lead to a high blood sugar level. This state is called *hyperglycaemia*. As this state arises from the diabetes itself, this comes under the legal definition of a disease of

the mind and therefore is classed as insanity, even though this is only a temporary state.

If the defendant takes too much insulin, this may reduce his blood sugar level, a state known as *hypoglycaemia*. The courts take the view that because this state is caused by an outside source, i.e. the taking of too much medicine, this does not come under the heading of a disease of mind and therefore is not insanity under the **M'Naghten Rules**. The defendant in such a situation is therefore able to put forward the defence of non-insane automatism which, if successful, entitles him to a full acquittal. The following two cases illustrate the strange (and unfair) results of these conclusions.

In **Hennessy 1989**, the accused was charged with taking away a conveyance and driving while disqualified. He had diabetes and argued that he failed to take his dose of insulin because he was suffering from anxiety, stress and depression and that this affected his blood sugar level. He contended that this led to the condition of hyperglycaemia and a state of automatism, thereby allowing him this defence. The judge decided instead, that this state raised the question of insanity because the hyperglycaemia had arisen from the diabetes itself, not from any outside source. Like Clarke and Sullivan before him, Hennessy did not wish to be tainted with the stigma of insanity. He therefore changed his plea to guilty but then appealed against the judge's finding.

The Court of Appeal upheld the finding of the trial judge. Lord Lane stated that stress, anxiety and depression 'constitute a state of mind which is prone to recur' and could not be classed as outside factors. This meant the defence of automatism was not available to the defendant, only the defence of insanity because of his disease of the mind.

This case can be contrasted with **Quick 1973**. The accused was a nurse in a mental hospital and convicted of occasioning actual bodily harm to a severely disabled patient. The defendant claimed that the attack occurred while he was suffering from hypoglycaemia, caused by low blood sugar in his blood and was unaware of his acts. He therefore argued that the defence of automatism should be available for him. The trial judge decided that this defence could not be used, only the defence of insanity so, once again, the defendant changed his plea to guilty and appealed.

The Court of Appeal decided that Quick's mental condition was not caused by his diabetes but by his use of insulin and alcohol, which were outside sources. It followed, therefore, that the defence of automatism should have been put before the jury and because it had not been, the appeal had to be allowed, albeit reluctantly.

Why is this distinction upheld?

The courts make such a distinction between conditions caused by an outside source, like a blow to the head causing concussion, or the wrongful use of medication, and diseases of the mind because, in the former case, the condition can easily be treated or avoided and is unlikely to recur. Where diseases of the mind are involved, however, which might well recur at a later time, the protection of the public is of paramount importance and the court needs to be able to make orders for suitable treatment and/or detention.

Sleepwalking

Such reasoning is apparent in the case of **Burgess 1991**, where the accused attacked his friend while watching television in her flat. She had fallen asleep and, while in this state, the defendant hit her over the head with a bottle and the video recorder and attempted to strangle her. When she cried out, he appeared to come to his senses and he voluntarily called

an ambulance for her. At his trial for malicious wounding, he argued that he remembered nothing of the events and must have been sleepwalking during the attack. He therefore put forward the defence of automatism but this was rejected by the trial judge, who argued, instead, that the evidence suggested insanity under the **M'Naghten Rules**. After being found not guilty by reason of insanity, the judge ordered that Burgess should be detained in a secure hospital.

The Court of Appeal upheld this verdict. Lord Lane approved of the cases of **Bratty** and **Sullivan**. He also noted the views expressed in the Canadian case of **Rabey 1977**. The Supreme Court of Canada had stated that 'the ordinary stresses and disappointments of life which are the common lot of mankind, do not constitute an external cause constituting an explanation for a malfunctioning of the mind which takes it out of the category of a "disease of the mind".' His opinion of the law was not affected by the later Canadian case of **Parks 1990**, where a man was acquitted when he allegedly drove over 20 kilometres while asleep and killed his mother-in-law! Lord Lane decided that while sleep is a normal condition, sleepwalking, and particularly violence in sleep, is not normal. He noted that the doctors for the defence and prosecution had given conflicting evidence. The prosecution had not believed that this was a case of sleepwalking at all but rather one of a 'hysterical dissociative state'. Lord Lane, therefore, upheld the judge's finding that this was 'an abnormality or disorder, albeit transitory, due to an internal factor, whether functional or organic, which had manifested itself in violence' and decided that it needed to be treated, even if recurrence of serious violence was unlikely. He did, however, agree that it was 'incongruous' to label such conditions as insanity and supported Lord Diplock's view, expressed in **Sullivan,** that Parliament could change the wording.

As not to know the nature and quality of the act he was doing . . .

It can be seen from the Rules, that the effect of the disease of the mind must be such that the defendant is 'unaware of what he is doing, or if he does understand this, he fails to appreciate that he is doing something wrong'.

The first part of this statement covers situations where the accused, because of his defect of reason, does not understand the physical nature and quality of his act. In **Kemp 1957**, the defendant's attack occurred when he had lost consciousness and, in **Burgess 1991**, the man claimed that he was asleep. Neither, therefore, knew the nature and quality of their acts. This part of the Rules would also act as a defence if a man threw his girlfriend from the roof of a building, in the belief that he was flying a kite, or, conversely, his girlfriend chopped off his head, thinking that she was chopping down a tree!

The second part of this statement covers a person who is aware of what he is doing but does not realise that he is doing something wrong. This may be harder to prove. In **Codere 1916**, the appeal court made it clear that the defendant will not be able to rely on such a contention just because he feels that he is not doing anything morally wrong, if he does know that his acts are legally wrong. The man who feels he is morally justified in killing prostitutes would not come under the Rules if he were able to appreciate that he was breaking the law. The case of **Windle 1952** also makes this position clear.

The defendant, a 40-year-old man said to be of weak character, was married to a much older woman who was believed to be insane. She often spoke of suicide and a workmate of the defendant, irritated by Windle's constant complaints about his unhappy home-life, suggested giving her 'a dozen aspirins'. The defendant, instead, gave her 100. A defence doctor believed that the accused was suffering from '*folie à deux*', a form of communicated insanity, but both sets of doctors agreed that Windle knew that he was performing a wrongful act. He had also mentioned to the police that 'I suppose they will hang me for this?' He was found guilty of murder and the Court of Appeal confirmed that the word 'wrong' in this context meant that the defendant knew 'that what he was doing was contrary to law, and that he had realised what punishment the law provided for murder'.

10.3.5 Suggested reform of the defence of insanity

We have noted that many doctors, lawyers and laymen have strong reservations about the current law on insanity. *The Draft Criminal Code* provides for reform of this area. It adopts, with limited amendments, the recommendations made by the Butler Committee. It approves of that body's suggestion that the verdict should be changed to one of 'not guilty by reason of mental disorder'. Clause 35 states that this would be established if it is proved that the defendant, at the time he committed the offence, was suffering from severe mental illness or severe mental handicap. Two medical practitioners, who are experienced in this field, must give evidence to this effect. Clause 36 states that a mental disorder verdict should be brought where the defendant acts in a state of automatism due to mental disorder, or, surprisingly, a combination of mental disorder and intoxication. It should also be brought where the fault for the offence cannot be established for this reason or where, because of his mental disorder, the defendant believes that an exempting circumstance existed.

▶ *Comment*

The law on insanity, particularly in relation to the **M' Naghten Rules** and the judges' interpretation of them, has been subjected to a barrage of criticism from a variety of sources. I have identified ten of these:

1. The Rules were formulated in 1843 and have never been updated.
2. The Rules are too restricted; they do not cover the defendant who is subject to an irresistible impulse that he knows is wrong but cannot control. The partial defence of diminished responsibility, reducing the liability from murder to manslaughter, does recognise this type of situation.
3. The Rules lay down a purely legal formula for establishing insanity; they have been criticised by the medical profession as not conforming to medical views of insanity.
4. They are also disliked by the people they were designed to protect, i.e. the defendants. The latter prefer to use the partial defence of diminished responsibility if the crime is murder. People suffering from epilepsy, diabetes and those who have committed crimes while sleepwalking are outraged to discover that the law labels them insane and, as shown in cases like **Clarke 1972, Sullivan 1984** and **Hennessy 1989**, often prefer to plead guilty rather than be tainted with such a stigma.
5. The judges themselves are uneasy about this development, as shown by the comments of Lawton L J in **Quick 1973**. He stated that 'Common sense is affronted by the prospect of a diabetic being sent to such a hospital when in most cases the disordered mental condition can be rectified quickly by pushing a lump of sugar . . . into the patient's mouth'. It is felt that the condition of too much sugar in the blood could be put right just as quickly. Lord Diplock in **Sullivan 1984** and both the trial judge and Lord Lane, in **Burgess 1991** urged Parliament to look into this matter.
6. The very different results from a finding of an illness caused by an inside source, such as hyperglycaemia, and an effect on the mind caused by an outside source, such as the wrong dose of medication causing hypoglycaemia, appear to most people to be irrational and unfair. In the first instance, the defendant could be locked away without a time limit being set, whereas in the second case, if automatism is accepted, the defendant will have a complete defence and will walk free from the court. It is a valid argument that the public needs to be safeguarded against violence from offenders who have mental disorders but it might also need to be protected from those who have attacks because they have not followed their correct course of treatment.
7. This is the only general defence where the onus is on the defendant to prove his insanity, instead of the prosecution having to prove that he is not insane. This again acts unfairly when the alternative defences of insanity and automatism are put forward. In the first case, the defendant must show, on a balance of probabilities, that he is not insane. In the second case, the prosecution will have the task of proving that the defendant was not acting as an automaton.
8. The defence is not available for the defendant who believes that what he is doing is morally right but who knows that the act is legally wrong. Such a person is also in need of medical help.
9. The state of the law on insanity has

been criticised by the Royal Commission on Capital Punishment, the Butler Commission and the Law Commission.

10. The old-fashioned terminology surrounding the law on insanity also sounds offensive to modern ears. Those who cause harm while suffering from illnesses like epilepsy or diabetes are obviously upset and outraged when the courts label them insane; it must add further pain when they are then found 'not guilty by reason of insanity' under the **Trial of Lunatics Act 1883**. Surely it would not have been too difficult a task for Parliament to have repealed the act and modernised the law, rather than merely amending it.

10.4 Non-insane automatism

We have just discussed the position where the defendant commits a crime but is completely unaware of this because he is suffering from a disease of the mind. This is an example of insane automatism. If, however, an outside factor causes him to act like an automaton, he may be able to use the defence of automatism.

The difference between insane and non-insane automatism

We have already observed that the consequences of the two states of mind are very different. With insane automatism, the verdict will be 'not guilty by reason of insanity' and the judge is obliged to make an order regarding treatment for the defendant. If non-insane automatism is proved, this results in a complete acquittal. The case of **Quick 1973**, noted under insanity, illustrates this. Another very similar example occurred in **Bingham 1991**.

The defendant, who had diabetes, was found guilty of the theft of a can of Coca Cola and a packet of sandwiches, worth just £1.16p. The trial judge would not permit him to put to the jury the defence that he was suffering from hypoglycaemia and had not been aware of any criminal activity.

The Court of Appeal affirmed that the courts had made a clear distinction between hyperglycaemia (an excess of sugar in the blood), which is classed as a disease of the mind and gives rise to the defence of insanity, and hypoglycaemia (a deficiency of sugar in the blood), which is caused by an outside source. If the latter is satisfactorily established, it shows that the accused is in a state of non-insane automatism, which is a complete defence. The court therefore decided that the judge should have directed the jury on this matter and allowed the appeal.

10.4.1 Establishing the defence of automatism

It is now necessary to establish when the defence of automatism will be allowed. The essence of the defence is that the defendant's actions are completely involuntary. Involuntary acts done after a blow to the head, or reflex actions after being attacked by a swarm of bees were cited as examples in **Hill v Baxter 1958**. In **Bratty 1963**, Lord Denning stated that the defence was limited to reflex actions, acts done as a result of a spasm, or acts committed while unconscious or while having convulsions. It was made clear in that case that an act is not involuntary simply because the offender could not resist the impulse to act or did not intend the consequences to take place. Some of the examples given in earlier cases will now come under the heading of insane automatism, after decisions such as **Sullivan 1984** and **Burgess 1991**. In the latter case, the Court of Appeal firmly decided that sleepwalking came under the heading of a disease of the mind, and therefore the defence of insanity applied, not automatism. In the light of these decisions, which have limited the scope of automatism, it is rather surprising to note the decision in **T 1990**. The court accepted that post-traumatic stress, which is surely a disease of the mind, could satisfy the criteria laid down for the defence of automatism, because this condition had been caused by the outside factor of a rape. A woman of 23 had allegedly been acting in a dream-like state during and after her involvement in a robbery. A psychiatrist diagnosed that, at the time of the crime, she was in a dissociative state and not acting with any conscious will. The judge therefore allowed the defence of automatism to be put before the jury and the girl was acquitted of the crime. It is arguable whether this decision is in line with other authorities although it may well have been a just one in the circumstances.

In **Whoolley 1997**, sneezing was accepted as an involuntary act and the defence of automatism allowed.

The defendant admitted that he was driving very close to the car in front in a queue of slow-moving traffic on the M62 near Manchester. He alleged that he suddenly had a sneezing attack and lost control of his HGV wagon. He crashed into the car ahead and this caused a 'domino effect' involving seven other vehicles. The court decided that an attack of sneezing could be the type of involuntary act that came under the defence of automatism and affirmed that a verdict of not guilty by magistrates was allowable.

Limits on the defence of automatism

In **Broome v Perkins 1987**, the defence of automatism was not allowed to a person suffering from diabetes who still had some control over his vehicle and this position was affirmed in **AG's Reference (No 2 of 1992) 1993**. In the case that had given rise to this reference, the jury had found a lorry driver not

guilty of the offence of causing death by reckless driving. He had driven 700 yards along the hard shoulder of a motorway before crashing into a parked car and killing two people standing in front of it. He alleged that he had been 'driving without awareness' after a long journey on a straight flat motorway.

The acquittal caused concern and, when the case was referred to the Court of Appeal, it was decided that the defence of automatism is not available where there was merely reduced or imperfect awareness and some degree of control still existed. The court stated that there had to be a 'total destruction of voluntary control' before the defence could apply.

Self-induced automatism

In addition to the limitations noted above, the defence of automatism may not be available even where the defendant is suffering from hypoglycaemia, if it is the defendant's own fault that he is in such a condition. The Court of Appeal addressed this matter in the case of **Bailey 1983**.

The defendant had suffered from diabetes for over 30 years and needed insulin to control his condition. He became very upset when his girlfriend had ended their relationship and befriended another man.

Bailey visited this man to discuss the position and after ten minutes or so complained of feeling unwell and requested a drink of water and sugar. He then said that he had lost his glove and as the other man bent to look for it, Bailey hit him over the head with an iron bar, which he had brought with him. The jury found him guilty of malicious wounding. Bailey appealed.

The Court of Appeal made it clear that automatism arising from the voluntary consumption of drink or drugs is not covered by the defence because the party concerned has been reckless at putting himself in this position, a decision which will be discussed further in the next part of the chapter. The same approach, however, is not normally taken towards someone who fails to take food after an insulin injection, unless he is aware that this might lead to 'aggressive, unpredictable and uncontrollable conduct', and it was felt that this fact was not generally known.

It was decided, therefore, that the jury had been misdirected on this point. Despite this finding, however, the Court of Appeal held that there had been no miscarriage of justice. It was believed that the jury would still have convicted Bailey on the facts; there was ample evidence that he had deliberately gone to the victim's home, armed with an iron bar, in order to teach him a lesson.

10.4.2 Reform of the defence of automatism

The Draft Criminal Law Bill 1989 upholds the defence in cases of spasms, reflex actions and convulsions. It would also allow automatism to be used when he is in a state of unconsciousness or asleep, thus covering the **Burgess** type of situation, a change many would welcome.

Activity

- Do you agree with the contention that the law on insanity is outdated, unfair and in urgent need of reform?
- Romulus and Remus are twins. They both suffer from diabetes. Romulus was studying so hard for his examinations that he forgot to take his insulin. He became very ill-tempered and attacked his law lecturer after the latter criticised his revision plan.
- Remus is more of a 'party animal'. He did not have time to eat, but took an extra dose of insulin and went off to a club. He was later informed that he had overpowered two of the club 'bouncers' after they had objected to his unruly behaviour at the bar.

Advise the twins, who both face charges of grievous bodily harm. Neither has any recollection of the incidents in question.

10.5 Intoxication

In law, the phrase 'intoxication' covers both excessive drinking and various forms of drug taking.

There are rare occasions where the drunkenness or the drugged state is not the fault of the accused at all and, if this is shown to the satisfaction of the court, he may well have a defence. As a starting point, therefore, the law makes a distinction between voluntary and involuntary intoxication.

10.5.1 Voluntary intoxication

As a general rule, the defendant will not be able to rely on the defence of intoxication if he has voluntarily put himself into that state and then committed a crime. In **DPP v Beard 1920**, the Lord Chancellor of that time made the

FIVE KEY FACTS ON INSANITY AND AUTOMATISM

- There are three possible times when the question of insanity arises, before the trial, at the time of the trial and at the time the offence was committed. Two doctors must agree on this and, if the case has reached the trial stage, a special jury must decide the issue taking the doctors' opinion into account. If the jurors hold that the defendant is insane, they must then examine the case against him and decide whether he did the act of which he is accused. If not, he will be released. If so, the judge will choose how to treat him from a range of orders although, in the case of murder, the defendant must be sent to a secure mental hospital (**Criminal Procedure (Insanity) Act 1964**, as amended).

- If the accused is thought to be insane at the time he committed the act (an issue that can be brought up by the defence, prosecution or the judge), the **M'Naghten Rules** are used to decide whether legal insanity exists. These state that there must be a defect of reason, caused by a disease of the mind, so that the defendant did not know the nature and quality of his act or, if he did know what he was doing, he did not realise that his act was wrong. The defendant must prove his insanity on a balance of probabilities. If proved, a special verdict 'not guilty by reason of insanity' is recorded.

- The term 'defect of reason' means a complete loss of reasoning powers; forgetfulness is not enough (**Clarke 1972**).

- The term 'disease of the mind' is wider than a disease of the brain; it includes any malfunctioning of the mind that affects reason, memory and understanding (**Kemp 1957**). It includes criminal acts committed while suffering from arteriosclerosis (**Kemp 1957**), in the midst of an epileptic fit (**Sullivan 1983**), while suffering from hyperglycaemia caused by diabetes (**Hennessy 1989**), and even where the defendant is sleepwalking or suffering from a blackout (**Burgess 1991**). It does not include illnesses like hypoglycaemia which are caused by an outside source (**Quick 1973**). In such cases, the complete defence of automatism is available.

- Denning's statement that 'any mental disorder which has manifested itself in violence and is prone to recur is a disease of the mind' now seems to have been widened to admit diseases of the mind where the violence is unlikely to recur (**Burgess 1991**).

- The defendant must either be unaware of the nature and quality of his act or not realise that he is doing something wrong (**Codere 1916, Windle 1952**).

- Automatism is divided into insane automatism, as above, to which the **M'Naghten Rules** are applied, and non-insane automatism, which is a complete defence, resulting in an acquittal. Non-insane automatism is sub-divided into involuntary automatism and self-induced automatism.

head, reflex actions after being attacked by a swarm of bees (**Hill v Baxter 1958**), other involuntary spasms (**Bratty 1963**), a dissociative state caused by a rape (**T 1990**) and an attack of sneezing (**Whoolley 1997**).

- Automatism cannot now be pleaded for sleepwalking (**Burgess 1991**) or for acts where the defendant still has the power to exercise some control over his actions (**Broome v Perkins 1987, AG's Reference (No 2 of 1992) 1994**).
- The defence will not be available if the accused has caused the situation by his own reckless conduct (**Bailey 1983**). The Court of Appeal felt that failing to take food after an insulin injection might not come into the category of reckless behaviour because it was not commonly known that such inaction could cause a diabetic person to act aggressively.

following statement:

Under the law of England as it prevailed until early in the nineteenth century voluntary drunkenness was never an excuse for criminal misconduct; and indeed the classic authorities broadly assert that voluntary drunkenness must be considered rather an aggravation than a defence.

Specific intent and basic intent crimes

During the nineteenth century, however, the judges began to allow intoxication to be a limited defence in some circumstances where the most serious crimes were involved and the person would otherwise be put to death or, at the least, transported to the colonies. It was gradually accepted that, while voluntary intoxication would never be a defence in crimes of basic intent, like assault, ordinary criminal damage, rape and manslaughter, it might be allowed as either a full or partial defence where crimes of specific intent are involved. Specific intent crimes are normally offences for which some extra element has to be proved before liability is established, although the crime of murder has also been included in this group. The following offences are examples of specific intent crimes:

- **Aggravated criminal damage.** This offence can only be established if a person destroys or damages property, with the intention of endangering life or being reckless whether life is endangered.

- **Theft.** This offence can only be committed when the offender dishonestly appropriates property belonging to another with the intention of permanently depriving the other of that property.

- **Gbh or malicious wounding under s18 OAPA 1861.** The defendant must have unlawfully and maliciously wounded or caused grievous bodily harm to another with the intention to do some grievous bodily harm.

- **Murder.** This occurs where there is an unlawful killing with malice aforethought.

All these crimes, with the exception of murder, which is treated as a special case, require some further intention to be established and, if this is not the case because extreme drunkenness or a deeply drugged state negatives this, it is felt that the offender cannot be found guilty; he cannot be shown to possess the appropriate *mens rea*. It will be seen from the cases, however, that, in many instances, he can be found guilty of a lesser offence, i.e. manslaughter instead of murder, basic criminal damage rather than the aggravated form and malicious wounding or grievous bodily harm under **s20**, instead of **s18**. The offence of theft causes difficulty, because no lesser offence exists to put in its place.

It is now necessary to look at some of the important cases concerning the two issues of basic and specific intent.

Basic intent crimes

As stated in **DPP v Beard 1920**, intoxication cannot be used as a defence for these crimes. A basic intent crime is a crime where the *mens rea* does not exceed the *actus reus* of the offence. This was stated in **DPP v Morgan 1976**. Examples among the crimes we have studied in this book are manslaughter, rape, malicious wounding or grievous bodily harm under **s20 Offences Against the Person Act 1861**, actual bodily harm and common assault and battery.

> ## ◀ Comment
>
> The reasoning behind the refusal to allow intoxication as a defence is that the act of getting drunk or putting oneself into a drugged state is a reckless course of conduct which, combined with a criminal act, will amount to recklessness in law and thus satisfy the *mens rea*. It is probably best to think of this as a policy decision on the part of the courts, rather than trying to reason it through, because there are difficulties with this in cases where **Cunningham**-style recklessness has to be shown.

Despite these problems, and despite what is stated in **s8 Criminal Justice Act 1967**, the rule that drunkenness is no defence in crimes of basic intent was categorically affirmed by the House of Lords in the case of **DPP v Majewski 1976**.

The defendant was convicted at Chelmsford Crown Court of three counts of actual bodily harm and three counts of assault on a police constable in the execution of his duty. Majewski was a drug addict and claimed that on the day in question he had consumed such large quantities of drugs and alcohol that he 'completely blanked out' and had no recollection of committing assaults in the pub in Basildon or later at the police station. The judge told the jury to disregard the fact that there could be a defence on this ground and the defendant appealed.

The House of Lords unanimously upheld the conviction. Their Lordships were obviously concerned about the social as well as the legal implications of allowing such a defence. Lord Salmon stated: 'If there were to be no penal sanction for any injury inflicted under the complete mastery of drink or drugs, voluntarily taken, the social consequence could be appalling'. Lord Elwyn-Jones stated that self-induced drunkenness had long been a problem. He went on to say that 'voluntary drug-taking with the potential and actual dangers to others it may cause has added a new dimension to the old problem'.

Majewski's convictions, therefore, were upheld and the defence denied him. Lord Elwyn-Jones approved of the case of **Beard**, and stated clearly that it was only in crimes of specific intent that drunkenness could ever provide a defence. Lord Salmon admitted that it could seem illogical to allow the defence in one class of case and not in another but felt that treating specific intent crimes differently was justified in order to alleviate the harshness that might otherwise be caused. He did not agree that basic intent crimes should be allowed the defence as the law had been clear on this subject for about 150 years and had not been seen to cause injustice. He believed that the rules were more necessary today, because of the increase in drug taking.

Another basic intent crime is rape and, as in **Majewski**, the defendant could not rely on his drunkenness to avoid liability. In **Fotheringham 1988**, the defendant was appealing against his conviction for the rape of a 14-year-old girl. She had acted as a babysitter for Fotheringham and his wife, and had gone to sleep in the matrimonial bed. The defendant claimed that he was very drunk and had got into bed and had sexual intercourse in the mistaken belief that the girl in the bed was his wife. He was appealing because the judge had directed the jury to disregard this fact.

The Court of Appeal upheld the rule that self-induced intoxication cannot be used as a defence to a crime of basic intent and stated that neither could the defence of mistake be raised, if this mistake were caused by self-induced intoxication. The case of **O'Grady 1987** (see Chapter 11) was held to be authority for this.

Specific intent crimes

It has been noted that, with regard to specific intent crimes, if the drunkenness is so advanced that the defendant has not been able to form the *mens rea* for the offence, he may be able to put forward the defence of intoxication. He will not often escape liability completely, because it is usually possible to convict him, instead, of a lesser basic intent crime. An example of this occurred in **Lipman 1970**.

The defendant and the victim were both addicted to drugs and, on the night in question, took LSD. The dead body of the girl was found a day later. She had suffered two blows to the head but had actually died of asphyxia from having part of a sheet crammed into her mouth. The man, an American citizen, had returned to his home country but was sent back to face trial for murder. He claimed that he had experienced a bad LSD 'trip', during which he had believed that he was descending to the centre of the earth and was being attacked by snakes, which he had tried to fight off. He argued that he had no knowledge of the real events and had not intended to harm the girl. Despite his claims, the jury found him guilty of manslaughter.

The Court of Appeal upheld this verdict. The court decided that he could not be found guilty of murder, a specific intent crime, if the intention to kill or cause grievous bodily harm could not be established. He could, however, be found guilty of manslaughter; there had been an unlawful act and a death had resulted. Manslaughter was a basic intent crime for which self-induced intoxication was no defence.

In **AG for Northern Ireland v Gallagher 1963**, the defendant was not able to show that he lacked the intention to kill. The prosecution claimed that the defendant harboured a grudge against his wife because she had been instrumental in arranging for him to be detained in a mental hospital. He therefore decided to kill her and bought a knife for this purpose. He also bought a bottle of whisky, either to give himself Dutch courage or to deal with his conscience after the event.

The jury convicted him of murder but this was quashed by the Northern Ireland Appeal Court. The House of Lords restored the conviction.

Lord Denning gave the main speech. He decided that there were only two possible defences; the first was insanity, the second, intoxication. Denning decided that insanity was not applicable here because, although the man was a psychopath, this state of mind was not active at the time he conceived of the plan to kill his wife. He also affirmed that the defence of intoxication was not available in a crime of basic intent and added that, even in a specific intent crime, it had to be shown that the degree of drunkenness was such that the defendant 'was rendered so stupid by drink that he does not know what he is doing'. Denning agreed that this had been established in the early case where a nurse at a christening had been so drunk that she had put the baby onto the fire, instead of a log of wood. He also quoted with approval a later case where a man had stabbed his friend several times, in the mistaken belief that it was a theatrical dummy in his bed, not a real person.

In **Gallagher**, however, the House of Lords decided that the defendant obviously knew what he was doing and had formed the clear intent to kill. Lord Denning made the following pronouncement:

> *My Lords, I think the law on this point should take a clear stand. If a man, whilst sane and sober, forms an intention to kill, and makes preparation for it, knowing it is a wrong thing to do, and then gets himself drunk so as to give himself Dutch courage to do the killing, and whilst drunk carries out his intention, he cannot rely on this self-induced drunkenness as a defence to a charge of murder, nor even as reducing it to manslaughter.*

The case of **Gallagher** did, however, affirm that the defence of insanity was available for both specific intent and basic intent crimes if the drunkenness had been so acute that it had led to a 'disease of the mind', as where the defendant was suffering from delirium tremens.

10.5.2 Involuntary intoxication

In the aforementioned cases, the offenders have deliberately taken alcohol or drugs. We now need to look at the position where the intoxication is involuntary. An example of involuntary intoxication would occur where the drink or drugs were given to the offender without his knowledge, as, for example where his drink has been 'spiked'. In such a case, the defendant might well have a defence, both in cases where the crime is a specific intent one and also where it is a basic intent one, provided that in the latter situation the defendant is not found to have been careless.

In the early case of **Pearson 1835**, it was stated that 'If a party be made drunk by stratagem, or the fraud of another, he is not responsible'.

Calming drugs

In some circumstances, the courts have gone further than this and have decided that the intoxication may also be involuntary even if taken deliberately, if it can be shown that the defendant believed that he was taking a drug to calm himself when, in reality, it had the opposite effect. In the case of **Hardie 1985**, noted below, it could be argued that the defendant was, at the least, misguided in taking drugs prescribed for his ex-girlfriend. Nonetheless, the Court of Appeal held that the defence of intoxication should have been put to the jury for that body to consider the matter.

The facts were as follows. Hardie's long-term relationship broke down and he was asked to leave the flat he shared with his girlfriend. He became very upset and during the day took several Valium tablets, after being reassured that they were 'old stock' and would not do him any harm.

He later fell asleep and claimed that he could remember very little after this time but while in this state, he started a fire in a wardrobe at the flat he was vacating. The jury found him guilty of arson but the Court of Appeal quashed the conviction. Parker L J stated: 'It is true that Valium is a drug and it is true that it was taken deliberately and not taken on medical prescription, but the drug is, in our view wholly different in kind from drugs which are liable to cause unpredictability or aggressiveness. It may well be that the taking of a sedative or soporific drug will, in certain circumstances, be no answer, for example in a case of reckless driving, but if the effect of a drug is merely soporific or sedative the taking of it, even in some excessive quantity, cannot in the ordinary way raise a conclusive presumption against the admission of proof of intoxication for the purpose of disproving *mens rea* in ordinary crimes, such as would be the case with alcoholic intoxication or incapacity or automatism resulting from the self-administration of dangerous drugs'.

The court distinguished the case of **Bailey 1983**, where the conviction had been upheld despite the judge's misdirection, on the grounds that the error in the law would not have made a difference to the outcome, and quashed Hardie's conviction.

The courts are not, however, prepared to extend this licence too far. In **Allen 1988**, it was affirmed that it was not available to a defendant who had been drinking wine in a voluntary way but had failed to realise the strength of it and had acted out of character as a result.

On the other side of the coin, the defendant who has, in truth, been involuntary intoxicated will not be able to use this as a defence if he had still retained the ability to form the intent to commit the crime in question. The House of Lords, in **Kingston 1994**, overturned the controversial quashing of the decision by the Court of Appeal and upheld the view of the trial judge that 'a drugged intent is still an intent'.

The defendant was involved in a business dispute with another couple and the latter decided to blackmail him. They knew that he had paedophiliac tendencies and arranged for him and their accomplice to visit a flat to which a 15-year-old boy had been lured. The latter had been given drugs and was asleep on the bed. The defendant was then invited to abuse the boy and was photographed and taped as he did so. Kingston claimed that he, too, had been drugged and had performed the unlawful acts while in this state. He asserted that, if he had not been so intoxicated, he would have been able to control his actions.

The Court of Appeal decided that, if this were indeed the case, the defence of involuntary

intoxication should be open to him. The House of Lords was clearly worried about the implications of such a move, and refused to allow this. The current state of the law, therefore, is that once the intent to commit the crime in question is proved, intoxication is no defence, whether the offence is one of basic intent or specific intent and whether the intoxication is voluntary or involuntary.

10.5.3 Possible reform of intoxication

Over the years, various suggestions have been put forward to reform this area of law. The Butler Committee suggested a new offence called dangerous intoxication, which would come into play when the defendant was acquitted of the main charge and which would carry a penalty of one year's imprisonment for a first offence or three years for subsequent ones. This proposal did not find favour with the Criminal Law Revision Committee. This body did not like the idea of the same penalty being applied, whatever the offence against the person and suggested, instead, clarifying the present rule laid down in **Majewski**.

Other reformers believe that it is unfair to treat an intoxicated person in the same way as if he were not drunk or drugged, and disapprove of the current restrictions put upon the defence of intoxication. The defence is more widely available in other jurisdictions, including Australia, Canada, New Zealand and South Africa. The Law Commission therefore in a consultation paper in 1993 suggested that UK law should follow similar lines and abolish the basic intent/specific intent distinction and allow the defence to be put forward in all instances. The responses to this were not favourable so the Commission now proposes to codify and clarify the present law, with only minor amendments.

FIVE KEY FACTS ON INTOXICATION

- The defence of intoxication is available for specific intent crimes if the defendant is so drunk or drugged that he is not able to form the *mens rea* for the offence in question (**DPP v Majewski 1977**). In most cases, the defendant will be found liable for a lesser crime instead, such as manslaughter instead of murder (**Lipman 1970**), basic criminal damage instead of aggravated criminal damage or gbh under s20 instead of s18. If intoxication is established where the crime is theft, the defendant is entitled to an acquittal.
- If the defendant has been shown to have formed an intent, the defence will not be available. An intent formed by a psychopath while he is not insane (**AG for Northern Ireland v Gallagher 1963**), or an intent formed by a person who has been drugged (**Kingston 1994**) will still amount to an intent.
- Specific intent crimes are normally those for which an extra intention has to be established beyond that required for the *actus reus*, although murder has been included in this category. The offences include grievous bodily harm under s18 **Offences Against the Person Act 1861**, aggravated criminal damage, theft and burglary.
- The defence of intoxication is not available for basic intent crimes (**DPP v Beard 1920, DPP v Majewski 1976, Fotheringham 1988**).
- If the intoxication is involuntary, then, prima facie, the defence will be available for both basic intent crimes and specific intent crimes (**Pearson 1835**). It might also be permitted even in cases where the drugs are deliberately taken, if they are believed to be calming drugs rather than stimulants (**Hardie 1985**).

Activity

Sushila was upset when she was passed over for promotion. She had a sleepless night so took some amphetamines to help her get through the following day. She then visited a local bar and consumed eight glasses of vodka in quick succession. She later regained consciousness at Billericay police station and was told that she had hit the barman over the head with her laptop computer because he wasn't serving her quickly enough and had assaulted the two policeman who had been summoned to take her away. Advise Sushila who has been charged with actual bodily harm, in relation to the defence of intoxication.

Decide how your answer would differ in the following unrelated circumstances:

a) the barman died and Sushila was charged with his murder.
b) A colleague had given Sushila several Valium pills, which had an adverse effect on her. She later discovered that she had set fire to the office before she left.

Self-Assessment Questions

1. What degree of criminal liability do the following groups possess?
   Children under 10?
   Children between 10–14?
2. What changes were made by the **Criminal Procedure (Insanity & Unfitness to Plead) Act 1991**?
3. What was decided in the case of **Antoine 2000**?
4. Define insanity under the **M'Naghten Rules** and state who has the burden of proof.
5. Using decided cases to illustrate your answer, explain why the effects of illnesses such as arteriosclerosis, epilepsy and diabetes might come under the **M'Naghten Rules**.
6. Why were the convictions of **Codere** and **Windle** upheld but **Clarke's** finding of guilt quashed?
7. Why were the defendants in **Whoolley, Quick** and **Bingham** entitled to an acquittal but not **Bailey**?
8. Distinguish between basic intent crimes and specific intent crimes, giving three examples of each.
9. Discuss the outcomes of the cases of **Majewski** and **Fotheringham**.
10. Why did the appeals fail in **Gallagher** and **Kingston** but succeed in **Hardie**?

Chapter 11

GENERAL DEFENCES II

11.1 Introduction

Our study of general defences continues with the defence of mistake. This will be followed by a discussion of three important and inter-related defences, i.e. those of necessity, duress and duress of circumstances. Lastly, the defences of self-defence and prevention of crime will be examined. These two defences are known collectively under the term private and public defence.

11.2 Mistake

Generally, making a mistake about the law will not provide a defence. In 1982, Lord Bridge stated that a fundamental principle existed that ignorance of the law is no defence in criminal law. If, for example, the defendant had led a very sheltered life and then killed someone who disagreed with his views, he would not have a defence to the crime of murder even though he may have been unaware that such an offence existed.

With mistakes of fact, however, there could be a defence if the mistake is such that it prevents the accused forming the *mens rea* necessary for the crime in question or, on the facts, there is some justification or excuse for the defendant's actions, as seen in the cases of **Williams (Gladstone)** and **Beckford**, mentioned later.

We have noted that special provisions allowing for certain mistakes may be found in the statute laying down the offence, as in the **Theft Act 1968** and **Criminal Damage Act 1971**.

Reasonable mistakes

The defence of mistake is also available in a more general way but, until the 1970s, its scope was fairly limited. Before this, the defence was only possible if the defendant could establish that his mistake of fact was a reasonable one and this was not always easy to prove. Fortunately, the accused in **Tolson 1889**, was able to satisfy the court that her mistake was both an honest mistake and a reasonable one to make in the circumstances.

The defendant's husband had deserted her and she later heard from others that he had been aboard a ship bound for America that had sunk with no survivors. Six years later, therefore, she went through a ceremony of marriage with another man. The husband then turned up again 11 months later.

Mrs Tolson was convicted of bigamy but this was quashed on appeal. Stephen J stated:

> The conduct of the woman convicted was not in the smallest degree immoral, it was perfectly natural and legitimate. Assuming the facts to be as she supposed, the infliction of more than a nominal punishment on her would have been a scandal. Why, then, should the legislature be held to have wished to subject her to punishment at all?

Tolson, while recognising the existence of the defence of mistake, nevertheless put restrictions on its use by deciding that the mistaken belief had to be both honestly and reasonably held. This view of the law held sway for many years but later became subjected to attack, culminating in the landmark House of Lords decision in **DPP v Morgan 1976**. This case widened the use of the defence and, in cases where subjective recklessness or intention had to be proved, allowed it to be used where the mistake was genuine but the belief was not necessarily a reasonably held one. It should be noted that while this wider proposition was clearly stated, it did not help the defendants in their particular appeal for reasons that are stated below. The facts of this extraordinary case were as follows:

The defendants were all in the RAF and spent the evening drinking together. Morgan then invited the others to have intercourse with his wife and stated that, if she protested, she did not really mean this and was doing so to increase her pleasure, which was shown to be completely untrue. The men were all convicted of rape but tried to argue on appeal that they believed that the woman was consenting and that the judge had misdirected the jury that their belief had to be a reasonable one.

Their Lordships admitted that there had been a misdirection and clearly stated that, in cases where intention or recklessness has to be proved, an honest mistake, even one that is not reasonably held, could provide a defence. In this particular case, however, the convictions were not quashed because the judges held that the jury would not have believed such a story and would still have convicted even if the point of law had been correctly put to it.

In **W (a minor) v Dolbey 1983**, a 15-year-old defendant was able to take advantage of this rule when he was convicted of malicious wounding. He successfully argued that he honestly believed that the air rifle he carried no longer had any pellets in it.

◀ **Comment**

Even after the landmark decision in **Morgan**, it was still widely believed that a mistaken belief had to be reasonable as well as honest in cases where the *mens rea* of the offence merely requires objective recklessness or negligence. After the decision in **B (a minor) v DPP 2000**, this position may well have changed. Professor Sir John Smith states in his commentary on

that case that, as regards to laying down any wider principle of mistake, the case of **Tolson** needs to be reconsidered in the light of later developments and that the words 'and reasonable' should now be removed. It will be remembered from Chapter 2 that in the case of **B (a minor) v DPP**, the House of Lords firmly decided that when *mens rea* was ousted by a mistaken belief, 'it was as well ousted by an unreasonable belief as by a reasonable belief'. This may well apply to **all** cases of mistake.

Mistake in relation to other defences

- **Self-defence**
  This widening of the defence of mistake was also upheld in two cases of alleged self-defence. The first was **Williams (Gladstone) 1987**, where the defendant mistakenly believed that he was watching a mugging. In fact his victim had been the one to see such a crime and had grabbed hold of a youth that had just robbed a woman. The defendant then attacked the man holding the mugger and inflicted actual bodily harm on him! His appeal against his conviction was successful on the grounds that he had made an honest mistake.

  Similarly, in **Beckford 1988**, a policeman who shot a man who had been terrorising his family, was able to use the defence of mistake because he had believed, wrongly as it transpired, that the victim was armed.

- **Intoxication**
  While the decision in **Morgan** has opened up the defence of mistake, it is still not available for mistakes that are made while in the state of voluntary intoxication. This was seen in the case of **Fotheringham 1988**, mentioned in Chapter 10 on intoxication, where the defendant was unable to use the

FIVE KEY FACTS ON MISTAKE

- There is normally no defence for mistakes about the law. When a mistake of fact has been made, a defence will exist if the mistake means that the *mens rea* of the crime cannot be established, as in **Morgan 1976** and **B (a minor) v DPP 2000** or it provides an excuse for the acts committed, as in **Williams 1987** and **Beckford 1988**.
- Some statutory offences specifically allow the defence of mistake (**Theft Act 1968, Criminal Damage Act 1971**).
- At common law, the original view was that an honest but reasonable mistake about the facts provided a defence (**Tolson 1889**).
- The House of Lords' decision in **Morgan 1976** made it clear that, for crimes where intention or subjective recklessness had to be proved (in this case, rape), the mistake did not need to be a reasonable one provided that the belief was honestly held, as seen in **W (a minor) v Dolbey 1989**. In **B (a minor) v DPP 2000**, the House of Lords decided that an honest but not necessarily reasonable belief, could be used as a defence against a charge of inciting a child under the age of 14 to commit an act of gross indecency. **Tolson** was not specifically overruled but is now unlikely to be followed in the cases not covered by **Morgan**.
- The defence of mistake may be available in cases where another defence is being claimed like self-defence or prevention of crime (**Williams (Gladstone) 1987, Beckford 1988**), but it cannot be used if the accused made the mistake as a result of voluntary intoxication (**O'Grady 1987, Fotheringham 1988**).

defence that he thought he was having intercourse with his wife rather than the babysitter. In **O'Grady 1987**, noted later in this chapter, the Court of Appeal would not allow the defence of self-defence to be used when, because of his intoxication, the defendant mistakenly believed himself to be in danger and attacked and killed his friend.

11.3 Necessity

The defences of necessity, duress and duress of circumstances are all connected and, for this reason, the key facts chart and the activities will encompass all three defences. In particular, duress of circumstances, only recognised by that name since the 1980s, is felt to be an

extension of the defence of necessity. In these three offences, the defendant is claiming that he did not want to commit the crime in question but either the circumstances or other people were forcing him to do this.

11.3.1 The scope of the defence of necessity

There has always been some doubt as to the actual extent of the defence of necessity in English law and this uncertainty was reflected in the comments of members of the Commission drafting the Criminal Code. They stated: 'We are not prepared to suggest that necessity should in every case be a justification;

we are equally unprepared to suggest that necessity should in no case be a defence.' The cases that have come before the courts also show this ambivalence towards the defence.

In early times, the defence was available in specific instances. For example, it was felt to be justifiable to pull down a house to prevent a fire spreading to others, to jettison the cargo of a ship to save lives or for a prisoner to escape if the jail in which he was kept imprisoned was on fire. Before the passing of the **Abortion Act 1967**, there was a defence to a charge of carrying out an illegal abortion if this was necessary to safeguard the life of the mother or, as in the case of **Bourne 1939**, a 14-year-old girl who had been raped.

In **Johnson v Phillips 1976,** it was held that a police officer, acting in the course of his duty, was permitted to order a motorist to disobey traffic regulations, if this action was felt to be necessary for the protection of people and property.

Extension of the defence

More recently, the courts appear to have extended the defence. In **Re F (Mental Patient: Sterilisation) 1990**, West Berkshire Health Authority, acting with the permission of the girl's mother, sought a declaration that it was not unlawful to sterilise a patient suffering from a very serious mental disability, after the girl had formed a sexual relationship with another patient. It was believed that a pregnancy would be disastrous to her precarious mental health. The Official Solicitor, acting on behalf of the girl who was not able to give her own consent to this operation, challenged the action, doubting its legality. The House of Lords came out strongly in favour of the Health Authority. Lord Brandon stated:

In many cases . . . it will not only be lawful for doctors, on the ground of necessity, to operate on or give other medical treatment to adult patients disabled from giving their consent; it will also be their common duty to do so.

In 1992, a doctor was allowed to perform a caesarean operation on a pregnant woman who, because of her beliefs, had specifically refused to give her consent to it. The doctor claimed that the operation was necessary to save the life of the unborn baby.

Similarly, in **Re A (children) 2000**, as discussed in Chapter 3, an operation was again considered to be necessary in order to save the life of Jodie, one of the famous conjoined twins. In this case, however, it would also lead to the death of Mary, the other twin. The twins both had a heart, a brain and a set of lungs but Mary's were not functioning properly and she only stayed alive because blood was being pumped through her body by Jodie's heart through their common aorta. If the twins were separated, Mary would die. The Court of Appeal had to decide whether the doctors would be killing this twin unlawfully if they embarked on such an operation or whether this action could be justified in the eyes of the law.

As we have already noted, the three judges came to a unanimous decision that the operation would be lawful. This seems to imply that their minds were as one on this subject but in fact, the routes by which each of them came to their conclusions were very different. Walker L J seemed to be of the opinion that the operation would be lawful, either because there was no intention at all to kill Mary or, at any rate, no murderous intent on the part of the doctors. The other two judges believed that, following **Woollin**, an intention to kill was present and that the operation would therefore be considered to be a murderous act unless a defence could be found.

Ward L J discussed several defences, including necessity but appeared to favour the defence of private defence, which will be examined later in this chapter. Brooke L J preferred the defence of necessity. With reference to the latter, he decided that the three requirements for its use, as put forward in 1887 by Stephen L J had been made out:

- The act was necessary to avoid inevitable and irreparable evil (harm).
- No more was planned to be done than was reasonably necessary for the purpose to be achieved.
- The evil to be inflicted was not disproportionate to the evil to be avoided.

It was acknowledged that principles of modern family law led to the conclusion that the interests of the stronger twin had to take precedence over those of the weaker one. The defence of necessity therefore was, as the reporter of the case stated, 'uniquely available to provide justification of what would otherwise be an offence of murder'.

◀ Comment

The result of this decision is that the defence of necessity has been extended quite considerably. For example, it was previously believed that the defence could never be used to justify a case of murder, as noted below. The Court of Appeal dealt with this by deciding that this prohibition does not apply where the victim has already been decided by the circumstances and is not being picked out as an alternative to another party. There has also been a development from what has been termed 'rights-based' doctrine of necessity, where the defence was used in the best interests of the person involved, as in **Re F** to cases of 'utilitarian' necessity, where the victim's rights may be overridden for the sake of another party. The Court of Appeal took pains to state that the case of **Re A** was an exceptional one but, as Professor Smith remarks, 'the decision is, whether it likes it or not, a precedent, and a very important one for the criminal law'.

11.3.2 Limitations on the defence of necessity

While allowing the defence in specific situations (and, at its narrowest, the case of **Re A (children)** could be seen as just one more specific example), the courts have been wary of expanding the defence in a more general way. Lord Hale, an early writer, made it clear that the defence was not available just because a person was hungry or unclothed. In the latter half of this century, Lord Denning, normally a champion of the underdog, was equally forthright when he stated: '. . . if hunger were once allowed to be an excuse for stealing, it would open a door through which all kinds of lawlessness and disorder would pass'. He was even less inclined to allow the defence to homeless people, arguing that, if it were allowed 'no one's house could be safe. Necessity would open a door which no man could shut'.

Until the case of **Re A (children)**, the courts were strongly influenced by the notorious case of **Dudley and Stephens 1884**, where the Divisional Court decided that the defence of necessity was not allowed as a defence to murder. Lord Coleridge claimed that if necessity was once allowed in such circumstances, it might 'be made the legal cloak for unbridled passion and atrocious crime'.

The two defendants, another man and a 17-year-old cabin boy had been adrift in the ocean in an open boat, 1600 miles from land. They had been without food for eight days and without water for six. They therefore decided to kill and eat the cabin boy, who had become very weak. Four days later, a passing ship discovered them. The men were charged with murder. The jurors obviously had some sympathy for the plight of the shipwrecked crew because, although they found that the defendants had indeed killed the boy, they wished to record a special verdict. This recognised the fact that the men had little hope of an early rescue and would probably have died if they had not committed the act. It was also acknowledged that the boy was likely to have died anyway although it was stressed that there was no greater necessity to kill him rather than one of the men.

The Divisional Court was not prepared to allow a defence in these circumstances. Lord Coleridge had sympathy with the suffering of the defendants and appreciated the difficulties of resisting temptation in such a dreadful situation but stated that the judges were:

often compelled to set up standards we cannot reach ourselves and to lay down rules which we could not ourselves satisfy. But a man has no right to declare temptation to be an excuse, though he might himself have yielded to it, nor allow compassion for the criminal to change and weaken in any

Honestly, I can see land.

manner the legal definition of the crime. It is therefore our duty to declare that the prisoners' act in this case was wilful murder, that the facts as stated in the verdict are no legal justification of the homicide; and to say that in our unanimous opinion the prisoners are upon this special verdict guilty of murder.

The men were sentenced to be hanged but the sentence was later commuted to just six months' imprisonment without hard labour.

Rather surprisingly, in **Buckoke v Greater London Council 1971**, Lord Denning decided that the defence of necessity was not even available for firefighters and other rescuers, if they contravened the traffic regulations in their race to the scene of danger. He did go on to say that they should be congratulated rather than condemned for their action and expressed the hope that they would not be prosecuted in the first place. One example noted by Smith and Hogan, of where a prosecution did not take place, concerned the behaviour of an army corporal at the time of the sinking of the Herald of Free Enterprise at Zeeebrugge. He told the inquest that he had ordered people near a young man on a rope ladder to push him off it,as he was preventing the rescue of others. The man had become petrified through cold and fear, and would not move despite all attempts to persuade him. The corporal and others involved were never prosecuted.

It should be noted that firefighters have now been given a special defence under the **Road Traffic Act 1988** in certain situations and other statutes also lay down specific defences akin to necessity as, for example, the **Criminal Damage Act 1971**, which allows a defence under s5(2) if the accused acted as he did in order to protect property he thought in immediate need of protection.

Conversely, the courts have decided that the common law defence is not available if the statutory provision expressly or impliedly precludes this, as shown in **DPP v Harris 1995**, a careless driving case.

Similarly, in **Cichon v DPP 1994**, the defendant was unsuccessful in his attempt to use the defence of necessity because the notorious **Dangerous Dogs Act 1991** (now amended) laid down an offence of absolute liability. The defendant, a nephew of the dog's owner, claimed that he had taken off the muzzle of the pit bull terrier in the park to allow it to be sick because it had kennel cough. Despite this, he was still found guilty, fined £50 and the dog ordered to be destroyed. Dog lovers will be pleased to note that the animal later won a temporary reprieve from its death sentence from the Divisional Court, after the owner challenged the fact that the hearing had taken place without her.

Despite the limitations noted above, it can be seen that the defence of necessity has expanded in several ways in recent years and differing views have been expressed about such developments. Along with this has come the recognition of a new defence, that of duress of circumstances, discussed below after duress of threats, which again tries to cater for situations where a defence is felt to be justified and once again has both supporters and detractors.

11.3.3 Possible reform of the defence of necessity

At present, there are no plans to change the common law rules on this defence, uncertain though they are. In 1977, the Law Commission had been in favour of abolishing the defence altogether. It was felt that it only covered rare cases and, where such a defence was felt to be necessary, it could be included in the relevant statute. In other cases, it was argued that the matter could be dealt with when deciding whether or not to charge the offender or when the defendant was sentenced. This view was strongly criticised at the time, causing the Commission to rethink the matter.

Their altered view has now been strengthened in the light of the development of the defence of duress of circumstances, for which they have given the seal of approval. In the Law Commission's Report No 218, *Legislating the Criminal Code – Offences Against the Person and General Principles, 1993,* and the Draft Bill accompanying it, special provisions are included relating to duress of circumstances. None are made concerning the wider defence of necessity but the Commission does recommend that it should remain as a common law defence, to be developed by the judges, as required.

11.4 Duress (of threats)

In these cases the act amounting to duress was caused by another person. This has come to be known as duress of threats.

Since the 1980s, another form of duress has developed which is actually closer to the defence of necessity, although many of the rules laid down for duress of threats have also been held to apply to this 'new' defence. This is known as duress of circumstances. It can be used when the defendant commits a crime as a result of threatening circumstances. The difference is that no one is ordering him to commit the crime, as with duress of threats. The development of this type of duress is described in 11.5.

11.4.1 The scope of the defence of duress of threats

Prima facie, the defence of duress by threats is available if the defendant is forced to commit a criminal act because another person is using force against him or another or threatening to do so. In **AG v Whelan 1934**, it was stated that the defence of duress should be available when the accused is subjected to:

> *threats of immediate death or serious personal violence so great as to overbear the ordinary powers of human resistance.*

If the case is heard in the Crown Court, the jury will decide this matter. With regard to magistrates' courts, it was decided by the Divisional Court in **A v DPP 2000**, that the magistrates should adopt a two-fold test. They should first decide whether the defence could be brought, but at this stage they should only consider whether the defendant had raised a defence fit to be tried; they should not try the case on its merits. This should only be done after hearing all the evidence.

The definition in **Whelan** now needs further examination:

At whom must the threat be directed?

The force or threat of it may be made against the defendant himself or against others, although how widely this extends is, at present, uncertain. It certainly covers threats to the defendant's family and appears to cover threats to cohabitees and other loved ones, as suggested in **Hurley and Murray 1967,** an Australian case. The Law Commission favours the view that there should be no restrictions on who is actually threatened, but it cannot be said with certainty that this is the current position.

What constitutes a serious threat?

It is obvious from the definition in **AG v Whelan** that the threat must be a really serious one; in **Valderrama-Vega 1985**, a threat to disclose details of the defendant's homosexual tendencies was not, on its own, enough to constitute duress. The defendant had been involved in a drug smuggling 'racket' concerned with importing cocaine from Columbia. He claimed that he committed the crimes because he and his family were threatened with death or injury if he did not comply. He also argued that the defence of duress should be available to him because he was under severe financial pressure and was therefore forced to turn to crime and also because threats to divulge his homosexual leanings had been made. The judge told the jury to discount the last two fears; he decided that they were not serious enough threats to amount to duress and the Court of Appeal agreed. The judge then went on to tell the jurors that they should only allow the defence if they were convinced that he committed the crimes solely because of the threats of violence and this part of his judgment was held to be a misdirection. Despite this, the conviction was upheld, as it was in the case of **Ortiz 1986**, where, once again the word 'solely' had been used by the judge. In this case, however, only one alleged threat had been made, a threat to harm the defendant's wife and child. Apart from this there had been substantial inducements to commit the crime in question; the defendant had received business advantages, nearly £90,000 in cash, a holiday for himself and his family and a flat in Chelsea, before the threats had been made. The jury refused to accept the defence of duress and convicted him of dealing in drugs and the Court of Appeal upheld this. That court did suggest, however, that it would be better not to direct the jury that the serious threat had to be the sole reason that the defendant committed the crime.

How immediate must the threat be?

The threat must be a reasonably immediate one. Normally, if there is plenty of time to obtain help and protection from other sources, the defendant will not be able to use the defence of duress. In some circumstances, however, the courts are prepared to look at all the circumstances of the case and may take a sympathetic view of the fears of the accused, as in **Hudson and Taylor 1971.** Hudson, a young girl of 17 and Taylor, aged 19, were the principal prosecution witnesses in a malicious wounding case but, through fear of retaliatory action from associates of the accused, changed their stories in court and ensured the acquittal of the defendant. The girls were later charged with perjury and put forward the defence of duress as they had been threatened with serious physical violence if they testified. They had then seen one of the men who had threatened them sitting in the public gallery at the trial, which reinforced their decisions to change their evidence. The jury convicted the girls after the judge made it clear that the defence was not open to them because the threats 'were not sufficiently present and immediate'.

The Court of Appeal disagreed. The court said that the prosecution needed to prove that the girls could have obtained protection and it was then up to the jury to decide the matter after considering the age of the offenders, the circumstances in which they found themselves and any risks which may have been involved.

The question of the immediacy of the threats was again at issue when the case of **Abdul-Hussain** and five others reached the Court of Appeal in 1998. The case actually concerned the defence of duress of circumstances, which the court first confirmed was available for a hijacking case. The defendants were fugitives, having fled to the Sudan from Iraq, where they had fallen foul of Saddam Hussein. They feared that they would be put to death if they were deported back to Iraq and they believed this to be imminent. They therefore decided to hijack an aeroplane bound for Jordan and effected this by the use of imitation weapons. The plane eventually landed at Stansted and after negotiations lasting eight hours, the defendants surrendered to the police. At their trial, the judge refused to put the defences of

necessity and duress to the jury because the threat was not seen by him as 'sufficiently close and immediate to give rise to a virtually spontaneous reaction to the physical risk arising'. The defendants appealed against their convictions.

The Court of Appeal affirmed the view taken in **Hudson and Taylor** that the threat must be imminent but need not be immediate, and questioned the later decision in **Cole 1994**, which had suggested otherwise. As a result, the court allowed the appeals on the grounds that the defence of duress of circumstances should have been left to the jury.

The defendant in **Heath 1999** was not so lucky. The same court decided that he had ample time to seek police protection when threatened by drug dealers and he had not done so because he was a heroin addict and did not want the police to be involved.

What constitutes 'ordinary powers of human resistance'?

This question was looked at in the case of **Graham 1982**. He was a homosexual who lived with his wife and his homosexual lover, King. Graham claimed that he was frightened of King, because he had been violent towards both Graham and his wife. Graham claimed that the Valium he was taking increased his fear and made him more susceptible to the bullying King. This made him agree to help in the murder of his wife. Mrs Graham was lured to the house after her husband falsely claimed that he had attempted suicide. She was then strangled by King with a flex from the coffee percolator. The prosecution claimed that Graham had helped with this and with the disposal of the body.

Graham's conviction for murder was upheld and the defences of intoxication and duress were rejected.

The Court of Appeal held that, if anything, the judge had been too favourable to the accused in his summing up and dismissed the appeal.

The test for establishing duress

In **Graham**, the proper test was said to be a two-fold one:

- Was the defendant impelled to act as he did because, as a result of what he reasonably believed the other had said and done, he had good cause to fear that, if he did not act as he did, death or serious injury would result?
- Would a sober person of reasonable firmness, sharing the characteristics of the defendant have acted in the same way?

It can be seen that in fact three different points have to be proved:

- the defendant's belief must have been a reasonable one,
- he must have good cause to fear that death or personal injury will result,
- a sober person of reasonable firmness, sharing the characteristics of the defendant, would have made a similar response.

Acceptable characteristics

The question as to which characteristics of the accused can be attributed to the sober person of reasonable firmness has occupied the attention of the court in the last few years.

In **Bowen 1996**, the prosecution claimed that the defendant had visited over 40 electrical outlets and had falsely obtained goods on credit in order to sell them to others and pocket the proceeds. The defendant, on the other hand, argued that he had only committed the offences because two men had threatened to use petrol bombs against him and his family if he refused and had not gone to the police because of his fear of retaliation. Evidence was put forward by the defence that Bowen only had an IQ of 68 and was especially vulnerable to threats.

The Court of Appeal held that these factors were not in the category of characteristics that could be taken into account. His low intelligence fell short of mental impairment and characteristics such as excessive vulnerability, pliability and timidity were not factors shared by a person of reasonable firmness. His appeal against his conviction for obtaining services by deception was therefore dismissed, as it had been earlier on the grounds of a personality disorder in **Hegarty 1994** and vulnerability falling short of a psychiatric illness in **Horne 1994**.

In **Bowen** however, an extension of the defence did take place even though this did not help the defendant in question. The court accepted that a recognised mental illness or psychiatric condition like post-traumatic stress disorder leading to learned helplessness, was among the characteristics that could be taken into account, along with age, severe physical disability, pregnancy and perhaps the person's sex.

11.4.2 Limitations on the use of duress

Voluntary participation in a criminal enterprise

Even if both parts of the test in **Graham** are satisfied, the defence will not be allowed to a person who has voluntarily joined a gang or voluntarily taken part in a criminal exercise and is then forced to take part in activities of which he does not approve. This point was established in **Fitzpatrick 1977**, where the defendant had voluntarily joined the IRA but had later tried to leave the organisation. Threats were then made against both him and his mother so he was 'persuaded' to take part in an armed robbery in which he shot and killed an innocent person.

The Court of Appeal for Northern Ireland said that:

> if a person voluntarily exposes and submits himself . . . to illegal compulsion, he cannot rely on the duress to which he has voluntarily exposed himself as an excuse either in respect of the crimes he commits against his will or in respect of his continued but unwilling association with those capable of exercising upon him the duress which he calls in aid . . .

It was also made clear in **Fitzpatrick**, that the ruling was not confined to proscribed organisations like the IRA and this was affirmed in the case of **Sharp 1987**. The latter had been involved in a series of armed robberies on sub-post offices and in the latest attack the shop owner had been killed by another member of the gang. Sharp tried to argue that he had only remained involved because the ringleader had threatened to kill him. The Court of Appeal reiterated that where the defendant:

> voluntarily, and with knowledge of its nature joined a criminal organisation or gang which he knew might bring pressure on him to commit an offence and was an active member when he was put under such pressure, he cannot avail himself of the defence of duress . . .

This view of the law has been extended to those who consort with drug dealers and then cannot pay their suppliers, as in the cases of **Ali 1995**, **Flatt 1996** and **Heath 1999** mentioned earlier. In all three cases the defence failed, even though the men claimed that they had only committed the offences in question because they feared death or serious injury if they did not comply.

The crimes of murder and attempted murder

In addition to the above limitation, the courts have also had to decide whether the defence of duress should be made available for all crimes even the most serious one of murder. The answer, at present is 'no'. Judicial opinion on this has changed over the years. In **DPP for Northern Ireland v Lynch 1975**, it was allowed for a secondary offender involved in a murder.

The defendant was ordered to drive a group of terrorists to the scene of the crime where they murdered a policeman. The defendant took no part in this but later drove the men away. He claimed that he would have been shot if he refused to help but, despite this, was convicted of murder.

The case reached the House of Lords where it was decided that the defence of duress was available for a secondary offender; a retrial was therefore ordered. Lord Wilberforce stated:

> Heinousness is a word of degree, and that there are lesser degrees of heinousness, even of involvement in homicide, seems beyond doubt. An accessory before the fact, or an aider or abettor, may (not necessarily must) bear a less degree than the actual killer: and even if the rule of exclusion is absolute, or nearly so in relation to the latter, it need not be so in lesser cases.

In **Abbott 1977**, the Privy Council had to decide whether the defence of duress was **ever** available to a principal offender. It was stated that this position had never been argued in an English court, although in Hale's *Pleas of the Crown* 1736 and Blackstone's *Commentaries on the Laws of England* 1857, it was accepted that duress was not a defence to murder.

In the present case, the defendant had taken part in a particularly horrible murder where the woman in question had been stabbed with a cutlass and then buried alive. The defendant alleged that he was forced to help because of threats made against him and his mother.

The Privy Council found it 'incredible . . . that in any civilised society, acts such as the appellant's, whatever threats may have been made to him, could be regarded as excusable or within the law'. The judges went on to state that the courts did not have 'the power to invent a new defence to murder which is entirely contrary to fundamental legal doctrine, accepted for hundreds of years without question'.

This precedent was not actually binding on the English courts but was clearly affirmed by the House of Lords in the case of **Howe and Bannister 1987**, a case in which their Lordships then went further and overruled the decision in **Lynch** regarding secondary offenders.

Howe and Bannister had been involved in the vicious murders of two young men, who were alleged to have 'grassed' on other gang members. The defendants had kicked and punched the first victim until he was near death but had not been involved in the final act of strangulation. In the second case, however, they had been the actual killers. After their conviction for murder, they argued that the defence of duress should have been allowed.

The House of Lords unanimously disagreed. Lord Griffiths stated: 'We are facing a rising tide of violence and terrorism against which the law must stand firm recognising that its highest duty is to protect the freedom and lives of those who live under it'. He was strongly of the opinion that the defence should not be available to the actual killer. He then went on to decide that it should not be allowed for a secondary offender either, saying that it was neither rational nor fair to make such a distinction. This was because, in many cases, the latter was just as blameworthy as the actual killer or often, as in the case of a contract killer, more so. He said that those who were obviously innocent of wrongdoing, as where a woman was forced to drive criminals to the scene of the crime, would not be prosecuted in the first place. He concluded his argument in

the following way:

> As I can find no fair and certain basis upon which to differentiate between participants to a murder and as I am firmly convinced that the law should not be extended to the killer, I would depart from the decision of this House in **DPP for Northern Ireland v Lynch 1975** and declare the law to be that duress is not available as a defence to a charge of murder or to attempted murder.

Lord Mackay was of the same opinion and questioned whether the law on duress was sufficiently precise to make it right for the House of Lords 'to introduce it for an actual killer for the first time in the law of England'. The judges also rejected the idea that duress should be a partial defence which, if successful, would reduce the offence from murder to manslaughter.

In **Gotts 1992**, the House of Lords confirmed that the defence of duress was not available on a charge of attempted murder either but only on a majority of three to two. As in the case of **Howe**, calls were made for Parliament to intervene and put the law on duress on a statutory footing.

In this case, a boy of 16 alleged that he had been ordered by his father to kill his mother otherwise he, instead, would be shot. He therefore stabbed his mother and seriously injured her but, fortunately, she survived. The defence of duress was not allowed at his trial so the boy pleaded guilty and was put on probation for three years. The House of Lords was eventually called upon to decide the matter. Lord Jauncey, for the majority, after reviewing the case of **Howe**, stated 'I can therefore see no justification in logic, morality or law in affording to an attempted murderer the defence which is withheld from a murderer'.

11.4.3 Possible reform of duress by threats

There has been little consensus on this and, as has been seen above, the judges in the cases of **Howe** and **Gotts** felt strongly that it was time for Parliament to intervene in relation to the defence of duress and clarify when the defence should, or should not be available. Some judges favour the complete abolition of the defence and believe that any circumstances excusing the defendant could be looked at when the defendant was sentenced. The minority in the case of **Gotts** felt that the defence should be available for all cases of duress, including murder. Similar confusion is apparent in the views of the Law Commission. This body has been looking at possible reforms on the law relating to duress since 1974 and, currently, takes a similar view of the defence to that of the minority in the cases mentioned above. In its latest proposals, found in the Law Commission Report No 218, *Legislating the Criminal Code: Offences Against the Person and General Principles 1993*, it suggests that the defence should be available for all crimes, including murder and attempted murder. It does, however, recommend that the burden of proof for this defence should be shifted to the defence, as it is with insanity.

Under these proposed reforms, a person will have a complete defence if the crime was committed because of duress of threats. The defendant must have committed the crime because he knew or believed that he or another was being threatened with immediate death or serious injury or before he or another could obtain 'effective official protection'. A threat to damage property would not suffice. He must also have believed that there was no other way of preventing the threat being carried out. When assessing the seriousness of the threat, the courts would be asked to take both a subjective and objective approach. The threat to the defendant must be 'one which in all the circumstances (including any of his personal characteristics that affect its gravity) he cannot reasonably be expected to resist'. The Commission felt that the more restrictive test in **Graham** was not in line with other defences, especially self-defence, and also felt that the present separation of characteristics that could be taken into account, and those that could not, was unsatisfactory. The amended law would therefore change this and would allow any of the characteristics that affect the gravity of the threat. There would be no requirement to show 'good cause' for the fear and all the defendant's characteristics could be taken into account.

The amended defence would not, however, be available to someone 'who knowingly and without reasonable excuse exposed himself to the risk of a threat', so presumably the existing rules on the voluntary joining of a criminal enterprise would remain.

Comment

The proposals are a mixture of the current law and new additions. A very important change is that the defence would be available for murder and attempted murder, thus conflicting with the views of the majority in the House of Lords in **Howe** and **Gotts.** The report suggests that if Parliament does not favour such a change, the defence could be used to reduce the crime from murder to manslaughter. Neither is a completely satisfactory approach. If the defence is allowed as a complete defence in cases of murder, a person who has taken the life of an innocent party would be entitled to a full acquittal, which could cause great distress to the victim's family. In such situations, the jury might be more inclined to reject the defence and find the accused guilty of murder. He would then be sentenced to life imprisonment, despite the threats made to him. The changes could also encourage people who might have taken a heroic stand to take the easier option. The defence would also become more subjective and could, with the help of clever lawyers, be utilised by less deserving defendants, who will not have to show the reasonableness of their belief in as strict a way as is currently the case in **Graham**. In **Lynch**, Lord Morris made the following point: 'Duress must never be allowed to be the easy answer of those who can devise no other explanation for their conduct'. Even where there is an obvious threat of harm to the defendants and more sympathy for their plight, many would argue against a full acquittal. Arguably, the vicious behaviour of defendants like **Abbott, Howe and Bannister** and even **Gotts** should not be allowed to go completely unpunished, however horrible the circumstances in which the defendants found themselves.

On the other hand, if the defence can only be used to reduce the crime to manslaughter, a person subjected to the most awful threats, which few could be expected to resist, would still be convicted of a serious crime and, in some circumstances, this would be unjust. It is true that the judge would have the discretion over the sentence and, in appropriate cases, the defendant could be given the minimum sentence to reflect the special circumstances, but he would still be stigmatised as a convicted killer. In addition, many have argued that Lord Hailsham's belief that the ordinary man should be expected to lay down his life rather than kill another is unrealistic. Even those who might be prepared to give up their own lives to save a stranger could yield if their children or other loved ones were the people threatened with torture or death. Even in less extreme cases, it could be argued that the law should not expect such heroism.

The proposed changes allow the threat to be made to 'another', which would deal with the current problem of how far it should be widened from threats to the person or his family.

The belief in the seriousness of the threat and its immediacy, would be viewed subjectively, but the threat itself would have to be one that the defendant 'cannot reasonably be expected to resist', thus retaining an objective element in the defence. An important change is that, under the reforms, more of the defendant's characteristics could be taken into account. The 'sober person of reasonable firmness' would disappear, which, it could be argued, might widen the defence in an unacceptable way.

Another important alteration suggested by the Law Commission concerns the burden of proof. It proposes that, in future, the onus should be on the defendant to prove the duress rather than placing the burden on the prosecution to disprove it, as is currently the law. This is a major reversal but is thought to have been included to make the other changes, such as allowing the defence for murder and attempted murder, more palatable to Parliament.

It remains to be seen whether any of these changes will be effected in the foreseeable future. The current attitude in Parliament appears to favour the increase of criminal liability rather than its reduction. It should also be remembered that other alternatives are available. One would be to abolish the defence completely and make allowance for the duress in the sentencing process, although such a move would be out of line with most other common law jurisdictions and, arguably, would be a step backwards rather than a reform. Another solution would be to retain the rule that duress is not a defence for murder but to change the mandatory aspect of the sentence, so that life imprisonment is not the only option. People against such a move would argue that the deterrent aspect would then be lessened.

11.5 Duress of circumstances – an extension of necessity

The defence of duress was, until recently, confined to threats from another person against the person or someone close to him. Any other kind of pressure on him was felt to come under the possible defence of necessity and, as has been noted, was not often allowed.

Since the late 1980s, however, a special defence has sometimes been permitted which has become known as duress of circumstances. The following cases show where it can or cannot be used.

11.5.1 The development of duress of circumstances

The origins of the new defence began with the case of **Willer 1986.** The defendant was convicted of the old offence of reckless driving. He had been persuaded by a broadcast on a Citizen's Band radio to drive to a shopping precinct in Hemel Hempstead to meet another enthusiast. The directions he had been given led him down a very narrow alley, where he was confronted by a gang of youths shouting that they were going to kill him. The gang surrounded the car, banged on it and tried to drag out the occupants. One of the men got into the car and started fighting. Willer decided that his only way of escape was to mount the pavement and drive through a small gap in the road. He made good his escape, driving very slowly but then discovered that one of his friends was missing. He returned the same way to try to find him but was unsuccessful and therefore went to the police instead. He was then charged with reckless driving which as the appeal court judge said was 'a very surprising

turn of events indeed!' The defendant's bad luck continued; he chose trial by jury but the assistant recorder refused to allow him to put the defence of necessity before that body.

The Court of Appeal decided that necessity was not the appropriate defence; this, they argued should have been duress. Watkins L J concluded: 'the assistant recorder upon those facts should have directed that he would leave to the jury the question as to whether or not upon the outward or return journey, or both, the appellant was wholly driven by force of circumstance into doing what he did and did not drive the car otherwise than under that form of compulsion, ie under duress'.

Further development of this new defence

It can be seen therefore how the defence started. It was developed further in the case of **Conway 1989**, another reckless driving case, although arguably one with a lot less merit. In this case the accused drove off erratically after two plain clothed policemen in an unmarked car approached him. His version of events (which was substantially different to that of the prosecution, who strongly maintained that the occupants knew they were policemen) was that one of his passengers had been in a car a few weeks earlier when one of the occupants had been shot and badly injured. This youth, called Tonna, was said to have been the intended target and had only narrowly escaped.

In the present instance, the defendant claimed that Tonna had shouted hysterically at him to drive off, when the two men, who, he alleged, had not identified themselves, approached the car. Believing them to be potential assassins, the defendant had driven erratically, and at high speed, in order to shake them off when they had followed him. The defendant was convicted of reckless driving but argued that he should have been allowed a defence. The Court of Appeal confirmed that:

necessity can only be a defence to a charge of reckless driving where the facts establish 'duress of circumstances' as in R v Willer . . . i.e. where the defendant was constrained by circumstances to drive as he did to avoid death or serious bodily harm to himself or some other person.

The same rules as duress of threats

The court agreed that 'a defence of "duress of circumstances" is a logical consequence of the existence of duress as that term is ordinarily understood, i.e. "do this or else".' The court continued: 'This approach does no more than recognise that duress is an example of necessity. Whether "duress of circumstances" is called "duress" or "necessity" does not matter. What is important is that, whatever it is called, it is subject to the same limitations as "do this or else" species of duress'. In this case, the court decided that the matter should have been put to the jury, even though they doubted that it would have made a difference to the verdict.

After **Conway**, therefore, it was clear that the new defence had been recognised but also that it was subject to the same limitations as duress, i.e. it was only possible to use it where there was a fear of death or personal injury.

This point was confirmed in the odd case of **Martin 1989**, yet another driving case. The defendant claimed that, even though he had been disqualified from driving, he had been forced to drive his stepson to work because his wife had threatened to commit suicide if he did not comply! Doctors had supported the view that she had suicidal tendencies and was capable of carrying out the threat. She had been shouting and screaming and making such threats because her son had overslept and she feared that he would be sacked if he were late for work.

Once again, although the Court of Appeal was sceptical as to the success of the defence, it decided that it should have been put before the jury. The court stated that the authorities were now clear and that:

English law does recognise a defence of necessity. Most commonly this defence arises as duress, that is pressure on the accused's will from the wrongful threats or violence of another. Equally however it can arise from other objective dangers threatening the accused or others. Arising thus it is conveniently called 'duress of circumstances'.

The Court of Appeal again made it clear that there are important limits to this new defence. The defendant must have good cause to fear that unless he acted in the way he had, death or serious injury would follow. It also had to be shown that a sober person of reasonable firmness, sharing the same characteristics as the accused, would have responded in the same way, i.e. the court affirmed that the test laid down in **Graham** is to be applied.

The defendant in **DPP v Bell 1992** was able to establish this when he drove off while under the influence of alcohol, because of his fear that those pursuing him intended to harm him. In addition, the fact that the defendant had only driven a short way before stopping, rather than all the way home, showed that he was acting reasonably. It was on this latter issue that the drink/driving convictions were upheld in the cases of **DPP v Davis** and **DPP v Pittaway** in **1994**, despite the defence of duress of circumstances being put forward. In the first case, the court felt that the fear engendered by the homosexual advances of a friend did not necessitate the defendant driving two miles while under the influence of drink. In the second case, the woman fearing an assault had reached her home safely and thus did not need to take out her car and drive elsewhere.

In the case of **Cole 1994**, the Court of Appeal decided that neither type of duress was available to the defendant. He claimed that he had robbed two building societies because he needed the money to repay moneylenders. He alleged that they had attacked him with a baseball bat and had threatened him, his girlfriend and their child with further violence if he did not find the money.

The Court of Appeal decided that the defendant could not rely on duress by threats because the moneylenders had not ordered him to rob the banks, i.e. the person making the threats had not nominated the crime to be committed. Neither could he put forward the defence of duress of circumstances, because the court found that the connection between the threat and the criminal act was not as close or immediate as in **Willer**, **Conway** and **Martin**, 'where the offence was virtually a spontaneous reaction to the physical risk arising'. The appeal court may have been alarmed at the escalation in the use of the defence because they echoed an earlier call for Parliament to legislate on the matter and decided that, in the meantime, the defence of duress should be rigidly confined to its present established limits.

It therefore comes as somewhat of a surprise to note the decision in **Pommell 1995**. The defendant had been convicted of being in possession of a firearm without a licence. He was discovered in bed with the loaded gun in his hand. He claimed that he took possession of the gun because a friend was threatening to shoot someone with it. The defendant added that he only pleaded guilty because the judge ruled that his failure to go to the police immediately deprived him of a defence. He now appealed against this finding. The Court of Appeal confirmed that, *prima facie*, the defence of duress of circumstances was available for all crimes except murder, attempted murder and some forms of treason, and also decided that a delay was not always fatal to the defence. The defendant had put forward possible explanations for the delay and

these should have been put before a jury. The appeal, therefore, was allowed, but a new trial was ordered. This would enable the jury to decide on the matter.

In **Cairns 1999**, the defence was allowed for charges of dangerous driving and wounding with intent. The victim, who had been drinking, spread-eagled himself across the bonnet of the defendant's car with his face up against the windscreen and, fearing for his safety, the defendant drove off with him still in this position. The defendant, who was said to be small and rather timid, claimed that he was also afraid of the victim's friends who chased after the car, shouting and waving their arms. They alleged that they were merely trying to stop the defendant driving away and that was why they had followed him.

When the car came to a hump in the road, the victim fell off the bonnet and the defendant drove over him, breaking his spine. The trial judge advised the jury that the defence was only available if 'actually necessary to avoid the evil in question' and the accused was convicted.

The Court of Appeal decided that this was a misdirection and the conviction was quashed. After **Martin**, the jury was asked to look at the defendant's perception of the threat and then consider whether he had acted reasonably and proportionately with regard to it. The Court also approved its direction in **Abdul-Hussain 1999**, mentioned earlier. It will be remembered that in this case, the Court of Appeal allowed the defence of duress of circumstances to be put forward in a case of hijacking. The potential scope, therefore, is very wide but, as it shares the same principles as duress of threats, it is not available for murder or attempted murder. It may also not be available for conspiracy or certain forms of treason, as suggested in **Abdul-Hussain 1999**. In the latter case, the Court of Appeal made its **fourth** plea to Parliament to put the defence on a statutory footing and thus set its boundaries.

'We seized plane to flee Taliban horrors'

STANSTED HIJACK TRIAL

By Paul Cheston, Courts Correspondent

AN AFGHAN university lecturer today told an Old Bailey jury how the horrors of the Taliban regime drove him to lead the armed hijacking of a plane and hold 170 passengers hostage at Stansted airport.

Ali Safi, 38, described how he was forced to watch a woman being stoned to death as her eight-year-old daughter begged for mercy for the "crime" – in the eyes of the Taliban – of leaving the house without being accompanied by a man.

He claimed the local authority arranged for lorry-loads of stones to be brought in and the leader of the Taliban's "department of prevention of crime and promotion of virtue" cast the first stone.

The father-of-three said his own son had died from a simple respiratory problem because the young boy was taken ill when he was away and the Taliban, under their hardline moral code, would not permit his wife to leave home alone to take the child to hospital. Safi himself was arrested for playing chess and as a punishment was beaten so badly with cables and a metal bar that his back turned the colour of an aubergine, the court heard.

On Fridays, he said, the local football stadium was turned into a punishment block where arms and legs were hacked off those who had offended the regime. He claimed the amputated limbs were hung from trees.

When the Taliban took control of the country in 1996, Safi said he saw death squads roaming the streets shooting on sight. They broke into a hospital next to his home and indiscriminately shot nurses and patients. Bodies were ordered to be left lying in the streets as deterrents despite the 40 degree heat and the threat of disease.

A few years earlier in Kabul he had seen the bullet-ridden body of President Najibullah, who had been overthrown by the Mujahideen, and his brother, hanging from a traffic pole in the middle of the street.

Safi is one of 11 defendants, aged between 20 and 38, said to have seized the plane which was originally on an internal flight from Kabul in February last year. They were armed with four handguns and explosive grenades.

They are accused of forcing it to fly across several former Soviet countries before eventually landing at Stansted where – in an operation costing £2 million – it was surrounded by armed police before the siege ended after 77 hours.

Safi, from the northern city of Masar-i-Sharif, said women who had once enjoyed the normal freedoms of the West were liable to be arrested and either stoned to death or subjected to public lashings for any breach of the ruthless and extreme moral code enforced by the Taliban.

"In one of the worst experiences of my life I saw a woman stoned to death who I knew because she lived in our area," he told the jury through an interpreter.

"I saw a hole being dug and the judge decide that she had left her house without permission of her husband. They placed her in the hole."

He said that the head of the "prevention of crime and promotion of virtue" committee was the first person to throw a stone and that the people who had been ordered to watch were forced to stone the woman to death.

Safi added: "They stoned her until the hole was full, then a doctor pronounced she was still alive so they kept on stoning her until she died. Her eight-year-old daughter was running around her begging people not to thrown stones at her mother."

Safi and nine other defendants deny hijack. The 11th defendant, who does not face that charge, has pleaded not guilty to possessing explosives and arms. The case continues.

Evening Standard, 31 October 2001

Meanwhile, the defence continues to develop. In **Shayler 2001**, it was decided that the defences of both necessity and duress, as developed, were *prima facie* available under the **Official Secrets Act 1989**. In the case at issue however, the appeal failed. The defendant tried to argue that he had only disclosed certain secret information to protect the public from harm but the court decided that he was unable to identify an imminent threat to the life or limb of that group.

No half-way house

If the defence of duress of circumstances succeeds, it is a complete defence, entitling the defendant to an acquittal. In **Symonds 1997**, the Court of Appeal decided that it was not correct in a dangerous driving case, merely to reduce the offence to careless driving.

11.5.2 Possible reform of duress of circumstances

The Law Commission has recognised the value of the defence of duress of circumstances and has included the defence in its Draft Criminal Law Bill 1993. These current proposals differ from what is in the *Draft Criminal Code*. The newer version would permit the defence to be used in crimes of murder and attempted murder, but would change the burden of proof, which would now be on the accused. This would bring this defence in line with what it proposed for duress of threats. Under Clause 26, the defence would be available for a defendant who only commits a crime because 'he knows or believes that it is immediately necessary to avoid death or serious injury to himself or another. The danger that he knows or believes to exist must be such that in all the circumstances (including any of his personal characteristics that affect its gravity) he cannot reasonably be expected to act otherwise'.

Comment

It will be seen from the suggested reforms that the defence of duress of circumstances has been firmly recognised by the Law Commission and would be extended to cover all offences including murder and attempted murder. The merits and possible problems with this are the same as those discussed under duress by threats. It can also be seen that the test in **Martin** has been watered down, although there is still an objective element when assessing the actions that he has taken in response to the threat. This might result in many more appeals, especially in relation to driving offences, and could overload an already over-stretched Court of Appeal.

Activity

- In small groups, or individually in written form, discuss the following question: 'At the present time, English law recognises the three separate, but related defences of necessity, duress and duress of circumstances. Is this a satisfactory state of the law?'
- Decide whether a defence of necessity, duress or duress of circumstances is available in the following scenarios:

Charles took part in the killing of James after Mary threatened to commit suicide if he refused to help.

Anne found herself surrounded by a hostile crowd in the middle of town. She saw George's Mercedes parked nearby, with the keys still in the ignition, so jumped in and sped away at 60 miles per hour. She has been charged with theft and dangerous driving.

William and Victoria were the only survivors of a plane crash. After 15 days without food, William killed and ate Victoria.

- Critically examine whether a relaxation of the current limits on the defence of duress, on the lines suggested by the Law Commission, would open the floodgates to a rush of possibly unworthy claims.

11.6 Marital coercion

This very limited defence only applies to a wife who can prove that she committed an offence other than treason and murder in the presence of, and under the coercion of, her husband.

The defence was originally formulated by the common law, under which it was presumed that a wife was acting under the coercion of her husband unless the prosecution could prove that she had taken the initiative. In 1925, however, the presumption was abolished by **s47 Criminal Justice Act 1927**. Currently, marital coercion only exists as a defence in such a situation. It is limited to wives who need to show that they are validly married. In **Ditta 1988**, Lord Lane seemed to have had doubts as to whether the defence could be extended to polygamous marriages.

Many feel that such a defence has little part to play in a more equal society. The Law Commission recommended its abolition back in 1977 but, as yet, no reform has been effected.

TEN KEY FACTS ON NECESSITY, DURESS OF THREATS AND DURESS OF CIRCUMSTANCES

- The defence of necessity, if allowed, is said to justify the commission of a crime; for this reason it is a very limited defence, confined to specific situations (**Bourne 1939, Johnson v Phillips 1976, Road Traffic Act 1988 (as amended), Re F (Mental Patient: Sterilization) 1990** and **Re A (children) 2000**). It is not normally available for the crime of murder (**Dudley and Stephens 1884**), (but note **Re A (children) 2000**), or where statutes do not intend the defence to be available (**Cichon v DPP 1994, DPP v Harris 1995**).

- Duress of threats provides an excuse for the commission of a crime. It is definitely available if the person or his family is threatened (**Hurley and Murray 1967**), and may well apply if others are at risk.

- It can only be used where the threat is to cause death or serious injury (**AG v Whelan 1934**) and a sober person of reasonable firmness, sharing the characteristics of the accused, would have acted in the same way (**Graham 1982**). The word 'characteristics' would include age, sex, mental impairment and post-traumatic stress disorder (**Bowen 1996**), but not a personality disorder (**Hegarty 1994**), excessive vulnerability, timidity or pliability (**Horne 1994, Bowen 1996**) or a low IQ (**Bowen 1996**). Threats to reveal someone's poor financial position or his homosexual tendencies are not enough (**Valderrama-Vega 1985**), but the threat of death or serious injury need not be the sole reason for the defendant's act (**Valderrama-Vega 1985, Ortiz 1986**).

- The threat must be imminent, without the prospect of getting official protection (**Heath 1999**), although the courts may look at extenuating circumstances, such as the age of the defendant and the belief that official protection is inadequate (**Hudson and Taylor 1971, Abdul-Hussain and Others 1998**).

- Even if the requirements for the defence are satisfied, it is not available for those who voluntarily join gangs or other illegal enterprises (**Fitzpatrick 1977, Sharp 1987, Ali 1995, Flatt 1996**). It is also not available for murder, whether for a principal offender (**Abbott 1977**), or a secondary offender (**Howe 1987**). Neither is it a defence for attempted murder (**Gotts 1992**).

- Duress of circumstances is an extension of the defence of necessity but has the same limitations as duress of threats. There is no actual threat from a person; instead it comes from the circumstances. If successful, the defendant is entitled to a full acquittal (**Symonds 1997**); it cannot be used to reduce a charge.

- The defence is available where the defendant fears that death or personal injury will result if he does not commit a crime in order to relieve the situation. He must, however, have good cause for his fear and the court must be satisfied that a sober person of reasonable firmness would have acted in a similar way (**Martin 1989**). Such a defence was first suggested in **Willer 1986**, although it was not specifically named as such until **Conway 1989**. These cases and **DPP v Bell 1992, DPP v Davis 1994** and **DPP v Pittaway 1994** all concerned driving offences but, in **Pommell 1995** and **Abdul-Hussain and Others 1998**, the Court of Appeal made it clear that the defence can be used for nearly all offences, even those against the **Official Secrets Act (Shayler 2001)** except some forms of treason, murder, attempted murder and possibly conspiracy.

- Despite this extension, it was stated in **Cole 1994** and on three other occasions that Parliament should legislate on the defence of duress and meanwhile it should be 'rigidly confined'.

- As in duress by threats, normally the defence of duress of circumstances can only be used if the threat is immediate (**Bell 1992**). It was felt that the danger had passed in **DPP v Davis** and **DPP v Pittaway** so the defence failed.

- In **Pommell 1995**, however, the Court of Appeal stated that if there were possible explanations for the delay, the matter should be put before the jury.

11.7 Public and private defence

The defences described below come under this blanket heading because a party may lawfully use force, provided that this is not excessive, in the defence of both public and private interests. He is therefore allowed to use such force in defence of the following:

- To prevent crime or assist in the lawful arrest of an offender or a suspected one
- To prevent a breach of the peace
- To protect his property or to prevent a trespass
- To protect himself from unlawful violence
- To protect himself from unlawful detention

11.7.1 The statutory offence

The law on the first two of the situations listed above was developed at common law but is now found under **s3 Criminal Law Act 1967**. This states that:

a person may use such force as is reasonable in the circumstances in the prevention of crime or in assisting in the lawful arrest of offenders or suspected offenders, or of persons unlawfully at large.

In the case of **Renouf 1986**, the defendant had been working on the forecourt of his garage when the occupants of a Volvo car drew up and threw things at him. He suffered an injury to his arm and his car windscreen was damaged. After calling to his wife to call the police, he followed the men in his car and eventually forced them onto a grass verge. He was convicted of reckless driving (still in existence at that time), but appealed. The Court of Appeal held that the possible defence under s3, that he was trying to assist in the lawful

arrest of offenders, should have been put before the jury and quashed the conviction.

In many cases of assault, this statutory defence is also open to a person who is personally threatened, in addition to the common law defence of self-defence, discussed below. While he is defending himself against the attack on his person or the person of another, he will, in most cases, also be preventing a crime being committed. The **Criminal Law Act** makes it clear that the common law defence remains in areas where the act does not provide a defence and in **Cousins 1982**, it was stated that both defences exist and can be used in conjunction with each other.

Defending property

S5 Criminal Damage Act 1971 provides a person with a defence if: 'he destroys or damages the property of another in order to protect his own property or that of someone else, provided that it is in immediate need of protection and the force used is reasonable'.

In earlier times, a person was allowed to stand firm and fight against the loss of his property whereas if the attack were against him personally, he was supposed to retreat from the danger where possible. In **Hussey 1924**, the Lord Chief Justice quashed the conviction of a man who barricaded himself in when threatened with alleged unlawful eviction. He then fired a gun through the door at the three people armed with household tools who were seeking to remove him, wounding two of them. It is extremely unlikely that a similar decision would be arrived at today but it is still clear that a person can seek the help of the law in protecting his property. In **AG's Reference (No 2 of 1983) 1984**, it was rather surprisingly decided that it was not unlawful for a person to make up petrol bombs to try to prevent crime and defend his property in an area where there had been extensive rioting and further threats were imminent.

11.7.2 Self-defence at common law

The subjective element

The judges have decided that a person may use reasonable force to protect himself or another person if he fears an attack or one actually occurs. The first part of this test is a subjective one, so even if the reaction is thought to be unreasonable by the ordinary man, the matter should be put before a jury for that body to decide the matter. The cases of **Williams (Gladstone) 1987** and **Beckford 1988**, discussed earlier, are authority for this.

Intoxication

While the belief in whether there is a need to act in self-defence is a subjective one, and an honest, albeit unreasonable belief may be enough, a different approach is taken if the defendant is merely making the mistake because he is intoxicated.

This point was made clear in **O'Grady 1987**. The defendant was addicted to drink and, on the night in question had consumed eight flagons of cider! He then retired to his flat with two friends. In the morning, one of these friends found him covered with blood and the other friend dead. O'Grady claimed that he and the victim had been involved in a fight in the night and when he had felt the victim he was cold. The defendant reported the matter to the police and argued that he had only acted in self-defence. When he was examined, a number of cuts and bruises were noted which might have supported his version of events, but he was still convicted of manslaughter. The Court of Appeal confirmed that the defence of self-defence would be available to a 'sober man who mistakenly believes he is in danger of immediate death at the hands of an attacker' but not to a person whose mistake was caused by voluntary intoxication.

No need to retreat

In the older cases of common law self-defence, it was suggested that the defence would fail unless the defendant could show that he had tried to retreat from the danger. In **Julien 1969**, however, the Court of Appeal decided that this was not essential but went on to state what action he did need to take:

> what is necessary is that he should demonstrate by his actions that he does not want to fight. He must demonstrate that he is prepared to temporise and disengage and perhaps to make some physical withdrawal.

In the following case, the Court of Appeal went further. In **Bird 1985** a 17-year-old girl was celebrating her birthday and became very upset when an ex-boyfriend appeared at her party with a new girlfriend in tow. He left after a heated argument but later returned alone and the argument continued. The defendant threw a glass of Pernod over him and a physical fight developed. Bird alleged that she was held up against a wall and had then lunged at the victim. The glass was still in her hand when she hit him in the face, causing him to lose an eye.

The Court of Appeal decided that the case of **Julien** had placed too great an obligation on the defendant to demonstrate that he did not wish to fight, which was not reflected in the later Privy Council decision in **Palmer 1971**. This case had decided that 'there are no prescribed words which must be employed in or adopted in a summing up'. The court also stated that the courts had gone too far when they said that the defendant must demonstrate a desire not to fight. This was not consistent with the rule that a person can use force, not merely to counter an attack, but also to ward off an attack honestly and reasonably believed to be imminent. It was felt that the defendant's demonstration that he did not want to fight was the best evidence that he was acting reasonably and in good faith in self-defence; but was no more than evidence to this effect.

Bird's conviction for wounding was therefore quashed.

The objective element

It has just been noted that the defendant's belief that he has to act in self-defence need not be a reasonable belief. The test is subjective. With regard to the actual force used, however, the courts have now made it very plain that only reasonable force can be used to counter the threat and that this is an objective test. This had been felt to be the law but some doubt was cast upon this view in the case of **Scarlett 1993**. A pub landlord forcibly ejected a drunken customer who then fell down the steps and was killed. The judgment seemed to imply that the test for deciding whether the force used was excessive was also subjective. This was firmly denied by the Court of Appeal in **Owino 1996**. The court said that if such a view were taken, it would allow a person who was merely threatened with a punch, to shoot the other and plead self-defence. The court concluded 'That clearly is not, and cannot be, the law'.

The use of excessive force

It has therefore been made abundantly clear that an objective view is taken when assessing whether the defendant has used reasonable or excessive force. Should the force be found to be excessive by this standard, the defence will fail and the defendant will be guilty of whatever crime has been committed. This is shown clearly in the cases of **Clegg 1995** and **Martin 2001** where the responses to the threats were held to be excessive.

In **Clegg 1995**, the defendant had been on a night patrol in West Belfast, in order to catch joy riders. His team was moving towards Belfast just beyond a checkpoint at a bridge. Clegg was not informed of the reason for the patrol but it was established at his trial that he did not believe the offenders were terrorists.

The car containing the victim was initially stopped at the checkpoint but then accelerated away in the centre of the road with its headlights full on. Someone in the checkpoint team shouted that it should be stopped and all four members of Clegg's team fired at it. Clegg's evidence was that he fired four bullets into the windscreen and one into the side of the car as it passed. He claimed that he had believed that a fellow soldier had been struck by the speeding car and that his life had been in danger. Scientific evidence, on the other hand, showed that the last shot had been fired when the car had already passed and was over 50 feet further along the road. The 18-year-old victim, a passenger called Karen Reilly, had been hit in the back. It also emerged later that the speeding car had not caused Private Ainbow's injuries. Instead, the soldiers were alleged to have deliberately stamped on his leg to make it look as though this had happened. Ainbow was later convicted of conspiring to pervert the course of justice.

There are no juries in such cases in Northern Ireland in view of the political situation; therefore it was the judge who found Clegg guilty of murder. He found that there was insufficient evidence for him to use **s3 Criminal Law Act** in his defence. The Court of Appeal disagreed but went on to decide that there had been no miscarriage of justice because the force used by Clegg with regard to the fourth shot had not been reasonable: it had been fired with the intention to kill or seriously injure the victim.

Nevertheless, the Court of Appeal called on Parliament to consider making a change in the law on this subject and, meanwhile, put a point of law to the House of Lords. This was whether a killing by a police officer or soldier in the course of his duty should be regarded as manslaughter rather than murder where the force used is excessive and unreasonable.

The House of Lords decided that it would be impractical to make a distinction between excessive force used in trying to prevent a crime or apprehend a suspect and any excessive force used in self-defence, particularly as the two often overlap. Their Lordships then reviewed authorities such as **Palmer 1971**, a Privy Council decision, **McInnes**, a Court of Appeal decision in the same year, and **Zecevic v DPP 1987**, an Australian case. They came to the conclusion that 'there is no half-way house. There is no rule that a defendant who has used a greater degree of force than was necessary in the circumstances should be found guilty of manslaughter rather than murder. . . . The defence either succeeds or it fails. If it succeeds the defendant is acquitted. If it fails, he is guilty of murder.' Clegg's conviction for murder therefore, was upheld. He was later allowed a retrial when fresh forensic evidence was produced and, in March 1999, his conviction was quashed. The judge decided that while much of Clegg's testimony was 'a farrago of deceit and lies' it could not be conclusively proved that he had fired the fatal shot.

The Norfolk farmer, Tony Martin, was less successful in his appeal. He had been found guilty of murder after using excessive force in self-defence when fatally shooting a 16-year-old burglar and injuring another.

The Court of Appeal agreed with the jury that the force used to repel the burglars had been excessive, no matter how great Martin's fears. The court was prepared instead to accept fresh evidence, allowing the partial defence of diminished responsibility to be put forward and, as noted in Chapter 4, the life sentence for murder was reduced to five years for manslaughter.

In the case of **Davenport**, as shown in the article overleaf, there were no such doubts as to whether the force used was excessive. The jury took only 15 minutes to decide that the defence of self-defence had been made out, thus allowing the defendant to walk free from the court.

Comment

In **Clegg**, their Lordships had the opportunity to 'bite the bullet' and change the rules so that a manslaughter verdict could be substituted for murder, in cases where excessive force was used in self-defence or prevention of crime. They preferred to maintain the status quo but if they had acted more radically, they would not have faced the criticism that they were acting alone or against informed opinion. Back in 1958, in the case of **Howe** (not the same **Howe** as in duress), the Australian courts had decided that a killing by excessive force in self-defence should be treated as manslaughter, not murder (although they later brought their law into line with the English courts). Our Criminal Law Revision Committee also favoured a more liberal defence and suggested a change in the law, as did a Select Committee of the House of Lords when its members looked into the question of murder and life imprisonment.

Whether such a change should only be effected in relation to the police and armed services, as some have argued or apply more universally is a contentious issue. Perhaps a stronger case can be made out for the police and armed services because of the tense situations in which they might find themselves, where the need for a split-second decision is vital. There are many that oppose making them a special case however, believing it to be dangerous to give more licence to certain sections of the community as this could lead to abuse.

It is submitted that the case for a change in the law with regard to this defence is overwhelming and that it needs to apply in a general way. None of us can foretell how we would act in a situation fraught with danger and should we use what the outsider regards as excessive force, we could be found guilty of murder, with no discretion about the sentence, sharing the same fate as a serial killer. If the jury members realize that this might happen, they could be tempted to bring in a not guilty verdict even in a 'grey area' case. This, in turn, could lead to injustice because on occasion some form of blameworthiness on the part of the defendant is present and the courts need to recognize this fact, particularly if fatal injuries have been inflicted. The answer is to introduce a partial defence, preferably by statute, reducing the charge to manslaughter in the same way as for diminished responsibility, provocation or the survivor of a suicide pact. The judge can then sentence in proportion to the degree of blameworthiness. Another, less satisfactory option is to leave the law as it stands but to give the judge discretion over the sentence to be imposed even in a case of murder. He can then decide upon the appropriate punishment after assessing the level of culpability.

FIVE KEY FACTS ON SELF-DEFENCE

- Most of the law on this subject comes from two main sources. **S3 Criminal Law Act 1967** allows a party to use reasonable force to prevent a crime or to assist in the apprehension of offenders and the common law defence of self-defence is available where a person uses reasonable force to protect himself or another or their property. In many cases, the two areas overlap, and can be used in conjunction with each other (**Cousins 1982**). In both areas, a defendant may use reasonable force to avert the danger, and the jury will decide the matter (**Renouf 1986**).
- The belief that an attack is imminent is decided on a subjective basis, so an honest but unreasonable belief will suffice (**Williams (Gladstone) 1987, Beckford 1988**), although this rule will not apply if the mistake is caused by intoxication (**O'Grady 1987**).
- There is no longer a need for the defendant to show that he has tried to retreat from the danger (**Julien 1969, Palmer 1971** and **Bird 1985**), nor need he now demonstrate that he has no desire to fight (**Bird 1985**).
- The question of whether the force used is reasonable is decided objectively (**Owino 1995, Martin 2001**), and will apply equally to the police and armed services (**Clegg 1995**).
- If the defence is successful, it results in a full acquittal; there is no half-way house, such as allowing the crime of murder to be reduced to manslaughter (**Clegg 1995, Martin 2001**). The defendant in such a case will have to find another defence, as in **Martin 2001**.

Jury clears father who killed intruder

Standard Reporter

A FATHER-of-five walked free today after being cleared of murdering an armed intruder who burst into his home.

Television engineer Garfield Davenport, 47, grabbed a kitchen knife and stabbed masked John Taffinder six times in the chest and arms. A jury took only 15 minutes to find him not guilty of murder after deciding he acted in self-defence.

The case comes a week after the murder conviction of Norfolk farmer Tony Martin was reduced to manslaughter by the Court of Appeal. He is now serving five years for shooting dead a 16-year-old burglar.

Mr Davenport's lawyer told Cardiff Crown Court it was "scandalous" that he was charged with murdering Mr Taffinder, a 34-year-old labourer.

The court heard Mr Taffinder bore a "grudge" against Mr Davenport's family over a faulty computer. He and another man went to their home in Whitchurch, Cardiff, at midnight. They were wearing face masks and armed with a claw hammer.

Prosecutor Paul Lewis QC told how Mr Davenport "decided to meet trouble with trouble". He said: "Instead of calling police, Davenport went into the kitchen and armed himself with a large carving knife. He opened the front door and there was a confrontation between himself and the two men.

"Davenport stabbed Mr Taffinder five times in the body and once in the arm. One wound was eight centimetres deep in Mr Taffinder's right lung. "Mr Taffinder, a father of one, collapsed after leaving the scene and was dead by the time emergency services arrived.

John Charles Rees QC, defending, reminded the jury of the Tony Martin case, saying: "The facts of this case are a million miles from that one. The burglars did not go to Mr Martin's case to do him grievous bodily harm. They went to steal.

"Mr Davenport attacked two hooded and armed men intent on doing him injury in his own home. He is not guilty of murder, not guilty of manslaughter and not guilty of any offence at all because what he did was perfectly lawful."

Mr Rees told how Mr Davenport was "petrified for his life" during the attack in May. He said: "This man burst in, forced him backwards and attempted to hit him with a hammer – and, in self-defence, he stabbed Mr Taffinder. He waved the knife at the other man and forced him out of the front door.

"These are men who are prepared to come to his home with masks and lethal weapons to cause damage."

Mr Davenport elected not to give evidence during the trial and did not comment after the verdict. But his wife Shirley said: "This is the way I hoped it would turn out. I never had any doubts."

Evening Standard, 8 November 2001

Activity

Fred had an argument with Wilma. He picked up some pebbles and indicated that he was going to throw them at her. Wilma could have deflected the blow quite easily but instead, picked up a boulder and hit Fred with it, fracturing his skull in two places. Fred later died in hospital.

Advise Wilma on the issue of self-defence.

11.7.3 Possible reform of the defence of self-defence

Clause 27 of the *Draft Criminal Law Bill* states that a person may use force to protect himself or another from harm or from damage to their property or to prevent a crime or breach of the peace. The use of force must be 'such as is reasonable in the circumstances as he believes them to be', which largely restates the present position, with its objective and subjective elements.

Self-Assessment Questions

1. Describe the principle regarding mistake laid down in the case of **Tolson 1889** and show how this has been affected by the cases of **Morgan 1976 and B (a minor) v DPP**.
2. Why were the appeals in **Williams** and **Beckford** successful but not those of **Fotheringham** and **O'Grady**?.
3. Why did the defence of necessity fail in the case of **Dudley and Stephens**? Why then did it succeed in **Re A (children)**?
4. Distinguish between duress of threats and duress of circumstances.

5. It was previously believed that the threat had to be an immediate one. How has this been affected by the decisions in **Hudson and Taylor** and **Abdul-Hussain and Others**?
6. Examine the different elements of the test for duress, as laid down in the case of **Graham**.
7. Using cases to support your answer, describe two groups of people who are unable to benefit from the defences of duress of threats and duress of circumstances.
8. Explain why the defendants were successful in their claims of duress of circumstances in **Willer, Martin** and **Abdul-Hussain and Others** but failed in the appeals in **Davis, Pittaway** and **Cole**.
9. Distinguish between **s3 Criminal Law Act 1967** and self-defence at common law. With regard to the latter, explain how the cases of **Williams** and **Bird** helped to expand this defence.
10. Why was the defence of public and private defence not originally available for the defendants in **Clegg** and **Martin**? What was the eventual outcome of these two high profile cases?

Chapter 12

PARTIES TO A CRIME

12.1 Introduction

In some cases however, more than one person will be involved. For example, two or more people may decide to carry out an armed robbery on a bank or to break into a house in order to steal. If they commit the offence together, they are considered in law to be joint principals. If one party merely helps the other to commit the crime, however, he is not considered to be a principal offender. Instead, he is known by a variety of names. He is normally known as a secondary offender, but could also be called an accessory or an accomplice. In some of the older cases, he may have been classed, rather confusingly, as a principal in the second degree. By whatever name he is known, the law takes a very strict attitude towards him and he is treated in virtually the same way as the principal offender. The law is to be found in a very old statute, which was amended by the **Criminal Law Act 1967**. **S8 Accessories and Abettors Act 1861**, as amended, states that:

> Whosoever shall aid, abet, counsel and procure the commission of any indictable offence . . . shall be liable to be tried, indicted and punished as a principal offender.

S44 Magistrates Courts Act 1980 ensures that the same approach is taken with regard to summary offences.

If this is the case, we need to examine why a distinction is made between principal offenders and accomplices.

- It could be important when sentencing in cases where the judge has some discretion over the matter.
- The *actus reus* and *mens rea* of secondary participation is different to that required for the principal.
- Where liability is strict, the prosecution will still have to prove that a secondary offender has *mens rea.*

12.2 The principal offender

It has been noted that the person who directly brings about the *actus reus* of the offence, i.e. the main perpetrator of the crime, is known as the principal.

It has also been seen in many cases throughout this book, that it is possible to have more than one principal.

The test to decide whether an offender is a principal or a secondary offender is to discover whether his act is the most immediate cause of the *actus reus* or whether he is merely helping that cause to be effected.

Innocent Agents

It is usually a simple matter to discover the principal but there are some difficult areas. One of these is where the apparent principal is unaware that he is involved in wrongdoing, another is where he is too young to be apprehended. In such cases, the perpetrator of the crime is known as an innocent agent and the person instigating the crime will be treated as the principal.

An example of the first type of innocent agent would be where a postman personally delivers a letter bomb to the victim, believing it to be a harmless parcel. It explodes and kills the recipient. Obviously, it would be very unjust to convict the postman of this crime; he is merely the innocent agent. The principal, therefore, would be the person sending the bomb. Similarly, in an unnamed case in 1665, a

Migrant 'Fagin' ran Tube gang of child pickpockets

By Patrick Sawer

AN ASYLUM seeker from former Yugoslavia ran a gang of child pickpockets, some as young as seven, preying on Tube commuters, it was claimed today.

Vaske Besic, 34, became a latter-day Fagin shortly after his arrival in Britain and was allegedly responsible for doubling the amount of pickpocketing offences on the Underground.

Police, who today named Besic as being behind the operation, are unable to say just how much the children stole during their 18-month campaign, but some were found with up to £2,000.

Besic, who was regularly seen dropping off children in his Mercedes at East Ham Tube station, controlled the activities of three extended families, it was claimed today as further details emerged of the scale of the pickpocketing operation, first revealed in the Standard on Monday. Up to 30 immigrants are thought to have been involved.

At one stage police resorted to using a dentist to examine the children's teeth to establish their ages and find out if they were above the age of criminal responsibility. One 14-year-old, who claimed to be under 10, was arrested more than 90 times. Another, now seven, was arrested 27 times and her eight-year-old sister 46 times.

The children would be returned to their home address, from where they would set out the next day to rob passengers in the West End.

Besic arrived on a false passport in Dover in autumn 1999, with his partner and four children. He sought asylum and said he was head of a gipsy family from Sarajevo.

Asylum was refused but he appealed and last May was granted exceptional leave to stay on the ground that gipsies in former Yugoslavia are an oppressed minority.

As police took action against the gang, the Besic family moved from East Ham, to Barking then Dagenham, finally disappearing altogether in June. So lucrative was the pickpocketing operation the family are not thought to have claimed benefits.

Last year the children were held responsible for doubling pickpocketing on the Tube to 10,626 cases. Police drafted in an extra 40 officers and in the 12 months to this September the number of offences fell to 5,035.

Det Insp Keith Griffiths, of British Transport Police, today appealed for anyone with information on the Besic family to come forward. He said: "They could be in Birmingham or Paris. I am most concerned about the children. They are suffering from neglect."

Attempts to prosecute arrested children were hampered by identification problems. Some were taken into care.

Evening Standard, 1 November 2001

daughter was instructed to give her father a potion to cure his cold. In fact, it was poison with which his wife intended to kill him. The wife was held to be the principal and the daughter was the innocent agent. The second type of innocent agency would exist if a modern day Fagin co-opted several children under the age of ten to engage in shoplifting on his behalf and ordered them to deliver the goods to him. The children could not be charged as principals because they would be under the age of criminal liability, as noted in Chapter 10; Fagin, therefore, would be the principal. A recent example of this can be seen in the article, left, a case deplored by genuine asylum seekers.

12.3 The different types of secondary offender

It can be seen from the **Accessories and Abettors Act 1861** that secondary offenders are those who aid, abet, counsel or procure the commission of a crime. It was stated in **AG's Reference (No 1 of 1975) 1975** that these words should be given their ordinary meaning. The judges of the Court of Appeal went on to state that Parliament must have intended each of the four terms to have their own, distinct meaning, otherwise one or two words would have sufficed. The four terms 'aiding, abetting, counselling and procuring' need, therefore, to be examined in more detail.

To aid

The term 'to aid' has been interpreted as 'to give help, support or assistance'. Normally, such help will be given at the time the crime is committed, although the cases show that this is not always the position.

To abet

The meaning of the term 'to abet' is 'to encourage, incite or instigate'. Again, it is felt

that such encouragement would normally be at or near the scene of the crime. In this way it can be distinguished from the term 'to counsel', which has been held to have a similar meaning 'to abet' but takes place before the crime is committed.

The terms 'aiding and abetting' imply some sort of action on the part of the secondary offender; a merely passive presence at the scene of the crime will not normally make a person liable. In **Bland 1988**, the defendant's conviction for aiding and abetting a dealer in drugs was quashed. The court decided that merely living with such an offender and perhaps having knowledge of his activities was not enough to incur liability; a more active involvement was required.

In the much earlier case of **Coney 1882**, the defendant's conviction for abetting a battery had also been quashed. The judge had not made it clear to the jury that a simple attendance at an illegal prize-fight was only evidence that the spectator may have been involved and was not, in itself, conclusive. If the jury had not been misdirected on this point and there had been some evidence that he had actively participated in the event, as, for example, by cheering and clapping, the jury could have rightly convicted him.

In **Wilcox v Jeffrey 1951**, a more active involvement was found by the Divisional Court. The defendant was the proprietor of a magazine called the *Jazz Illustrated*. He had attended a concert at which a celebrated American jazz musician had played his saxophone, in direct contravention of an **Aliens Order** that prevented him from performing while in the UK. There was no direct evidence that the magazine owner had actively participated at the concert, but he had attended and had later written an article for his magazine, describing the performance in glowing terms. Taken together, these actions by the defendant were considered by Lord Goddard, the Lord Chief Justice, to be enough to constitute aiding and abetting the contravention of the Order.

A party could also be held to be an aider and abettor in cases where he is held to be under some sort of duty to control the other party, as in **Tuck v Robson 1970**. The defendant was a licensee of a public house called the Canterbury Arms, which was visited by the police after closing time. They discovered 12 people still drinking and three of these were charged and convicted with consuming intoxicating liquor out of hours. The licensee was charged with aiding and abetting the crime.

The Divisional Court decided that he had knowledge that the offence was being committed. A more difficult matter was whether he could be said to have assisted in its commission. The court decided that there was enough evidence that he had aided and abetted the offenders. He had failed to eject the customers or even to withdraw their permission to be on the premises, when he possessed the requisite authority to take such a course of action.

To counsel

This also involves the giving of advice and encouragement but usually takes place before the crime takes place.

An example of counselling can be seen in the case of **Calhaem 1985.** The defendant was infatuated with her solicitor and wished to remove his girlfriend from the scene. She therefore hired a private detective called Zajac to murder her. Zajac claimed that he had no intention of committing the crime but was going to pretend that he attempted the murder but was unsuccessful. He alleged that he visited the girlfriend's house with this plan in mind but then panicked and killed her because she screamed after he had gained entry.

Despite this contention, Zajac was convicted of murder and Calhaem was found guilty of being a secondary offender. She appealed on the grounds that the judge had not directed the jury that her counselling of the contract killer had to be a substantial cause of the killing. She unsuccessfully tried to argue that it was not her words or actions that had persuaded the killer to commit the crime.

The Court of Appeal agreed with the trial judge that the word 'counsel' merely meant to 'advise, solicit or something of that sort' and decided that there was no implication in this word that there had to be a causal connection between the counselling and the crime. It will be noted below that a different view is taken with regard to the word 'procure'.

To procure

In **AG's Reference No 1 of 1975 (1975)**, this term was held to mean 'to produce by endeavour'. Lord Widgery gave a more detailed explanation of this when he added 'You procure a thing by setting out to see that it happens and taking the appropriate steps to produce that happening'. It was also decided in this case that procuring may also take place when the principal offender has no knowledge of this. In most cases of aiding, abetting and counselling there will have been some form of contact between the principal and secondary offenders, 'some meeting of the minds', as stated by Lord Widgery C J.

He decided that this was not necessary in the case of procuring. The judge stated, 'there are plenty of instances in which a person may be said to procure the commission of a crime by another even though there is no sort of conspiracy between the two, even though there is no attempt at agreement or discussion as to the form which the offence should take. In our judgment the offence described in this reference is such a case'. What is felt to be necessary, however, is some sort of connection between the acts of the secondary offender and the actual crime committed.

In this case, the defendant had 'spiked' the drinks of his friend with spirits, knowing that the other would later be driving home. The friend was charged with a drink driving offence under the **Road Traffic Act** in force at that time and the defendant was charged as an aider, abettor, counsellor and procurer.

The friend was convicted but the judge decided that there was no case to answer in relation to the secondary offender. The **Attorney General's Reference** was a result of the disquiet felt about this decision. The Court of Appeal decided that a person acting in such a way should have faced trial for two reasons. First, he had acted secretly in lacing the drinks of his friend. The latter was therefore unaware of the alcohol consumed and was unable to take precautions to avoid committing an offence. Secondly, as a direct consequence of the added spirits, the friend had driven with the excess alcohol in his blood. This provided the causal link between the actions of the alleged secondary offender and the principal offender, which was felt to be essential in cases of procuring.

To sum up, therefore, a secondary offender can be charged with all four types of secondary participation, aiding abetting, counselling and procuring but can be found guilty if just one of these is satisfied. Normally, the accomplice will counsel and procure before a crime is committed and will aid and abet during the course of an offence. With aiding, abetting and counselling there is usually some contact between the principal and the accessory in relation to the crime to be committed but this is not necessary for procuring. What is required here is some sort of connection between the acts of the secondary offender and the eventual crime.

12.4 The *actus reus* of participation

It has to be proved that the alleged secondary has done something positive to assist or encourage the committing of the offence or has taken some steps to procure its commission. It was noted above that a passive presence at the scene of the crime would not, on its own, be enough to constitute liability. In **Clarkson 1971**, the conviction of two soldiers for abetting a rape was quashed because they had not participated in any way; they had merely been present at the time the crime took place. It is not necessary, however, to prove that the actions of the accomplices had any utility in the committing of the crime or even to prove that any incitement or encouragement was heeded, as was shown in the case of **Calhaem,** mentioned earlier.

Can the accomplice withdraw without incurring liability?

The very early authority of **Saunders and Archer 1573** suggests that this is possible. It appears however, that a mere show of repentance will not be sufficient and the offenders will need to take positive steps to indicate that their assistance is at an end. It was stated in **Whitehouse 1941** that they will need to:

> serve unequivocal notice upon the other party to the common unlawful cause that if he proceeds upon it he does so without the further aid and assistance of those who withdraw.

In some cases, the accomplice will need to go further and neutralise the effect of any aid he has given, such as taking back the car he has stolen or making the other surrender the weapon that was supplied. He will find it more difficult to avoid liability if his change of heart comes about at the scene of the crime. In

Becerra and Cooper 1975, the defendants and another man broke into the house of an elderly woman and attacked her, after hearing that she kept large sums of money there. Becerra was not engaged in the cowardly attack on the defenceless woman but used a knife to cut the telephone wires. Cooper later took control of this knife and moved towards the kitchen to look for the money. The men were then disturbed by the arrival of the tenant of the first floor flat who had heard the commotion and come to investigate. Becerra called to the others 'Come on, let's go!' and he and the third man escaped through a window. Cooper was unable to get away and, in the ensuing struggle, the tenant was fatally stabbed.

Becerra tried to argue that his withdrawal from the scene of the crime meant that he was not liable for this murder. The Court of Appeal refused to accept this and his conviction was upheld, as it was in Baker 1994, where the defendant had taken part in the stabbing of the victim before stating that he wanted nothing more to do with the violence. If the attack is not pre-planned and the violence of the perpetrator is more spontaneous, the other party might be able to withdraw more easily, as suggested in Mitchell and King 1999.

12.5 The *mens rea* of secondary offenders

For the *mens rea* of secondary liability to exist, the prosecution must show two things:

- That the accomplice had knowledge of the type of crime to be committed.
- That he had the intention to aid, abet, counsel or procure the principal offender.

Knowledge that a crime is to be committed

It was stated in Johnson v Youden and Others 1950 that, before a person can be convicted of aiding and abetting the commission of an offence, 'he must at least know the essential matters which constitute that offence'. In Bainbridge 1960 it was decided that the defendant need not know of the precise crime that is to be committed, provided that he possesses, not mere suspicion 'but knowledge that a crime of the type in question was intended'.

Six weeks before any criminal activity took place Bainbridge used a false name and address to purchase oxygen-cutting equipment. This was used later by the principal offenders to cut through the windows, the doors, and the safe of the Midland Bank in Stoke Newington. Bainbridge was charged with being an accessory to the burglary but tried to argue that he did not know the purpose for which the equipment was being used. He claimed that while he suspected that something illegal was going on, he believed that his purchases were merely being used for the breaking up of stolen goods or something similar.

The Court of Appeal held that while it was not enough merely to show that the defendant knew that some sort of illegal activity was planned, it was not necessary to show that he knew the exact time and place of the intended crime. The court decided that the judge had explained the matter well to the jurors, who had obviously not believed the defendant's story. His conviction, therefore, was upheld.

The House of Lords took the matter further in the case of DPP for Northern Ireland v Maxwell 1978. The defendant was a member of a prohibited terrorist organisation, the Ulster Volunteer Force and, being a local man had guided other terrorists to a public house called the Crosskeys, which was owned by a Catholic.

There a bomb was planted and the fuse ignited. The defendant was not involved in that activity and had not, at any time, had the bomb in his possession. Despite this, he was convicted. He appealed on the grounds that it had not been proved that he knew the type of crime that was going to be committed. The House of Lords was called upon to decide whether an accomplice could be convicted if 'the crime committed by the principal, and actually assisted by the accused, was one of a number of offences, one of which the accused knew the principal would probably commit.' Their Lordships firmly held that the answer was 'yes'.

Viscount Dilhorne explained their decision in the following way:

An accessory who leaves it to his principal to choose is liable, provided always the choice

is made from the range of offences from which the accessory contemplates the choice will be made.

He acknowledged that the lower court had gone further than earlier cases but added that 'it is a sound development of the law and in no way inconsistent with them. I accept it as good judge-made law in a field where there is no statute to offer guidance'.

Is recklessness or negligence enough?

The law seems to be undecided as to whether the accomplice's knowledge that an offence is probable is enough to make him liable, i.e. it is unclear whether he can be found guilty when he is merely reckless about whether a crime is committed.

In **Blakely, Sutton v DPP 1991**, there was a clear statement by the Divisional Court that objective or inadvertent recklessness is not sufficient to constitute liability but less certainty as to whether subjective recklessness would suffice. In this case, the two women defendants had 'spiked' the drink of the first defendant's lover to stop him returning home to his wife. They intended to tell him what they had done but he left before they could do so. He was convicted of a drink driving offence and the defendants were found guilty as accessories. The women obviously intended that the defendant should drink the alcohol but, equally obviously, did not intend that the man should drive and thereby commit the offence. The court had to decide whether their convictions should be upheld on the grounds that they should have contemplated that the man's actions in leaving and driving were probable.

The Divisional Court quashed their conviction because the magistrates had used the **Caldwell** test of recklessness. The court was definite that this type of recklessness was insufficient to create liability. The judges were less clear with regard to **Cunningham**-type recklessness, although they did suggest that it was best to avoid the word 'reckless' altogether when deciding upon the *mens rea* of secondary offenders.

While the position with regard to subjective recklessness may be in doubt, mere negligence on the part of the alleged secondary offender is definitely insufficient to incur liability. In **Callow v Tillstone 1900**, a vet was negligent in his examination of a carcass of meat and declared it to be sound. The meat was later offered for sale and the owner was convicted of the strict liability offence of selling unfit food. The vet's conviction as an accessory, however, was quashed. He had not intended to be an accomplice and, as noted below, this point must also be shown for a secondary offender, even when the offence in question is a strict liability one.

The intention to aid, abet, counsel or procure

In addition to the knowledge that a crime will be committed, the prosecution must also prove that the accomplice had the intention to do the acts that assisted or encouraged the commission of the crime.

In **National Coal Board v Gamble 1959**, the Coal Board, via the actions of one of its employees, was found guilty of aiding and abetting because the intention to assist the principal offender was apparent, even though there was no benefit to the accomplices. The employee of the Coal Board operated a weighbridge and informed a lorry driver that his load was nearly four tons overweight. The driver decided to take the risk and the operator supplied him with a ticket permitting him to leave the premises. The driver's employers were later found guilty of contravening the **Motor Vehicles (Construction and Use) Regulations 1955** and the National Coal Board was convicted as a secondary offender.

An equally strict line was taken in **Garrett v Arthur Churchill (Glass) Ltd 1970**, where the defendant's conviction for knowingly being involved in the exportation of goods without a licence was upheld, even though he was merely an agent and the goods actually belonged to the other party.

Is motive relevant?

It was noted in Chapter 2 that, provided that an intention to commit the crime is proved, the offender's motive is normally irrelevant. This position does not appear to have been followed in **Gillick v West Norfolk Area Health Authority 1986.** Victoria Gillick, the intrepid campaigner for support of family values, sought a declaration that doctors would be acting illegally if they prescribed contraceptives to girls under the age of 16 without obtaining the consent of their parents. It was contended that, by such an action, the doctors were aiding and abetting the commission of unlawful sexual intercourse.

The House of Lords decided that the doctors would not have the intention to commit such a crime if they followed the guidelines that had been laid down, limiting such provision to exceptional cases. Lord Scarman stated:

> The bona fide *exercise by a doctor of his clinical judgment must be a complete negation of the guilty mind which is an essential ingredient of the criminal offence of aiding and abetting the commission of unlawful sexual intercourse.*

This was clearly a policy decision and he did go on to say that if a doctor gave the contraceptive treatment merely to facilitate the girl's unlawful sexual intercourse he may well be guilty of secondary liability.

12.6 Problem areas

12.6.1 If the principal offender is acquitted

It is now necessary to examine whether the accomplice can still be held liable if the principal is acquitted.

This is possible as long as the *actus reus* of the main offence has been committed and the secondary offender has the *mens rea* for participation. The courts are then prepared to combine the two elements and convict him. This complicated principle is best understood by looking at the appalling behaviour of the two husbands in the cases described below and the obvious desire of the courts to convict them.

In the case of **Bourne 1952**, a man forced his wife to have sexual intercourse with a dog. This is illegal but mercifully the wife was not charged. If she had been brought to court, she would have been able to plead the defences of marital coercion or duress and, hopefully, would have been acquitted. Because the *actus reus* of the crime was held to exist, however, the court was able to convict the husband for aiding and abetting the illegal act.

The decision in **Cogan and Leak 1976** is perhaps less easy to justify, although it is clear why the Court of Appeal was reluctant to quash the conviction. Leak wished to punish and humiliate his wife after she had refused him money so on his return from a drinking session, he forced her to have sexual intercourse, first with him and then with his drinking partner, Cogan, while the husband looked on. The unfortunate woman was said to be sobbing quietly throughout the ordeal. Later, Cogan was charged with rape and Leak with procuring this offence. Leak could not be charged with his own rape of his wife because, at that time, it was not an offence for a

husband within a marriage to have sexual intercourse without his wife's consent.

Both men were convicted at first instance but appealed. Cogan's appeal was successful, following the questionable decision of the House of Lords in **Morgan 1976** in the interim period, which held that an honest belief that the other had consented could be a defence to a charge of rape; the belief did not have to be a reasonable one. Leach tried to argue that, as the principal had been acquitted, his conviction as an accomplice could not then stand and, brutal though his behaviour was, there could be said to be some merit in this argument. If Cogan's conviction had been quashed, it was arguable whether the crime of rape still existed.

The Court of Appeal, however, refused to quash Leak's conviction. Lawton L J took a robust approach to this problem, roundly declaring that an acquittal would be 'an affront to justice and to the common sense of ordinary folk'. He found that a rape had, indeed, been committed and confirmed that Leach had procured this offence. He rejected the appellant's arguments and stated, 'Here one fact was clear – the wife had been raped. . . : The fact that Cogan was innocent of rape because he believed she was consenting does not affect the position. . . In the language of the law the act of sexual intercourse without the wife's consent was the *actus reus*; it had been procured by Leak who had the appropriate *mens rea*, namely his intention that Cogan should have sexual intercourse with her without her consent'.

This possible expansion of the law was followed in the case of **Millward 1994**. The defendant was charged with aiding, abetting, counselling and procuring his employee to commit the offence of causing death by reckless driving. The vehicle in question was a tractor, with a trailer attached. The hitch on the tractor was defective and during the journey, the trailer became detached from the tractor and hit another vehicle. The driver of this car was killed. Both employer and employee were originally convicted but the employee's conviction was quashed on appeal. Millward tried to argue that the acquittal of the principal meant that the *actus reus* of the offence had not been committed because the recklessness of the employee had not been made out.

The Court of Appeal decided that the *actus reus* did still exist; it consisted of the taking of the vehicle onto the road in a defective condition so as to cause the death. It was stressed that procuring does not require a joint intention between the accessory and the principal, thus allowing the accessory to be convicted even when the principal is acquitted.

The court approved of the reasoning in **Cogan and Leak** and distinguished the earlier case of **Thornton v Mitchell 1940**, where the facts were somewhat similar to those in **Millward**. In the earlier case, a conductor had given inadequate signals to the driver of a bus who was trying to reverse and this had resulted in a fatal injury to a pedestrian. The conductor's conviction for aiding and abetting the careless driving of the principal was quashed on appeal because the driver of the bus had been acquitted. The Divisional Court clearly decided that, as the *actus reus* of careless driving no longer existed, there was no crime for the secondary offender to aid and abet.

12.6.2 If the liability of the secondary offender is different

Liability of the secondary offender for a different offence to that of the principal is possible, provided that both offences share the same *actus reus*. This was not held to be the case in **Dunbar 1988**. It was alleged that

Dunbar wanted to see her lover dead but she claimed that this comment was made while she was intoxicated. It was shown that she suspected that the co-defendants might break into the flat of her lover and, in the course of the burglary, might inflict some harm upon the woman. Dunbar argued strongly however, that she had not envisaged that death or grievous bodily harm might result. The Court of Appeal quashed her conviction for manslaughter. The trial judge had not made it clear to the jury that, if the defendant had not contemplated the possibility that death or grievous bodily harm might occur and had only suspected that some lesser harm might be inflicted, she could not be found guilty of manslaughter because the crime that she had contemplated was different to the one committed.

12.6.3 When the principal offender is a victim

It was established in the early case of **Tyrrell 1894**, that the alleged accomplice cannot be found guilty of aiding and abetting if the offence in question was actually created to protect him or another. In this case an under-age girl was charged with aiding and abetting a man to have incestuous sexual intercourse with her but was acquitted. The court felt it to be wrong that she should face criminal proceedings when the act had been designed to protect young women in similar circumstances.

TEN KEY FACTS ON PRINCIPAL AND SECONDARY OFFENDERS

- The main perpetrator of a crime is called the principal offender; in some cases, there may be more than one principal. If an innocent agent is involved, a person may be convicted as a principal even though he is not at the scene of the crime. Innocent agents are those without knowledge of the crime or those who lack capacity.

- People with less involvement are called secondary offenders. They may also be known as accomplices or accessories. Secondary offenders are liable to be tried and punished in the same way as principal offenders (**s8 Accessories and Abettors Act 1861**, as amended and **s44 Magistrates Courts' Act 1980**).

- They will fulfil this role if they have aided, abetted, counselled or procured the offence. In **AG's Reference (No1 of 1975) 1975**, it was stated that these words should be given their ordinary meaning. All four terms may appear on the indictment but the secondary offender can be convicted if just one of these forms of assistance is proved.

- Aiding and abetting usually takes place at the scene of the crime. Aiding means giving help, support or assistance; abetting means encouraging, inciting or instigating the crime. A purely passive presence at the scene of the crime will not incur liability, unless the person is involved in other ways or has the authority to control the others (see **Coney 1882**, **Clarkson 1971** and **Bland 1988**, and contrast with **Wilcox v Jeffrey 1951** and **Tuck v Robson 1970**).

- Counselling means inciting or encouraging, or 'to advise or solicit or something of that sort' (**Calhaem 1985**). This will take place before the crime takes place. Liability may still be incurred even where the principal offender does not heed the advice (**Calhaem 1985**).

- The term 'to procure' means 'to produce by endeavour', i.e. to set out to see that the crime happens, but there is no requirement that the principal has to know of these actions. There must, however, be some causal connection between the steps taken by the alleged accomplice and the actual crime committed (**AG's Reference (No 1 of 1975) 1975**).

- The *actus reus* of participation requires the activities of aiding, abetting, counselling or procuring, i.e. something active to assist the commission of the crime, although it is not necessary for the help to have been of any use. A secondary offender may still be liable even when the principal offender has been acquitted, so long as the *actus reus* of the crime is still held to exist. This will then be merged with the mens rea of the accomplice (**Bourne 1952, Cogan and Leak 1976** and **Millward 1994**). This will not be the case if he contemplated a different offence (**Dunbar 1988**).

- Accomplices may be able to withdraw from their criminal activity without incurring liability, but must take steps to make this position clear to the others involved in the crime (**Whitehouse 1941**). In many cases, they will need to go even further and will need to neutralise the effects of any help they have already given, such as taking back the weapons supplied. The later the withdrawal, the less likely it is that the courts will believe it is genuine (**Beccera 1975, Baker 1994** but this might be possible if the violent acts are more spontaneous, **Mitchell and King 1999**).

- Two points have to be established before the *mens rea* of participation is satisfied. First, there must be knowledge that the crime is to be committed (**Johnson v Youden and Others 1950**) or, at the very least, **Cunningham**-style recklessness that an offence might happen (**Blakely, Sutton v DPP 1991**). It appears from the cases of **Bainbridge 1960** and **DPP for N.I. v Maxwell 1978**, that it is enough for the accused to be aware that a particular type of crime might be committed or one from a range of crimes.

- Secondly, there must be an intention to assist the principal (**NCB v Gamble 1959, Garrett v Arthur Churchill Glass Ltd 1970**). He has to have the *mens rea* of intending to do the assisting, even where the offence committed is a strict liability one, as in **Callow v Tillstone 1900**. He need not, however, intend that the actual crime should be committed. **Gillick** appears to have been decided on its own particular facts.

Activity

- Barry recruited two children to steal mobile phones for him from a local store. Peter was 12, Wendy was 9.

Assess the possible liability of Barry, Peter and Wendy in relation to participation.

- Thelma is jealous of her friend Louise, who has just passed her advanced motoring test. She secretly laces Louise's orange juice with gin, knowing that the latter will be driving home. Louise is later charged with driving a motor vehicle with excess alcohol in the blood.

Discuss Thelma's involvement.

- In **Rook 1993**, the defendant was convicted of being a secondary offender to the crime of murder. The case involved a contract killing in which the taxi driver, Afsar, arranged for three men to kill his wife. The men had at least two meetings in which they discussed the ways of carrying out the crime and Rook had asked for money 'up front' to help pay for the new clothes they would need after the event. He then had second thoughts about being involved and did not turn up at the pre-arranged murder spot. The other two men dragged the unfortunate woman from the car in which she was travelling with her husband and brutally murdered her. Rook was convicted with the others but appealed. He argued that he had never intended the woman to be killed and that he had merely tagged along to see how far the others would go. He then claimed that he had tried to stall them and had believed that if he did not turn up at the appointed place, the others would not go ahead with the crime.

Imagine that you are a judge of the Court of Appeal and decide whether Rook's appeal should succeed. Give clear reasons for your answer.

12.7 Joint enterprises

In the situations mentioned earlier, the decision as to who will fulfil the role as principal offender and who will be classed as a mere accessory has usually been obvious. In some instances, however, the position is not so clear, especially where two or more parties embark on what is known in law as a joint enterprise. Professor Sir John Smith states that the essence of a joint enterprise 'is that the parties have a common purpose to commit an offence – a common purpose which, like conspiracy, is usually evidenced by the concerted action of the parties'. The parties all know that the others have this same purpose. In such a case, if one of the parties commits an offence the others are also liable for it, even if this crime goes beyond the common purpose, provided that it is an act that could have been foreseen by the others.

Smith would argue that there is little difficulty with such cases and that the ordinary rules of primary and secondary liability should be applied. In cases where the joint criminal enterprise fails and one party is alleging that he is less at fault than the other, all that then needs to be worked out is whether he is, in truth, a secondary participator or whether he should be classed as a joint principal.

In the case of **Stewart and Schofield 1995**, however, the Court of Appeal refused to uphold such a view and decided that the law should take a stricter approach in cases where the parties involved have set out together on a criminal escapade. Hobhouse L J stated:

The allegation that a defendant took part in the execution of a crime as a joint enterprise is not the same as an allegation that he aided, abetted, counselled or procured the commission of that crime. A person who is a mere aider or abettor is truly a secondary party to the commission of whatever crime it is that the principal has committed . . . In contrast, where the allegation is joint enterprise, the allegation is that one defendant participated in the criminal act of another. This is a different principle. It renders each of the parties to a joint enterprise criminally liable for the acts done in the course of carrying out that joint enterprise.

The facts of this case are depressingly all too common. Heather Stewart bought some cigarettes from a 'corner shop' and noted the shopkeeper removing a wad of money from the till and putting it in his pocket. She then met up with two men, Lambert and Schofield, and suggested that they should steal this money. They took with them an iron bar and a knife and returned to the shop. Schofield acted as a lookout and the other two went into the shop, where the Pakistani shopkeeper was beaten so badly with the iron bar by Lambert that he died a few days later. The attackers left with less than £100. When the offenders were later charged, Stewart and Schofield tried to argue that they had not imagined that the shopkeeper would be more than threatened and that they had not known that Lambert was so full of racial hatred that he would use excessive force. They therefore claimed that the attack had not formed part of the joint enterprise on which they had embarked. Despite this claim, they were found guilty of manslaughter.

The trial judge had relied on the statements made in **Reid 1975** that where the parties are engaged on a joint plan and carry offensive weapons, there was always a likelihood that one of them would use them and cause death or serious injury. In such a case, if the injury had not been one that the others intended, they could not be found guilty of murder, but they could, instead, be convicted of manslaughter.

The appellants tried to argue that this decision no longer represented the law, as it did not stand with other later Court of Appeal decisions. The judges reviewed these but decided that there was no conflict. Hobhouse L J concluded:

The question whether the relevant act was committed in the course of carrying out the joint enterprise in which the defendant was a participant is a question of fact not law. If the act was not so committed then the joint enterprise ceases to provide a basis for a finding of guilt against such a defendant. He ceases to be responsible for the act. This is the fundamental point illustrated by R v Anderson and Morris and R v Lovesey, R v Peterson. But it does not follow that a variation in the intent of some of the participants at the time the critical act is done precludes the act from having been done in the course of carrying out the joint enterprise, as is illustrated by R v Betty and R v Reid.

The appeals against the convictions therefore failed.

Uncertainty remains, however, as to how much variation of the plan can take place before it is considered to be outside the scope of the joint enterprise. It appears that the party in the joint enterprise who did not commit the final act will not escape liability if he knew that the other might commit such an act. This principle was laid down by the Privy Council in **Chan Wing-Siu 1985** when it stated:

Where a man lends himself to a criminal enterprise knowing that potentially murderous weapons are to be carried, and in the event they are in fact used by his partner with an intent sufficient for murder, he should not escape the consequences . . .

The court went on to say, however, that the test of *mens rea* is subjective, i.e. what the accused contemplated, but added that this could be inferred from his conduct and any other evidence throwing light on the matter. The court made it clear that liability would not be incurred unless the defendant thought the risk was a real or substantial one, but preferred not to use just one term to describe it. In the event, the convictions were upheld.

In **Hyde and Others 1991**, the Court of Appeal approved of the statements in the above case and stated:

> If B realises (without agreeing to such conduct being used) that A may kill or intentionally inflict serious injury, but nevertheless continues to participate with A in the venture, that will amount to a sufficient mental element for B to be guilty of murder if A, with the requisite intent, kills in the scope of the venture.

In this case, the convictions for murder of the three defendants, who had kicked and punched another person outside a pub, were upheld, despite the fact it was impossible to say who had inflicted the fatal blow.

The Privy Council went further still in **Hui Chi Ming 1991** and upheld the defendant's conviction for murder, even though the others in the venture were only found guilty of manslaughter in an earlier trial.

It was inevitable that some of the numerous appeals on this subject would need to be examined by the House of Lords. In **Powell and Daniels 1997**, the House of Lords took a similarly tough attitude as the Privy Council towards the imposition of liability where the actions of the person inflicting the fatal injury were foreseeable by the others in the joint enterprise. Their Lordships made it clear that in cases like murder, where only intention will suffice for *mens rea* in relation to the actual perpetrator of the crime, such a strong degree of blameworthiness does not have to be proved for the other parties in the joint enterprise. They can be found guilty if they merely foresaw that the perpetrator might commit such an offence.

In this case therefore, the convictions for murder were upheld for all three of the members of the joint enterprise, when one of them shot and killed a drug dealer.

Where the final act is not foreseen

If the others in the joint enterprise did not foresee the final act of the actual perpetrator of the crime, they will not be fixed with equal liability, as can be seen in the following cases.

In **Mahmood 1995**, the 15-year-old defendant and the even younger driver were 'joy-riders' (an unfortunate term for something that so often ends in tragedy), and were chased by the police after their erratic driving was noted. The driver jumped out of the car while it was still moving and Mahmood was believed to have followed. The empty car, still in gear, mounted a pavement and struck a child's pram, killing the ten-month-old baby inside.

The Court of Appeal thought that the passenger may well have contemplated that someone could be killed or injured by the other's dangerous driving but not that the car would be abandoned in such a way. The conviction for manslaughter was quashed.

In **English 1997**, too, the conviction was not upheld. The defendant and another had been involved in attacking a policeman with wooden posts but the other party suddenly pulled a knife and stabbed the policeman, causing fatal injuries. The House of Lords followed an earlier Northern Ireland decision in **Gamble 1989**, where the defendant had been expecting to take part in a 'knee-capping' and had not foreseen that the victim would have had his throat cut. Their Lordships decided that English's conviction for murder could not be sustained.

In **Greatrex 1999**, a group of men attacked the victim but then one of them produced an iron bar and inflicted a fatal blow. The defendant's conviction was quashed because the trial judge had told the jury that the defendant could be convicted if he intended to inflict serious injury on the victim and had not directed that body on the difference in the acts.

How should the defendant be dealt with?

The appeal courts have come to different conclusions on this. While certain principles have been established and may well be binding on them, different issues may be involved in the appeals, giving the judges a certain amount of flexibility. The following decisions might be taken:

• To release the defendant from all blame in relation to the act of the perpetrator by quashing the conviction and leaving it at that, as seen in the cases above.
• To order a retrial and leave a new jury to decide the matter.

This approach was taken in **Uddin 1998**. The defendant's murder conviction was quashed but a new jury was left to decide whether the perpetrator's act in stabbing the victim went beyond the common purpose of the joint enterprise. The defendant had been involved in kicking the victim and repeatedly hitting him with a billiard cue.

• To find the defendant guilty of a lesser offence.

Rather controversially, the Court of Appeal of Northern Ireland decided on this option in **Gilmour 2000**. The defendant had driven three others to a housing estate, and waited for them while they threw a petrol bomb into a house where the six occupants were asleep. Three children died in the resulting blaze. The defendant was charged with the murder of the young boys, the attempted murder of the three adults and with arson. The court of first instance found him guilty of the three murders, not guilty of the three attempted murders but guilty of causing grievous bodily harm in one case and attempting to do so in the other two cases. The case of arson was not pursued.

The thrust of the defendant's appeal was whether he realised that the petrol bomb was to be used by the others to cause really serious harm. The court learned that as a normal rule, the throwing of petrol bombs did not cause such serious injuries, only minor fires, and that it could therefore be said that the defendant had not foreseen the tragic consequences that resulted in this case. He may also have been unaware that a larger bottle than average had been used to make the bomb.

The Court of Appeal therefore quashed the murder convictions but went on to decide that the defendant could be found guilty of manslaughter instead. The judges decided that a party acting as an accessory to a principal who carried out a plan that had been contemplated by both of them, could be liable for the degree of offence appropriate to the intent with which he had acted. In this case, the defendant had intended that a petrol bomb would be thrown in order to cause a fire so he could be found guilty of manslaughter. While questioning some of the statements made in Stewart and Schofield, the court decided that the basic principles enunciated in that case could be relied upon and applied to this new situation.

Comment

Professor Sir John Smith questions the correctness of this decision. Among the other points he makes, he argues that the facts of the case are comparable to **Gamble**, **Powell** and **English**, where a manslaughter conviction was not imposed. He also questions whether this is truly a case of joint enterprise, deciding that it falls more easily into the category of secondary liability. It was debatable whether the accused took part in any pre-arranged plan. According to him, he had been roughly awakened in the middle of the night and ordered to take part in this operation, which, according to his version of events, 'he did not do willingly'. It could therefore be argued that he was merely giving reluctant assistance rather than joining in a common purpose.

Further appeals on this subject and the degree of blame to be imposed for participation in a joint enterprise appear to be inevitable.

For any of the above principles to apply, some form of joint enterprise must be established. It was confirmed in **Petters and Parfitt 1995**, that if the parties act independently of each other but wish to achieve the same result, and it cannot be proved that they intended to assist or encourage the other, then they are not liable for the acts of the other. If a killing takes place in such circumstances, and it is impossible to prove who did this, both of the parties must be acquitted. This can lead to the distressing result that a crime goes unpunished, as sometimes occurs where a child has been killed, but it is impossible to prove which of the parents is responsible.

12.8 Suggested reform on secondary offenders

The Law Commission has studied the law relating to accessories on several occasions. The most recent proposals are in their Consultation Paper No. 131, entitled *Assisting and Encouraging Crime.* The Commission invites comments on their proposals for radical changes in this area. It is suggested that two new offences should be created, one of assisting crime and the second on encouraging crime and to make them inchoate offences. This would mean that they are not dependent

on the main crime having to take place.

- First, a person would be guilty of assisting crime if he knows or believes that another party is doing an act (or will do one), which will involve the commission of a crime and he does any act to assist this. To widen liability, the clause states that assistance includes the giving of advice about how to commit the offence and advice on how to avoid detection or arrest.

  The person will also be liable if he assists a principal and knows or believes that the latter intends to commit one of a number of offences (i.e. the **Bainbridge** type of situation).

- The offence of encouraging crime will arise where the offender solicits, commands or encourages the principal to do acts which would involve the commission of an offence by the principal and intends that such acts should be done.

  The help should be brought to the attention of the principal but the latter does not need to be influenced by it. It is also not necessary that the offender should know the identity of the principal, nor even have any particular group in mind, provided that he intends that his communication will be acted upon by any person to whose attention it comes.

If effected, these changes would mean the abolition of aiding, abetting and counselling and also the abolition of the common law offence of incitement, which is dealt with in Chapter 13. The Commission believed that there might also be a need for another new offence to cover procuring, in cases where there is no communication about this with the principal. It remains to be seen whether any of these far-reaching proposals will be acted upon.

FIVE KEY FACTS ON JOINT ENTERPRISE

- When two or more people embark upon a joint criminal venture, this is known in law as a joint enterprise. Despite the misgivings of Professor Sir John Smith, the appeal courts have upheld the view that such cases are to be treated differently to those of ordinary secondary liability.
- In cases of joint enterprise one party is held to participate in the criminal acts of another and will be criminally liable for the acts done in the course of carrying out the joint enterprise (**Stewart and Schofield 1995**).
- The participator in the joint enterprise will still be liable, even where the acts of the other vary from what was originally planned, provided that they are in the range of acts contemplated by him (**Stewart and Schofield 1995, Chan Wing-Siu v R 1985, Hyde 1990, Powell and Daniels 1997**). The test, however, is subjective. The defendant must believe that the risk of the harm occurring is a substantial one but this can be inferred from the conduct of the defendant and any evidence throwing light on the matter (**Chan Wing-Siu v R 1985**).
- If the act is outside the contemplation of the defendant he cannot be found liable (**Gamble 1989, Mahmood 1996, English 1997 and Greatrex 1999**). In some circumstances, a retrial may be ordered, as in **Uddin 1998**. In the controversial case of **Gilmour 2000**, a manslaughter conviction was substituted instead of murder.
- If no joint enterprise is found, and it cannot be established who inflicted the injury, the parties must be acquitted (**Petters and Parfitt 1995**).

12.9 Assistance after the crime

Only assistance before or during a crime can render a person liable as an accomplice. There is no longer such a concept as an 'accessory after the fact'; this was abolished in 1967.

There are, however, specific crimes that may be committed if help is given after a crime has been committed.

Bentley trial unfair through flawed summing-up

Before Lord Bingham of Cornhill, Lord Chief Justice, Lord Justice Kennedy and Mr Justice Collins [Judgment July 30]

Having regard to the evidence adduced at trial the jury, if properly directed, would have been entitled to convict Derek Bentley of murder as the offence was then constituted, before the abolition of constructive malice and the introduction of the defence of diminished responsibility.

However, since the trial judge in his summing-up failed to direct the jury on the standard and burden of proof, to give sufficient direction on the law of joint enterprise, or adequately to summarise the defence case, made prejudicial comments about the defendants and their defences and indicated that the police officers' evidence, because of their bravery on the night in question, was more worthy of belief than that of the defendants, Bentley was denied the fair trial to which he was entitled and his conviction was in consequence unsafe;

The Court of Appeal, Criminal Division, so held, when, on a reference by the Criminal Cases Review Commission under section 9 of the Criminal Appeal Act 1995, it allowed an appeal on behalf of Derek Bentley by his niece, Maria Bentley-Dingwall, and quashed his conviction for murder following a trial before Lord Goddard, Lord Chief Justice, and a jury at the Central Criminal Court on December 11, 1952.

On November 2, 1952, Christopher Craig, aged 16, armed with a knife, a revolver and ammunition, and Bentley, aged 19, who had knife and a knuckle-duster, went on a warehouse-breaking expedition. At about 9.15pm they were observed climbing into a warehouse premises in Croydon and the police were called, arriving at the site at about 9.25pm.

DC Fairfax and PC Harrison, finding that the defendants had climbed on to the roof pursued them there and a third officer followed. DC Fairfax arrested Bentley who was then, on the three officers' evidence, heard to shout: "Let him have it, Chris". Craig fired at DC Fairfax, slightly injuring him. Bentley broke away, but that officer grabbed him and removed the knife and knuckleduster which he found in Bentley's pockets.

Thereafter, Bentley remained wholly docile beside the officer, offering no incitement and, on the police evidence, making various remarks which showed concern for his and their safety. Craig continued firing, and shot dead a fourth officer, PC Miles, as that officer reached the roof probably a little before 9.57pm.

On the way to the police station Bentley was alleged to have said "1 knew he had a gun but I didn't think he'd use it" and his statement under caution recorded: "I did not know Chris had one until he shot".

Following a two day trial, he was convicted with the jury's recommendation to mercy. He was sentenced to death, the only sentence then permitted, his appeal was dismissed on January 13, 1953 and he was executed on January 28. On July 29, 1993 he was granted a royal pardon in respect of the death sentence and execution.

Taken from a Law Report published in *The Times*, 31 July 1998

Activity

Answer the following questions on the article on page 258:

- Which crime were the offenders Craig and Bentley said to have committed and why did Bentley's conviction arouse such controversy?
- Describe three ways in which the trial judge, Lord Goddard, was said to have misdirected the jury.
- What was the latest decision of the Court of Appeal in respect of Bentley?

Self-Assessment Questions

1. State two other names for an accomplice.
2. Give two examples of innocent agents.
3. Define the following expressions, giving examples of each:
   To aid
   To abet
   To counsel
   To procure
4. Using decided cases to illustrate your answer, explain how the *actus reus* of participation is established.

5. Describe the two elements that have to be shown before the necessary *mens rea* of a secondary offender is proved. Give cases to support your findings.
6. What steps must a secondary offender take in order to withdraw from the commission of the crime without incurring liability?
7. Citing case examples to back up your answer, decide when it is possible for the secondary offender to remain liable after the acquittal of the principal.
8. What is meant by the term 'a joint enterprise' and why is this treated differently from secondary liability?
9. Why were the convictions upheld in the cases of **Stewart and Schofield, Chan Wing-Siu, Hyde** and **Powell and Daniels** but quashed in **Mahmood, English** and **Greatrex**?
10. Why has the decision in **Gilmour** attracted criticism?

Chapter 13

INCHOATE OFFENCES

13.1 Introduction

Inchoate offences are incomplete offences. The parties involved may well have desired that a crime should go ahead, but circumstances beyond their control may have prevented this. For example, an offender may have planned to murder another, he may have raised the gun to shoot him, taken careful aim but then, for some reason, the gun does not fire. In another case, an armed robbery may have been plotted but the sudden re-routing of the security van may have prevented the planned ambush. In yet another scenario, a person may have been pressurising his friend to blackmail a business acquaintance, but this friend may have had 'cold feet' and decided to pull out of the venture. Not unnaturally, even though the main crimes did not go ahead, the law still takes the view that the people involved in these activities should be punished. In the first instance, therefore, the offender would be charged with attempted murder. In the second case, the wrongdoers might also be charged with attempt or might, instead, be charged with conspiracy. In our last example, the party exerting the pressure on his friend might be guilty of incitement. These three offences, therefore, are the subject of this chapter and will be dealt with alphabetically.

13.2 Attempt

The law of attempts is now governed by the **Criminal Attempts Act 1981**, which came into force on 27 August 1981. Before the passing of this Act, the rules had been formulated at common law.

S1(1) Criminal Attempts Act 1981 states that a person will be guilty of attempt if:

with intent to commit an offence to which this section applies, a person does an act which is more than merely preparatory to the commission of the offence.

S4(1) lays down the punishment and it will be noted that this may be severe. The subsection states that 'the attempt is punishable to the same extent as the substantive offence'.

13.2.1 The *actus reus* of attempt

The *actus reus* of attempt will exist where the party 'does an act which is more than merely preparatory to the commission of the offence'.

The law makes a clear distinction, therefore, between acts which are undertaken merely to prepare for the crime in question and acts done after this time which will then amount, in law, to an attempt to commit the actual offence. With regard to earlier acts, the party may be guilty of other, less serious offences, as, for example, obtaining a gun and ammunition unlawfully or stealing a car, but he will not, at this stage be guilty of the attempt to commit the main crime. For this to occur, he must do something more substantial and with a closer connection to the crime in question. Before the **Criminal Attempts Act** codified the law on attempts, the Court of Appeal in **Davey v Lee 1968** took the view that it had to be 'a step towards the commission of the specific crime, which is immediately and not merely remotely connected with the commission of it'. In **DPP v Stonehouse 1978**, the House of Lords approved of the early description in **Eagleton 1855** that 'Acts remotely leading towards the commission of the offence are not to be considered as attempts to commit it; but acts immediately connected with it are'. Their Lordships therefore decided that 'the offender must have crossed the Rubicon and burnt his boats'. The Law Commission, when formulating the changes in the law of attempt, decided that there was 'no magic formula' to work out when enough has been done to amount to an attempt but decided that it must be 'more than merely preparatory'. With this as a guide the question of whether the defendant had done enough to be convicted of attempt could then be left to the jury's good sense.

More than merely preparatory

In **Jones 1990**, the defendant was unable to accept that his ex-mistress had formed a serious relationship with another man, Michael Foreman. Jones purchased four guns and shortened the barrel of one of them. On the day of the crime, he drove to the school where Foreman was dropping off his child and jumped into the victim's car. He then pointed the loaded gun at Foreman and stated 'You are not going to like this'. The victim managed to grab the gun and throw it out of the window and then escaped himself, despite a cord pulling him back. The police later arrested the defendant who also had a knife with him. They recovered his holdall, which contained a hatchet, some ammunition and a length of cord and his car, in which they found was a large quantity of English, French and Spanish money.

Jones claimed that he had only intended to kill himself and appealed against his subsequent conviction. He argued that he had at least three more acts to do before he could be said to be ready to kill anyone; i.e. he had to remove the safety catch on the gun, to put his finger on the trigger and thirdly, he had to pull that trigger.

The Court of Appeal agreed that the acts of obtaining the gun, shortening it, loading it, putting on a disguise and going to the school were merely preparatory to the commission of the offence. The judges added, however, that 'once he had got into the car, taken out the loaded gun and pointed it at the victim with the intention of killing him there was sufficient evidence for the consideration of the jury on

the charge of attempted murder'. The appeal, therefore, was dismissed.

In other cases, the matter is less clear-cut. In **Gullefer 1990**, the defendant had placed a bet of £18 at a greyhound stadium in Romford. The dog was not performing well so, in the final stages of the race, the defendant climbed over the fence and onto the track and tried to distract the dogs. He hoped that this action would result in the race being declared null and void and in the eventual return of his stake money from the bookmaker. Unfortunately for Gullefer, he was no more successful in this plan than he was with his gambling and he was charged with attempted theft. His luck changed for the better, however, when his appeal was heard and his conviction was quashed. The former Lord Chief Justice, Lord Lane, decided that the attempt could not be said to begin until the defendant embarked upon 'the crime proper'. Gullefer's actions when he jumped onto the track, therefore, were merely acts in preparation for the later crime of theft and, at that time, he could not be said to be guilty of an attempt.

The decisions in the case of **Campbell 1991** and **Geddes 1996** are rather more disquieting. In the first case, the defendant was arrested within yards of a post office, armed with an imitation gun and was convicted of attempted armed robbery. In the second case, Geddes had been discovered by a teacher in the boys' lavatory block at a school in Brighton. He had no authority to be there and left when challenged, discarding his rucksack as he went. This was found to contain a large kitchen knife, ropes and a roll of masking tape. He was later convicted of attempted false imprisonment.

Both convictions, however, were quashed on appeal on the finding that the acts were not more than merely preparatory. While the appeal court appeared to be convinced in both cases that the defendants had the necessary intention to commit the crimes in question, they nevertheless felt bound to conclude that the actions were not advanced enough to merit a conviction.

The Court of Appeal took a more robust approach in **Attorney General's Reference (No 1 of 1992) 1993** and decided that a defendant could be found guilty of rape without the need to show that he had tried to penetrate the woman's vagina, provided that there was enough other evidence of attack.

13.2.2 The *mens rea* of attempt

It will be noted when looking at the definition of attempt in **s1(1)** that the mental element required for the crime of attempt is an intention to bring about the offence. The section states that a person will be guilty of attempt if 'with intent to commit an offence', he does an act which is more than merely preparatory to the commission of the offence. In relation to the attempt to commit the actual crime, therefore, recklessness behaviour is not sufficient to incur liability.

This was clearly affirmed by the Court of Appeal in **Millard and Vernon 1987**. The defendants were football supporters who were charged with attempted criminal damage. They had systematically pushed against a wooden wall at the ground. The prosecution alleged that they had done this in conjunction with each other in order to damage the line of planking, whereas the defendants strongly denied that they were acting with intent to damage the stand, or that they were acting in cohort. Despite this, they were convicted so they appealed on the ground that the judge had misdirected the jury about the need to establish intention. It was contended that recklessness was not enough, even though this state of mind would suffice for the full crime of criminal damage.

The Court of Appeal agreed with this reasoning and quashed their convictions. The same view would be taken if the defendant was charged with attempted grievous bodily harm under **s20 Offences Against the Person Act 1861**. If the offence had been carried out, the offender could be convicted if he either intended to inflict grievous bodily harm or was reckless about this. For the charge of attempt to inflict grievous bodily harm to succeed, however, only intention will suffice. With the crime of murder, the defendant can be found guilty if it is proved that he intended to kill or to cause grievous bodily harm. For the crime of attempted murder, the wrongdoer must be shown to have had the intention to kill; the intention to cause grievous bodily harm is not enough and, if this is all that can be proved, the defendant must be acquitted.

We now need to see how this intention to commit the crime can be established. It is primarily a jury matter. In **Mohan 1976**, decided before the **Criminal Attempts Act 1981**, the Court of Appeal said that intention meant:

> a decision to bring about, in so far as it lies within the accused's power, the commission of the offence which it is alleged the accused attempted to commit, no matter whether the accused desired the consequence or not.

In attempted murder, therefore, the fact that the defendant foresaw that his actions might cause the death of the victim would not be enough. As in the full crime of murder, however, if the defendant foresaw that death was a virtually certain consequence of his actions, this would be strong evidence from which the jury would be entitled to find that the wrongdoer had the necessary intention. In **Walker and Hayles 1990**, discussed earlier in Chapter 2, the Court of Appeal was prepared to accept a direction of the trial judge that the jury could infer that the defendant had the necessary intention if he foresaw that there was a very high degree of probability that death would result, although it was made clear that the court preferred the words 'virtually certain'.

In this case, the convictions for attempted murder were upheld. The appellants had thrown the victim from a third floor block of flats because it was believed that he had ill-treated Walker's sister. The Court of Appeal confirmed that it was necessary to show that the appellants had intended to kill the victim and that the intention to cause really serious harm was insufficient for attempted murder. The court found, however, that this had been proved and that the statements made by the trial judge did not amount to a misdirection. This case now needs to be read in the light of the judgment of the House of Lords in **Woollin 1998**, mentioned in Chapter 2. It is almost certain that the words 'highly probable' would now be considered insufficient; the defendant must have foreseen that death was a virtually certain consequence of his actions.

To summarise therefore, to be found guilty of attempted murder, the defendant must have intended to kill and the jury will decide this fact after the direction formulated in **Woollin** is given. Intention must also be proved for the offences of attempted grievous bodily harm, attempts relating to lesser forms of assault, attempted theft and attempted criminal damage. It is also clear from the Law Commission's report that it was envisaged that intention had to be proved for **all** criminal attempts and with regard to all aspects of the offence in question. This uniform approach has not always been followed and a different view has been taken in respect of the offences of attempted rape and attempted arson, as will be noted below.

Crimes where lesser *mens rea* will suffice

With certain offences, intention still has to be proved with regard to the actual conduct, but a lesser degree of blameworthiness, i.e. recklessness, may suffice in relation to the circumstances in which the crime was committed. These exceptions are best explained by looking at the cases of **Khan 1990** and **AG's Reference (No 3 of 1992) 1993**.

In **Khan and Others 1990**, a 16-year-old girl had gone to a house with five boys after a visit to a disco and other boys had joined them. It was alleged that three of the boys had raped the girl and that four others, the defendants in this case, had attempted to do so.

The defendants were convicted of attempted rape but claimed that the judge had misdirected the jury on the *mens rea* required for this offence. They said that it had not been proved that they had intended to commit all aspects of the offence. They agreed that they intended to have intercourse with the victim, but argued that they thought that the girl was consenting.

The Court of Appeal decided that the *mens rea* necessary for attempted rape was the same for the complete offence:

> *namely an intention to have intercourse plus knowledge of or recklessness as to the woman's absence of consent. No question of attempting to achieve a reckless state of mind arises; the attempt relates to the physical activity; the mental state of the defendant is the same.*

The court believed that this interpretation of the law was desirable because it 'did not require the jury to be burdened with different directions as to the accused's state of mind, dependant on whether the individual achieved or failed to achieve sexual intercourse'.

The same approach was taken and expanded upon in **AG's Reference (No 3 of 1992) 1994**. The offence in question was attempted arson, being reckless whether life be endangered under **s1(2) Criminal Damage Act 1971**. The defendants were acquitted because the judge ruled that, on a charge of attempt, intent to endanger life was required; recklessness was not sufficient. The Court of Appeal decided that this was wrong and said that it was enough for the defendants to be in one of the states of mind required for the commission of the full offence.

To sum up, therefore, the *mens rea* required for attempt is intention in relation to committing the actual crime but in certain limited circumstances, recklessness will suffice with regard to the circumstances in which the crime is committed, provided that the full offence allows this lesser degree of *mens rea*. This seems to be confined to cases of attempted rape and attempted aggravated criminal damage.

 **Comment**

One can see why the Court of Appeal was reluctant to see the offenders go unpunished in the situations described in the previous two cases. It has to be admitted, however, that the two decisions have 'muddied the waters' considerably and made the law very uncertain regarding the *mens rea* of attempt. In respect of the offences of rape and aggravated arson at least, the court appears to have changed that which has been clearly laid down by Parliament. With regard to other crimes, the courts have been definite in their opinion that intention only will suffice so, at present, a two-tier system operates which is extremely difficult for juries (and students!) to understand and will surely lead to further appeals.

One solution would be for Parliament to make it clear that the *mens rea* required for an attempt should be the same as for the full offence. Another would be for the House of Lords to overrule the decisions in **Khan** and the **Reference** and state that intention is needed for all aspects of every offence. This, however, is unlikely to happen. After the appeal in **Khan** was dismissed, the

Appeal Committee of the House of Lords rejected the defendants' application to appeal to that House, thereby tacitly agreeing with the decision of the lower court. The third way is to accept the different treatment for these crimes. The Law Commission was originally in favour of demanding intention for all the aspects of a crime but came to believe that this approach was too narrow and now agrees with the changes effected by case law.

Attempting to commit the impossible

Before leaving the subject of *mens rea*, it has to be decided whether a person can be guilty of an attempt to commit a crime, even though the crime itself is, for some reason, impossible to commit. Examples of this could occur where a gang member attempts to shoot and kill an informer while he is asleep in his bed but, unbeknown to him, another gang member has already strangled the man. Alternatively, a wrongdoer might be attempting to smuggle 50 crates of whisky into the country but the plan has been discovered and the bottles now contain cold tea. The question that needs to be asked is whether such people could be convicted of attempting to commit a crime because, as has been noted, the crime itself is now impossible. The House of Lords has made it clear that the answer to this question is 'yes' but, over the last two decades, the decisions of that court have swung alarmingly from one view to the other on this subject.

In **Haughton v Smith 1975**, which was decided before the law on attempts was put into statutory form, the police seized a quantity of stolen corned beef but allowed the lorry to continue on its journey under the control of a disguised policeman. At the end of its route, the people unloading the consignment were arrested and later convicted of attempting to handle stolen goods. The case reached the highest appeal court where their Lordships decided that the conviction for attempt could not be sustained if the crime itself was not possible.

The **Criminal Attempts Act 1981** clearly intended to reverse such decisions. **S1(2)** states that

> *A person may be guilty of attempting to commit an offence to which this section applies even though the facts are such that the commission of the offence is impossible.*

Despite this plain wording, however, the House of Lords again quashed a conviction, this time in the case of **Anderton v Ryan 1985**.

Mrs Ryan had confessed that she had bought a video cassette recorder for £110 in the belief that it was a stolen one and was charged with both handling and attempted handling of stolen goods. In the event, the prosecution did not believe that it would be able to establish that the goods had been stolen, so the first charge was dropped and only the attempted handling charge pursued. The magistrates refused to convict but the Divisional Court supported the prosecution's appeal on the point of law. The House of Lords quashed the conviction, obviously believing that it would be unjust to find liability in a case such as this, despite what was laid down in **s1(3)**.

In **Shivpuri 1987**, the House of Lords overruled this decision, made less than two years earlier. The defendant had been arrested by customs officials on his return from a visit to India. While there, he had been approached by a dealer in drugs who had offered him £1,000 to take control of a suitcase in Cambridge, the contents of which he was later to distribute to others. He believed that the drugs were either heroin or cannabis. He was later arrested in Southall, London, as he handed over a packet to a third party. This packet and the others in the lining of his suitcase were found to contain

a harmless vegetable matter like snuff, not harmful drugs. The defendant argued, therefore, that his conviction for attempting to be knowingly concerned in dealing with a prohibited drug should be quashed on the grounds that the complete offence was impossible.

The case reached the House of Lords. The point of law on which that body was asked to decide was stated in the following, lengthy way: 'Does a person commit an offence under **s1 Criminal Attempts Act 1981** where, if the facts were as that person believed them to be, the full offence would have been committed by him, but where on the true facts of the offence which that person set out to commit was in law impossible, e.g. because the substance imported and believed to be heroin was not heroin but a harmless substance?'

The House of Lords decided that the answer was 'yes'.

Lord Bridge felt it was necessary to start with the Act itself (although he did not really explain why he had not taken that approach in **Anderton**!). He said it had to be decided whether the defendant had intended to receive, store and pass on to others packages of cannabis or heroin, to which the answer was clearly yes. It then had to be established whether he had done an act which was more than merely preparatory to the commission of the offence and, again, the answer was yes. Lastly, it had to be examined whether this act required anything further than this. **S1(2)** indicates that the answer to this is no; the defendant, therefore, must be found guilty.

The learned judge then questioned whether this result could stand with the earlier decision in **Anderton v Ryan** and decided that it could not. His conclusion, therefore, was that **Anderton v Ryan** was wrongly decided and that he and his fellow judges 'fell into error' in their desire to avoid convicting Mrs Ryan and others in her situation. He was obviously

FIVE KEY FACTS ON ATTEMPTS

- The law on attempts is in the **Criminal Attempts Act 1981**; the maximum punishment is the same as for the complete offence.
- The *actus reus* exists where a party does an act which is more that merely preparatory. The jury will decide this issue but the conviction may be quashed if that body has not been directed properly on the matter or the acts cannot be said to be directly connected to the crime (**Gullefer 1990, Campbell 1991, Geddes 1996**).
- The mental element needed for the attempt is intention, which was said in **Mohan 1976** to mean a decision to bring about the commission of the offence whether or not it was desired. Intention must be proved for attempted murder, attempted assault in all its forms, attempted theft and attempted basic criminal damage. For attempted murder, there has to be an intention to kill, not merely to cause serious harm, as in the complete offence, and it appears that the direction in **Woollin** may now be required. This would mean that the jury is not entitled to find intention unless the defendant foresaw that death was a virtually certain consequence.
- Recklessness about the actual commission of the offence is not enough (**Millard and Vernon 1987**). In attempted rape and attempted arson, however, although the offender must intend to commit the sexual intercourse or criminal damage, he may still be convicted if he is reckless about the woman's consent in the first instance or reckless about endangering life in the second situation (**Khan 1990, AG's Reference (No 3 of 1992) 1994**).
- The House of Lords in **Shivpuri 1987** clearly affirmed s1(2) **Criminal Attempts Act** and upheld that it is possible to be convicted of attempting to commit a crime, even though the actual offence may not have been possible.

influenced by the strong criticism of this ruling given by Professor Glanville Williams in the *Criminal Law Journal* in 1986. Lord Bridge stated ruefully, 'The language in which he criticises the decision in **Anderton v Ryan** is not conspicuous for its moderation, but it would be foolish, on that account, not to recognise the force of the criticism and churlish not to acknowledge the assistance I have derived from it'. Their Lordships unanimously decided to overrule **Anderton v Ryan**, using the rights given under the Practice Statement of 1966 to do so and dismissed the appeal in **Shivpuri**. The position is, at last, crystal clear; a person can be found guilty of attempt, even though the actual crime is impossible.

Before leaving the question of attempts, it is important to note that certain crimes cannot be attempted. These are attempting to conspire, attempting to aid, abet, counsel or procure and attempting to assist an offender after the commission of a crime.

13.3 Conspiracy

A conspiracy is an agreement between two or more people to do an unlawful act. Until the passing of the **Criminal Law Act 1977**, conspiracy was a common law offence and covered a wide range of activities, including a conspiracy to commit a tort such as trespass. The Law Commission believed that the offence should be confined to agreements to commit crimes but felt that certain areas of the law needed to be discussed more fully. When the **Criminal Law Act** was passed, therefore, two forms of common law conspiracy were retained for what was supposed to be an interim period. Over 20 years later, this position remains so the law on conspiracy is an uncomfortable mix of statute law and common law.

Three main forms of conspiracy need to be looked at. These are:

- Conspiracy to commit a crime, an offence defined in the **Criminal Law Act 1977**.
- Conspiracy to defraud, a common law offence.

- Conspiracy to corrupt public morals or outrage public decency, also created at common law.

13.3.1 Conspiracy to commit a crime

As stated, this offence is to be found in the **Criminal Law Act 1977**, as amended by the **Criminal Attempts Act 1981** and the **Criminal Justice Act 1987**.

S1 states that the offence of conspiracy to commit a crime will take place when a person agrees with another person or persons to pursue a course of conduct which, if carried out, will amount to or involve the commission of an offence, or would do so if something had not happened making the offence impossible to commit.

Conspiracies to commit a crime are often known as **s1** conspiracies. The punishment is laid down in **s3** but this, too is complicated. In cases of murder and other very serious crimes, the maximum is life imprisonment; in other cases punishable by imprisonment, the maximum sentence should not exceed the maximum for the main offence.

The *actus reus* of conspiracy

The *actus reus* of conspiracy to commit a crime is satisfied if the party agrees with another or several others to pursue a course of conduct which, if carried out will amount to or involve the commission of an offence. There must, therefore, be some form of agreement about the course of conduct to be pursued, although, if several people are involved it is only necessary for the offender to have agreed with one of them, provided that this is not a spouse or a child or the intended victim. In **Chrastney 1991**, the defendant tried to argue that she had only discussed the matter of supplying Class A drugs with her husband. The Court of Appeal rejected her appeal, as she had known that other conspirators were involved in the plan. It would have been different if she had been completely unaware of the involvement of others.

The *mens rea* of conspiracy

When looking at the position relating to the *mens rea* required for conspiracy, the Law Commission made it clear that there should only be liability if the defendant intended to commit the offence. The Bill introduced into Parliament originally stated that the defendant and his fellow conspirators 'must intend to bring about any consequence which is an element of the offence'. Unfortunately, this clause was deleted from the statute because the whole phrase, of which this was only a part, was felt to be too complicated. Instead, intention can be implied from the wording of **s1(1)**, when it states that a person must agree with another to pursue a course of conduct. **S1(2)** also states that, in cases where the full offence can be committed without the offender having knowledge of any particular fact or circumstance necessary for the commission of the offence, such a person cannot be found guilty of conspiracy unless 'he and at least one other party to the agreement intend or know that the fact or circumstance shall or will exist at the time when the conduct constituting the offence is to take place'. This means that even in cases where recklessness, negligence or strict liability suffices for the complete offence or a part of it, this is not enough for conspiracy to commit such crimes; here, an intention must be proved.

The difficulties arising from Anderson

Given these statements of the law, therefore, it is very surprising to note the comments of the House of Lords in **Anderson 1986**.

The defendant, while in Lewes prison, had agreed, in return for payment, to help a temporary cellmate facing very serious charges, to effect an escape from prison. The prisoner's brother and another man were also involved. After his release, Anderson had provided some diamond wire but was then involved in a car accident and took no further part in the plan. He tried to argue that he did not possess the *mens rea* for conspiracy. He claimed that he had never intended for the agreement to go ahead and had never believed that it could succeed. He stated that, instead of giving any additional help, he was going to go abroad with the money paid up-front. The House of Lords dismissed his appeal against his conviction but the reasoning of Lord Bridge when reaching such a decision has been seriously questioned. He came to the rather startling conclusion that the conspirator did not need to intend that the pre-arranged plan should actually take place.

He accepted that it was a necessary ingredient for the defendant to agree that a course of conduct should be pursued, which would then lead to the committing of an offence. Nevertheless, he decided that it was not necessary for the prosecution to prove that each and every conspirator should intend that the crime should be committed.

This view of the law ensured that Anderson's conviction could be upheld. It also makes it easier for the prosecution to convict those who only play a subordinate role in the planning of a crime and who do not really care whether or not the offence is carried out, so long as they are paid for their part in the proceedings. It has, however, been sharply criticised by academics. The wording of **s1(1)** seems to imply that the defendant must have an intention to pursue the course of conduct which, if carried out would amount to or involve the commission of an offence. In addition, **s1(2)** specifically demands that the offender must be shown to have knowledge or intention, before being convicted of conspiracy to commit certain crimes, such as strict liability offences and ones for which recklessness might suffice for the full offence. It would, therefore, be extremely odd if intention were required for these offences but not for all the others where a higher degree of *mens rea* is needed for the complete offence.

Anderson was distinguished on this point by the Court of Appeal in Northern Ireland, in the case of **McPhillips 1990**, where the defendant was found not guilty of conspiracy to murder. His conviction was quashed because it was believed that he had intended to give a warning that a bomb was primed to go off at a disco at 1am, the busiest part of the night, while the other conspirators had not.

If the statements mentioned above in **Anderson** had been followed, it would have been immaterial that McPhillips did not intend the crime to go ahead. The court, however, seized on another part of Lord Bridge's judgment, where he suggested that special consideration should be given to honest citizens who might find themselves caught up in a conspiracy and feel obliged, for a time, to go along with the plot. The court conveniently overlooked the fact that McPhillips was far from innocent in other respects and had definitely been involved in the criminal activities.

Lord Bridge's *dicta* that a conspirator may still be found guilty when he does not intend that the crime should be committed, was also ignored in **Edwards 1991**. There was a conspiracy to supply amphetamine, an illegal drug, but there was some doubt as to whether the defendant intended to supply another drug instead, which was not illegal. The Court of Appeal held that a direction by the trial judge that the defendant could only be convicted if he intended to supply amphetamines was held to be correct. If **Anderson** had been followed, a different answer would have been given.

Must the conspirator play a part in the proceedings?

Another part of Lord Bridge's judgment that has also given rise to problems was his contention that the defendant is only guilty of conspiracy if he intended to play some part in the proceedings.

Professor Sir John Smith calls this 'a novel dictum' and notes that it is unsupported by authority. It also creates a loophole through which many offenders could escape, especially ringleaders, and others in a similar position, who organise events and then leave it to others to carry out the 'dirty work'. In **Siracusa 1990**, the Court of Appeal decided to address the issue, even though it was not directly pertinent to the appeal the court was hearing. The court decided in this drug smuggling case that participation in a conspiracy could be passive as well as active. The judges decided tactfully that Lord Bridge could not have meant what he said! O'Connell L J remarked 'We think it obvious that Lord Bridge cannot have been intending that the organiser of a crime who recruited others to carry it out would not himself be guilty of conspiracy unless it could be proved that he intended to play some part himself'. Be that as it may, there is no getting away from the fact that he did clearly state that the necessary *mens rea* would only be established if 'the accused, when he entered into the agreement, intended to play some part in the agreed course of conduct in furtherance of the criminal purpose . . .'. The appeal court did, however, make it clear that to secure a conviction, the right charge must be brought. If an offender is alleged to have conspired to import heroin, then that is what must be proved, not that he imported cannabis; if another drug is involved, this should be stated instead or as an additional charge.

Comment

It can be seen that the Court of Appeal has been making valiant efforts to limit the effect of these two statements by Lord Bridge and, that, so far, their attempts to do this have gone unchallenged and may be said to represent the law as it currently stands. It might have been clearer if the Court of Appeal had stated that Lord Bridge's second statement was merely *obiter* and that the court did not feel able to follow it.

13.3.2 Conspiracy at common law

The first point to note is that **s5 Criminal Law Act 1977** states that, subject to certain listed exceptions, the offence of common law conspiracy is abolished.

The exceptions consist of conspiracy to defraud (**s5(2)**) and conspiracy to corrupt public morals or outrage public decency (**s5(3)**).

Conspiracy to defraud

Reforms of this area of law have been promised for decades. The **Criminal Law Act** specifically retained it as a common law offence, while abolishing most other forms of common law conspiracy, in anticipation of fairly early reform. This never materialised; instead, in 1994, the Law Commission decided that a comprehensive review of the whole law of dishonesty was necessary. This will, of course, include the offence of conspiracy to defraud. In the meantime, however, it remains as a common law offence, along with conspiracy to corrupt public morals and outrage public decency.

Conspiracy to defraud acts as a safety net to ensure that certain offenders do not escape punishment, which, as seen in **s12 Criminal Law Act 1977**, can be up to a maximum of ten years' imprisonment. If there is a conspiracy to commit a substantive offence, the common law offence of conspiracy to defraud will not be normally needed because conspiracy under **s1** of the **Criminal Law Act 1977** can be charged. Common law conspiracy is, however, useful in the following situations: where the prosecution finds it difficult to establish any deception, where the fraud is not directly inflicted and in cases where no loss has been caused to the party defrauded.

In **Scott v MPC 1975**, the defendants had persuaded employees of a cinema to make copies of films without the permission of the owners which they then intended to show for a profit. The House of Lords upheld the conviction for conspiracy to defraud, claiming that it was enough that dishonesty and injury to the interests of another had been established. Their Lordships made it clear that there was no additional requirement to show that a deception had been practised.

The House of Lords was again involved in the case of **Hollinshead 1985**. The defendants manufactured devices which, when fitted, caused electricity meters to under-record the amount of electricity used. They tried to argue that they were not guilty of conspiracy to defraud because they had not been involved in any agreement to use the boxes; they had merely sold them to a middle-man.

The House of Lords upheld the convictions, stating that it was enough that the defendants had arranged to put the boxes into circulation for the sole purpose of causing loss to the electricity boards.

In both the cases mentioned above, actual loss would have resulted from the conspiracy. The House of Lords had, however, already made it clear in **Welham v DPP 1961** that it is not always necessary, in the offence of conspiracy to defraud, to show that another party has suffered loss, so long as an intention to defraud is apparent. Examples cited included cases where the conspiracy to defraud was against a public authority or the holder of a public office and where a drug addict forged a doctor's certificate to obtain drugs from a chemist.

In **Moses and Ansbro 1991**, the defendants had unlawfully helped immigrants to obtain work permits to which they were not entitled. The Court of Appeal decided that there was a clear conspiracy to defraud; the defendants were acting dishonestly and contrary to their public duty. There was no additional need to show that economic loss had been caused by their actions.

Similarly, in **Wai Yu-Tsang 1992**, the Privy Council upheld a conviction for conspiracy where the defendant had agreed with others not to enter certain dishonoured cheques in the records of a bank in order to help safeguard the bank's reputation. The judges decided that the term 'conspiracy to defraud' should be given a wide meaning; it was enough if there was 'simply an intention to practise fraud on another or an intention to act to the prejudice of another man's right'.

Elements of conspiracy to defraud

The *actus reus* of conspiracy to defraud could be said to be an agreement between two or more people to bring about an unlawful object. The *mens rea* would be satisfied if this was done intentionally, even if this was for a benign purpose, as confirmed in the above case.

S5 Criminal Law Act 1977, as amended, provides that either statutory conspiracy or conspiracy to defraud can be charged if there is any overlap between the two.

Conspiracy to corrupt public morals or outrage public decency

The re-emergence of this type of common law conspiracy caused disquiet among some academics. This was mainly due to certain comments uttered by the House of Lords in the case of **Shaw v DPP 1962**, which seemed to suggest that these top judges had the power to watch over the nation's morals and adapt the law for this purpose. When one looks at the material currently available in magazines, on late-night television and on the Internet, one can see that they were largely unsuccessful in holding back the tide of change!

The defendant had been convicted of the crime of conspiracy to corrupt public morals after he had published a magazine called the *Ladies' Directory*, in which the names and addresses of prostitutes were listed. He had fallen foul of the law because, in some instances, the names were accompanied by photographs of the women, together with the details of the sexual perversions they practised.

The House of Lords upheld the view of the Court of Criminal Appeal that a substantive offence of corrupting public morals did, in fact, exist and affirmed that it was therefore possible to conspire to commit this offence. Shaw's conviction was upheld.

It was the speech of Lord Simons that caused the furore. He suggested that the courts not only had the duty to uphold the law but also the power to conserve the moral welfare of the State. He claimed that it was their duty 'to guard it against attacks which may be the more insidious because they are novel and unprepared for'.

In **Knuller v DPP 1973**, the House of Lords was invited to overrule its decision in **Shaw**. Not only did their Lordships refuse to do this, they confirmed that there was also a common law offence of outraging public decency and that therefore it was possible to conspire with others to commit this crime.

The defendant in **Knuller** had been involved in the publication of a magazine alleged to be of interest to those holding 'progressive views'.

The offending advertisements contained details of homosexual men who were obviously hoping to attract responses from like-minded people. The charge claimed that this material encouraged the readers 'to indulge in such practices, with intent thereby to debauch and corrupt' their morals.

Lord Simon denied that the judges have the right to create new criminal offences; that, he said, was a matter for Parliament. He decided that what they could do was to ascertain whether there were any existing offences that might cover the matter in question. If this were the case, they could then apply that law to the new circumstances. After reviewing the authorities, he decided that there was indeed an existing offence of outraging public decency and a corresponding one of conspiring to do this. He believed, however, that the latter offence should only be invoked in exceptional circumstances. He stated that the word 'outrage' was a very strong word and 'goes considerably beyond offending the susceptibilities of, or even shocking reasonable people'. He acknowledged that standards are constantly changing and said that the jury should be reminded that we live in a multi-faceted society with a good record of tolerance for minority views.

In this particular case, therefore, although the existing offences relating to outraging public decency were recognised and upheld, the actual conviction was quashed because the behaviour in question did not satisfy the definition of the word 'outrage'.

The Court of Appeal decided that there was sufficient outrage in the case of **Gibson 1990** and upheld the conviction of an artist for the substantive offence of outraging public decency.

Gibson had displayed examples of his work in a gallery to which the public had free access. One of the exhibits was a pair of earrings, each of which had been made from a freeze-dried human foetus of three or four months. The court obviously believed that most members of the public would find such material offensive. It was also decided that the prosecution did not have to prove that the defendant intended to outrage public decency; all that was necessary was to prove that the publication or display was deliberate.

13.3.3 Conspiring to commit the impossible

S1 Criminal Law Act 1977 makes it clear that a statutory conspiracy can take place even though the full offence is impossible. It is believed that, following the case of **Shivpuri**, relating to attempts, similar rules would also be applied to common law conspiracies if the matter came up.

13.3.4 Conspiracies where a foreign element is involved

The last point to be considered relating to conspiracies is the position where the conspiring is done abroad but the crime is to be committed in the UK. It will obviously be of great advantage if the enforcers of law and order can act as soon as possible to prevent the crime taking place. The courts have done their best to help this process.

In **DPP v Doot 1973**, the House of Lords held that a conspiracy may, in some circumstances, be a continuing process. Where, therefore, an unlawful arrangement was made abroad to import cannabis into the UK, it was decided that all the conspirators could be charged with the offence when one of their group landed in England. Their Lordships stated that:

A conspiracy does not end with the making of the agreement. It will continue so long as there are two or more parties to it intending to carry out the design.

TEN KEY FACTS ON CONSPIRACY

- The rules relating to conspiracy to commit a crime are laid down in the **Criminal Law Act 1977. S1(1)** defines the offence.
- The *actus reus* is agreeing with another or others that a course of conduct will be pursued, which if carried out in accordance with their instructions, will necessarily amount to the commission of an offence (or would do so if the crime was not impossible).
- From the rather obscure wording of the statute, it appears that the defendant must intend that the offence should be carried out, but the House of Lords in **Anderson 1986** decided that the defendant was guilty even when this was not established. The Court of Appeal, however, did not follow this reasoning, in either **McPhillips 1990 or Edwards 1991** so the law on this point is far from clear.
- In **Anderson**, the House of Lords also stated, *obiter*, that the alleged conspirator must have intended to play some part in the commission of the offence. The Court of Appeal in **Siracusa 1990** decided that the House of Lords did not really mean to state this! The law on this point also remains uncertain. Academics appear to favour the views of the Court of Appeal on these issues
- The common law offences of conspiracy to defraud, and conspiracy to corrupt public morals and outrage public decency, have been specifically retained by **s5 Criminal Law Act 1977**, although all other common law conspiracies were abolished by that act.
- The term 'conspiracy to defraud' is given a broad meaning. The offence may be committed even when the motives of the perpetrators of the fraud are not necessarily bad (**Wai Yu-Tsang v The Queen 1992**). It may also arise in cases where there is no deception (**Scott 1975**), or no financial loss (**Welham 1961, Moses and Ansbro 1991**), or even where there is no direct link with the person who might commit the crime (**Hollinshead 1985**).
- The maximum punishment is ten years' imprisonment.
- The House of Lords has confirmed that the common law offences of corrupting public morals and outraging public decency do still exist and, therefore, so do the corresponding offences of conspiring to do these things (**Shaw v DPP 1962, Knuller 1973**).
- It was made clear by the Lords, however, that it has no residuary power to create new criminal offences and also that the offences of outraging public decency and conspiring to do this should be reserved for really offensive cases. The Court of Appeal in **Gibson 1990** felt that the display of a freeze-dried foetus made into an earring was such an example.
- The Court of Appeal decided in the same case that it is unnecessary to prove that the defendant had the intention to outrage public decency, so long as his publication of the material was deliberate.

This very useful interpretation enabled the conspiracy to be thwarted and the crime prevented.

In **Liangsiriprasert v Government of the USA 1991**, the Privy Council took this reasoning a stage further and decided that even if an overt act like the above could not be proved, it was still possible to decide that a conspiracy existed. The court argued that:

> The only purpose of looking for an overt act in England in the case of a conspiracy entered into abroad, can be to establish the link between the conspiracy and England or possibly to show that the conspiracy is continuing. But if this can be established by other evidence, for example the taping of conversations between the conspirators showing a firm agreement to commit the crime at some future date, it defeats the preventative purpose of the crime of conspiracy to have to wait until some overt act is performed.

The Court of Appeal approved of this extension in **Samson 1991**.

In the cases just mentioned, the arrangement made abroad had to involve conduct which amounted to a crime in this country, otherwise no liability existed. **S1(4) Criminal Law Act 1977** makes this very clear. Amendments to the Act, however, also allow a person to be charged with conspiracy if acts are done in this country in preparation for a crime to be committed abroad. **S1A** refers. In addition, the **Sexual Offences (Conspiracy and Incitement) Act 1996** extends liability for conspiracy to paedophiles who conspire in this country to commit unlawful sexual acts outside the UK.

13.4 Incitement

This is the last of the inchoate offences and is mainly a common law offence, although there are some specific offences of incitement which have been put in statutory form. Examples are inciting a person to commit murder, inciting others to mutiny or inciting racial hatred.

The remaining part of this chapter will examine common law incitement. The current position is that incitement to commit a summary offence is only triable summarily, whereas an incitement to commit an indictable offence is triable on indictment. This might seem obvious but it was not always the law. An odd feature of the law which does remain is that, while the punishment for an incitement to commit a summary offence cannot exceed that given for the full offence, the courts have the discretion to set the punishment when the offence is tried on incitement. This means that, theoretically at least, the inciter could receive a higher sentence than the person committing the offence. This could be a useful deterrent in combating terrorist attacks.

13.4.1 The meaning of incitement

Incitement occurs when a person urges another to commit a crime or 'reaches or seeks to influence the mind of another'. The courts have decided that incitement can be effected by suggestion, argument, persuasion and, as stated in **Race Relations Board v Applin 1973**, even by threats or other pressure. Incitement will often be verbal but it is possible to put the words in writing and thereby incite members of the public. In the early case of **Most 1881**, the incitement seemed obvious when the defendants urged certain members of the community to rise up and assassinate the heads of state. In **Invicta Plastics Ltd v Clare 1976**, however, the conviction of the defendant company was also upheld when they merely put an advertisement in a motoring magazine drawing attention to their product called Radatec, an instrument which could be used to help evade police speed traps.

The Divisional Court held that, when looking at the advertisement as a whole, there was clear evidence of incitement.

The incitement does not have to be successful but it must be shown that there was incitement to commit an actual offence known to law. In **Whitehouse 1977**, a loophole was disclosed when a man was accused of inciting a young girl of 15 to have incestuous intercourse with him. **S11 Sexual Offences Act 1956** states that it is an offence for a woman of 16 or over to permit her father and other close relatives to have sexual intercourse with her but under-age girls are not included. Therefore, Whitehouse could not be found guilty because he was being charged with inciting a girl to commit a crime which, under statute, she was incapable of committing. The court also held that he could not be liable for inciting his daughter to aid and abet him to have sexual intercourse with her! The judges were understandably reluctant to decide that young girls in these appalling situations should be tainted with the suggestion that they, also, have done wrong. The case of **Tyrrell 1894**, which decided that victims like this should not be held liable for aiding and abetting the commission of a criminal offence, was cited with approval. The defendant, therefore, was found not guilty in the current case but the judges suggested that Parliament should step in and plug this loophole in the law. This was effected very speedily and **s54 Criminal Law Act 1977** lays down that it is an offence for a man to incite to have sexual intercourse with him a girl under the age of 16 whom he knows to be his grand-daughter, daughter or sister.

Another offender who escaped liability when he was obviously guilty of wrongdoing was **Curr**, a case decided in 1968. The defendant ran a highly lucrative business of advancing money to women with large families and in return taking their Family Allowance books to cover the debt, plus a large sum in interest. He handled between 40 and 80 such books a week and made a profit of around 800 per cent on

the deals. He employed a team of women to cash the signed vouchers for him and was charged with inciting them to commit offences under the **Family Allowances Act 1945**. The crime that he was alleged to have incited was committed when a person received family allowance knowing that it was not properly payable or receivable by him or her. The Court of Appeal quashed the man's conviction, arguing that while it was obvious that the defendant knew that he was acting illegally, the prosecution also needed to establish that the women agents knew that they were committing a crime. This matter had not been properly put before the jury so the court felt obliged to quash the defendant's conviction for incitement of such an offence. He must have been laughing all the way back to the Post Office!

The team drafting the *Criminal Code* strongly criticised this decision, arguing that it was not necessary to prove that the person who was being incited had to know that an offence was being committed. It was felt to be enough that the defendant had such a belief. **Curr,** however, is a Court of Appeal decision that has not been overruled. It must, therefore, reflect the state of the law at the present time.

13.4.2 The *mens rea* of incitement

It is necessary for the prosecution to prove that the defendant intended to bring about the criminal result and used persuasion or pressure to do this, although the offence incited need not actually take place. The early decision in **Higgins 1801** makes this position clear and the judges affirmed this in **Whitehouse 1977**. From the decision in **Curr 1968**, discussed above, the defendant must also believe that the person incited will have the necessary *mens rea* to commit the crime in question or, at least, another crime requiring the same *mens rea*. If he does not believe this, they could be in the position of innocent agents and he could be the principal offender, provided that he was charged correctly.

13.4.3 Incitement of crimes which are impossible to commit

The law on the subject of whether a person can be found guilty of incitement when the crime in question is impossible to commit is rather confused. Since the case of **Fitzmaurice 1983**, it is also out of line with the statutory position taken for the crimes of attempts and conspiracy to commit a crime.

In **McDonough 1962**, the defendant's conviction for inciting a number of butchers to handle stolen meat carcasses which he believed were in a cold store, was upheld. He tried to argue that his conviction should be quashed because, at that time, the carcasses were not, in fact, in that place and there was some doubt as to whether they had ever existed. The Court of Appeal held that the essence of the offence lay in his suggestion to the other parties that they should receive the meat that he believed was stolen.

The Law Commission felt that this was a sensible line to take and, with regard to attempts and conspiracy, Parliament made it clear when it passed the **Criminal Attempts Act 1981** that the defendant may still be liable even if the actual offence is impossible.

The position with incitement, however, is now confused because of the later decision in **Fitzmaurice 1983**, which limited the cases where liability could still exist. The defendant was convicted of inciting three men to commit a 'wages snatch'. At his father's request, he had recruited the men allegedly to rob a woman walking from her workplace to the National Westminster Bank. In fact, the defendant's father had hatched a complicated plot to recover reward money by informing the authorities that there was an impending raid on a security van. He had therefore dissuaded his son from taking part but had arranged for him to assemble the gang. He then intended that they would be discovered outside the bank, wearing masks and carrying imitation firearms. The son was completely unaware of his father's plot but after it was discovered, he was charged with incitement.

He tried to argue that he could not be guilty of inciting the other men to commit a crime that could not, in fact, be committed. The Court of Appeal held that it was immaterial that the defendant's father was not planning a real offence at all because the defendant obviously believed that he was arranging for the men to commit a robbery in Bow and such an offence was not impossible to perform. The conviction, therefore, was upheld.

It can be seen from this that, despite the upholding of the conviction, the judges have not decided that an offender can still be guilty of incitement even though the crime is impossible, as is now the case with attempts and statutory conspiracy. A far more limited rule has been laid down in relation to incitement. If the incitement is a specific one, such as inciting another to kill a third party when, in fact, that person is already dead, the inciter cannot be found guilty. If, however, the incitement is a more general one, as, for example, that the other wrongdoers should rob a woman carrying wages outside a bank in Bow, as was the case in **Fitzmaurice**, then the defence of impossibility would not prevail.

◀ Comment

It is difficult to understand why the Court of Appeal did not take this chance to put the law on incitement, in respect of crimes that are impossible to commit, on the same footing as attempts and conspiracy. It was clearly the intention of both the Law Commission and Parliament that the defence should not be available for inchoate offences.

FIVE KEY FACTS ON INCITEMENT

- Incitement is a common law offence. If tried on indictment, the courts have the discretion to set the punishment.
- The *actus reus* is committed when the offender suggests, urges, persuades, threatens or pressurises the other to commit a crime (**Race Relations Board v Applin 1973**). Incitement can be effected orally or in writing (**Most 1881, Invicta Plastics v Clare 1976**). The offender must be inciting the other to commit a crime known to law; if there is no such offence he cannot be found guilty (**Whitehouse 1977**). If the crime does exist, then it does not matter if the inciter is unsuccessful in his attempts to persuade the other to commit it.
- The *mens rea* of incitement is an intention to bring about the required result, plus persuasion or pressure on the person targeted (**Hendrickson and Tichner 1977**).
- The controversial case of **Curr 1968** also decided that the person incited must have the *mens rea* to commit the offence in question. While this decision has been criticised, it has not been overruled.
- **Fitzmaurice 1983** appears to have limited the previously wide interpretation of liability for incitement when the actual crime has been impossible to commit, as laid down in **McDonough 1962**. It now appears to be the law that the offender will only be guilty if the offence is a general crime that it might have been possible to commit. It is important to realise that this approach is at odds with the other inchoate offences where the **Criminal Attempts Act 1981** specifically states that there can be liability to attempt to commit a crime that is impossible, or to conspire to do so.

13.5 Suggested reform of inchoate offences

It has been seen that a measure of reform of the law on conspiracy to commit a crime was effected by the **Criminal Law Act 1977** and changes made to the law on attempts made in the **Criminal Attempts Act 1981**. Reform of the law of deception is under review and, within this, the law on conspiracy to defraud. The offence of incitement has not been subjected to such a degree of scrutiny. The Draft Code team did investigate whether to change the name of the offence but at that time, decided to retain it. Clause 47 of the Draft Code defines incitement. This states that a person will be guilty of incitement if: (a) he *incites another to do or cause to be done an act or acts which if done, will involve the commission of the offence or offences by the other; and (b) he intends or believes that the other, if he acts as incited, shall or will do so with the fault required for the offence or offences.*

Clause 50 of the Code, if ever enacted, provides for a common approach to be taken with regard to impossibility. It states that *'a person may be guilty of incitement, conspiracy or attempt to commit an offence although the commission of the offence is impossible, if it would be possible in the circumstances which he believes or hopes exist or will exist at the relevant time'.*

As noted under Chapter 11, however, the Law Commission is now in favour of abolishing the crime of incitement altogether and is, instead, in favour of creating two new inchoate offences of assisting and encouraging crime.

Activity

Decide whether the following wrongdoers can be charged with an inchoate offence, giving full reasons for your answers:

Pablo, Gustav and Salvador met to enjoy their weekly drink together and discussed the possibility of stealing the Crown Jewels. Salvador, a glass merchant, promised to provide the equipment to cut the glass behind which the jewels are kept. Unbeknown to the friends, their conversation was taped and they were arrested. Salvador claimed that he had never intended to take part in the crime itself and had never really believed that it was going to take place.

Vincent decided that shock tactics were needed if ever his work was to attract the attention of art critics. He therefore created a sculpture made up of dead hedgehogs, which had been killed by passing motorists! He then displayed this in the centre of his free one-man exhibition at the local Town Hall.

Claude was at a racing track. The horse he had backed, called Monet's Folly, was trailing at the back of the field. Claude fired an air pistol close to the track, trying to distract the leading horses. He was hoping to get the race called off and thereby retrieve his stake money. His plan failed miserably and he was later charged with attempted theft.

Jacques is a student activist, who fiercely opposes the contraction of art courses at Chagall University. He placed an advertisement in the Student Quarterly Review urging students to rise up and kill the Chancellor. The Chancellor, however, is aware of the strength of feeling that his reforms have engendered and has employed a team of bodyguards to keep a 24-hour watch over him.

Self-Assessment Questions

1. Where is the law on attempts to commit a crime and what is the punishment?
2. Giving cases to support your answer, describe the test for deciding whether an attempt has been made.
3. What is the *mens rea* for attempt in cases of murder, grievous bodily harm under s18 and gbh under s20?
4. Why have the decisions in **Khan 1990** and **AG's Reference (No 3 of 1992)** caused difficulties with regard to *mens rea*?
5. What is the position if a person attempts to commit a crime but the actual crime turns out to be impossible?
6. Define a criminal conspiracy and state where the law is to be found.
7. Why did the House of Lords decision in **Anderson** cause problems with regard to the *mens rea* of conspiracy and how has this been dealt with in subsequent cases?
8. Describe the conspiracy to defraud in the following cases:
   Scott
   Hollinshead
   Moses & Ansbro
9. Which offences were resurrected in the cases of **Shaw** and **Knuller**?
10. Define incitement, giving two case examples. Explain why the case of **Fitzmaurice** has caused problems.

Chapter 14

VICARIOUS AND CORPORATE LIABILITY

14.1 Introduction

This chapter begins by looking at the principle of vicarious liability and explains how this operates under criminal law; it then moves on to discuss the liability of corporations. It will be seen that there have been calls to extend the criminal liability of companies in the light of several well-publicised disasters and we need to see whether the proposals to do this are workable and fair.

14.2 Vicarious liability

Under the principle of vicarious liability a person or company may be held liable for the criminal acts of another. The principle is far more common in civil law under the law of tort, where one of the most notable examples is the liability of an employer for the acts of his employees, provided that these are committed in the course of his employment.

Under criminal law, however, liability for the acts of another is naturally more strictly contained. This can be seen in the early case of **Huggins 1730**. The defendant was the warden of the Fleet prison in London and was charged with the murder of a prisoner. The prisoner died after being imprisoned in an unhealthy cell. Huggins was held to be unaware of this fact so therefore escaped liability, even though his employee was found guilty. The judge made it clear that there were important differences in the way the principle should be used in civil law and criminal law. In the latter instance, he stated that the parties 'must each answer for their own acts, and stand or fall by their own behaviour'. Over the years, however, the strength of this statement has been diluted and, in limited circumstances, it has been felt to be right to impose criminal

liability on a party even though the acts in question have been committed by someone else. In this chapter we shall discover when such action is deemed appropriate but, before this is examined, the differences between vicarious liability and strict liability need to be stressed.

14.2.1 The differences between strict liability and vicarious liability

It was noted in Chapter 2 that many statutes impose strict liability on a party. The offender may well be liable, even though he had no intention to commit the crime of which he is accused, was not reckless as to whether it was committed and may even have taken all possible care to ensure that it was not committed. Under the principle of vicarious liability, the offender is liable, not for his own acts, but for the criminal acts of another. In practice, there may be little difference in the effect. For example a company may be prosecuted for polluting a river because a statute makes the company strictly liable if such pollution takes place. Under the principle of vicarious liability, the company may also be found guilty along with an employee, if the latter has been charged personally with the crime.

14.2.2 The operation of vicarious liability in criminal law

As stated, the principle of vicarious liability under criminal law is more restrictive in its operation than under the law of tort. Under criminal law, such liability is only imposed in specific instances: These occur:

- where a statute expressly lays down such liability,
- where the acts of an agent are held to be the acts of another,
- where the delegation principle is held to apply.

These three situations need to be looked at in turn although it should be noted that there is a large measure of overlap between the first two.

Where a statute lays this down

Such statutes are usually of a regulatory nature. If they impose a legal duty on a person or, more often, a company, that body will be liable along with the person charged if the company has failed to ensure that the duty has been performed or obeyed in the way required. In **Mousell Bros Ltd v London and North Western Railway Co. 1917**, the court stated:

> while prima facie *a principal is not to be made criminally responsible for the acts of his servants, yet the legislature may prohibit an act or enforce a duty in such words as to make the prohibition or the duty absolute; in which case the principal is liable if the act is in fact done by his servants.*

Where the acts of an agent are counted

The case of the **Duke of Leinster 1924** illustrates this point well. The Duke was an undisclosed bankrupt who was convicted of obtaining credit without disclosing his true financial status. In fact it was his agent who had arranged for the credit, despite being instructed not to. The Duke was still held to be liable.

In many cases under this head, an employer is held liable for the actions of his employees. An example of this is the case of **Coppen v Moore (No 2) 1898**, where the employer owned six shops and in one of them, a sales assistant had

sold a ham, which she had described as 'a Scotch ham'. The employer had given clear instructions that the hams in his stores were to be described more generally as 'breakfast hams' but, despite this, he was convicted of selling goods to which a false trade description was applied. The court stated why he was liable: 'It cannot be doubted that the appellant sold the ham in question, although the transaction was carried out by his servants. In other words he was the seller, although not the actual salesman'.

A strict approach

This approach is often used where the relevant statute uses the word 'sells' or 'keeps' or when the party is charged with 'presenting' a play even if he is far away at the time. The reasoning behind such a seemingly hard approach is to gain the conviction of the person thought to be the real culprit, even if this is only caused by his failure to employ suitable staff or to take sufficient care in the running of his business. In appropriate cases, therefore, the courts are prepared to extend the meaning of the statute in order to achieve this purpose.

The words of Morland J in **National Rivers Authority v Alfred McAlpine Homes (East) Ltd 1994** help to illustrate why this approach was taken in one emotive area. The company was convicted of polluting a river, after employees of the company discharged wet cement into it. The judge stated that:

> to make an offence an effective weapon in the defence of environmental protection, a company must by necessary implication be criminally liable for the acts or omissions of its servants or agents during activities being done for the company. I do not find that this affects our concept of a just or fair criminal justice system, having regard to the magnitude of environmental pollution.

Limitations

There is obviously a limit to the lengths to which the courts will go when stretching the meaning of the words in the relevant statute in this way. The approach is obviously inappropriate where the wording denotes some activity by the offender that cannot realistically be imputed to the employer, such as the word 'drive'. In addition, it is felt that it should not be used where the statute uses words like 'knowingly'. It might be considered to be too great an extension to import the *mens rea* of the employee to the employer in these circumstances, although, as will be seen below, this is done under the delegation principle. Under this second head, the principle is confined to offences of strict liability.

Where the delegation principle is said to apply

Use of such a principle can, on occasion, make a party liable even in cases where some form of *mens rea* is necessary for the commission of the offence and even where he has delegated the duty to someone else, as in **Allen v Whitehead 1930**. The defendant, a licensee of a café, left the management of it to another and just visited it once a week. He was convicted under the quaintly-worded section of the **Metropolitan Police Act 1839** of 'knowingly permitting prostitutes or persons of notoriously bad character to meet on the premises'. He was found liable despite the fact that he had instructed his manager not to allow prostitutes to visit the café and had displayed notices to that effect!

The Divisional Court adopted such a rigid stance because it was felt that otherwise the statute would be completely ineffective, or 'rendered nugatory' as one judge put it. He went on to say 'This seems to me to be a case where the proprietor, the keeper to the house, had delegated his position to a manager so far as the conduct of the house was concerned; he had transferred to the manager the exercise of

discretion in the conduct of the business, and it seems to me the only reasonable conclusion is, regard being had to the purpose of this Act, that knowledge in the manager was knowledge in the keeper of the house. I think, therefore, that this case ought to go back to the learned magistrate, with a direction to convict'.

This approach can seem very odd to a layman and perhaps the opposite of what one might expect. Despite this, the same view was taken in **Linnett v Metropolitan Police Commissioner 1946**, where a co-licensee was liable for permitting disorderly conduct on the premises even though he had delegated control to another. To confuse matters further, the courts developed a rule that the delegation principle only applied where there was a complete delegation by the owner or occupier. This again appears to be an odd decision; one might reasonably assume that the opposite approach would have to be taken and that the more the person remained in control, the more likely it would be that he was liable. When looked at more carefully, however, this interpretation ensures that an owner or occupier is not able to escape liability just because he absents himself from the premises. The principle can be used in cases where it might be difficult or non-productive to charge the actual offender. Be that as it may, this approach meant that owners were able to deny liability if they had not delegated the whole of their authority to another and the person committing the offence had acted without authority, like an employee in another part of the building.

The strangeness of this common law rule was examined by the House of Lords in the case of **Vane v Yiannopoullos 1964**, and reluctantly accepted as the correct view of the law. The owner of a restaurant had been charged with 'knowingly' supplying liquor to people who had not eaten in the restaurant, which contravened the terms of his licence. He was on one floor of the building and the waitress, who had unlawfully sold the alcohol was on another. The owner argued that he was unaware of the actions of the waitress so could not be said to have committed the offence 'knowingly'. The first instance court agreed that he did not have the necessary *mens rea* and the charge was dismissed. The prosecutor appealed and the case eventually reached the House of Lords, which dismissed the appeal.

Lord Reid accepted that it would be difficult on occasions to enforce such statutes without the delegation principle. He added, however, that if it had not been so firmly established for over half a century, he would be very tempted to challenge such a rule, which made a person liable even though the *mens rea* of the crime said that he had to commit the offence 'knowingly'. Because of the well-established authorities, he concluded that it was now 'too late to upset so long-standing a practice'.

An unsatisfactory distinction

Lord Reid admitted that the distinction that had developed between full delegation where the owner was liable, and partial delegation where he might not be, was 'hard to justify'. Despite this, he was not prepared to abolish it in this particular case because such a move would then make the defendant liable.

In **Winson 1969**, the Court of Appeal accepted that the doctrine of delegation still formed part of English law and held that it also applied to licensing laws.

The whole matter was thrown into confusion again in **Howker v Robinson 1973**, where the Divisional Court applied the doctrine of delegation in a case where there was only partial delegation.

The landlord had been serving in the public bar, while his barman had served drinks illegally in the lounge bar. The appeal court used **Winson** as a precedent to show that the doctrine still existed. They simply accepted it as a fact that the magistrates had found that delegation had taken place and upheld the conviction. In fact, it was clear that only partial delegation existed in this case and that therefore, under this principle at least, the licensee should not have been convicted. It has been persuasively argued that this case was wrongly decided.

14.2.3 Arguments for and against vicarious liability

Five points in favour
- Without it, it will be hard to obtain a conviction. The comments of the judges in **Mousell Ltd v London and North Western Railway Co 1917** and in **Vane v Yiannopoullos 1964** illustrate this.
- The principle helps to keep standards high. It stops employers 'cutting corners' in order to reap greater profits and ensures that they choose their staff with care.
- Without the delegation principle, licensees and other employers not on the premises at the relevant time could simply argue that they were unaware of any violation of the law.
- The principle ensures that the person in charge retains proper control over his business even when he is not present or transfers such responsibility to someone capable of understanding and obeying the law.
- It can be argued that it is not too onerous to impose liability in this way, as the offences are only those of a quasi-criminal status.

Five points against
- The most important point is that it is unjust to penalise a party for the wrong of another, particularly in cases where he cannot possibly know of the wrongdoing. It goes against the principle that criminal liability only be imposed on the person committing the offence. A criminal conviction is still seen as a serious matter, despite the fact that the offence is only a regulatory one. It might

well have serious implications for future business activities.

- It is felt to be even more unjust when the offence requires *mens rea* and the *mens rea* of another person is imputed to the person vicariously liable, as can happen under the delegation principle.
- A person or company can still be liable even where steps have been taken to ensure that the offence is not committed, as in **Coppen v Moore (No 2) 1898, the Duke of Leinster 1924** and **Allen v Whitehead 1930**.
- It has not been conclusively shown that the principle does have the effect of raising standards. As noted above, in many cases the person charged has tried to ensure that the law is obeyed. In other cases, he may be completely unaware of the infringement.
- The principles of vicarious liability in criminal law have not been laid down by Parliament, instead they are judge-made and, as can be seen under the delegation principle, often move completely away from the intention of Parliament. This can be seen when a person is found vicariously liable, but knows nothing about the infringement and the statute contains the word 'knowingly'.

14.2.4 Possible reform of vicarious liability

The *Draft Criminal Code* of 1989 would, if enacted, reform this area of law. It would drastically restrict the scope of vicarious liability. Probably the most important change would be to abolish the situations where the *mens rea* of the actual offender is also attributed to the employer or other person, so the delegation principle would no longer apply. Under Clause 29, such a person would only be liable if this is specified in the offence. In addition, an employer would only be liable in cases where the wrongdoer was acting within the scope of his employment, or as an independent contractor.

Activity

- Discuss whether the principle of vicarious liability in criminal law has any part to play in a modern and just society.
- Russell owns a very successful restaurant called *The Tenors*. He has put Luciano in charge of the establishment while he concentrates on his singing and just visits on a Sunday to check the books and count the profits! He is outraged to find that he has been charged with contravening the terms of his drinking licence. He has discovered that Luciano has been serving drinks without meals to the impoverished students, studying at the Figaro School of Music, close to the restaurant.

Advise Russell. How would your answer to the second question differ if Russell maintained control of the ground floor restaurant and left Luciano to deal with the first floor patrons?

14.3 Corporate liability

This subject is connected to the above, in that a corporation may sometimes be found vicariously liable for the acts of its employees. In addition, a corporation may well be liable in its own right under one of the ways mentioned below. In such a situation, the company itself will be charged as the principal offender, rather than being charged along with another offender, as in the case of vicarious liability.

A corporation therefore is a legal body, an artificially created organisation with directors managing the business and, in theory at least, the shareholders controlling it. The most common example of a corporation is the private or public limited company, a type of organisation which became widely recognised in the middle of the nineteenth century.

In the distant past, a corporation could not be found criminally liable because a personal appearance was needed in court. That problem was solved by using a complicated procedure which enabled an attorney to appear on the corporation's behalf in the Court of King's Bench but such a tortuous route became unnecessary with the passing of the **Criminal Justice Act 1925**. A corporation may now appear in court through a representative and we need to examine the circumstances under which it will become liable. It is convenient to discuss this under three headings.

When the principle of vicarious liability is invoked

A company may be held vicariously liable in the same way as a natural person, and the same principles, discussed above, will apply to that body. In the cases of **Mousell Ltd v London and North Western Railway Co 1917** and **National Rivers Authority v Alfred McAlpine Homes (East) Ltd 1994**, mentioned earlier, the respective companies were found guilty of an offence through the acts of their employees and were charged alongside them. In the first case, the company was liable for evading freight charges, in the second situation for being involved in the pollution of a river.

Where the statute expressly makes a corporation liable

Some statutes will expressly make a corporation liable and often such liability will be absolute. In such cases there will be no problems with having to prove that the company possessed mens rea, as necessary in the cases mentioned below. It should also be noted that the word 'corporation' or 'company' does not have to be expressly stated. **The Interpretation Act 1978** states that the word 'person' includes a body of persons corporate or unincorporate (the latter phrase includes clubs, societies and partnerships), unless otherwise stated.

There are obviously some offences that a company cannot commit as, for example, the crime of murder. The general rule is that a company cannot be convicted of a crime for which it cannot be sentenced, so it can only be convicted of offences where a fine can be imposed. With murder, the only sentence is one of life imprisonment. Over the years, the courts have also added the crimes of incest, perjury and rape. In an important ruling, however, in **P&O European Ferries (Dover) Ltd 1991**, it was decided that a company could be held liable for manslaughter. The defendants had tried to argue that an old definition existed, identified by Coke in the seventeenth century and applied in the USA and New Zealand, stating that a killing had to be 'of a human being by a human being'. Therefore, it was argued, a company could not be liable. Turner J disagreed, but made it clear that liability will not be easy to establish. He stated:

> A company may be vicariously liable for the negligent acts or omissions of its servants and agents, but for a company to be criminally liable for manslaughter – on the assumption I am making that such a crime exists – it is required that the mens rea and actus reus of manslaughter should be established not only against those who acted for or in the name of the company but against those who were identified as the embodiment of the company itself.

Where the doctrine of identification is used

Where an offence requires mens rea, therefore, there has to be some way of finding this within a company structure because an inanimate body obviously has no mind. The courts have addressed this problem by developing the doctrine of identification. This is done by looking for the personnel in the company who are said to be 'the directing mind and will' of the organisation. The phrase was first used back in 1915 in **Lennard's Carrying Co Ltd v Asiatic Petroleum**.

The identification principle was taken further in three cases in 1944. **In DPP v Kent and Sussex Contractors Ltd 1944**, it was held that the intention and belief of a responsible agent of the company could be imputed to the company itself. This case was quoted with approval in **ICR Haulage 1944** where, again, the company tried to argue that, not being a natural person it could not have a mind, honest or otherwise so could not be indicted, in this instance with conspiracy to defraud. The Court of Appeal decided that knowledge and intention of the agent involved in the conspiracy could be imputed to the company. In **Moore v Bresler 1944**, matters were taken even further and the company involved was found guilty of making false tax returns, via the company secretary and a branch sales manager even though this action on their part was designed to defraud the company itself. This decision has been criticised and the provisions of the *Draft Code*, if ever enacted, would not make a company liable in cases where the acts of the controlling officers, as they are known in the Code, were done with the intention of causing harm to the company.

In **Robert Millar (Contractors) Ltd and Millar 1970**, the courts went further still and found the managing director of a company liable for counselling and procuring causing death by dangerous driving. He had allowed a heavy lorry and trailer to be taken out on the road, laden with 18 tons of bricks, knowing that the front offside tyre was badly worn. The tyre burst, the driver lost control and the lorry crashed into a car travelling the other way, killing all the occupants, a family of six. The driver, who had also known of the dangerous state of the vehicle and had complained about it many times, was found guilty of dangerous driving but treated leniently by the judge, with a modest fine and a disqualification. The company, however, was fined £750 and the managing director was sent to prison for nine months. The appeal was dismissed.

The brains and hands of a company

In **H L Bolton (Engineering) Co Ltd v T J Graham and Sons Ltd 1957**, Lord Denning delivered his interpretation of the doctrine of identification in his own inimitable style. He likened a company to a human body and went on to say:

> It has a brain and nerve centre which controls what it does. It also has hands which hold the tools and act in accordance with directions from the centre. Some of the people in the company are mere servants and agents who are nothing more than hands to do the work and cannot be said to represent the mind or will. Others are directors and managers who represent the directing mind and will of the company and control what it does. The state of mind of these managers is the state of mind of the company and is treated by the law as such.

This statement was quoted with approval by the House of Lords in **Tesco Ltd v Nattrass 1972**, the leading case on the doctrine of identification. The facts were very simple. A pensioner tried to buy a packet of washing powder at a price that had appeared in advertisements and in Tesco's shop window but was told that the only packets left were at the normal price. A sales assistant put out the full price packets, after discovering the special offer packets had all been sold, but failed to inform the manager that more should be ordered.

The pensioner complained and the company was convicted under the **Trade Descriptions Act 1968**. Tesco relied on a defence in the Act. This states that liability will not arise if the person charged can prove that he has taken all reasonable precautions and exercised all due diligence to avoid the commission of the offence and show that the offence was committed by 'another person'. The branch manager was duly named as that person but the magistrates took the view that he was part of the company and convicted Tesco. The House of Lords disagreed. Their Lordships decided that the branch manager was too far down in the scale of command to be part of the 'directing mind or will' of the company. To be in such a position, Lord Reid felt that the company member needed to be part of the board of directors, the managing director or perhaps be one of the other superior officers. Viscount Dilhorne included a person in actual control of the operations of a company and who is not answerable to anyone else.

In **Boal 1992**, an assistant general manager at a large bookstore was not held to be in such a position, therefore no liability was incurred under the **Fire Precautions Act 1971** for the company's breaches of its fire certificate. In **Seaboard Offshore v Secretary of State for Transport 1994**, the owner of a ship had his conviction overturned. One of his ships had put to sea within three hours of a new chief engineer joining it. This employee had been given no time to study the workings of the ship and as a result, had succeeded in flooding the engines.

The magistrates originally found the company liable but the House of Lords quashed the conviction. This court decided that, while the **Merchant Shipping Act 1988** did impose a duty to ensure that the ship operated in a safe manner, the owner could discharge this and not fall foul of the criminal law, by showing that he had taken reasonable steps to comply with the provisions.

These decisions show that it is not easy to gain a conviction under the identification principle but there has been some small movement on this issue. In **Redfern 1993**, the Court of Appeal stressed that the important point to establish was whether the person committing the offence had true powers of management. In two civil cases in 1995, **Meridian Global Funds Management Asia Ltd**, and **Re Supply of Ready Mixed Concrete Co**, the Privy Council and the House of Lords respectively

were prepared to widen the principle to enable it to cover personnel other than directors. For example, a financial investment manager was held liable.

Manslaughter cases

In more serious criminal cases, the identification principle still causes many difficulties. This was highlighted after the sinking of *The Herald of Free Enterprise*, a roll-on, roll-off ferry, just outside Zeebrugge harbour in March 1987. The ferry had left the port with its bow doors left open and the ship capsized, causing the death of nearly 200 passengers. It was the job of the assistant bosun to ensure that the doors were shut but he was asleep at the time. The captain was responsible for the ship setting sail safely but had no way of confirming whether or not the doors were shut. These two employees were charged with manslaughter along with directors of the company and the company itself but the case against all seven parties collapsed. While it was established that there was a high degree of mismanagement within the company, the prosecution needed to prove more than this. The test at that time was for reckless manslaughter and the judge came to the conclusion that it could not be established there was an obvious and serious risk of death or serious harm occurring by operating the ship in this manner. The system in use was said to have operated for over 60,000 crossings without previous trouble and was also adopted by other ferry operators. Neither had any outside bodies, such as the insurers and the Department of Trade, imposed higher standards. With regard to the operation of the company itself, the Sheen Report in 1987 came to the conclusion that the company was 'infected with the disease of sloppiness'. Because of the state of the law at that time however, several separate errors could not be combined, under what was called the 'aggregation principle' to make the company liable for reckless manslaughter. The case collapsed. The only positive point to come from the whole sorry mess was the affirmation by Turner J that it was possible, as a matter of principle, for a manslaughter charge to be brought against a company in its own right.

We noted in Chapter 5 that such action has taken place in the case of smaller companies. It was comparatively easy in the cases mentioned there, to establish liability under the existing identification doctrine. For example, in **Kite and OLL Ltd 1996**, both the company itself and the managing director of the outdoors activity centre in question were found to be liable for gross negligence manslaughter. The company was fined and Kite was jailed for four years, although this sentence was cut in half on appeal.

The identification principle and larger companies

With regard to larger companies, there has been a conspicuous lack of success. No manslaughter charge was sustained after the Kings Cross fire, the P&O ferry case, as noted above, the Clapham rail crash or the Southall train disaster in West London. In the latter case, there was some consolation in the fact that the company, Great Western Trains, was found liable for breaches of the **Health & Safety at Work etc Act 1974** and was fined the exceptionally large sum of £1,500,000. The collapse of the manslaughter case also led to an **Attorney-General's Reference (No 2 of 1999) (2000)** under which we noted earlier, the Court of Appeal decided that a company could be convicted of gross negligence manslaughter in the absence of evidence as to the defendant's state of mind. Unfortunately, the same reference also established that a company could not be convicted of gross negligence manslaughter if there was no evidence establishing the guilt of an identified human being.

Comment

The identification principle is therefore the only way to establish liability for gross negligence manslaughter against a company at the present time. In the reference, mentioned above, the Court of Appeal rejected the opportunity to introduce the 'aggregation principle', allowing several individual failures to be added together to illustrate the grossly negligent behaviour. This was rejected in the **P&O** case but at that time subjective recklessness had to be proved. Now the standard is one of gross negligence and the standard is an objective one so a case for change could be made out. Professor Sir John Smith was strongly critical of the court's failure to accept this.

Many other commentators have argued that a change in the law is urgently required. The Law Commission recognised this concern several years ago and put forward workable proposals for reform in 1996. Until the adverse criticisms made after the latest rail disasters, these were gathering dust. In 2000, the Home Office decided to produce its own proposals for reform, which are noted below. There is still criticism that the Government of the day is dragging its heels on these, as the following article illustrates.

14.3.1 Possible reform of corporate liability

The Law Commission specifically addressed this issue after heeding the depth of feeling on the subject and recognising that some sort of reform was essential. In *Law Com. No. 237, part VIII*, this body recommended the creation of a new offence of corporate killing. This would arise where a management failure of the company was the cause, or one of the causes of the person's death and the failure constitutes conduct falling far below what can

A law long overdue

Companies should face charges of 'corporate killings', says **Gary Slapper**

GLANVILLE EVANS was killed when the bridge he was working on collapsed and he fell into the River Wye. The company that employed him had clearly been reckless but an attempt to convict it for manslaughter failed. That was in February 1965.

Since then more than 31,000 people have been killed at work or through commercially related disasters like train crashes. Safety reports have shown that management failures are responsible in most cases but the number of prosecutions for manslaughter since the death of Evans has been 12 and the number of companies convicted has been three. Each year, however, the law has no difficulty in convicting more than 200 ordinary people for killing through carelessness while engaged in antics of various sorts.

Last week the police, the TUC and the Director of Public Prosecutions all called for a new law on corporate manslaughter. The families of four men killed in horrifying circumstances while repairing Avonmouth Bridge released a statement after the company had been convicted of regulatory safety offences and fined. They said: "Considering the gross and appalling failures of the companies and the assets of the companies, we do not feel this fine will have the deterrent effect necessary to force companies to ensure that safety is paramount above profit and to ensure that such an accident could not happen again." In the same week Euromin Ltd, the company responsible for the death of Simon

Jones, decapitated on his first day at work in Shoreham Docks, was also convicted of serious safety law violations but not one that has "killing" as a part of the offence.

There are now more than one million companies in England and Wales and their activities permeate every pore of social life. It is a reasonable expectation that the considerable body of people and rules used to protect customers, investors and rival businesses from financial irregularity will be matched by laws to protect life and limb. For the early part of its history, the company lay outside the criminal law. "It had no soul to damn, and no body to kick," observed Lord Thurlow, the 18th-century Lord Chancellor. Certainly, the practice of excommunicating corporations had been pronounced contrary to canon law by Pope Innocent IV at the Council of Lyons in 1245.

The main difficulty in using the current law of manslaughter to proceed against corporate bodies is that the rules were evolved in relation to individuals. This means that they are concerned with things like evaluating the state of mind of the defendant, and companies do not have easily identifiable "minds". For a while in the Middle Ages, certain clerics could escape liability for serious crimes by pleading "benefit of clergy". They were effectively outside the normal law. Today we see that as unjustifiable and rather bizarre, and it is likely that today's legally privileged status afforded to companies will, in future, be regarded in the same way.

Under current law, the courts must look at the conduct of senior company officers who are taken to personify the company. These are what Lord Denning once referred to in a renowned anthropomorphic metaphor as people who act as the "brain and nerve centre" of the company. There must, however, be at least one fully culpable officer; a company will be acquitted if, through a diffuse management or chaos, various directors each knew only part of the full picture.

In its report *Legislating the Criminal Code: Involuntary Manslaughter* (1996), the Law Commission recommended a new offence of "corporate killing". It said it saw no reason for companies effectively to remain exempt from the law of manslaughter and recommended that there should be a specific offence of "corporate killing" broadly comparable to "killing by gross negligence" on the part of an individual. A company would become liable for prosecution if a "management failure" by the corporation resulted in death, and the failure constituted conduct falling "far below what can reasonably be expected of the corporation in the circumstances". The corporation would be judged simply by the results of its collective efforts.

Innovation is often an agonisingly gradual process in law. The Law Commission's 1996 report was ignored, causing Mr Justice Scott Baker, the trial judge in the manslaughter prosecution of Great Western Trains in 1999, following the Paddington crash, to ask why the report had been permitted "to lie for years on a shelf gathering dust". New legislation on corporate killing has been intermittently promised as due "in the near future" for more than ten years. The Government produced a draft law in May last year but a Bill again failed to appear in this year's Queen's Speech.

The 1965 death of Glanville Evans and those of the Avonmouth workers in 1999 are bridged by a long curve of law that conspicuously failed to protect many of the 30,000 victims of commercial incidents who died in that span. A much better legal bridge to the future has been designed. It remains to be seen whether there is the political will to build it.

The Times, 11 December 2001

reasonably be expected of the corporation in the circumstances.

As stated, at first no one seemed to be in any hurry to implement these proposals. It took several years and two further rail disasters before there was any action. This came in 2000, when the Home Office published a consultation paper *'Reforming the Law on Involuntary Manslaughter: The Government's Proposals'*. Rather surprisingly, these go further than was suggested by the Law Commission. As that body suggested, a new offence of corporate killing is recommended but the Home Office has recommended that liability should also extend to non-corporate businesses, such as partnerships and sole traders.

The new offence of corporate killing

The Home Office proposals adopt the terminology of the Law Commission for the actual offence. A corporation would therefore be guilty of corporate killing if:

a) a management failure by the corporation is the cause or one of the causes of the person's death; and
b) that failure constitutes conduct falling far below what can reasonably be expected of the corporation in the circumstances.

Such failure on the part of a company would arise:

a) ' . . . if the way in which its activities are managed or organised fails to ensure the health and safety of persons employed in or affected by those activities: and

TEN KEY FACTS ON VICARIOUS AND CORPORATE LIABILITY

- A person or company may be liable under the principle of vicarious liability for the criminal acts of another, although liability is more restricted than in civil law. It will arise in three main ways: where a statute states this (**Mousell Ltd v London and North West Railway 1917**), where the acts of an agent can be imputed to the other (**Coppen v Moore (No 2) 1898, Duke of Leinster 1924** and **National Rivers Authority v Alfred McAlpine Homes (East) 1994**), and where the delegation principle applies (**Allen v Whitehead 1930, Linnett v MPC 1946, Vane v Yiannopoullos 1965, Winson 1969**).

- The second head is confined to offences of strict liability but, under the third head, the *mens rea* of the party committing the offence can be imputed to the person delegating the authority.

- The delegation principle only applies where the whole of the authority has been delegated (**Vane v Yiannopoullos 1964**). **Howker v Robinson 1973**, a Divisional Court decision, is felt to be wrong on this point; it certainly conflicts with the House of Lords' decision in **Vane**.

- The principle of vicarious liability can apply to a company in the same way as to an individual (**Mousell Ltd v London and North West Railway Co 1917, National Rivers Authority v Alfred McAlpine Homes (East) 1994**).

- A company may also be liable on its own account in two ways: first, where a statute expressly states this and secondly where the doctrine of identification is used.

- This applies if those with the 'directing mind and will' of the company have committed the offence (**Lennards Carrying Co v Asiatic Petroleum 1915, DPP v Kent and Sussex Contractors 1944, ICR Haulage 1944, Moore v Bresler 1944, H L Bolton v T J Graham 1957, Robert Millar (Contractors) and Millar 1970**). This can still apply even where the offence committed by a person with a directing mind is defrauding the company (**Moore v Bresler 1944**).

- Lord Denning talked of those at the brain and nerve centre, for whose actions the company would be liable and the mere 'hands' of the business, where the company was not liable under this doctrine (**H L Bolton v T J Graham 1957**). The Court of Appeal found the company liable where the employee had 'true powers of management' (**Redfern 1993**), but the employees were not held to be part of the 'directing mind and will' in **Tesco v Nattrass 1972**, or **Boal 1992**.

- In a dangerous driving case, the company may be liable for counselling and procuring (**Robert Millar (Contractors) and Millar 1970**).

- A company may be liable for most offences, except murder, bigamy, rape and incest. It can be liable for manslaughter (**P&O European Ferries 1991, OLL 1994**), but convictions are rare. They have only occurred where the company is a small one and it is easy to identify the 'directing mind' (**OLL 1994**).

- The courts are not prepared to use the 'aggregation principle' to impose liability on a company even though the test has changed from recklessness and several errors could amount to gross negligence (**P&O European Ferries 1990, Great Western Trains**).

b) such a failure may be regarded as a cause of a person's death notwithstanding that the immediate cause is the act or omission of an individual'.

It will be noted that the offence is carefully worded to try to ensure that the company cannot simply pass the liability on to another. The new offence will run parallel to the existing offence of gross negligence manslaughter and would also co-exist with the proposed new offence of manslaughter by reckless killing, should this change be effected by Parliament. Unlike these two offences, however, it is not necessary to find that the conduct of one particular individual has caused the death. Liability can be imposed where the standards as a whole fall far below that what is expected. The offence would be an indictable one and the sanctions would be an unlimited fine and/or a remedial order.

Other changes recommended by the Home Office

An important one is the proposal to extend liability from corporations alone to other undertakings. The Government wished to include schools, hospital trusts, charities which are not incorporated, partnerships and sole traders, i.e. 'any trade or business or other activity providing employment'.

Another radical change is the inclusion of secondary liability, which could affect individuals associated with the undertaking in question. The Law Commission was against this measure.

The consultation paper also canvasses views as to whether Government should create a separate offence for individuals who 'substantially contribute' to the corporate killing and asks whether this should carry a term of imprisonment.

Comment

In his well-reasoned article *Corporate Killing – Some Government Proposals, Criminal Law Review* 2001, page 31, Bob Sullivan, Professor of Law at Durham University, states that 'the Government has grasped a major truth. Deterrent incentives to promote greater safety will have the most immediate and direct impact if they are targeted at individual managers who have or should have assumed responsibility for safety matters'. He goes on however, to express concern over both the proposals mentioned above, arguing that the first measure could be unfair on small businesses with unlimited liability. A partner, for example, could find his personal assets at risk if there was a big fine to pay. It could lead to the partnership breaking up and jobs being lost. He also feels that the proposal to permit secondary liability to be imposed on individuals for corporate liability 'is misconceived' and 'would constitute a significant extension of the law of homicide'.

Activity

- It has been argued that the rules relating to the liability of corporations are weighted too much in favour of the company, at the expense of the victims of their negligence. Critically evaluate whether the suggested new offence of corporate killing will redress this imbalance.

- Executive Coaches Ltd is a large organisation running a fleet of luxury coaches nationwide for businessmen who dislike flying or are concerned about the reliability of the train service. Competition is fierce and the directors have recently suggested several cost-cutting measures, including making the drivers work longer hours, faster turn-round times and longer intervals between servicing the vehicles. Will, the manager of the Westchester branch has expressed his disquiet at these measures but was told he should stop complaining and get on with the job or he could find himself without one.

  Grace, one of his drivers, was on her second shift of the day. One of the front tyres on her coach burst and because of her tiredness Grace may not have acted promptly enough to evade serious harm. The coach overturned and 30 passengers were killed. Advise the directors of Executive Travel, Will and Grace who have all been charged with manslaughter.

Self-Assessment Questions

(If the subject of vicarious liability is not part of your course, attempt the last five questions only).

1. Explain what is meant by the term 'vicarious liability' and distinguish this from the doctrine of strict liability.
2. Why was the conviction quashed in the early case of **Huggins**?
3. With cases to illustrate your answer, describe the three ways in which vicarious liability can be imposed.
4. Why has the delegation principle caused problems and what is the position today?
5. Give four arguments in favour of retaining vicarious liability and four against this.
6. Explain why it was impossible, in the past to find a company criminally liable. How was this resolved?
7. Describe the three ways in which a company can be held vicariously liable in criminal cases.
8. Describe Lord Denning's interpretation of the identification doctrine, as quoted in **H L Bolton Ltd** and applying this, explain why the company was not liable in **Tesco v Nattrass**.
9. Explain why the prosecution succeeded in **OLL** but the cases against **P&O** and **Great Western Trains** collapsed.
10. How have the findings in the **Attorney-General's Reference (No 2 of 1999)(2000)** affected this position? Explain why, if reforms were to be enacted, it would be easier to find a company criminally liable for the proposed new offence of corporate killing.

Chapter 15

BRINGING IT ALL TOGETHER

15.1 Introduction

Well, you've made it! Hopefully, you now have a good knowledge of the key topics. Before attempting to revise, set down which of these are required for your particular board. Changes have been effected recently so be careful! Know exactly which substantive offences you need to study, and which of the general defences are included in your course. The same applies to inchoate offences; some boards only ask for knowledge of attempt, not conspiracy or incitement. Note however, that a topic might come up in a more general way as, for example, **aggravated** criminal damage, which though not required now for OCR (basic criminal damage is still needed), is still important when looking at **Caldwell** recklessness.

Remember that the chapters are set out in a distinctive way to help you in your studies. Apart from the law on general defences, all the law on a particular topic will be found in one chapter.

In addition remember that:

- **The Key Facts charts summarise the current state of the law**
  You need this knowledge to deal with both problems and essays in the Activities' sections and the examination.

- **The comment sections discuss some of the problems arising from the state of the law**
  This information is not needed for problem questions but is necessary to help you obtain a wider view of the state of the law for use in discussion and with the essay questions in the exam.

- **The proposals for reform are indicated separately in the text**
  These are not needed for problem questions but are very important for discussion and essay work, as they indicate the changes that might be made in the future.

From the information gathered from the text and from these sources, you are then ready to undertake:

- **The Self-Assessment questions at the end of each chapter**
  These ensure that you go through the text and extract the relevant information. After this you should have a good understanding of the legal principles in that area.

- **The activities appearing regularly through each chapter**
  These contain a mix of discussion topics, essays and problems. They have been carefully selected to ensure that you develop a wide knowledge of the topic, the ability to analyse and evaluate the legal principles and the expertise to apply these principles to relevant factual situations.

15.2 Highlights of Chapters 1 to 14

The following are my suggestions on the important points; remember that those setting the papers for the various boards may well have different ideas so heed the advice of your tutors on this.

Chapter 1

Chapter 1 should be carefully read. It contains important information on the layout of the book, the appeal courts and a reminder of the importance of precedent in English law.

It is very important to understand the workings of the appeal system when studying criminal law. Many of the cases concern 'grey' areas that these courts have helped to solve. The Divisional Court hears appeals from the magistrates' court or the Crown Court where there has already been an appeal there from the lower court. If there is an important question of law, there may be a further appeal from the Divisional Court straight to the House of Lords. The vast majority of appeals concerning indictable offences and triable either way offences where the case is dealt with in the Crown Court, are dealt with by the Court of Appeal. Remember that, on the criminal side of the law, the House of Lords will only deal with points of law of general public importance. The normal stopping place is the Court of Appeal.

Remember the importance of the doctrine of precedent. If a precedent is laid down by a sufficiently high court, that decision will be binding on the lower court unless it can be distinguished. The Court of Appeal is often bound by decisions of the House of Lords, which it might, on occasion, prefer not to follow. It can choose not to follow the Privy Council, as can be seen under provocation and, in a more limited way, it may also choose not to follow its own earlier rulings, as noted under actual bodily harm.

Chapter 2

There are several important areas in this chapter. When looking at the *actus reus* of a crime, you should note the 'state of affairs' cases, like **Larsonneur**, and, particularly, the area on omissions. When studying *mens rea*, remember that the question of intention is to be decided by the jury and that **Moloney** has established that in most cases no extra help on the meaning of intention will be given. What has caused problems is where the defendant is

claiming that it was not his intention to kill, i.e. where only an oblique intent exists. In **Woollin 1998**, the House of Lords approved of the direction in **Nedrick** which confirmed that the members of the jury decide on the question of intention but also have their discretion limited in cases of murder. Here, 'they are not entitled to find the necessary intention unless they feel sure that death or serious bodily harm was a virtual certainty (barring some unforeseen intervention) as a result of the defendant's actions and that the defendant appreciated that this was the case'. There is likely to be a question on this, probably in essay form, requiring you to bring in some of the problems arising from this decision, as discussed in the Comments section.

Remember that two types of recklessness exist in English law, **Cunningham** and **Caldwell** recklessness and remember that the first type is needed for all assault cases. The latter is now reserved for criminal damage alone. Know how this came about. Be able to discuss the strictness of **Caldwell** in cases like **Elliott** and also know that the House of Lords is only prepared to recognise a lacuna, or loophole, in very limited circumstances. This will probably come up as an essay question or be combined with a problem on assault of some sort or with a problem on criminal damage. Questions on negligence will normally be confined to gross negligence manslaughter, as described in Chapter 5. Questions on strict liability often take the form of an essay but remember to answer the question set and not give a mere list of advantages and disadvantages.

Note the very important case of **B (a minor) v DPP 2000**, where the House of Lords extended the principle in **Sweet v Parsley** and firmly decided that *mens rea* is an essential ingredient of an offence, even in age-related offences unless Parliament has expressly or by implication indicated otherwise. There could well be a question concerning this so, in the words of the news-sellers 'read all about it'! If there was a problem on this, it could be combined with the defence of an honest but not necessarily reasonable belief.

Chapter 3

In Chapter 3 it is vital to learn the definition of murder, so that you can identify when it is not established and manslaughter can be pleaded. The subject of causation, often in the form of a problem is a popular area. One of the most important points to remember is that it will take a very special event to break the chain of causation. Know the cases on this, particularly **Blaue, Malcherek, Dear, Jordan, Smith, Cheshire and Mellor.**

With regard to murder, know that it is a common law offence, there is no statutory definition. Know also that the year and a day rule has been abolished and note the difficulties of establishing birth and death. Note also the importance of the **AG's Reference (No 3 of 1994) 1996**. It may be manslaughter or perhaps even murder when a foetus is injured, the baby is then born alive and then dies.

Be aware that in **Re A (children) 2000**, the Court of Appeal recognised an extension of the situations where a homicide may be lawful, i.e. where the killing is necessary to save the life of another. Note the interaction of several areas here. Under **Woollin**, the death would have been unlawful unless a defence could be found and two of these were suggested, utilitarian necessity and private defence. Study these points by linking the information found in Chapter 2 (intention after **Woollin**), Chapter 3 (lawful homicide) and Chapter 11 (the defences of necessity and private defence). Note that the House of Lords decided in November 2001, in the case of **Pretty**, that an assisted suicide remains unlawful.

Chapter 4

This deals with voluntary manslaughter and is a fertile ground for both problems and essays. Know that the law is mainly in the **Homicide Act 1957**. The limited defence of diminished responsibility, reducing murder to manslaughter, could be linked to the general defence of insanity, which is available for all crimes but has a stigma attached. Know the definitions of both diminished responsibility and insanity and the criticisms of both defences. Note that in **Martin 2001**, the Court of Appeal accepted the defence of diminished responsibility, after a self-defence plea failed. The court accepted fresh evidence showing that the defendant had a paranoid personality disorder.

Know the three elements of provocation and be able to apply them in a clear way to a problem situation. Be aware that the concept of the reasonable man continues to give trouble and note the latest cases on this, particularly **Smith 1998**, where the House of Lords decided that the Court of Appeal was right to extend the characteristics that may be attributed to this mythical figure, and the Privy Council was wrong for trying to curtail them. **Camplin** is still the main authority but has now been extended by **Smith**.

Chapter 5

As mentioned earlier, gross negligence is back, so study this carefully. Know when this will be found, quoting cases like **Adomako, Edwards, Kite** and **Woodburn** but be aware of the difficulties in establishing this offence against large companies. Link with the information in Chapter 14 on corporate liability, particularly in relation to corporate killings and the need, at present to use the identification principle with all its attendant difficulties. It is a relevant topic so it could well come up. In an essay, discuss the reforms suggested by the Home Office and its adoption of a possible new offence called corporate killing, where an individual does not have to be identified.

In a problem question look out also for a death that was not intended but arises from an unlawful and dangerous act. This could be a case of constructive manslaughter so note the three elements that need to be established. Be aware of the Law Commission's wish to abolish this offence and create instead new offences of reckless killing, and killing by gross carelessness. This, too, could be a good area for an essay or it could make a good problem with having to establish an unlawful and dangerous act.

Chapter 6

Chapter 6 is a very large chapter containing all the non-fatal offences against the person. You need to know the *actus reus* and *mens rea* of each one, from assault and battery up to grievous bodily harm with intent. Be aware that the harm can be indirectly inflicted. Note that abh can be established with the *mens rea* of a common assault and that the *mens rea* for a **s20** offence is merely 'some harm' but for liability under **s18**, there must be an intention to cause gbh. Be able to pinpoint the other differences between **s18** and **s20**. Note the restrictions on the defence of consent, after the decisions of the House of Lords and the European Court in **Brown**, but note **Wilson**, which has opened matters up again! Note that the courts have been prepared to accept that words can amount to an assault, as can psychiatric harm (**Constanza, Ireland**), but note that the **Protection of Harassment Act** now provides a more direct way of obtaining help against stalkers.

Chapter 7

There is nearly always a question on theft in the exam. It is important to understand the *actus reus* and *mens rea* and be able to apply **ss2–6** to problem situations. There are several problems for you to tackle in this chapter, which should help with this. Know the specific defences laid down in the Act. Appropriation of property is still a favourite area so know the case of **Gomez** and the cases after this, particularly **Hinks 2000**. You should also be able to decide when someone is or is not dishonest under the Act. Look at **s1** and **s2** and the case of **Ghosh**.

Know that the definition of theft must first be satisfied for robbery and burglary and then add the additional elements. The latter may come up in a problem situation but the largest part of your time should be explaining the elements of theft. Blackmail again, is likely to be included in a problem, rather than having its own treatment.

Chapter 8

Chapter 8 examines making off without payment and the deception offences. Be very clear as to which of these you need to study. It should be remembered that, after **Gomez**, anyone satisfying the definition of **s15** would also be guilty of theft. Know the differences between the elements for theft and deception. The two often come up together. You need to memorise the *actus reus* and *mens rea* of the other deception offences and **s3 Theft Act 1978**. If you know the elements of each offence, with cases in support, you will do really well in this area.

Chapter 9

This gives detail on basic criminal damage and the aggravated offences under **s1(2)** and **s1(3)**. Know what is meant by the terms damage and destruction and be aware of the defence of lawful excuse under **s5**. Note the difference between the basic and aggravated offences. Under **s1(2)**, the property need not belong to another but know that the life must be endangered by the damaging or destroying of property. Note that the defence of lawful excuse does not apply to the more serious offences. Remember that **Caldwell** concerned criminal damage in both the basic and aggravated forms, and **Shimmen** relates to the basic offence. Be able to discuss both the damage and the *mens rea* needed for the offences. Remember that damage by the use of fire is arson under **s1(3)**.

Chapter 10

Chapter 10 concerns the first four of the ten general defences. Note that the presumption that no liability exists for 10–14-year-olds has been removed by Parliament. We looked at the defence of insanity earlier but note the case of **Antoine 2000**, which decided that diminished responsibility cannot be brought up when the defendant has been found unfit to plead through insanity.

Know the three elements of the defence with cases to support and the criticisms of the M'Naghten Rules. The defence could also be combined with automatism, which is a complete defence; note the cases on hypoglycaemia (remember 'o' for outside source) and compare with hyperglycaemia, which could be insanity. Examiners also like intoxication! Remember that the rules differ for basic intent crimes, for which intoxication is no defence, and specific intent crimes, where it may be, although it will usually only reduce the crime, apart from cases of theft. Note the important ruling in **Kingston**, however, that a drunken intent is still an intent. Watch out for involuntary intoxication.

Chapter 11

This concerns the other general defences. The defence of mistake may not come up alone but could be combined with others like intoxication or self-defence or with strict liability (**B (a minor) v DPP**), theft or criminal damage. The defences of necessity, duress of circumstances which is an extension of this, and duress of threats should all be learned together and the elements of each known well. This area could come up in the exam because of the extension of necessity after **Re A (children)** and duress of circumstances after **Abdul-Hussain**. Know that the restrictions on the defences of duress of circumstances and duress of threats are the same, so the defendant must be a sober man of reasonable firmness. The courts are still deciding which of the characteristics of the defendant can be attributed to him. Neither defence, nor the defence of necessity can be used for murder, either as a principal or as an accomplice, nor can it be used for attempted

murder. Self-defence and the prevention of crime are also popular areas and may well be the subject of a problem question, in which too much force is used and a death results. At present, this is still murder unless a partial defence can be put forward, as in **Martin 2001**.

Chapter 12

Chapter 12 concerns parties to a crime and you need to learn the differences between principal and secondary offenders and aiders, abettors, counsellors and procurers. This may well come up as a problem question. Be able to distinguish between this type of secondary liability and those who only conspire or incite. You also need to know how the *mens rea* for participation is established. Note that the law is hard on those who embark on a joint enterprise. They will be liable along with the other unless the latter does something completely unexpected or they make a truly effective withdrawal. Know the latest cases on this fertile area.

Chapter 13

Chapter 13 describes the different types of inchoate offences, attempt, conspiracy and incitement. You need to be able to identify each type of offence and know the *mens rea* required. It could come up as a problem question, along with a substantive offence, or you might be asked to compare them or be asked whether common law conspiracy should remain. Remember that you can be found guilty of incitement, attempt and statutory conspiracy, even though the main crime is impossible.

Chapter 14

Chapter 14 concerns the area of vicarious and corporate liability and the latter could be a popular area with the promise of reforms in this area. The first part of the chapter nearly always arises as an essay question and is easy to learn, but it is likely that corporate liability will be combined with manslaughter by gross negligence.

15.3 A revision plan

You are probably inundated with advice on revision so this is only intended as a brief guide. Your lecturers will give you valuable help with this. The most important point is try to enjoy your revision and you can do this if you don't leave it all until the last minute. Most successful revision entails careful planning to avoid last minute panics and attendant loss of confidence.

I have known a few students who have managed to learn the whole of the course in just three or four weeks but one of these students was a policeman! Such a course is not to be recommended if you wish to keep your health, looks and sanity!

If you are answering the problem questions as you learn each area and discussing the other topics, you will be pleasantly surprised when you start your formal revision to discover just how much you know already. I would suggest that, before you begin your concentrated revision, you should re-read as much of your work as possible, not with the object of learning it all but just to get the whole picture. It is important to start with a general view of the subject before zooming in on particular topics. At this stage, it is advisable to write down all the areas you need to learn, to know from the start the revision route that you are going to take. You can then condense down and down and, by examination day, just have cards of the main points, to trigger your memory. It is important, when dividing up your work, not to set yourself impossible tasks:

- Take a small area at a time, read the information, take notes and ask yourself what you have learned.
- Have periodic breaks and give yourselves treats. The diet can be reactivated after the exam!
- Work with friends. One excellent way to revise is to teach the subject to another.

Your positions can then be reversed and you can take notes as your friend explains the matter to you. Remember, you are not in competition; you are all hoping to obtain high grades. A word of warning, though! Don't talk with your friends on the day of the exam, either before or afterwards. This can cause unnecessary and usually unfounded panic or depression.

15.4 Examination technique

The following ten points may help you in the exam room:

- **List the subjects studied**
  In those first tense moments when you are waiting to start, jot down the various topic areas; use the chapters of this book as a guide.

- **Read the paper carefully**
  When the examination gets under way, don't start writing immediately, however great the temptation. It is advisable to spend several minutes reading the paper, remembering to turn over the page if appropriate. There may well be a 'doddle' of a question lurking there!

- **Draw up a plan**
  Both essays and problems require some planning before you start.

- **Make an effective start**
  The examiner may be marking hundreds of scripts so you need to make an impact with your first words. A brief explanation of the course your answer is to take works wonders, as it puts the examiner on the same track as you immediately.

- **Cite authority**
  Remember also that the examiner is looking for your knowledge of the law, so remember that it is vital to back up your answer with

appropriate case law or relevant Acts of Parliament. Don't spend valuable time writing out all the facts of a case, a brief explanation to convince the examiner that you know your stuff will suffice; it is the principle of law that is the most important part. If you can't remember the name of the case, don't panic; put in brief facts and quote the principle coming from it. If you can't even remember that, put in general information and you may pick up some marks. You cannot get any from a blank page!

- **Time yourself properly**
  Should you run short of time, be ruthless. Stop one question and continue with the next and finish with notes if you are completely out of time at the end. It is surprising how much information you can put down in this way in roughly the same time as writing one complete sentence. The latter will only give you minimal marks, whereas examiners are sympathetic if there appears to be a genuine time problem, especially if you have written a lot before this.

- **Leave some space after each question**
  You can then return to it at a later time if you have something extra to add.

- **Structure your answer**
  A good essay will have an introduction, a middle and an effective conclusion, hopefully bringing in the title or indicating in some other way that you have answered the question set by the examiner and not what you were hoping he would ask. In problem questions, several issues may be involved. Deal with the substantive offences first and then see if there are any specific or general defences. There may be more than one party involved and you will need to see if the others are joint principals or secondary offenders or, alternatively, whether any inchoate offences exist.

- **Check your answers**
  If you have enough time, read through and correct your answers. You'll be surprised sometimes at the odd things you write in the stress of the moment.

- **Forget about it**
  Finally, after having finished the exam, put it all behind you until result time. The very best of luck to all of you!

TABLE OF CASES

TABLE OF STATUTES AND STATUTORY INSTRUMENTS

Criminal Law

INDEX

Page numbers in bold type refer to Key Facts panels.